The Fourth Marine
Brigade in World War I

Also by George B. Clark

*The United States Military in Latin America:
A History of Interventions through 1934* (2014)

*The American Expeditionary Force in World War I:
A Statistical History, 1917–1919* (2013)

Battle History of the United States Marine Corps, 1775–1945 (2010)

*United States Marine Corps Generals of World War II:
A Biographical Dictionary* (2008; softcover 2014)

*The Second Infantry Division in World War I: A History
of the American Expeditionary Force Regulars, 1917–1919* (2007)

Decorated Marines of the Fourth Brigade in World War I (2007)

*The Six Marine Divisions in the Pacific:
Every Campaign of World War II* (2006)

*Hiram Iddings Bearss, U.S. Marine Corps:
Biography of a World War I Hero* (2005)

Edited by George B. Clark

*United States Marine Corps Medal of Honor Recipients:
A Comprehensive Registry, Including U.S. Navy Medical Personnel
Honored for Serving Marines in Combat* (2005; softcover 2011)

By John W. Thomason, Jr., and
Edited by George B. Clark

*The United States Army Second Division Northwest of
Chateau Thierry in World War I* (2006)

All from McFarland

The Fourth Marine Brigade in World War I

Battalion Histories Based on Official Documents

GEORGE B. CLARK

McFarland & Company, Inc., Publishers
Jefferson, North Carolina

LIBRARY OF CONGRESS CATALOGUING-IN-PUBLICATION DATA

Clark, George B., 1926–
The Fourth Marine Brigade in World War I : battalion histories based on official documents / George B. Clark.
    p.   cm.
Includes bibliographical references and index.

ISBN 978-0-7864-9699-0 (softcover : acid free paper) ∞
ISBN 978-1-4766-1813-5 (ebook)

1. United States. Marine Corps. Marine Brigade, 4th.
2. United States. Marine Corps. Marine Regiment, 5th. Battalion, 1st.
3. United States. Marine Corps. Marine Regiment, 5th. Battalion, 2nd.
4. United States. Marine Corps. Marine Regiment, 5th. Battalion, 3rd.
5. United States. Marine Corps. Marine Regiment, 6th. Battalion, 1st.
6. United States. Marine Corps. Machine Gun Battalion, 6th.
7. World War, 1914–1918—Campaigns—France.
8. World War, 1914–1918—Regimental histories—United States.
I. Title.

D570.3484th C53 2015   940.4'5973—dc23   2015009931

BRITISH LIBRARY CATALOGUING DATA ARE AVAILABLE

© 2015 George B. Clark. All rights reserved

No part of this book may be reproduced or transmitted in any form or by any means, electronic or mechanical, including photocopying or recording, or by any information storage and retrieval system, without permission in writing from the publisher.

Cover image: Corporal Noyes V. Moore (center), commanding officer of the machine-gun squad, 96th Company, 2d Battalion, 6th Regiment, pictured at Quantico in 1917 (author)

Printed in the United States of America

*McFarland & Company, Inc., Publishers
Box 611, Jefferson, North Carolina 28640
www.mcfarlandpub.com*

Table of Contents

Preface   1

Introduction   3

Abbreviations   4

1. Fourth Brigade of Marines   5
2. First Battalion, Fifth Marines, 1917–1919   26
3. Second Battalion, Fifth Marines, 1917–1919   67
4. Third Battalion, Fifth Marines, 1917–1919   106
5. First Battalion, Sixth Marines, 1917–1919   149
6. Second Battalion, Sixth Marines, 1917–1919   185
7. Third Battalion, Sixth Marines, 1917–1919   214
8. Sixth Machine Gun Battalion   251

Chapter Notes   279

Bibliography   281

Index   285

Preface

This is the story of the 4th Marine Brigade as part of the Second Division, American Expeditionary Forces, serving in France between 1917 and 1918 and after, briefly in the Occupation of Germany, and their arrival in the New York City area in August 1919. This was the original Marine unit in France.

The Second Division was a premier unit that saw more action, and captured more ground, plus probably killing and capturing more of the enemy, than any other division in that war, including the vaunted First Division. It was composed of two infantry brigades, an artillery brigade, an engineer regiment, signal unit, trains, and a miscellaneous group of smaller units particular to a U.S. Army division at that period of time. The 3d Brigade of Infantry was composed of the 9th and 23d Infantry Regiments, both with enviable records of service, especially the 9th. That unit had already served with the U.S. Marines in China and the Philippines earlier in the 20th Century. The 2d Division also had the 5th Machine Gun Battalion as a part of that brigade as well as support services.

This book is organized into seven separate battalion oriented units plus a smaller chapter dedicated to the entire Fourth Marine Brigade. Most of the maps for the war will be found in that first chapter. The other seven chapters will have occasional maps dedicated to those battalions exclusively. The chapters include the First, Second, and Third Battalions of each of the two regiments, 5th and 6th Marines, plus the 6th Machine Gun Battalion. Much of the text is from original documents.

Chapter 1, the 4th Brigade, is told briefly, whereas the other seven are in as much detail as possible. That all depended upon the officers in charge at the time. Some were great record keepers, while others weren't concerned with posterity and kept little documentation. All records directly imported are exactly as was sent to their recipients with no changes or additions except those within brackets [ ], which I added. Those in parentheses ( ) were added by someone to the original record. Some read as though the perpetrator was a kindergarten student, while others appear as though William Shakespeare was attempting a new play.

I can't accept responsibility for the various spelling errors, or the abbreviations used, nor periods, commas or other usage in the documents. They are printed as written. Original operation reports were good sources of information because the preparer had time to collect his wits and to find out from his officers and men what happened at any particular period. As far as the major body of messages is concerned, they were selected because I thought they were most important and informative.

The formation is simple. The Fifth Marines comes first because it is natural order, as do each of its battalions beginning with the First Battalion, Fifth Marines, usually shown as 1/5. The Sixth Marines follow, and the Sixth Machine Gun Battalion follows, told in order, by each of its companies.

Introduction

Except for sixty or so junior Army officers, and several Navy medical officers, the 4th Brigade was composed entirely of Marines. The 5th Marines, a regiment formed at Vera Cruz, Mexico, on 13 July 1914, was the senior unit and was inhabited by many Marines of lengthy service. The 6th Marines was formed at Quantico in 1917 by a modest number of old-timers and mostly new recruits. The 5th arrived in France in July 1917 as sort of an orphan until General John J. Pershing prepared a second division in late 1917. The commanding officer of the 4th Brigade, Colonel Charles A. Doyen, USMC, was appointed to command briefly the Second Division. That, incidentally, was the first time a Marine ever commanded a division.

Major General Omar Bundy was the intended commanding officer of the division, and when he arrived Doyen went back to the 4th Brigade. Training began in mid-winter 1917-1918 and in mid–March the division went into trenches in the Toul area with various French units to train for trench warfare. In mid–May the division was released and went into quarters to the west of Paris for rest and more training.

They were intended to relieve the First Division farther north, but the Germans launched a major attack which soon threatened the city of Paris. The French begged Pershing to release any U.S. units he had to help them stem the tide. He provided two divisions, the Second and Third. Both earned their keep, the Third down around the city of Chateau Thierry and the Second in an area which became known because of a major position: Belleau Wood.

The division, especially the 4th Brigade of Marines, earned a reputation as a steadfast unit of superb fighting men. It was a thirty plus day affair and the Marines suffered unusual casualties among officers and men. Following a brief rest, next came Soissons, which badly hurt the 6th Marines. After more rest at Marbache, the men had an easier battle for the St. Mihiel salient. Next was a bitter affair that lasted ten days at Blanc Mont in which the 5th Marines were badly hurt, some say worse than at Belleau Wood. The attack along the Meuse River and finally the Armistice on 11 November 1918 followed, then occupation of part of Germany until mid–July 1919. The men went home for parades and disbandment of the 4th Marine Brigade at Quantico on 13 August 1919. Following is their story, told as much as possible in official records.

Abbreviations

Awards: United States

DSC—Distinguished Service Cross
MoH—Medal of Honor
NC—Navy Cross
SS—Silver Star citation, later a medal

Awards: French

CdG—Croix de Guerre
B—Bronze
S—Silver
G—Gilt
P—Palm, the highest grade
LH—Legion of Honor

Other Abbreviations

AEF—American Expeditionary Forces
AWOL—absent without leave
Bn, Btn or Batt—Battalion
CG—commanding general
CO—commanding officer
Co—Company
CR—center of resistance
Hdqs or Hqrs—Headquarters
Inf—Infantry
IO—intelligence officer
MG—Machine Gun
NCO or non com—noncommissioned officer
NG—National Guard
OP—observation post
PC—post of command
USA—U.S. Army
USMC—U.S. Marine Corps
USN—U.S. Navy
USR—U.S. Army Volunteers

Rank: United States

Pvt—Private
PFC Private First Class
Cpl—Corporal
Sgt—Sergeant
Gy Sgt—Gunnery Sergeant
1st Sgt—First Sergeant
Sgt Maj—Sergeant Major
2d Lt—Second Lieutenant
1st Lt—First Lieutenant
Capt—Captain
Maj—Major
Lt Col—Lieutenant Colonel
Col—Colonel
BGen—Brigadier General
MGn—Major General
LGen—Lieutenant General
Gen—General
Co—Commanding Officer

1

Fourth Brigade of Marines

France

The 4th Brigade was officially formed on 23 October 1917 to be a part of the forthcoming Second Division (Regulars), American Expeditionary Forces (AEF), with Brig. Gen. Charles A. Doyen, USMC, in command. In fact, for a period of time, on 26 October 1917, Doyen commanded the newly constructed Second Division, until Maj. Gen. Omar Bundy arrived on 8 November 1917 and relieved him.

Brigadier General Charles A. Doyen issued General Order No. 1, 4th Brigade of Marines, on 25 April 1918. In it he stated that he had assumed command of the Northern Sector in "obedience to orders from the Commanding General of the 33d Infantry Division." The sector included the sub-sectors Moulainville and Ronvaux.

General Order No. 3 of the brigade, dated 1 May, designated Maj. Edward B. Cole as brigade machine-gun officer. And on the same date, five Marine officers were detached from the brigade and ordered to the 3d Division, which had just arrived in France. The 3d was listed as a "regular" division but was short of senior officers, especially those with combat experience, and the 4th Brigade had more field officers than they could use. Major Robert L. Denig was assigned to command the 1st Battalion, 30th Infantry; Maj. Edward W. Sturdevant to the 3d Battalion, 30th Infantry; Maj. Robert F. Adams to the 3d Battalion, 38th Infantry; Maj. Harry G. Bartlett to the 2d Battalion, 7th Infantry; and Maj. Littleton W. T. Waller, Jr., to the 8th Machine Gun Battalion. Within a few months most of the officers would be back with their beloved Marines, but only after Belleau Wood and Soissons were over. Waller was the only one who would return sooner to the brigade.

One of the most controversial actions during this period was the dismissal of Brig. Gen. Charles Doyen from command of the brigade he had formed, trained, and led. Doyen, who had failed his army physical exam, was relieved by U.S. Army General John J. Pershing and sent back to the States, with a modestly worded salutation. It is true that Pershing also refused to keep any officers of the AEF who couldn't meet the exacting physical and mental standards set for them, and many deserved to be sent home. This action would have the most profound impact upon relations between George Barnett, commandant of the Marine Corps, and John J. Pershing, head of the American Expeditionary Forces, and upon Army and Marine Corps attitudes toward one another for many years to come. The corps saw it as another attempt by Pershing and his cronies to minimize the 4th Brigade's independence and usefulness in France. It was no great secret that Pershing was not in favor of accepting any Marines in France and only took what he couldn't refuse because of the political and interservice machinations of Barnett, who worked very well behind the scenes in Washington.

There was a certain level of rancor in the brigade because Doyen was not only well-liked, he was highly regarded professionally. It was he who had pulled together and trained the team who would go on to such fame in the future. The official historian of the period, Edwin N. McClellan, briefly notes that on May 6, 1918, Brig. Gen. James G. Harbord assumed command of the brigade, relieving Brig. Gen. Doyen, who had been ordered to the United States on account of his physical condition. Brig. Gen. Doyen relinquished command of the brigade most unwillingly, and the reasons for his relief are best set forth in the words of the citation of a Navy Distinguished Service Medal posthumously awarded to him:

> By reason of his abilities and personal efforts, he brought this brigade to the very high state of efficiency which enabled it to successfully resist the German army in the Chateau-Thierry sector and Belleau Woods. The strong efforts on his part for nearly a year undermined his health and necessitated his being invalided to the United States before having the opportunity to command the brigade in action, but his work was shown by the excellent service rendered by the brigade, not only at Belleau Woods, but during the entire campaign when they fought many battles.

Pershing sent a letter to Doyen in which he said, "Your service has been satisfactory and your command is considered one of the best in France. I have nothing but praise for the service which you have rendered in this command." Pershing cabled home that Doyen "is an excellent officer, has rendered most valuable service and has brought his Brigade to his efficiency. I very reluctantly return him to the United States." General Omar Bundy, divisional commander, recommended that Doyen be promoted to major general with the statement that "it is a well-recognized fact that the excellent condition of this brigade is due largely" to Doyen. Pershing, in order to quickly close whatever doors Bundy might have opened, added a postscript to Bundy's statement which expressed his regrets that Doyen's "physical condition prevents a recommendation for his promotion to major general to which he might otherwise be entitled."

One additional person made comment about Doyen's relief. On 30 April Holland Smith wrote in his diary:

> The General received notice today that he had been found physically disqualified and Gen. Harbord, the Chief of Staff of Gen. Pershing was to relieve him. We are all saddened as we feel this is the first blow. The Brigade is broken-hearted. We feel like a lost soul. May God help us in our humiliation and give us the courage to do the best we can to beat the Boche. We prophecy [sic] now that the marines will be withdrawn from France or that we may form a casual division and be under [unknown].

The diary continues raving about the loss of Doyen and the consequently lowered morale among the brigade officers. Doyen and Smith met with Wendell C. Neville and he, too, was "quite sad." Of course, Neville was anticipating a promotion to brigadier general and may have expected that he would get the brigade should that promotion happen soon. On 2 May, Maj. Holland Smith's entry said, "We expect to make a fight against the Army's decision. We have always been fortunate in our fights with them. Tomorrow many officers are to be courtmartialed for [blank]. It is going to be bad for the morale. General D. [Doyen] is President of the Court. Puryear [Major Bennet, Jr.], Mealy [unknown, perhaps Manney?], Shearer [Maurice F.] and some of the captains are among the no. to be court-marshalled [*sic*]."

Brigadier General James G. Harbord, U.S. Army, had been Pershing's chief of staff. He had also been a personal friend of many years and presumably, when it became known that Doyen was going home, Harbord had an inside track. For him to qualify for higher rank he had to have a field command.

Harbord got the brigade, and even though the senior officers welcomed him in an emotional statement that used the Marine oath "Semper Fidelis" to express their loyalty to him, it would not be the same as before, for anyone. Harbord led the brigade through the worst and their performance was such that later he was promoted to command the division. According to Harbord's memoir, Pershing had told him that he was getting the best brigade in the AEF and "if it fails I'll know where to place the blame." It didn't fail. They made him look very good, even though they paid a heavy price to do so.

Harbord wrote a very kind letter to Doyen, as did the commanding general of the French 33d Division, under which the brigade had served. Brigadier General Charles A. Doyen, accompanied by his aide, 1st Lt. Benjamin S. Goodman, arrived in New York on 22 May 1918, just two weeks before the brigade would be ordered into the bloodiest single day in all of Marine Corps history.

One young officer remained as aide-de-camp to the new commander of the brigade. That was 1st Lt. Fielding S. Robinson. On 7 May 1918, Harbord appointed 2d Lt. R. N. Williams II, USA, as Goodman's replacement. Major Harry R. Lay returned from Langres and replaced Maj. Holland M. Smith, who had been acting as brigade adjutant during Lay's absence. Smith was assigned as brigade liaison officer on 16 May 1918—this move probably had something to do with Smith's part in the "cabal" then brewing.

Another officer got into trouble; I can find no record of his trial, but he was "dismissed from the service of the U.S. by the Auth. of the Commander-in-Chief of the AEF. Notice of dismissal received May 30, 1918." He is listed as Capt. John C. Foster, a member of the 7th Company, 1st Lt. Edward L. Burwell, Jr., commanding. Too bad; Foster might have been of some value in the weeks ahead.

Verdun

Movement for additional training was made toward a section known as the Verdun Sector in mid–March, and the Second Division joined with French soldiers in the trenches for two months. They really didn't gain much except to learn what a disaster trench warfare was for the infantryman. Actually, this type of warfare was completely opposite what Pershing had in mind for the American army.

Temporary Brigade Adjutant Maj. Holland Smith went one full month between entries, from 10 March till 11 April. On that date he noted that a German airplane was "driven back by shell fire. The Boche passed close over our heads and the [blank] had to hustle back." The following day he made an interesting entry that indicated that a U.S. naval gun mounted on a train flat car was close by. "Today the large 13" fired on a city [Conflans] 30 kilometers away.

And the other guns were firing too and we had quite a day of it. Tomorrow the reprisal will come." The reprisal, he noted, was the violent gas attack upon the 74th Company described in the history of 1/6. He also made a strong comment about a beating that the 9th Infantry inflicted upon the Germans, "killing, it is reported, 60 men and capturing 10 men and two machine guns."

Their time was nearly over and they had in truth learned a great deal about trench warfare and been bloodied in a relatively quiet sector. It was time for the Marines to be pulled out of the lines. The brigade had spent the better part of two months in trenches on the front lines when they were withdrawn on 14 May and transferred to an area around Vitry-le-Francois, northwest of Paris, for open-warfare training. It wasn't long before the area was deemed unsuitable for training, so the brigade moved by train and a two day road march to Gisors—Chaumont-en-Vexin, which was just north and slightly west of Paris. Headquarters was located at Bou-des-Bois. There the brigade learned many lessons of war that would assist them in the operations to come in June. Not many Marines ever got any closer than the thirty or so miles to the great city of Paris. Instead, they spent what little free time they had in the towns and villages around them. One of the towns close by was named Marines, a fact that wasn't lost on the members of the brigade, and the name remained in many memories of those who survived the dark days ahead.

Marines stringing wire at Verdun.

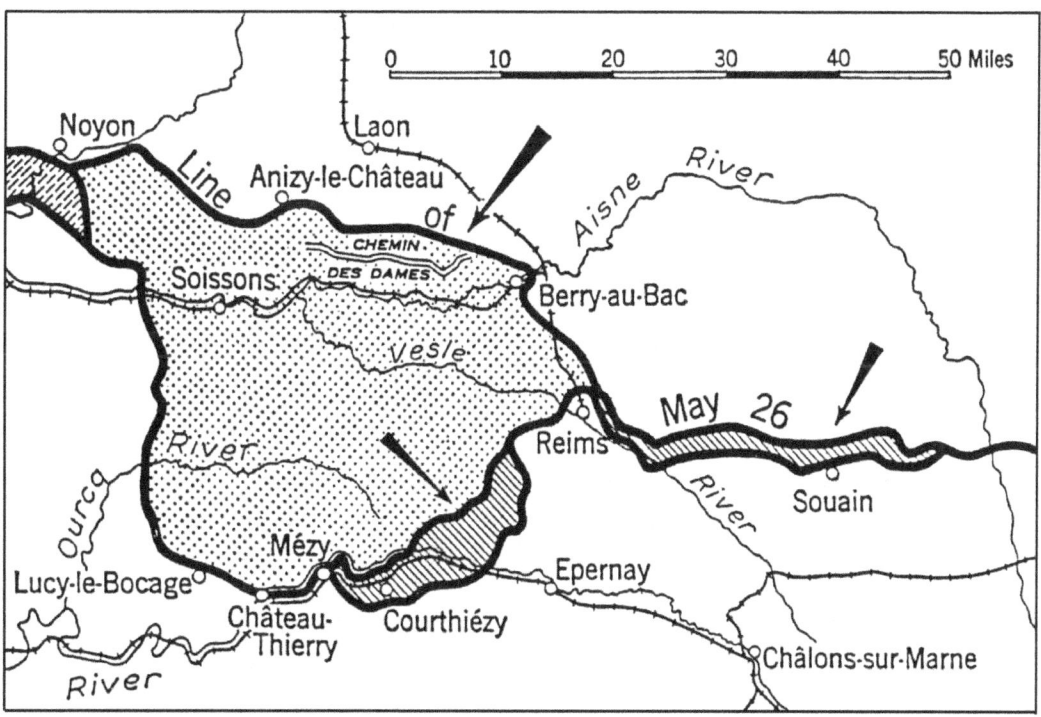

Top: Three senior members of the 4th Marine Brigade at Verdun. They are, from the left, Major Holland M. Smith, Colonel Charles A. Doyen, and Lieutenant Colonel Frederic M. Wise. *Bottom:* Map showing German Army advances into France in 1918.

The first time the German army had gotten that close to Paris was in 1914, when the French forces, riding in Paris taxicabs, rode into history. Paris was the hub of France. From it extended the spokes along which all commerce, supplies, and just about every important item necessary for a continuance of the war by France had to be conveyed. If the Germans continued their advance, Paris must fall. If Paris fell, France would fall, and if France should fall, the armies of the allies would fall too. There would be no tomorrow. The British in the north would be forced to cross the English Channel should the German sweep in the south successfully reach the coast. The fledgling American army had no real base such as the French and British armies had. They would be cut off from their home base more than three thousand miles away. No American fleet could possibly provide a Dunkirk retreat for the American soldiers in France; there were too many of them now.

At this time a division of American regulars was within calling distance. The 2d Division was an amalgamation of four of the finest infantry and three of the best artillery regiments, plus the pickings of the engineers and service troops in the entire U.S. military forces. The 3d Division was also nearby and would gain great glory for their defense of the bridge at Chateau-Thierry and later the Marne River line. The Rock of the Marne, they would be rightly called, for slamming that door to the all-victorious German army in July 1918. Victorious until they met up with the rough and ready juvenile delinquents from across the ocean.

Belleau Wood

The Bois de Belleau was elevated above the surrounding wheat fields. On the eastern side of the wood a paved road ran between Belleau in the north and Bouresches in the south, and continued on a few miles to Vaux. Another road, along the western frontage, ran south from Torcy to Lucy-le-Bocage. South of the woods ran a dirt road westward from Bouresches to Lucy. The woods lay within the triangle formed by these three roads. The wood was approximately a mile long, a half mile across at its widest, and four hundred meters at its narrowest. During this period, the trees were in full leaf, and under the trees the ground was choked with undergrowth through which men could not pass easily. There was a deep ravine along the southern edge and a narrow unimproved road within the forest. Another ravine, cutting from the western side, ran northeast to southwest in a slightly angled direction across the narrow part of the wood.

1 June: The German order of battle had five divisions of the Von Conta Corps facing the French and the 2d Division. Conta's mission was to provide a defensive flank for the thrust to the Ourcq by Winckler's 25th Corps. It wasn't to be Conta's task to aggressively attack along the line but just to keep pace with Winckler's men. But the local German command kept up the probing, always looking to attain better positions on the south side of the Clignon. Consequently, the area continued to be active. While the 2d Division was taking up its positions on that first day, the Germans were doing what they were paid to do and did so well, namely to overcome resistance along the Clignon line toward its confluence with the Ourcq.

The French order of battle facing the Germans was the 43d Division, under General

Michel, with attached units of cavalry and elements of five or six infantry regiments. That division would take up left flank liaison with the 4th Brigade all during the coming campaign. They would continue to do their duty and do it well.

2 June: At 0300 the 2d Battalion, 2d Division Engineers, arrived to begin developing fortifications for the Marines starting at Lucy-le-Bocage and working westward. For the balance of the fight before, in, and around Belleau Wood, the engineers would work and then fight. In attacks made later in the month by the decimated Marine brigade, the engineers would advance with the Marines and fight as infantry. Each rifle company was, initially, allocated one platoon of engineers, but as casualties among the engineers increased, those numbers were reduced. For many good reasons, Marines had a high regard for their buddies of the 2d Engineers.

Harbord directly passed along orders, as he did those to Maj. Julius Turrill later when he placed 1/5 brigade in reserve. All during the action in June, it was common for Harbord to bypass his regimental commanders and send orders from his command post to nearly every lower level: to battalion and occasionally even down to company level.

Fourth Brigade Headquarters was beginning to shape up and settle down. Harbord advised Col. Preston Brown, his chief of staff, that his communications "are in much better shape than yesterday," that liaison was working regularly and that he had telephone communication with "both regimental hdqrs. and ... HQ. of my M.G. bn., and through the latter, with the bn. nearest it, which is the bn. at the critical point on the line"—Holcomb's 2/6.

The lack of maps at practically every level, from top to bottom, became an increasingly serious problem. When French maps finally became more readily available, they were badly flawed anyway. Most had been developed in the previous century and many changes had not been recorded. With all the movement and readjustment of location, over ground they hadn't had an opportunity to reconnoiter, it is surprising that the Americans performed as well as they did.

Most everyone in the division had moved somewhere on 2 June, and consequently the men had little rest and less food. By 3 June the front was beginning to stabilize, even though there had been much lost motion and great confusion. There was some digging of trenches, especially around Triangle Farm, Lucy, and in the Bois St. Martin, but largely the men wearily dug foxholes. Rather than to meet a standard, they were dug to satisfy the individuals' own concern for protection from bursting artillery shells. According to several reports, some Marines, hungry, exhausted, and in a somewhat mutinous manner, swore they wouldn't dig another hole. Many expressed their opinion that they "were going to be bumped off anyway and if so they wouldn't have to tolerate any more shelling." Usually a shell dropping close by would terminate whatever antagonistic attitude they had toward "management" and the digging would commence again, immediately if not sooner.

After midnight the 43d Division notified Harbord that French troops would be issued an order "to retake the position they have just lost. The American troops will maintain at all costs the line of support they occupy."

3 June: Harbord in his daily report to Bundy summarized the important happenings of the day. He mentioned what happened to Williams of the 51st Company: "The French line has fallen back nearly to our own line, practically on our whole front. In one case, a retreating French officer gave an order in writing to an American officer to fall back from the position which we have been holding. The order was not obeyed."

This was the famous order given to Capt. Lloyd W. Williams, of the 51st Company, for which his response, "Retreat, hell! We just got here," set the tone for the entire brigade. Williams, ever the professional, requested that the French "kindly not shorten their artillery range," for they might hit him. That night Maj. Holland McT. Smith sent a message to both regimental commanders and to Major Cole: "Gen. Harbord directs that the necessary steps be taken to hold our positions *at all costs*" (emphasis in original). The situation was getting hairy and everyone in the brigade knew it.

Ben Berry's 3/5, which had been serving as corps reserve, was returned to brigade control and now, as brigade reserve, relocated to the woods southwest of Marigny.

4 June: Two companies from 1/5 were assigned to help Col. Frederic M. Wise and were directed to Hill 142, which was just to the east and north of Champillon. For some reason, no one seemed able to locate that place. The distance was approximately a half mile and this location would continue to dog everyone who was sent to fill it. What made matters even worse was that the main road between Torcy and Lucy went right through the area. Any advance made by German forces south would naturally take this easiest pathway. The 4th Brigade's entire position would thus be in serious trouble, greatly affecting the 2d Division, the entire line, and ultimately the war.

The French withdrew and turned command of the area to Gen. Bundy and the 2d Division. The area now controlled by the 2d Division stretched from Monneaux, at the base of Hill 204, to Le Thiolet, then to Lucy, to Hill 142, and finally to Les Mares Farm. Brigade command then issued orders that altered nearly everyone's current position. Headquarters of the brigade moved itself from Issonge Farm a half mile southward to La Loge, where it was less exposed to German observation.

The Germans suddenly became very active. Unknown to the 4th Brigade, they had moved into the Bois de Belleau and were organizing a defense that would stymie the Marines for the next three weeks. The 461st Infantry Regiment was now in liaison with the 10th Division at the southwest corner of Belleau Wood near Bouresches. They also established positions along the south face of the woods to the base of Hill 181 and then northward along the woods' western edge. Patrols of the 237th Regiment penetrated the Bois St. Martin just north of Lucy. Some of them operating near Lucy picked up a 6th Marine corpse, which was carried back to the intelligence section. It was the first American they had seen, but he would not be the last. There would be enough Americans to go around. More than enough to satisfy even the Germans. And, likewise.

That evening, in his daily report to General Bundy, Harbord proudly advertised the fact that "the Brigade Headquarters were honored this afternoon by a visit from the Commander-in-Chief [Gen. Pershing] who expressed his satisfaction of the work of the Marine Brigade." Pershing had every reason to be satisfied. His 2d Division was certainly better than any other division of the AEF, although he would have put his money on his "pets" of the great 1st Division.

The only record of a reconnaissance in the 4th Brigade was that performed by 2d Lt. William A. Eddy of the 6th Regiment. The disaster that would come on 6 June was directly

Top: Belleau Wood long after the war terminated. *Bottom:* German trenches at Belleau Wood.

caused by failure to reconnoiter the ground to be taken. Harbord would be quoted later as saying something like, "I thought the French had done all of that." If that was a reasonably correct quotation, brigade headquarters didn't know what was before them and consequently the regiments didn't know either. Worse, no one in charge took it upon himself to do anything about it.

Top: A one-pounder crew at Belleau Wood. *Bottom:* The Supply Company, 2d Division, delivering to the 4th Marine Brigade at Belleau Wood.

A view of Belleau Wood from Bois St. Martin.

5 June: Field Order No. 8 from the 2d Division at 1000 on this date said the 4th Brigade's area of responsibility ran from Triangle to eight hundred meters north of Champillon on the Bussiares road. The 5th and 6th Marines were to occupy the ground left to right running eastward. Berry's 3/5 would relieve 1/6 on the line and 1/6 would constitute Army (21st) Corps reserve. Division headquarters was instructed to move from Montreuil-aux-Lions a mile and a half southwest to Bézu-le-Guëry.

Harbord issued orders to Catlin and Neville that "on arrival of the troops of the 167th French Division to relieve that portion of your line west of but not including Champillon you will cause guides to be furnished to conduct them to their positions.... When they are in position you will withdraw your left battalion [2/5]." Harbord issued additional orders to both regimental officers for changes in the lines after dark. (Sometimes they made sense, sometimes not. To the hole-digging enlisted Marine, they made no sense at all.) Essentially, the area covered by the 4th Brigade would be substantially reduced. It would contract over a mile on the south and another half mile on the northwest. The 23d Infantry would move northward to fill the gap between the 9th and 6th Regiments. Most but not all of the Marines would be in position for the following day's activities.

6 June: The disaster would occur. The first to be slaughtered was 1/5 at Hill 142, then, at 1700, came 3/5's opportunity and at the same time 3/6. Both paid a heavy price going into the woods. Meanwhile, on its own, 2/6 was also chewed to pieces going after the town of Bouresches. It was a dismal day for the 4th Brigade. Harbord managed to reduce personnel in four battalions of the six he had. Fortunately, 2/6, though greatly reduced, was successful, or at least the twenty something men left from the 96th Company in Bouresches were.

For the next few days Harbord tried nothing spectacular. Then on 10 June he sent 1/6 in to the same location that 3/6 was forced to relinquish. They, 3/6, suffered gas casualties and 1/6 caught more.

11 June: Then 2/5 was given its opportunity to cleanse the wood of Germans on this date. Because of errors in judgment, they too took a terrible beating, or at least their 51st Company paid a heavy price. The battalion, however, was much more successful than either 3/6 or 1/6 had been insofar as taking territory within the woods.

Colonel Wise and 2/5 continued advancing against strong German strongpoints, paying more in personnel cost than any unit should. Eventually, they had captured about 75 percent of the woods. But, by this time someone had the sane idea that the Marines of the 4th Brigade were not only greatly reduced in manpower, but were also exhausted and starved after two and half weeks in constant combat with little food.

The 7th Infantry, a "regular" regiment of recent draftees from the 3d Division, were brought in to relieve the brigade of Marines. They tried, but were hopelessly untrained and inadequate against the very professional German soldiers they faced in Belleau Wood.

The Marines were brought back on about the 22 of June and were furious that much of what they had gained through a fearful loss of life had been lost and had to be retaken.

But now 3/5, with a modest number of replacements, was awarded the task of taking the entire Belleau Wood still held by the enemy. Major Maurice Shearer had replaced the badly wounded Maj. Benjamin S. Berry in command of the battalion. On 26 June, Shearer shouted loud and clear, "BELLEAU WOODS NOW U.S. MARINE CORPS ENTIRELY."

For a few more days, until relieved by the incoming 26th National Guard Division, the Second Division remained in the area, then for about two weeks they relaxed, ate, cleaned, and trained down near the Marne River. Swimming was a favorite activity and it helped to rid the men of fleas.

Then, on or about the 15th of July the men were made ready, mounted French camions, and were driven northward toward the ancient city of Soissons. After a horrible, exhausting ride, they dismounted and made their way eastward through the Foret Domaniale de Retz.

Soissons

The coming action in Soissons would be bloody. The first day was a complete fouled-up mess. The 5th Marines had a peculiar movement. They were to move in a northerly-easterly direction and according to the maps hardly anyone saw, they were to move to a certain location then turn in southerly-easterly and proceed to push the enemy back. To the 5th's right flank, the 9th Infantry Regiment followed the 5th's pattern and also went astray. Both plunged into the sector of the French Moroccan Division, which was slow coming along. After taking the village of Chaudun, the 5th, now recognizing their error, turned southerly back into their original pathway. The 9th had made that move earlier.

In fact, due to a lot of different officers of various commands getting involved, the 5th Marines would be scattered all over the battlefield that day. When the day was finished it would take some doing to bring them back into formation and control.

18 July: On this morning, the 5th Marines, the 9th and 23d Infantry Regiments, followed an artillery rolling barrage and by the end of the day had advanced miles toward the towns of Tigny and Villemontoire. Their losses in manpower were very costly and at the end of the day, the three regiments were exhausted. The 6th Marines were in a support position all day.

19 July: Due to circumstances beyond the men's control, the 6th Marines, whose turn it was, all alone, to advance and captured those towns, were late jumping off and were slaughtered. They advanced as far as possible, but left so many dead and wounded on the plains behind them, they were forced to give up and dig in. The following morning, French troops came in to relieve them and occupy their foxholes.

After Soissons the Second Division was badly in need of replacements and a complete rest. They had performed miracles in two major battles while suffering extensive casualties. They were assigned to duty in a sector known as Marbache. Here they lasted nearly a full month and suffered few losses of manpower. Their next move was to join Gen. Pershing's army in the effort to reduce the St. Mihiel Salient. This had been in existence since the early days of the war and though the French had tried several times to eliminate it, each time they failed with huge losses.

A Stokes mortar crew in action at Soissons.

Marines boarding camions on 16 July 1918, headed for Soissons.

The First American Army along with numerous French divisions encircled the salient and by 12 September were ready to retake it. It was Pershing's first combat command in France and frankly, it was, compared to every other fight in France, a push-over. Unknown to anyone on the Allied side, the Germans were making preparations to withdraw from their exposed position and were in the process on 12 September. Yet, surprised though they were, the Germans put up quite a scrap.

St. Mihiel

At St. Mihiel, the French Infantry Divisions were assigned to the west and north while seven of the American divisions were along the south. All, that is, except the 26th National Guard Division which, for some reason, was assigned within the French zones. Their advance, by the way, was led by Marine Colonel Hiram I. Bearss, leading the 102d Infantry of that division.

After the successful battle, the Second Division had once again been assigned to the French in their part of the front, west of the Argonne Forest. This coming battle in the Champagne region, for the massif at Blanc Mont, would be as deadly for the division, and especially the 5th Marines, as had been Belleau Wood. Most of the outspoken veterans of the 4th Brigade said it was worse.

A bunker built by the German army while they occupied the St. Mihiel salient.

After a few movements about France, the Second Division made its way to Suippe and Somme-Py, two towns lying beneath Blanc Mont. This location was another early conquest of the German armies in 1914 and they had held it since, even though the French had tried numerous times to throw them out. It was essential to relieve the large cathedral city of Rheims, which the Germans overlooked from their heights.

Plans made, mainly by the French in command, were for the 2d Division to advance up the heights on 2 October. That plan was rescinded and instead it was on for the 3 of October, and Maj. Gen. Lejeune and his staff prepared a variation on the French plan. The two brigades were split, one on each side of the Bois de la Vipère with the 4th Brigade to take the massif.

Blanc Mont

The order of battle was as what had become usual: a regiment advanced in a column of battalions with the other regiment in a supporting role. In this case, the 6th Marines would go first, followed by the 5th Marines. Two/six was given the post of honor, namely to be first. Major Ernest Williams, a Medal of Honor man from Santo Domingo in 1916, led 2/6. Williams was followed by 1/6, led by Major Frederick Barker, then 3/6 by Major George Shuler.

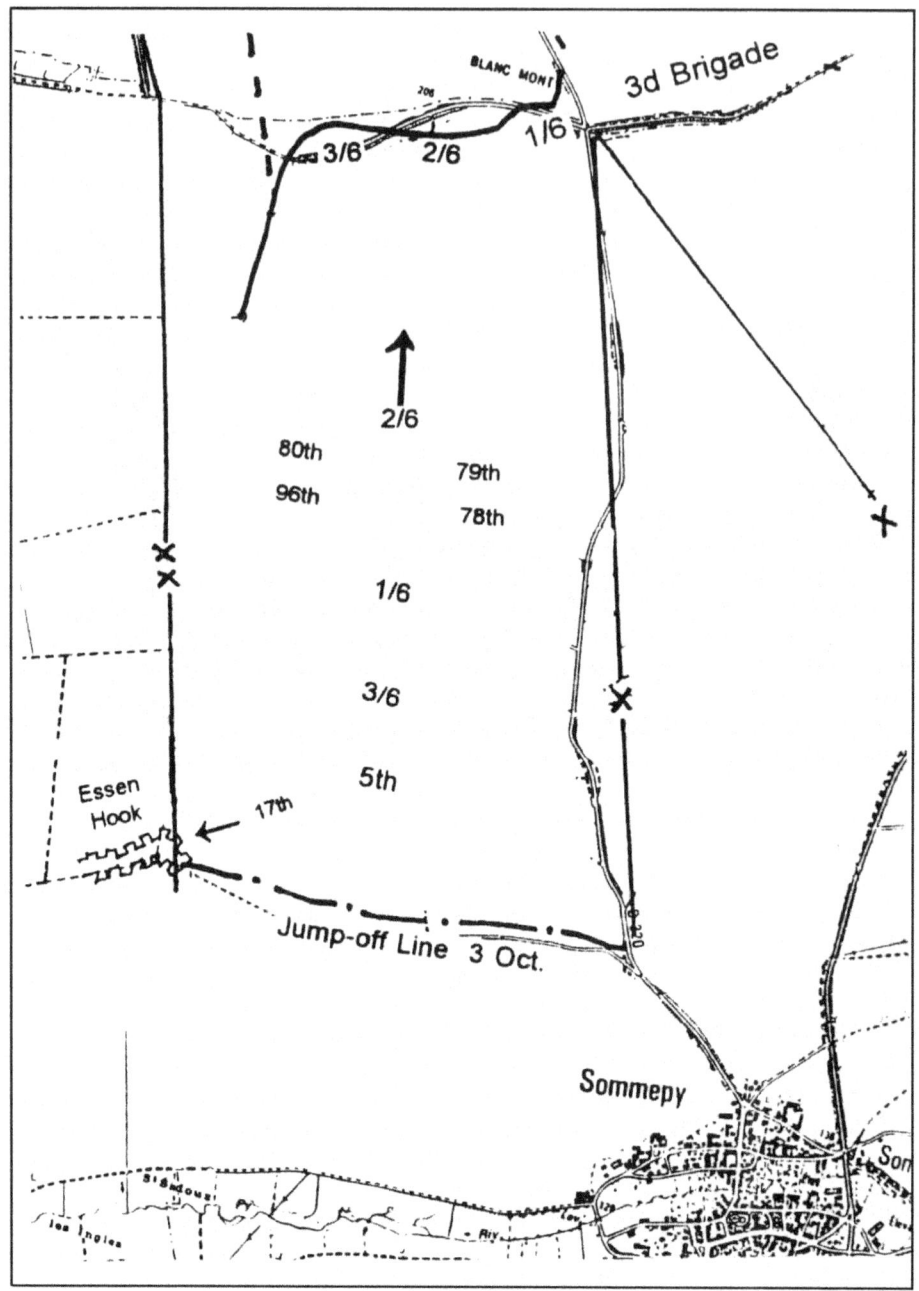

Blanc Mont. Attack of the 4th Brigade, led by the 6th Marines on 3 October 1918.

The 17th Company, 1/5, led by Capt. LeRoy Hunt, was charged with taking out a very strong German point known as Essen Hook. They did, turned it over to the French (it was in their sector) and joined their comrades of the 5th Marines later that morning. Soon afterward the French lost the Hook, leaving the rear of the 4th Brigade exposed to the enemy.

Meanwhile, as the 6th advanced up the incline, the French on their left flank did not advance. That left the entire flank open to German assault, which they took advantage of. The 6th and 5th Marines had a fight on their hands, both front and left all the way up.

About noon the 6th Marines were on the massif, but unknown to them, the hill was honeycomb with caves and strong points. Though the 6th Marines had taken Blanc Mont Ridge, they were loaded with enemy forces beneath and around them. It would take several more days for the Marines to truly own Blanc Mont.

The following day the orders were for the 5th Marines to advance up the road toward St. Etienne and take that town. This was the fatal part of the 4th Brigade on top of Blanc Mont. The formation along the road was: 3/5 leading, 2/5 in support, and 1/5 in reserve. Soon after arriving in that formation, the enemy—machine guns in well-prepared in various hardened bunkers and artillery well position on heights—opened up on the 5th Marines. Major Henry L. Larsen of 3/5 called for support from Maj. Robert E. Messersmith and 2/5, which ran off the road to the west and Larsen's left. That did little and the Germans changed pattern and began chewing up 2/5, and Messersmith called for Maj. George Hamilton to move 1/5 to his left. The latter moved immediately and now three battalions were on line. Trouble for 1/5 began at once. As 1/5 moved forward the Germans seemed to concentrate on his formation. It was hell. Several companies did what they could to move forward and

Drawing of a dressing station at Blanc Mont.

Top: A machine-gun block-house built by the German army at Blanc Mont. *Bottom:* A group of Marine officers of the 5th Regiment, including Colonel Wendell C. Neville (seated left) and Lieutenant Colonel Logan Feland (seated right).

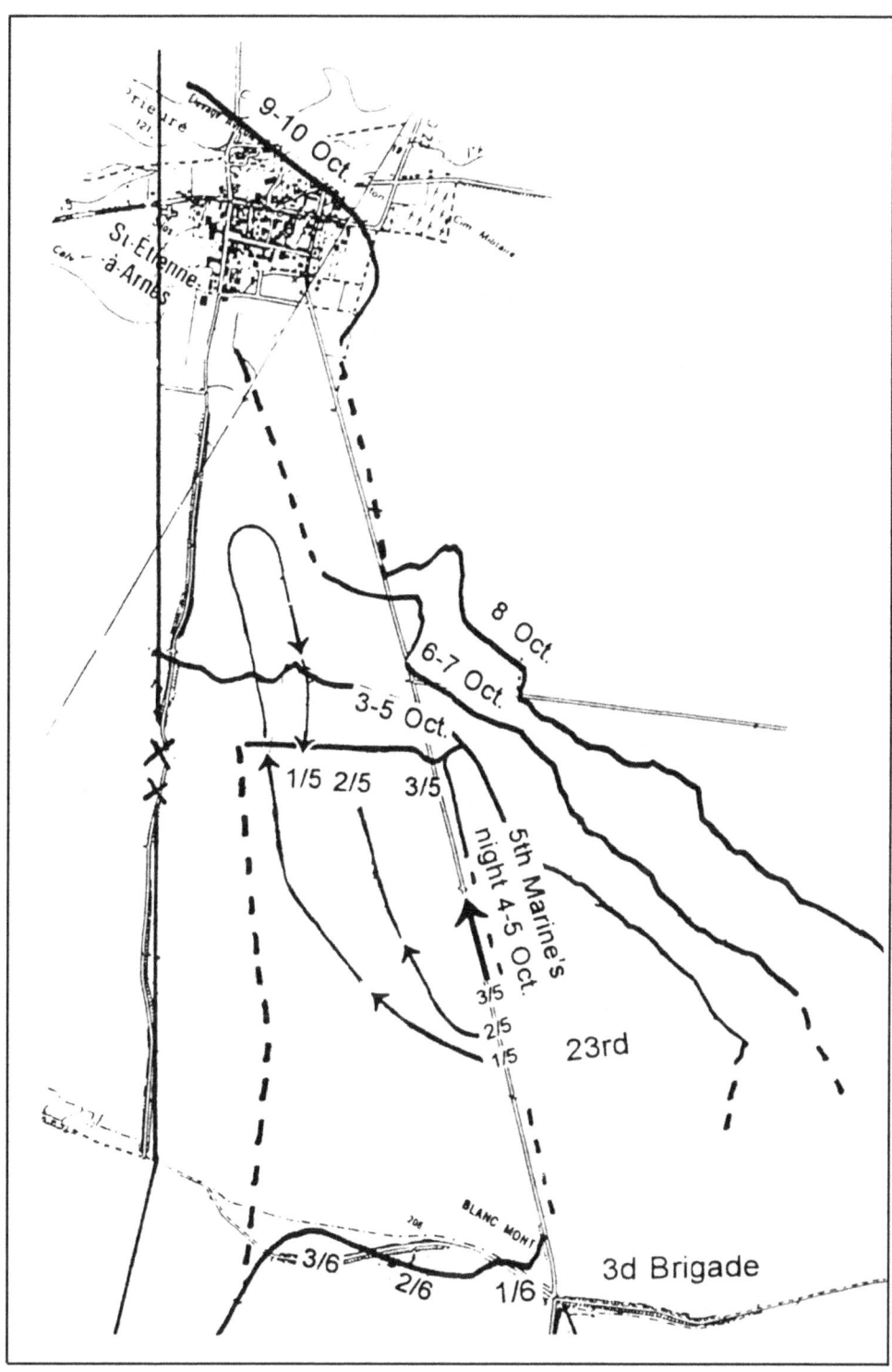

Attack by the 5th Marines on 4 October 1918, showing advance of 1/5 toward St. Etienne and subsequent positions of the 6th Marines and portions of the 23rd Infantry during the following six days.

get up close to the enemy, but the artillery and machine guns created a terrible scene. The veterans, the very few that remained, called that place "The Box." Captain John W. Thomason, Jr., a member of 1/5, later wrote the best account in his magnificent work *Fix Bayonets*.

The Marines had to fall back to the road and brace for the anticipated counter-attack, which was mainly artillery and machine gun fire all day and into the night. The remnants, about 10 percent of the numbers that went forward that day, had no more fight left in them. They remained out of action, just on the defensive, until the Second Division folded its tents and removed themselves from that area on or about 10 October.

The 6th Marines continued until they too were decimated. Meanwhile, a brand new division, the 36th "Cowboys" from Texas and Oklahoma, came in to relieve the Second Division and took over those positions the latter division had conquered with their blood.

From this time, the division moved about; soon after the debacle at Blanc Mont, the French requested more assistance and the division marched to their relief. But that was rescinded. Meanwhile, they continued to receive replacements. However, because of the great flu epidemic, many of the men died on the ships coming over to France or were sick upon arrival and were hospital bound. Instead of being able to contribute to the restoration of the 4th Marine Brigade, not due to any fault of their own, they were an instant drag on the hospital services, those that survived.

General Pershing's two armies had been engaged not many miles east of where the Second Division had been fighting. His First Army, composed of few veterans and many hastily trained troops, were badly handled in their part of the struggle known as the Argonne from late September to middle October. Now he and some of them were going to make another try to reach the Meuse River before an armistice went into effect. The Allies and Germans had been talking about such a situation for some time and everyone wanted to be in the "best location" when and if one came about.

Meuse-Argonne

The rebuilt Second Division, still badly understaffed, was given a most important position in the lineup to begin their advance on 1 November. On that date they were to jump off from the road connecting the towns of Landres and St. George. On that date the 4th Brigade was to lead off with the 3d Brigade in support. The 6th Marines were on the left and the 5th Marines on the right. Order of battle for both regiments was the first battalions, followed in the 6th by 3/6, then 2/6 in reserve. In the 5th it was 2/5 in support and 3/5 in reserve.

The artillery barrage went off at 0330 and the jump-off at 0530. Each unit made its first and second objectives that day and were well onto their third. The 3d Brigade took over and they made a grand effort. Brigades alternated until the division reached a point on or about 7 November when General John A. Lejeune called it quits until bridging equipment was brought up.

The 6th Marines, plus 3/5, were selected to cross the Meuse River just north of the town of Mouzon, and 1/5 and 2/5 plus a battalion from the 89th Division were sent below the village of Villemontry; both on the night of 10-11 November. Of course, by this time, an agreement was in effect calling for an armistice at 1100 that next morning and no soldier or Marine wanted to die now that the war was just about over. Other ideas surfaced, and those bright eyes decided how wonderful it would be if the Marines took additional ground from the enemy before the agreement went into effect. They wouldn't be going, of course, just the Marines and a few soldiers from the 89th Division. No one as important as Maj. Gen. Charles P. Summerall, commanding the 5th Corps, of which the Second Division was a part.

Afterward, the entire Second Division marched into Germany to occupy a section of the country. The 4th Brigade was assigned territory around the city of Coblenz, and the brigade headquarters mainly in or around Niederbieber. The men mostly were given light duties, some on river (Rhine) patrol, guard duties, rest, relaxation, anything but fighting. On or about 15 July 1919, trains were loaded and the division went toward the coast and eventual shipment home. Most arrived at Hoboken, New Jersey, on or about 8 August. After a few parades and assignment to Quantico, they were discharged on 13 August, at least those Marines who had had enough of the corps. Those who decided they wanted to continue being active remained behind.

2

First Battalion, Fifth Marines, 1917–1919

Battalion Headquarters
17th [A] Company
49th [B] Company
66th [C] Company
67th [D] Company
Medical Unit

Commanding Officers

From	To	
May 1917	23 Sept. 1917	Major Julius S. Turrill
24 Sept. 1917	24 Oct. 1917	Lt. Col. Logan Feland
25 Oct. 1917	18 Jan. 1918	Capt. George W. Hamilton
19 Jan. 1918	12 March 1918	Maj. Edward A. Greene
13 March 1918	19 Aug. 1918	Maj. Julius S. Turrill
20 Aug. 1918	28 Aug. 1918	Capt. Raymond F. Dirksen
29 Aug. 1918	19 Sept. 1918	Lt. Col. Arthur J. O'Leary
20 Sept. 1918	14 Dec. 1918	Maj. George W. Hamilton
15 Dec. 1918	15 Jan. 1918	Capt. LeRoy P. Hunt
16 Jan. 1919	20 March 1919	Maj. George W. Hamilton
21 March 1919	13 Aug. 1919	Maj. LeRoy P. Hunt

The assembling of the units of the First Battalion, Fifth U.S. Marines, under the command of Major Julius S. Turrill, at Quantico, Virginia, during the last two weeks of May 1917 marked the beginning of the formation of the 4th Marine Brigade.

The 66th and 67th companies were formed from prospective battleship's guards at the Norfolk Barracks, and were joined in Quantico a few days later by the 49th Company, whose ranks had been augmented by the USS *New Hampshire*'s guard, commanded by 1st Lieutenant George W. Hamilton. The battalion was made complete by the arrival of the 15th Company from Pensacola, Florida.

Following a brief period of drill on the banks of the Potomac, the battalion entrained for Philadelphia on 9 June 1917. On the occasion of this first movement as an organized unit, many different kinds of inscriptions were chalked upon the coaches. None were in a modest type and informed potential readers—the yet quite unawakened citizens along the route—that it was to be "Berlin or Bust" as far as the First Battalion of the Fifth Marines was concerned.

After tenting for three days in the busy League Island Navy Yard, the battalion quietly embarked, 20 officers and 790 men strong, aboard the *DeKalb*, formerly the enemy ship *Prinz Eitel Friedrich*, which had engaged in high piracy before its internment in American waters. The embarkation was conducted after the fashion of the corps, with no demonstration and with the greatest unconcern on the part of the troops. The *DeKalb* remained in home waters for two days, and on 14 June 1917, weighed anchor off Stapleton, New York, and set out upon a zigzag course eastward in convoy.

Conditions aboard the transport were somewhat cramped, but calm weather prevailed, and the voyage was accomplished with little hardship. The only notable incident occurred at 2230 on 22 June 1917, when two enemy submarines were sighted from the lookout. A light sea was running, and phosphorescent glow of the whitecaps furnished a means for spotting the enemy craft. Two torpedoes missed the *DeKalb* by a narrow margin. Meanwhile, the guns of the transport fired a salvo at the submarines, and at full speed the ship plunged away from the scene of the near disaster and encountered no other U-boats during the remainder of the trip. Part of the *DeKalb*'s guns were manned by members of the battalion, who demonstrated their prowess in target practice from day to day during the voyage.

Around the old piano in the forward quarters of the ship, the members of the battalion improved acquaintances, and by the time the convoy glided into the welcome harbor of St. Nazaire, France, on 26 June 1917, the unity of the four companies had become marked. On June 27, 1917, the battalion disembarked, was greeted enthusiastically by the citizens of St. Nazaire, and went into camp on the western outskirts of the city. The Fifth Regiment had been assigned to the First Division of the Army, units of which had crossed in the *DeKalb*'s convoy.

The battalion remained in this seaport camp for over two weeks, entraining on 15 July 1917 for Naix-Auxforges, in the Department of the Meuse. The trip was made in the little French boxcars, but pleasant weather was again an alleviating factor. Throughout the two-day journey the men were warmly greeted by the French, and upon reaching Naix on 17 July 1917, found the villagers, in gala attire, standing along the little main street, over which a banner of welcome had been suspended. Naix furnished the First Battalion comfortable billets for the summer, and it was here that the long, hard period of training began.

Practice entrenchments were dug among the peaceful hills of the region, and the organization to a man entered with a zest into the task of studying modern warfare. A battalion of Alpine Chausseur, the 30th, was stationed nearby for the purpose of cooperating in instructing the Americans, and the high character of that organization, both as soldiers and men, had a lasting influence upon the First Battalion. The two units found that they had much in common, and through the remainder of the war the Alpine Chausseur and the U.S. Marines were devoted brothers-in-arms. Social relations with the natives were here, as in succeeding localities, developed to a cordial extent, the French women from the first assuming a maternal benevolence toward the young men from over the seas. While at Naix the battalion was twice inspected by General John J. Pershing, who was accompanied upon one of the tours by General Philippe Petain of the French Army. "The finest body of men under our command" was the consensus of opinion of the general staff after the inspection of the 5th Regiment. The strenuous course of training was highly effective upon the health of the men, and September 1917 found the battalion in superb physical condition.

In the middle of the month General William L. Sibert, commanding the First Division, bade farewell to the 5th Marines upon the occasion of their being detached from that army unit, and on 23 September 1917, the First Battalion, minus the 15th and 67th companies, entrained for Breuvannes, Haute-Marne. The 15th company was detached from the First Battalion at this time and soon joined the newly named Sixth Machine Gun Battalion. Its place in the organization was not filled until January 1918, when the 17th company joined. The 67th company departed for England, where it remained on detached duty at the American rest camps in Southampton, Winchester, and Romsey until 7 March 1918, when it rejoined the battalion in Breuvannes. Major Turrill accompanied the 67th Company to England, and during his absence the battalion was commanded, in turn, by Lieutenant Colonel Logan Feland, Captain George W. Hamilton, and Major Edward A. Greene.

Upon its arrival in the Breuvannes area the 5th Regiment was attached to the 2d Division, whose other regiments later became the 6th Marines, the 9th and 23d Infantry, the 12th, the 15th, and the 17th Field Artillery, and the 2d Engineers.

The winter of 1917-1918 proved a rigorous season in the Breuvannes area, and the light wooden barracks occupied by the battalion were of slight protection from the cold. But the hardiness of the men increased during the period. A spirit of unrest, a longing for action, became marked, especially so when it was learned that the First Division had proceeded to the front early in the winter and was engaging the enemy.

Thanksgiving, Christmas and New Year's Days were celebrated in little Breuvannes with as much of the home observance as it was possible to reproduce under the circumstances. Keen interest was aroused in football, and the battalion was creditably represented by teams from its companies in contests arranged with other units of the regiment.

In January 1918, the battalion was reinforced by the 12th and 26th companies (both disbanded 31 December 1917); the strength of the respective companies was increased to the combat size of 250 men by spreading those men throughout the four other companies.

This battalion, especially, seemed to fight, outstandingly, with heavy losses, just four days of the entire period they were in France. The first was on 6 June at Hill 142, followed by 18 July at Soissons, on 4 October at Blanc Mont and lastly, the last night of the war, 10–11 November. They were, to the best of my knowledge, the only Marine battalion to have just those very heavy days; all the other five infantry battalions had bad days which went on steadily.

Verdun

Travel orders finally arrived, and on 17 March 1918 the First Battalion entrained at daybreak. A day's journey brought the unit to Lemmes, a short distance from Verdun. Disentraining under cover of darkness, the battalion set out upon a frying night march, made under great difficulties, which brought the organization at an early hour on the morning of the 18th to Camps Douzaine and Nivolette, reserved positions in the old French sector southeast of Verdun. On 28 March 1/5 relieved 3/6 at Mont-sous-les-Côtes and with a French regiment held the extreme left flank; a divisional section. In the meantime, on 13 March, Maj. Julius S. Turrill had relieved Maj. Edward A. Greene in command of 1/5. About this time the arrangement for machine gun company support had developed and the 77th Company of the 6th Machine Gun Battalion was assigned to 1/5.

A week later, after a single day had been spent in the trenches at a point opposite the two camps, the battalion hiked toward Verdun and, on the first day of April 1918, took over the lines before Moulainville and Aix, in the sector known as Meuse Heights, relieving French troops. The lines in this sector had remained stable since the early days of the war, in spite of the fact that the costly struggles for the possession of the Verdun strongholds had been staged a few kilometers to the left. The tranquility of Meuse Heights was due chiefly to the fact that the terrain rendered any extensive operation scarcely worth the price.

During the six weeks that followed, the battalion gained invaluable experience in trench warfare at the cost of minimum casualties. The only contact with the German forces was gained by patrols and by a raid that was launched successfully by a French-Marine force out of Aix. The entrenchments in the sector were for the most part in low ground, and the accommodations consequently damp and crowded. But the long period of training had placed the health of the battalion beyond the effects of any of the unsanitary factors that existed from this period on.

17 April: A patrol of 66th Company, 5th Regiment Marines, and French soldiers earned another commendation in Government Order No. 35, for their successful attack on the night of 17 April 1918, out of Fix, near Demi-Lune. Second Lieutenant Max D. Gilfillan and Sergeant Louis Cukela were awarded the Croix de Guerre and were cited in Government Order No. 35 for their individual actions. Corporal John L. Kuhn was killed in action, and he and Pvts. George C. Brookes and Walter Klamm were also cited. The patrol encountered a German patrol, and in the resulting firefight they suffered an additional two Marines wounded and two missing.

18 April: Report of that raid by Colonel Neville to commanding general, Second Division: "A raiding party was composed of 2nd Lieut. M. D. Gilfillan U.S.M.C. and 30 men, 1st Battalion 5th Marines, Lieut. Francois Viaud, Sous Lieut. Louis Charpain and 30 men of the 20th Regiment, French Army, (four stretcher bearers, American accompanied the party). Mission: To take prisoners and if possible to bring back arms, equipment and tools. Starting point: LA FIEVETERIE. Hour 11:10 p.m. April 18, 1918." Neville briefly explained what happened on the raid without describing the casualties suffered. They returned at 1145. On the night of 20-21 April, 1/5 was relieved by 3/5. The rest of April was, more or less, ordinary for 1/5.

10 May: The 49th Company was out on patrol when they ran into a German patrol. The latter yelled "*Halte*" and down on the dirt went the Marines. They were greatly outnumbered, but managed to drive the Germans off. The loss was one second lieutenant, Vernon L. Somers, wounded (Killed in action at Belleau Wood on 6 June). Somers was greatly praised by his men as doing "excellent work." Beneficially, they captured a wounded German officer.

On 10 May a special commendation for Pvt. Bernard Yoakam, a runner in the 66th Company, was presented to Maj. Turrill from, of all people, Maj. Gen. Bundy, 2d Division, for refusing medical treatment for a wounded hand.

14 May: The regiment was relieved, and the First Battalion entrained at Ancemont for a daylight trip to Vitry-le-Francois, from which Vitry-en-Perthois was reached that evening on foot. In that pleasant village the battalion was billeted for a week, after which it entrained for Boury, northwest of Paris, to await further orders. This brief period out of the lines was perhaps the happiest in the history of the battalion. Losses had been practically nil in the Meuse Heights, and the confidence gained during that period brought the spirits of the men to the zenith. Then too, there was a goodly percentage of men in the ranks of each company who had served in the Marine Corps for years, and who represented the traditions of the corps. Subsequent battles caused this group of the older Marines to dwindle to the merest handful, but they left behind them, in the minds of the younger sea-soldiers, the traditions of which they were so proud. The columns whistled and sang while on the march during this period, and racy songs were adopted in number. Chief among these was "Parlez-vous," whose catchy melody appeared suddenly from an unknown source, but whose verses were added to daily from the ranks of the songsters.

Private Joseph Feingold of the 67th Company told of the refitting and reorganization of the 1st Battalion after they left the Verdun front because "we were pretty well down on clothes and food." He added that his company, after lengthy road marches, was now billeted in "barns and farmyards" in the small village of Buerry. It was while in this relatively quiet zone that the division received its call to proceed to the Chateau-Thierry Sector, without delay.

Decoration Day 1918 was passed peacefully, but on the following morning, 31 May 1918, the battalion boarded camions (trucks) and whirled east over the white highways on the famed hurry call toward Chateau-Thierry (Bois de Belleau). Major Turrill sent an order to the 67th Company for one sergeant to report to Regimental Headquarters at Boury at 1115. "He will carry two marching panels, also lunch: RUSH." Though ordered by Turrill, it was signed by Sergeant Russell R. McDanel of the 67th Company.

The meeting, near Meaux—with a long, plodding procession of refugees, for the most part women and children, trudging westward under heavy burdens—acted upon the men that afternoon like a powerful stimulant, bringing the situation home to every member of the battalion, and instilled a tense demand for vengeance. The organization slept in the open on the night of May 31, a short distance east of Meaux, and continued to live in bivouac during the entire drive.

Belleau Wood

1 June 1918: a long march brought the battalion close to the lines. At 0820 Turrill sent a message to Neville: "Arrived at this position 6:15 a.m. (Old 3d Bn position)."

2 June: There had been a nearly three-mile break in the French line and troops were needed to fill it. Turrill and 1/5 were transferred to support the 23d Infantry. Sometime after midnight, Col. Paul B. Malone, USA, with his 23d Infantry, reinforced by Turrill plus two companies of the 5th Machine Gun Battalion and a company of engineers, were all roused out of their sound sleep. They had orders to march about six miles north and west of Lucy to fill the gap in the French line from Bois de Veuilly westward to Gandelu. By daylight on 2 June the Americans were in position with Turrill at the Bois de Veuilly at 0625.

Unconnected elements of French troops were scattered along the line and Marines of 1/5 reported that they had found vagrant Frenchmen looting Les Mares Farm, which was located about a half mile west and north of Champillon. Lieutenant Colonel Logan Feland, assistant regimental commander of the 5th Marines, who was scouting along the line, found a French regimental commander personally serving a machine gun, while his staff and such men as could be gathered were holding back the German advance from the Clignon Heights. The French officer told Feland, "Looting is very bad at times like these. Everything goes. As soon as we can reorganize, we shoot a few of them, and it stops."

At 0950 Turrill reported to Colonel Paul B. Malone, CO, 23d Infantry, that he and 1/5 were based 500 yards south of Premont and that he had made contact "with the Col. commanding the 133d Inf., the left unit of the 43d Div. [French Infantry] ... Have placed one officer and platoon at PREMONT [Prément] with instructions to get in contact with your rt. Co.... Expect to have some machine guns on the ridge S. E. of PREMONT. Have patrolled entire front."

Malone responded at 1525: "Have you established your Bn. observing station? If so, where is it? Indicate on your sketch." And again at 1745: "Your Bn. and M. G. Co. with you will move at once to LES GLANDONS where further orders will be given you. South of Prément." At 1800 Malone ordered: "Send platoon of Engineers now with you to report to CO 3d Bn., on your left." At 1812 Malone advised Turrill that his battalion was being relieved by 2/23, and to report to Neville at Pyramide as brigade reserve.

2 and 3 June: At midnight 1/5 was withdrawn to support positions near the Pyramide, where Neville had established his headquarters. That next morning at 0930 Turrill reported to Neville about his relief: "One man killed and ten wounded of the 49th Co. One man in 17th Co was hit in head by H. E. fragment, not a severe wound. I am at [Pyramide] Farm buildings near Pyramide Monument."

As the afternoon developed, it soon became apparent that the situation on the left of the 2d Division was not as threatening as originally believed. The line formed by the 23d Infantry Regiment, Turrill's 1/5 and the French dismounted cavalry was holding everywhere. Consequently, the Germans were making little progress in their attacks south of Clignon Brook. In mid-afternoon Harbord sent orders to Turrill that he and 1/5 were to withdraw from support of the 23d Infantry. As we have seen, his battalion would now become brigade reserve.

A message at 1800 from "Dr. Shea" at 1/5 Headquarters was sent to Captain George W. Hamilton, commanding officer of the 49th Company: "Send all bandsmen to Bn. Hqrs. after dusk." Twenty-five minutes later Hamilton replied: "The 49th company has no bandsmen. Other companies have been notified." (It appears that the bandsmen were being collected to help with the wounded.)

It was impossible for the officers and men to realize what a tremendous crisis hovered in the vicinity. The French forces were in the depths of despair, and the rapid withdrawal that they had been forced to make had taken from them the pride and determination that alone could stem the tide. As for the men of the battalion, the situation in prospect held no terrors. The crack units of the German Army were coming on, and the "Leathernecks" had been given the honor post in the Allied project of stemming the enemy's sweeping advance. Late that day Harbord ordered: "Turrill's 1st Bn now Brigade Reserve."

4 and 5 June: The daylight hours were spent under the cover of the Bois de Veuilly, near Marigny. On the latter day a number of enemy shells directed with fatal accuracy caused the battalion's first extensive casualties, and the incident served to fill to the brim the cup of the avengers. Meanwhile, the 17th and 66th Companies of 1/5, just released from the 23d Infantry, were assigned service with Lt. Col. Wise's 2/5 at Les Mares Farm. Shortly afterward, with some machine guns from the 8th Company they were sent to fill that gap between them and the 6th Regiment. The distance was approximately a half mile and this location would continue to dog everyone who was sent to fill it. What made matters even worse was that the main road between Torcy and Lucy went right through the area. Any advance made by German forces south would naturally take this easiest pathway. The 4th Brigade's entire position would thus be in serious trouble, greatly affecting the 2d Division, the entire line, and ultimately the war.

As it developed, Brig. Gen. Harbord, commander of the 4th Brigade, under French direction, decided to take the important position known as Hill 142. The only unit available was 1/5, but it was short half its component units. Orders were issued for Turrill to begin his operation early on the morning of 6 June. His two companies had spent most of these two days under partial cover. Their travel during the previous days had caused a serious morale problem; neither company had been fed during this period. This would fester even during the attack on 6 June.

In the meantime he received a request from Neville to report his manpower, and following was his response:

	Officers	*Men*	*Total*
17th	6	239	245
49th	6	234	240
66th	5	239	244
67th	5	241	246
	22	953	975

Additionally, 1/5 had two doctors, thirteen corpsmen, ten U.S. Army Signal Corps men, 17 USMC Headquarters signal men, eight bandsmen plus a sergeant major and four orderlies. However, 1/5 only had 11 officers and 475 enlisted Marines for that descent down to Hill 142. Later Turrill reported that 11 men from the four companies were missing, naming them, and three named were from the 49th Company and were in the hospital.

Turrill, who was slated to launch a major attack the following morning at 0345, hadn't yet received his orders at this late hour of 2100. Late receipt of orders was a common occurrence in the 4th Brigade all during the war due to sloppy administrative work.

6 June: Early morning found two companies of 1/5 deployed for combat a short distance east of Champillon on top of Hill 176. Late orders had made it impossible to bring up food. It would be later afternoon before supplies finally came up.

2. First Battalion, Fifth Marines, 1917–1919

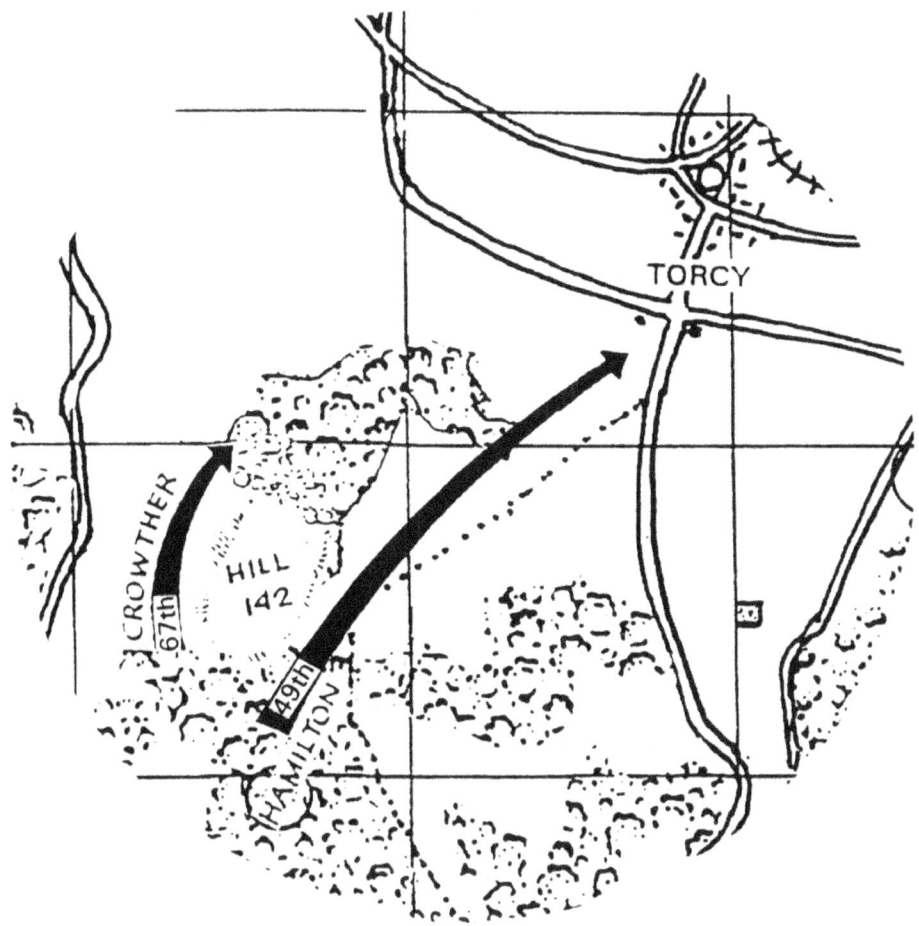

The attack by 1/5 on 6 June 1918.

The orders for attack down from Hill 176 on to Hill 142 had not reached Major Turrill until midnight on June 5–6, and the orders designated that the companies be in position three hours later. At the appointed hour the stage was set for the deadly drama that was to follow. There was very little artillery available in the emergency, but all such handicaps were forgotten when the H hour, 0345 a.m. arrived, and the battalion was deployed, pieces loaded and bayonets fixed. The 49th Company, Capt. George W. Hamilton, and the 67th Company, 1st Lt. Orlando C. Crowther, were the only two companies available. The 17th, Capt. Roswell C. Winans, and the 66th, 1st Lt. Walter T. H. Galliford, were still with Wise and 2/5 at Les Mares Farm. Later that morning, after the initial assault, when the two companies were released by 2/5, they reached Hill 142 and were immediately entered into defensive positions on that hilltop.

When he heard the whistle blow, 1st Sgt. Daniel Hunter of the 67th raised his cane up and then down toward their target, yelling, "Let's go." The hour had come, and the assaulting waves moved out, down the hill and then across the first wheat field, barely visible in the early morning mist, into their first mortal combat with the enemy. During this day's battle every man in the organization was called upon to give the best that was in him, and to a man, the unit responded.

Out ahead and down below lay Hill 142, an elongated height extending approximately north and south. The course of the 49th Company lay along the crest and on the right flank of the hill, bearing nearly due north, while the 67th Company's course led to the lower slopes and ravine west of Hill 142. Alternate woods and grain fields covered the region, and it was nearly surrounded from the enemy direction by commanding heights.

The two assaulting companies had advanced but a short distance when the enemy opened a machine gun barrage, and from that moment there was little cessation of fire until the noon hour. The enemy forces opposing the Marines included two of the most highly trained units in the Imperial Army, the 28th Infantry Regiment, better known as "The Kaiser's Own," and the 362d Infantry Regiment.

One of the first casualties was 2d Lt. Walter D. Frazier of the 49th Company, but there were many more, including most of the officers and many non-coms. After Pvt. John Kukoski of the 49th and his comrades ran into a German machine gun, they were all either killed or wounded. Alone Kukoski charged a machine gun and with utmost bravery captured it and its crew, including one officer, forcing them to carry the gun back to brigade headquarters.

But the man that held it all together was Capt. George W. Hamilton, skipper of the 49th. He displayed the highest type of courage and leadership on that first day of the battle when his command was under decimating fire from machine guns on their front and both flanks. At the attack upon Hill 142, his depleted company and the 67th continued forward. They jumped off at 0350 and by 0700, after taking severe casualties, his company and the 67th—which had lost all but one officer—dug in on the hill. His courage and competence were decisive factors in the success of the attack. He earned his Oak Leaf Cluster for a second Distinguished Service Cross the same day. While his men were digging in he saw 12 German machine gunners approach and proceed in setting up their Maxims. He and Gunnery Sergeant Charles F. Hoffman rushed forward with bayonets and after killing several, the balance were routed. Hamilton always carried a Springfield rifle; he and the sergeant captured their machine guns. This undaunted bravery served to inspire the men in his regiment and incited them to heroic efforts. It also served to earn Hoffman a Medal of Honor (his real name was Ernest Janson and a Silver Star was issued in that name).

The 49th Company was loaded with heroes that day. Sergeant John Casey, although wounded during a counterattack, refused to go to the rear since he was senior man of the group. He remained with his men, refusing to accept medical attention until assured that his men were properly dug in and the enemy had retired. Sergeant Raymond P. Cronin, while under heavy machine gun fire, attempted to establish liaison with an adjoining French unit, during which he was killed. Sergeant John H. Culnan, while assisting a wounded man to the rear, was himself wounded in the head, but carried out his mission, succeeding in bringing the other wounded man to the dressing station (he was promoted to 2d lieutenant). Sergeant Arthur F. Ware, while under heavy machine gun fire, attempted to establish liaison with an adjoining French unit, during which he was killed in action.

First Lt. Jonas H. Platt of the 49th was seriously wounded in the leg early in the engagement but continued to direct operations not only of his platoon but of another. He charged and drove off the crew of an enemy machine gun, supervised the disposition and digging in of a large part of his company and yielded command only when exhausted from pain and loss of blood. Another from the 49th who didn't fare so well was 2d Lt. Vernon L. Somers, who was killed in action 6 June 1918. An enlisted man later decorated was Cpl. Eugene W. Wear of the 49th who, with a private, went out into an open field under heavy shell and machine gun fire and succeeded in bandaging and carrying back to Allied lines a wounded comrade. Many men of the company earned medals that day, most were Silver Star citations or French Croix de Guerres, or both.

It appears that Hamilton was of the impression that he and his company were to continue down the hill and towards the village of Torcy. It wasn't until later that he received orders to withdraw back onto Hill 142, but a number of his men remained in the village, some eventually dying there.

The 67th Company wasn't far behind. The leader of the 67th that day was 1st Lt. Orlando C. Crowther, and although only temporarily in command, he displayed the highest type of courage and leadership. After all the men near him had been killed or wounded, he captured one machine gun and crew unaided, and while attempting to take a second, was himself killed. Private John Harris continued firing his automatic rifle in action after being wounded in the face, and Pvt. Arthur Hopper continued advancing with his platoon after being wounded in the arm. When Pvt. Joseph M. Baker's platoon of the 67th was suffering from casualties from the fire of a hidden machine gun, he exposed himself to a heavy fire to take up a position on the flank of the enemy gun. He attacked and killed the gunner by rifle fire and then rushed the gun, killing the crew with his bayonet. Meanwhile, Sgt. John V. Fitzgerald directed a flank attack on an enemy machine gun position all the while exposing himself to its fire. At about the same time, Cpl. Prentice S. Geer had become isolated when the enemy counterattacked his group, then he courageously charged with a bayonet and, with the assistance of his comrades, captured a machine gun crew and repulsed the attack at that point (he was promoted to 2d lieutenant).

While those men were killing Germans, Cpl. Arnold D. Godbey volunteered to rescue wounded men from a field swept by machine gun fire and snipers. Carl Norstrand, the battalion's sergeant major, and Godbey carried three men to shelter. Runner Pvt. John M. Fackey, while carrying messages, also assisted wounded to shelter under heavy enemy fire. A little later, Cpl. Charles G. Hawkins assisted in the reorganization of his company under heavy enemy fire.

One of the bravest Marines was old-timer 1st Sgt. Daniel A. Hunter, who fearlessly exposed himself and encouraged all men near him, although he himself was wounded three times, twice down, twice up then down forever. He died of his wounds later that same day.

At some point, according to an after-action report by Turrill, after the two companies had arrived on Hill 142 and were pushing into the woods on the north end, a platoon from the 66th Company, under 1st Lt. Max D. Gilfillan, arrived by Turrill's side. Later, at about 0430, the balance of the 66th arrived and went into line as did elements of the 8th Machine Gun Company. Not long after, Winans and the 17th Company arrived and was placed to Hamilton's right. The semi-official history suggested that the 17th Company arrived first and ignored completely the arrival of the 66th Company. The records aren't clear on that matter, but there is no question that each endeavored to support both the 49th and 67th Companies in their agony. Captain Keller E. Rockey, battalion adjutant, reported to Neville at 0537: "17th Co. going into deployment from old 1st line—8th M. G. Co. already forward. Things seem to be going well—No engineers are in evidence—Can something be done to hurry them along—The advance is about one kilometer. Major Turrill is up forward with the line."

Captain Albert P. Baston of the 17th, although shot in both legs while leading his platoon through the woods at Hill 142, refused treatment until he personally assured himself that every man in his platoon was under cover and in good firing position. His "skipper" was Capt. Roswell Winans, who distinguished himself in leading his company up on the right of the 49th Company on Hill 142, where he well organized his position, held steadfastly and stood some counterattacks. Winan's company was in support in the first stage, and then took an active part. His skill, fortitude, and high personal courage contributed loyally to 1/5's success (he had earned a Medal of Honor at Santo Domingo in 1916). Another platoon leader, 1st Lt. Robert Blake, was later decorated because, when the line was temporarily held up, he volunteered and maintained liaison with the 49th Company, continually crossing and re-crossing an open field on Hill 142 swept by intense machine gun fire. Later in the engagement he established liaison with a French unit on the left flank crossing a wheat field under heavy machine gun and sniping fire and returned with valuable information.

Displaying great courage and devotion to duty in delivering messages upon numerous occasions, Pvt. Ernest Borah, through severe shell fire that day, volunteered to bring up ammunition for a captured German gun and exposed himself to machine gun fire. He would also be decorated later at Blanc Mont. Platoon leader 2d Lt. Earl W. Garvin showed great courage and daring when, after repelling two counterattacks, led his platoon in a brilliant charge against a machine gun position, captured the gun and crew and immediately turned the gun against the enemy. Later he captured another machine gun. During the early months of the war, 2d Lt. Bernhardt Gissell of the 4th Brigade, U.S. Army showed high qualities of leadership and personal bravery in command of his platoon and led them under heavy shell fire in repulsing a counterattack of the enemy. A man who was always in the thick of it, Sgt. Maj. Carl J. Norstrand of the 17th, when his presence was not demanded in the performance of his normal duties of his office, volunteered to rescue wounded men from a field swept by machine gun fire, and continued this heroic work with the aid of other volunteers until all had been recovered (he was later promoted to 2d lieutenant). Gunnery Sergeant Sidney Thayer, Jr., leading thirty-one others, by conduct showed the highest qualities of courage, aggressiveness, and judgment under trying conditions. Under machine gun and shellfire in the woods, much of the time in darkness, due to their work in reorganizing and continuing the fight, the advance was carried on. Thayer was promoted to 2d lieutenant in the 43d Company. Private Clarence D. Hathaway of the 17th earned a Silver Star citation, later the medal, during the action at Hill 142. He and two others gave first aid to Sgt. Paul J. Robinett, who had been badly wounded in the chest and lay in an exposed position swept by machine gun, rifle and artillery fire, after which they moved him to a shelter. The other two were Pvt. Virgil E. McClain, also of the 17th, who came along later and carried him to a dressing station singlehandedly. The third was Sgt. Amor L. Sims, who would later serve as a general officer during World War II.

The U.S. Navy supplied the 4th Brigade with numerous medical services, mainly doctors and what later became known as corpsmen. Lieutenant Richard O'B. Shea, USN, of 1/5, was with the men that day and treated the wounded under heavy bombardment, showing utter disregard for his own personal safety. He would have been accompanied by enlisted corpsmen, but I don't have that data about them.

The 66th Company had heroes on the 6th but not many were highly decorated. Included were 1st Lt. Max D. Gilfillan, who was badly wounded on 6 June while leading his men into action. Previously he had been awarded a Silver Star citation (later a medal) at Verdun. One man who couldn't be kept down was Marine Gunner Henry L. Hulbert, who displayed extraordinary heroism during an attack on the enemy's lines, during which time he constantly exposed himself to the enemy's fire without regard for personal danger, thereby assuring the delivery of supplies. First Sergeant Thomas J. McNulty was another man of the 66th who was badly wounded while leading and encouraging men of his company, displaying courage of the highest order. Finally, Gy. Sgt. Edward T. Bayman was decorated for gallantry in action at Belleau Wood; from June 6 through June 18, he organized a position for defense under heavy fire.

The morning's objective lay along the northern extremity of Hill 142, a position which commanded the terrain on all sides. The attack orders were issued too late to permit fully acquainting the subordinates with the plan of assault, and when the 49th company reached the objective with approximately 90 percent of its officers and non-commissioned officers already on the casualty lists, the men pressed on down the northeastern slope of the hill toward Torcy, holding tenaciously to their additional gain until recalled to the designated objective line. One of the casualties that day from the 49th was 2d Lt. William C. Peterson, USA, who was killed in action 6 June 1918.

Some Marines never made it back to Hill 142. Bodies were found many years later, some in the buildings of Torcy, with German enemy lying alongside. Meanwhile, at 0805, Captain Lloyd W. Williams reported to Turrill that under orders from Lt. Col. Logan Feland, he and three of his platoons from his 51st Company, 2/5, were on hand and under Turrill's command.

Brave deeds and cool leadership went hand in hand on that day. The enemy's pride was shaken but not broken by the first attack, and he stood his ground more firmly than he did in any subsequent encounters with the Marines. Hand to hand engagements were fought in numbers on 6 June; and to the Leathernecks' notion, hand to hand engagements offered the only means of satisfying an avenging spirit long pent up.

The objective was reached before the sun was high, and by mid-morning the first of a series of enemy counterattacks had been successfully stemmed. The teams who had become experts in handling the Chauchat automatic rifles were decimated early in the battle, but the trusty Springfield in the hands of men who had confidence in the weapon saved the day and completely confounded the enemy with the accuracy. When he realized that all the officers in the 67th Company were down, Capt. Hamilton combined it with the 49th and assumed command of both.

Individual deeds of heroism were legion. For a year the battalion had trained faithfully and awaited its chance, and the long-postponed day of action was welcomed. It was its own reward. All were heroes.

Before the morning was over, at 0900 Turrill was reporting that he had four machine guns captured on the "last objective—would like a Co. (at least) near where the 5th and 6th Regt. joined." Less than an hour later he requested that the retired French "be persuaded to come up on our left. Suggest shelling *beyond* our objective. Need Chauchat amm. & Springfield amm. also stretchers—also M. G. amm. Berry [commanding, 3/5] is fighting in woods on my right, woods not shown on map [Bois St. Martin]." Fifteen minutes later Neville told him he was sending up ammunition, and Turrill replied: "I have no men to carry this up." At 0945 Turrill was again stating, "NEED AMMUNITION. Winans [Capt. Roswell, commanding, 17th] advancing on my right cleaning out woods."

Then at 0950 came probably the most plaintive report anyone would or could send on that morning. It was from Capt. George W. Hamilton, commanding officer, 49th Company, who was most responsible for the success of the attack and capture of the target, Hill 142.

> Elements of this Company and the 67th Company reached their objective, but because very much disorganized were forced to retire to our present position which is on the nose of hill 142 and about 400 yds. N. E. of square woods. (Square woods N. E. of figures "142").
>
> Our position is not very good because of salient. [Their position was like a nose sticking out northward with enemy on both sides.] We are intrenching and have 4 machine guns in place.
>
> We have been counter-attacked several times but so far have held the hill. Our casualties are *very* heavy. We need medical aid badly, cannot locate any hospital apprentices and need many. We will need artillery assistance to hold this line tonight.
>
> Ammunition of all kind is needed.
>
> The line is being held by detachments from the 49th, 66th, and 67th Company & are very much mixed together.
>
> 9:50 a.m.   George W. Hamilton
> No Very Pistols. All my officers are gone.   G.W.H.
> 1. Art fire on front beyond objective.
> 2. Men to carry ammunition.
> 3. Tools.
> 4. Stretchers.
> 5. Med. Attendance.
> 6. Food.
> 7. Push Berry up to our right.
> 8. Another M. G. Co.

At 1115 someone (unnamed) complained to Neville that 12th Field Artillery was "shelling our trenches, Bn. Hdqts. severely at present." At 1210 Hamilton wrote Turrill asking that artillery be notified of his position and fire to his front in order to "stop constant enemy activity and save our ammunition." And he emphasized his need for ammo and hospital apprentices to dress wounds. "We could evacuate later. Need water badly. Need Very pistols & illuminating rockets." For the next few hours Turrill was pressing for Berry to come up on his right. Otherwise he would have to fall back. "A strong attack on our right would finish us." More demands for ammunition, water, and food. At 1400 he reported that 60 men had delivered food, water and ammunition.

At sometime that day, no hour indicated, Winans wrote to Rockey complaining about the weak condition of Hamilton's left. "Just now the Germans are attacking Hamilton's left working around on him. I sent 10 then 20 men to help and protect his flank." He added, "We need more reinforcements, food, ammunition. Hamilton is OK."

Earlier in the day, Maj. Ben Berry of 3/5 had received orders to spread his battalion toward the north to make contact with Hamilton's group. Captain Peter Conachy's 45th Company was to be the connecting link. The connecting platoon was led by 2d Lt. Edward B. Hope, but for some reason, all during the period that 1/5 remained at Hill 142, that connection never occurred.

Captain Roswell Winans and his 17th Company came along to Hamilton's far right and remained there until the battalion was eventually relieved later in the month. This was where Hope was supposed to be.

7 June: Turrill sent a message to Neville at 0725 in which he requested that dead be buried in Champillon and that he would send dead to that town. He also mentioned that Capt. Peter Conachy, commanding officer, 45th Company, 3/5, had attacked enemy on his right at 0400.

Turrill provided a list of casualties and replacements to regiment for the 6 of June:

Unit	Officers	Men	Officers	Men
Bn. Hq	0	10	0	0
17th Co.	2	111	1	40
49th Co.	4	160	5	111
66th Co.	6	102	5	55
67th Co.	4	161	3	112
	16	544	14	318

I find no officer deaths listed on 6 June for the 66th Company, so all six casualties listed above must have been wounded. One of the officer replacements for the 49th Company was 1st Lt. John W. Thomason, Jr. One of the enlisted replacements for the 67th Company was Pvt. Elton Mackin.

A message from Turrill to Neville was listed as received at 12:26 a.m. but was really 12:26 p.m.: "10:17 a.m. Some activity by our artillery. Aeroplanes overhead. Enemy dropping shells south of here." Then he added that French soldiers were entering the square woods: "10:37 A party of the 8th M. G. Co. reported a ration dump south of Champillon. Am sending a party of engineers to bring them here. A wounded Boche prisoner just going by."

Someone wrote the following message on the 7th: "The 1st Bn. 5th Marines were hardly in position to make an attack owing to heavy losses yesterday morning. 67 Co. loss Lieutenant Crowther, [Francis] Kieren, [Aaron] Ferch and one other [2d Lt. Thomas W. Ashley]. 49th Co. Lieut. Simons [2d Lt. Vernon L. Somers] and all other officers except Capt. Hamilton." Dead were 2d Lt. Walter D. Frazier; 2d Lt. William C. Peterson, U.S. Army Volunteers; wounded, 1st Lt. Jonas H. Platt plus 320 enlisted Marines. Sometime that day, Winans told Turrill he had "two platoons of engineers ... they are digging 2d line positions for us. Have I the authority to keep them here until we get reinforcements? We have lost fifty percent and can't do our own digging. We would like a doctor if possible and chauchat ammunition."

The tension lessened after the first day, and from 7 to 9 June the battalion clung to the ground gained, repelling counterattacks and strengthening its position. Allied artillery had been rushed to the scene at the outbreak of the battle, and the positions of the enemy were shelled heavily during this period and until the great enemy retreat was taken up. The semi-official history nowhere mentions that replacements for the losses suffered by 1/5 on 6 June arrived on 7 June. They included mostly officers and men from the 5th Base Detachment.

8 June: Corporal August W. Meyers of the 17th Company voluntarily crossed a field covered by machine gun and sniper fire to carry information to a section on the left in the woods that the enemy were advancing up the ravine to attack. His reward was two Silver Star citations and two Croix de Guerres.

9 June: At 0115 Turrill wrote to Hamilton: "Am sending at the request of the French 100 men and two machine guns to hold the square woods northwest of our left (Winan's). The 50 men you sent me this a.m. I am sending to lines. Also I would like to have you send me another 50. This is a temporary arrangement, to help the French out. EXPEDITE." (I believe the directions are incorrect. It should read "northeast of our right" because those woods were to the front and right of Hill 142 and Winan's 17th Company was on the right flank.)

The Germans launched a major attack upon 1/5's positions, especially where the 17th Company was located. First Lieutenant Robert Blake, with eleven men, including Privates Harry Hess, Frederic E. Beausoleil, Charles P. De Grange, William K. Stach, William H. Behr, John F. Stasky, Charles A. Brooks, and Clifford A. Burke, stood up to machine gun fire and advancing German waves, helping to break up their attack upon a position defended by the French. Burke was killed by the enemy fire.

Lieutenant Colonel Fritz Wise demanded Williams and his 51st Company be returned to 2/5 since he was now being prepared for a major attack in a few days. It was approved and once again, Turrill was down to his four badly depleted companies.

During these past few days, Cpl. Robert C. Pitts, of the 17th Company, was awarded a Distinguished Service Cross (later a Navy Cross was added) for extraordinary heroism in action. During the attack between the 6th and 10th he advanced with the most gallant bravery to an attack outside his sector in order to support and rescue his comrades of the 116th Regiment of French Infantry. He was promoted to 2d lieutenant.

12 June: First Sergeant Murl Corbett of the 49th Company, finding himself one of a few remaining non-commissioned officers left alive after a desperate attack by the enemy, organized a defensive position under heavy fire, withstanding numerous counterattacks. On the night of 12 June he led a patrol of three men into the enemy's lines, secured valuable information, and although wounded in the eye, assisted in carrying from No Man's Land men more seriously wounded than himself, refusing evacuation until receiving peremptory orders from his company commander (Hamilton). Realizing that his battalion was hard-pressed for non-commissioned officers, he left the hospital without permission, returned to the front lines, and brought up reinforcements under heavy shell fire at a critical time. He retired in 1938 a lieutenant colonel.

13 June: Captain Roswell Winans and his 17th Company were ordered to move toward Belleau Wood and to make contact with 2/5. Details about Wise's command were very vague and Winans assigned the task to 1st Lt. Robert Blake and his platoon to make the reconnaissance. Blake and his men crossed the Torcy-Lucy road and entered the woods, finding many dead Marines as they moved along. After a bit, they came across a corporal and a few men from 2/5 that had been left there a few days before to cover 2/5's left flank. Blake and platoon returned and divulged the information gleaned to Winans. He was soon ordered to take his entire command and go into the woods himself.

Winans followed directions and entered the wood. As he did so, he noted German planes overhead and realized they were spotters for their artillery. Pulling back out, a few minutes later artillery intensely bombarded that part of woods they had been in. After awhile, when the bombardment ceased, Winans sent a few men into the woods to try to find Wise.

15 June: The 17th Company was released from 1/5 to support the ongoing attack within Belleau Wood. Winans requested reinforcements and Turrill sent him one platoon from the 49th Company and one platoon from the 66th Company. The 49th Company supplied the 17th Company with ten men, including Privates Claude R. Garvey, Marion A. Koch, Charles McK. Hagen, Earl S. Linder, Clarence G. Martin, Samuel C. Mullin (also spelled Mullins), Alonza R. Runyard, and Charles E. Wells, led by Sgt. Edwin S. Van Galder, as reinforcements. They were sent back to their company for ammunition which was badly needed, necessitating their passing through a heavy shrapnel barrage and exposure to fire from a nest of machine guns, returning through the same barrage and delivering the ammunition to Capt. Thomas Quigley, 17th Company, at an opportune moment.

At daylight, the 17th moved into the woods with support from four machine guns of the 8th MG Company. Shortly afterward they managed to push the German defenders aside and drive across the woods. They met 2/5 coming up from the right at about 0730. It was at about this time that Winans had been wounded in the foot and Quigley of the 49th

Left: Private Abner Frey, a member of the 17th Company, 1/5 Battalion. *Right:* Captain Roswell Winans, commanding officer of the 17th Company, 1/5, at Belleau Wood, where he was wounded on 14 June 1918.

The 5th Regiment of Marines marching in Paris on 4 July 1918.

replaced him. It was also at this time that the Germans were strengthened and the 17th was forced on the defensive.

Later that morning, at 0820, Capt. Thomas Quigley sent Neville a message, which arrived at 1130: "The 17th Company in the BOIS DE BELLEAU was attacked by a force of the enemy with 4 heavy and several light machine guns and have withdrawn to their former position. Winans shot through the foot. Quigley in command of the 17th Company."

16 June: On this date Sgt. John Johnston of the 67th Company was decorated with a Silver Star citation for gallantry in action in conducting rations and ammunition to his company during an enemy bombardment. Corporal Earl P. Wilson, also of the 67th, was also awarded a Silver Star for carrying a message from an artillery observation post to the artillery position during enemy bombardment.

17 June: Upon relief by the 7th Infantry late that evening, 1/5 moved back to Saacy-sur-Marne, a reserve position. The 2d Battalion, 7th U.S. Infantry, assumed their position.

24 June: Turrill informed Harbord at 0235 that he was in place in the Gros Jean Woods and located south of Paris-Metz Road.

25 June: Turrill and his 1/5 were called back to the old sector on June 25 for two full weeks more of strenuous duty in and about what had become known as "Hell Wood."

27 June: Turrill and 1/5 replaced 1/6 in St. Martin's Wood as brigade reserve.

28 June: At 2200 Harbord ordered 1/5 to the "woods N. W. of Lucy night of June 29-30 as Brigade Reserve."

30 June: A message from Harbord to both Neville and Lt. Col. Harry Lee of the 6th Regiment at 1100 said: "The 2d Battalion 5th Marines will be relieved as soon as possible after dark tonight by the 1st Battalion, 5th Marines."

It appears, though I lack any record, that Lee was given command of 1/5; at 1130 he sent Turrill a message: "Am inclosing your orders and five copies of the map of the sector.

Upon completion of relief please furnish this office with detailed sketch of your dispositions by company units. Get in touch with Maj. Ralph S. Keyser [commanding officer, 2/5] as soon as possible for your reconnaissance, as indicated in the order. Let me know anything that this office may do for you and keep me advised constantly of events."

1 July: Message from Lee to Turrill: "Please take measures today through your O. P.'s and tonight by patrols to gain any information of the enemy's position, strength and works always keeping in mind the desirability of securing identification, preferably prisoners, and keeping this office informed frequently of events, and if anything is needed by you do not hesitate to ask."

4 July: Message from Lee to Turrill: "Your note just received. You are mistaken about date of relief. You are to be relieved night 5-6th. Apparently there was some question about 1/5 performing a patrol. The patrol is ordered by Brigade who was here in person this morning.... Force called for which you must supply—25 men 1 Officer. Your relief will be 2nd Battalion of the 103rd [26th National Guard Division] who tonight will be in the same woods as you are now.... I repeat they will relieve you night 5-6th."

4 and 5 July: Lieutenant Colonel Hiram Bearss, with one officer and twenty-five men from the 67th Company, made a raid upon the German positions south of Torcy. In the process they killed two Germans and captured two more while procuring much valuable information.

Lieutenant Colonel Julius S. Turrill, incidentally, earned a Distinguished Service Cross, later a Navy Cross, two Silver Star citations, a Legion of Honor and two Croix de Guerre, both with Palm, for what he did on 6 June 1918, displaying extraordinary heroism and setting a splendid example in fearlessly leading his command under heavy fire against superior odds.

On 4 July 1918, fifty members of the First Battalion took part in an inspiring parade in Paris, during which the Marines were heavily "shelled" with bouquets and hailed as the saviors of the gay city.

9 to 15 July: The battalion was billeted in Crouttes, worn out, but well satisfied with the task it had completed. They spent most of their time swimming in the Marne River, repairing their gear and clothes, resting, and eating real food for a change.

Soissons

16 to 20 July: Beginning with 21 July and ending on 25 July, Major Turrill, commanding officer, 1/5, wrote a most comprehensive report of the experience at Soissons. It is long but included here because of the importance of the detailed information about what happened to 1/5 at Soissons.

> About 10 p.m. July 16th Bn. left Saacy-sur-Marne in camions.
> About 8:20 a.m. July 17th Debussed at R.R. Station north of Brasson.
> About 10:20 a.m. July 17th Bivouaced on improved road 2K south of Taillefontaine.
> 9:40 p.m. 17 July started march to attack. Were followed by 2nd and 3rd Battalions. Left 20 percent of Bn. Marched eastward along road to CARREFOURE DU SONT DU CERF, where we expected to find French guides to take us to our position of attack. They were not there. The march to this point was made under the greatest difficulty as the road was packed with wheel

traffic of all sorts and it was necessary to march in single file in the ditch on the right side of wood. Even the ditch was blocked at various points by wagons or camions, which had slipped off the road. Rain with consequent slippery clay mud added difficulties. Being in the woods, it was so dark that one could not see ones hand before the face. Several men were injured by horses or wagons. Under the conditions it was impossible to progress through the woods at side of wood. No guides being at above mentioned cross roads, we turned our march to the N. E. along the National Maubeuge road to an ammunition dump, where we took enough ammunition to give each rifleman 2 extra bandoleers. It was not necessary to draw many as the 1st Bn. supplied itself with 2 extra bandoleers per man before leaving Crouttes. The march was continued. (Long packs were thrown off on side of road before turning N. E. at the cross-roads—this was done to expedite march). At the intersection of 169.7 with the National road, a barbed wire obstruction was encountered, here we turned into woods and deployed on the north side of road, with the 66th Co. [William L. Crabbe] on right and the 17th Co. [LeRoy Hunt] on left, the 67th Co. [Frank Whitehead] was in support. The 49th Co. [George Hamilton] came up about 10 minutes later and went to the left to establish liaison with Moroccans. We covered the front in the woods from the National Road to the Route Chretiennette. A few Frenchmen were seen, and some trenches where we started our deployment. Our barrage commenced while we were deploying. Before the completion of our deployment, some of the 2nd Bn. came up on our right. The German barrage came down on us at this time. About 20 minutes after our barrage commenced, orders were given by me to advance.

About 6:30 a.m. 18 July moved Bn. P.O. to point 171.3-288.5. From this point a line of skirmishers, on line 172.4 could be seen fighting. Also 7 or 8 Tanks were engaged. The information from front was very meager. The line kept advancing. About 9:00 a.m. advanced Bn. P.C. to point 172.3-289.0. About 9:20 a.m. 18 July, moved P.C. to intersection of line 172.5 with National Road Maubeuge. While here, efforts were made to locate lines and establish liaison. Captains' Platt and [Robert] Yowell [20th and 16th] companies came up as a support with 3 bandoleers of ammunition apiece. (The 67th Co. had been sent into line about 8 a.m.) Platt's and Yowell's companies with some of the 49th Co. formed a new support at 5:15 p.m. which happened to be the time we received the order. As soon as possible I started for VIERZY with Bn. Hdqters and the above mentioned support. Two men were wounded before reaching VIERZY. The advance was made thru wheat fields to south of MAISON–NEUVE FERME, thence along wood to 300 yards N. E. of Beaurepaire Ferme, thence thru the fields to VAUXCASTILLE through northern end of that town to VAUXCASTILLE-VIERZY road. This indirect advance was necessary to avoid other troop and firing batteries. At western edge of latter town halted to locate the 3rd Brigade which we were to support. About 5 minutes after this halt, the 8th M.G. Co., came up and Capt. [John H.] Fay told me he had orders from the C.G. 3rd Brigade to occupy the eastern edge of town with his Co. At this time, I thought from the information received, that there was an American line to the east and south of town. While we were standing in the road, snipers opened up on us. I sent a couple of squads to follow the ridge and slope north of town to drive out the sniper or snipers. I still thought that our lines were as stated above, to the east and south of town and that a stray German had been missed in the advance and that he was using his opportunity to the beat advantage. At this time, I was sent for by the C.G. 3rd Brigade and went back down the road about 50 yards around a bend out of range of the sniper, where I met him. He asked me what my orders were and I told him they were to "support the 3rd Brigade." He drew attention to the time, which was 8 p.m. and expressed the opinion that I should have been there earlier. I told him I rec'd the order at 5:15 p.m. and came as soon as we could. I gained the impression that he thought I should have rec'd different orders. His excitement and anger gave me the impression that there had been some miscarriage of plans and that the person responsible therefor had not as yet been ascertained. I assured him that I had carried out the orders I had received as promptly and as well as I could. Further I told him that I had about 150 men there, which were all I could get hold of under the circumstances. He then ordered me to take the town of VIERZY and "keep going" until I took the town of HARTENNES ET TAUX and hold a line to the N. W. corner of the BOIS D'HARTENNES.

And when I had accomplished this mission I was to report the fact to him. This was to be done in case the 23rd Inf. did not come up and make the attack. The front we were to attack was 1500 meters, with the town of HARTENNES ET TAUX at the south end, and was nearly 6 kilometers into the enemy's territory. (I omitted to say that just before reaching Vauxcastille I received a note from Col. Upton 9th Inf. to join him. In view of my orders did not do so.)

By 9 p.m. 18 July, had reached the eastern edge of Vierzy. During our advance and when we had gone four-fifths of the way through VIERZY the 23rd inf. came through the north edge of the town and pushed on through our lines. We captured quite a good many prisoners (one group of 56 men were captured in southern part of town by 3 or 4 men). After the 23rd Inf. passed, I assembled the Marines and proceeded to the western slope of a ridge just east of the cemetery, which is at the southeastern corner of VIERZY. There I found a battalion of the 23rd (Major Fechets—spelling uncertain) deployed. I deployed a few yards in rear of his lines. Here we spent night. The shelling was continuous but not heavy. Most of shells did not strike on this slope but near it. There were a few wounds from fragments. About 4:30 a.m. 19th July, the Bn. of 23rd advanced six or seven hundred yards. We remained stationary. Liaison was effected with Col. Malone, under whose orders we were placed. He left us where we were all day.

Around 4 p.m. received orders from Col. [Logan] Feland that we were to assemble in tunnel in VIERZY. Where I went to reconnoiter the location of tunnel. While at Regimental P. C. received word from Captain Hamilton, 2nd in command [of 1/5], that the enemy was dropping air bombs on battalion and that they had shifted some guns so as to enfilade the slope Bn. was in, and that an immediate move was necessary to avoid unnecessary losses. I, at once, sent the order for him to bring Bn. to tunnel which he did without any losses. Bn. reached tunnel before dark. Remained in tunnel until about 2 a.m. 20 July, when we moved to vicinity of CARREFOURE DE FOURNEAUX where we remained all day and night.

Quite a little information as to what was going on was obtained from wounded and from runners from the front lines. The most of the latter failed to return to their companies when sent to the front. They got lost intentionally or otherwise. Some messages from the front lines were not received until 10 or 12 hours after hour of sending.

J. S. TURRILL, Major, U.S. Marines.

The formation of 1/5 for the advance was: the 49th on the left flank, the 17th Company, then the 66th. Captain Whitehead with the 67th Company was in support. To 1/5's right was the 2d Battalion. In the meantime, enemy airplanes rendered the advance from this point on a considerable problem. Sweeping low over Allied lines, the German aviators operated their machine guns upon the infantry with considerable effect.

The 17th Company under the direction of Capt. LeRoy P. Hunt, finding its left flank exposed because the French Colonial forces had not moved forward, boldly swerved to the left across the front of the 49th Company and against organized resistance captured the village of Chaudun, located well within the French division's sector. The 49th Company was also on this caper. The advance of the 2d Division was further confused by a sharp turn to the right which many of the Marine companies missed, continuing directly ahead into that French zone.

This minimized danger from the exposed flank, and then, after Hunt recognized that he was way out of his sector, the 17th regained its course and closed on the 66th Company. The advance toward Vierzy continued. The 49th Company was now on the far left once again. Second Lieutenant Murl Corbett was the officer commanding the platoon of the 49th which was charged with maintaining liaison with the French Senegalese. One of his men, Sgt. Joe Carter, followed a tank with two Moroccans, in spite of intense machine gun fire. He captured 63 prisoners, one of them an officer. For some reason, he was not awarded a DSC but later received a Navy Cross.

Two Marines earned the highest award that day and both were from the 66th Company. Sergeant Louis Cukela displayed unusual heroism, resourcefulness and utter disregard of personal danger in the Foret de Retz. This non-com advanced single-handed against an enemy strong point that was holding up Allied lines. He captured the first gun from the rear, killing the crew at their posts with his bayonet, and by the use of German hand grenades he bombed out the remainder of the strong point. In this operation he captured 4 prisoners and 2 undamaged machine guns. He was promoted to 2d lieutenant and awarded both an Army and Navy Medal of Honor plus two Silver Star citations. The French awarded him a Legion of Honor, and their equivalent of the U.S. Medal of Honor, a Medal Militaire, plus two Croix de Guerre, with Palm, and the Italian government awarded him an Italian War Cross.

Sergeant Matej Kocak, also in the 66th Company, was awarded the Medal of Honor, Army and Navy, for advancing ahead of the line and capturing a machine gun and its crew. Later that day he took command of several squads of French African troops and led them forward in the advance. He was later killed in action at Blanc Mont on 4 October 1918. Other medals he was awarded included two Silver Star citations, the French Medal Militaire, a Croix de Guerre with Palm and the Italian War Cross. Another 66th Company man, Pvt. Albert A. Taubert, went out in advance of the line of his company into the fire of a machine gun that was shooting at him and captured the gun and crew. His awards were a DSC and Navy Cross.

Captain Percy Cornell, skipper of the 49th Company, dashed forward with several men in the Bois de Retz and silenced a machine gun which had annihilated the advance wave of the adjoining company and was causing heavy casualties in his own company. By this heroic act he saved the lives of many that would otherwise have been cut down, and he earned two Silver Star citations and a French Croix de Guerre with Palm. The 49th Company had two more identifiable heroes that day. One was Sgt. Roland G. St. Louis, who while acting as a volunteer guide was killed in action for his trouble. Another 49th Company man, 1st Lt. John W. Thomason, Jr., with his company gunnery sergeant and six additional Marines, destroyed a German machine gun nest which was impeding the advance of his company and battalion. They killed thirteen Germans and captured 2 machine guns. His courage and leadership was exceptional. He, you might recognize, was a very important author and illustrator of books, mainly about Marines.

Private John F. O'Brien of the 67th Company reacted when his company was held up and subjected to a severe machine gun fire. Private O'Brien, having ascertained the location of the machine gun, alone and single-handed crawled into the enemy's lines, came upon the machine gun crew from the rear, surprised them, and compelled their surrender. His gallant and courageous action enabled his company to advance.

Later that day, Maj. Gen. Harbord gave Brig Gen Hanson Ely, commanding general of the 3d Brigade, control of the 5th Marines. Ely ordered 1/5 to take Vierzy by 1600. At 1715, Turrill, with what remained of 1/5, was at Vauxcastille, near the castle overlooking Vierzy. An Army lieutenant colonel belabored Turrill for not moving forward. Turrill tried to explain that he only had twenty men, all headquarters men with just pistols, but the officer said,

"They are Marines, aren't they major?" Turrill and his remnants of 1/5 went down and took Vierzy.

19 July: Turrill sent several messages on this date. At 0700 he wrote: "My P. C. is at Cemetery S. E. of VIERZY. Have about 150 men in battalion." Another at 1325: "Have only about 20 men of 49th Co. & Hdqrs. Detachment of 1st Bn. Also there are Capt. Yowell with 70 men of 16th Co., Capt. Platt with 40 men of 20th Co., Capt. Quigley with about 35 men of 47th Co. The above less 45th & 47th Cos. were my support before I came here. Total men here is about 200 plus Hdqrs.—235." He added: "Have notified Gen. [Hanson] Ely of above. Neville by [Major Harry R.] Lay."

This was the end of this battle for the 5th Marine Regiment. The 6th Regiment of Marines [see later chapters] took over and were shattered. Following this, the 2d Division units were apportioned to a different sector more or less to rest and rebuild after the catastrophic two campaigns of June and July. Meanwhile, Maj. Gen. John A. Lejeune became commanding general of the 2d Division, and Col. Neville, now Brig. Gen. Neville, assumed command of the Fourth Brigade. Logan Feland, long second in command of the 5th Regiment, became a full colonel and the commanding officer.

Marbache

25 July: The First Battalion was relieved from the Soissons sector, and by a series of marches and brief encampments, and transportation by rail from Nantieul to Nancy, reached the Pont-a-Mousson sector on 6 August. In this sector the battalion occupied a reserve position well back of the lines, and the two weeks spent here afforded comparative relaxation to the men who for two long months had performed assault and line duty with practically no respite.

9 August: The First Battalion took up a support position behind 2/5 in the western sub-sector.

17 August: The battalion set out upon a two-day hike to Govillers. At this point Julius S. Turrill, now a lieutenant-colonel, left the battalion, which was successively commanded by Captain Raymond F. Dirksen (20 to 28 August), then Lieutenant-Colonel Arthur James O'Leary (29 August to 19 September), and finally Major George W. Hamilton for the balance of the war.

After five days of practice upon a rifle range in the area, the First Battalion was billeted in Parey-St.-Cesaire, where it remained from 19 August to 1 September. This period, brief though it was, afforded an opportunity of giving valuable practice to the replacement men, who now filled the ranks in large numbers.

25 August: This was the day of the parade, a parade to award medals to deserving men. Thirty-eight Distinguished Service Crosses were awarded to the 4th Brigade plus numerous French awards.

1 September: The long march to the St. Mihiel sector began. The distance was covered in easy stages, chiefly by night, and on 12 September the First Battalion took up the divisional attack in support of a battalion of the 9th Infantry.

St. Mihiel

10 September: A message from Feland but signed by Capt. John Fay—former commanding officer, 8th Machine Gun Company, now adjutant, 5th Regiment—directed the 1st Bn to detail 1/2 of a platoon under an officer to liaison with 2/6, which would be on their left while 1 additional platoon with an officer to liaison with the regiment (5th Division) was on their right.

12 September: The 1st Battalion was located in the Bois-de-la-Rappe. A later official report listed "company 'D' [67th] in the trenches west of LIMEY. The 1st Battalion occupied a support position in the Ravine South of the road leading east of LIMEY south of the position of the 3rd Battalion. About 6:00 a.m., the leading Battalion (3rd) was ordered to advance to the old French front line trenches; the 1st Battalion following in support." Another report from Col. Feland dated 11 September also listed Company D (67th) under the command of the 2d Battalion.

13 September: Near the evening the 1st Battalion relieved a battalion of the 9th U.S. Infantry in the front lines immediately north of Jaulny. That night they were located in a ravine supported by the 8th Machine Gun Company. A report from Feland to Neville also mentioned that "the 45th and 49th Companies have not been located." (I believe, rather than the 49th, it was really the 47th Company, the 49th being in the 1st Battalion.)

14 September: During the afternoon, Lieutenant-Colonel J. S. Turrill was ordered to Jaulny to take charge of the operations of the 1st and 3rd Battalions.

15 September: About 11:00 a.m., Company B (49th) was placed under command of Major M. E. Shearer (commanding officer, 3/5) with a view to his using it to support his right and to assist in establishing liaison with the 6th U.S. Infantry, 5th Division. "Liaisons were established and maintained with the 6th U.S. Infantry on our right and by a platoon from Company 'A' [17th] under Lieutenant [Leonard E.] Rea."

Night of 15-16 September: The 3rd and 1st Battalions were relieved by two battalions of the 309th U.S. Infantry, 78th National Army Division, and the whole 5th Regiment moved in the Bois-de-l' Heiche.

The hasty retreat of the enemy forces in the first day's battle on the 12th was encouraged by the perfect work on the part of the 2d Division's artillery. On the following day, the First Battalion took over the front line on the northern outskirts of Jaulny, and stayed in position during the three remaining days in the sector.

The casualties sustained by the battalion during this drive, 4 deaths and 202 lesser casualties, were considered remarkably light for the amount of fire to which the unit was subjected.

During the combat at St. Mihiel, 2d Lt. Leonard E. Rea of the 66th Company displayed unusual heroism, coolness, zeal, and good judgment at the southwest corner of the Bois de Bonvaux, 12–16 September 1918. This officer was in command of the combat liaison group between this regiment and the 5th Division on the right. Due to the rapid movement of the line, this duty was most dangerous, and it was performed by him in an exceptionally efficient manner.

I cannot locate any highest honor awards to Marines of the 1st Battalion during this campaign. There were numerous Silver Star citations and various Croix de Guerres.

Hiking out of the St. Mihiel sector on 16 September, the battalion traversed Toul and on the 21st was billeted in Mont-le-Vignoble. Four days later the organization entrained for Chalons-sur-Marne. After two days in Courtisole, near Chalons, the unit was transported by camions into the heart of the Champagne sector, where, going into the lines beyond Somme-Py on 2 October, and jumping off on the following morning, the 5th Regiment added another laurel to its wreath.

Blanc Mont

Blanc Mont was a commanding eminence and the French had made many costly attempts to control it. The secret of the enemy's success in stemming these attacks lay in the fact that the sole portion of the Hindenburg line remaining in German hands traversed this sector. Another major factor was that they had controlled this territory since 1914 and had developed remarkable and hard positions. An intricate double system of trenches known as the Essen and Elbe trenches at the bottom of the high rise rendered the position formidable. The situation was rendered the more complex by the fact that Allied forces had gained a foothold in a part of these trenches, and that at points contact with the enemy was a matter of mere yards, a most precarious situation for the side unfamiliar with the intricacies of the entrenchments.

The 2d Division arrived in the area on 1 October and a plan developed by Major General Lejeune and his two brigade commanders was for the entire division to advance across a split front until they met atop the ridge, and there they would join for an advance upon the town of St. Étienne. The French army, located on both flanks, was to advance with the 2d Division. It didn't and the losses to the 2d Division, especially the Fourth Brigade, were horrendous.

2 October: A message with no names was sent from 1/5: "The 1st Battalion has occupied the trench d'Essen this morning, without resistance." They relieved two French regiments at 0735.

Colonel Feland sent Lt. Col. Arthur J. O'Leary a message at 0530 telling him he ordered Messersmith (commanding officer, 2/5) to send four machine guns of the 23d Company to the front line on left of Hamilton's (now commanding officer, 1/5) position to relieve the French, who were having a bad time. At 0530 Hamilton sent Feland a message that he had sent an intelligence officer to locate "the companies [French] on the left. The French major here says that his right company has reported being relieved, but as yet none of my company commanders have sent in any word. I am very much afraid the guides sent us did not know the way, as even my guide got lost." Feland responded: "Did French major consider the relief complete? Do you consider it complete?"

At 0955 Capt. Francis S. Kieren, 49th Company commanding officer, sent Maj. Hamilton a message that his platoon was in the front-line trench of Essen with no opposition. And at 1020 Hamilton reported to Feland that enemy vacated the Essen trench all along the sector of the regiment.

Original orders were for the attack to begin that morning, but by 1110 that was changed when Lejeune insisted on changing the French plan for one of his own. Hamilton reported that he and a French officer had made a reconnaissance of the lines and spotted Germans in the Bois de Vipère: "All trenches are filled with French dead, but because the area was exposed he could do nothing about it."

At 1745 2d Lt. Miller V. Parsons, 16th Company, 3/5, reported that he was liaison officer with 1/5. At 1900 Feland sent around orders that the attack would take place at 0630 on 3 October.

3 October: The chief of staff, 2d Division, was notified by 1st Lt. Carl J. Norstrand, 17th Company, "In the afternoon of Oct. 2, 1918, orders were received for the 17th Company, 5th Marines to attack the next morning. At the time these orders were received the 17th Co., was holding the left flank of the 5th Marines, the undersigned being in command of the 3rd Platoon which was in positions in the Trench d'Essen on the left front of the company some distance northwest of Somme-Py." Feland sent Hamilton at 0440 to take Essen Hook, located to the regiment's left front, in French territory, and told him to "keep a bright look out on your front before moving over and report promptly any developments there."

It fell to the lot of the 17th Company (Captain LeRoy P. Hunt) to attack a hook-like salient of the enemy position which menaced the 4th Brigade's left flank security. This the 17th accomplished with great success. Through the densest barrage of shell and machine gun fire that it had ever faced, the battalion performed its advance as coolly as ever, and digging into the chalky surface of Blanc Mont, formed its line and prepared to hold.

Norstrand described what the 17th Company had to put up with in their attack: "Upon reaching to within a distance of 800 meters from the hook, the machine gun fire became so intense as to temporarily stop our advance.... He described what measures were taken to continue the attack:

> A machine gun was set up and another was held in reserve and a messenger was sent to the Battalion Commander with a request for a one-pounder or 37 mm gun, the latter arriving within a very short time. Targets were designated by the Company Commander, Captain LeRoy P. Hunt, and due to excellent marksmanship both of the one-pounder and machine gun crews, at least four enemy machine guns were put out of commission. We were not able to resume the advance and at the distance of about 300 meters I was ordered to proceed with my platoon around the enemy's right flank and to attack from there. Lieut. [Edward E.] Lindgren with the 4th Platoon was to execute a similar flank attack from the left while Lieut. Gillis A. Johnson with the 1st Platoon supported by Lieut. [Jacob] Lienhard with the 2nd Platoon were to make a frontal attack. The platoon leaders were all second lieutenants.

Norstrand continued by describing his part in the action. He was held up by enemy machine gun fire, and requested a machine gun to help clear his front. "By the aid of this machine gun commanded by Lieut. [Alfred] Wilkerson [Wilkinson of the 8th Machine Gun Company] I was enabled, on account of the very short range (less than 200 yards) to effectively reduce the enemy fire and the order was now given to assault. Here he adds that the assault did not happen because the "Germans surrendered. "That was when the French occupied the Hook. The Company rejoined the Battalion about 11:00 or 11:30 a.m. the carrying out of the above mission having occupied the entire forenoon from about 7 a.m. on." Norstrand then lauded Hunt like any smart subordinate would.

All the other three companies, the 49th, 66th and 67th, participated in the assault, and supported the advance by the leading Sixth Marines. Second Lieutenant Robert E. Conner of the 49th Company, a former enlisted man, was killed in action while brilliantly leading his platoon up the hill. After his platoon leader, 2d Lt. Dave W. McClain, was hit, Sgt. Guy M. Yeaton of the 66th assumed command of and brilliantly led his platoon up the hill toward Blanc Mont Ridge.

At 0735, 2d Lt. Henry C. Murray, 67th Company, reported to Feland that 1/5 "went over at 7:00 a.m. and are advancing along the front. Tanks are coming up." He added that 1/5 Post of Command was moving to Trench du Pacha. A few minutes later Murray stated that 1/5 was "advancing slowly along the line—considerable artillery activity. The third and second batts. have passed through the 1st batt."

Hunt reported to Hamilton at 0915: "The Hook and hill to left still holds out. Have sent the platoon to work with French and tanks. Resistence at present pretty stiff. Getting them gradually. We will get there in the end." Hamilton then advised Feland that 1/5 was being held up at Essen Hook and asked, "Shall I leave one company and advance the other three or sit tight until the nest is cleared out?" Feland's response a few minutes later was rather bland and didn't address Hamilton's question about leaving the 17th Company behind.

Captain Leroy Hunt and his company spent six hours of severe fighting, reducing the Essen Trench and capturing 300 prisoners. Later, after the French army moved into Essen Trench, the 17th Company joined the balance of the 1st Battalion farther up the hill. Not long after, the French were driven out and the 17th had to go back down and retake Essen Hook. Meanwhile the French army was not moving beyond that point, which made the experiences of the Marines extremely difficult. Liaison between the various French and American units was maintained with the greatest difficulty during this engagement, and gaps occurred in lines that seriously threatened the Fourth Brigade and success of the battle.

Feland sent Hamilton a message at 1135 in which he had sent a 37mm gun. Additionally he wanted Hamilton to locate the posts of command of both 2/5 and 3/5 and "see that he gets this [copy of #22 sent to 2/5 at 0725]. THIS IS IMPORTANT. Send location of Bn. P. C's. Are 2nd and 3rd Bns ahead of you?" Message #22 was directions to Maj. Messersmith to fill in any gaps in 6th Regiment's lines and to the west where the French weren't.

Hamilton's message to Feland at 1305 stated: "Heavy machine gun fire from our left flank and woods to northwest. Am dropping off the 17th Company, with orders to move N. W. to top of the ridge where they can get afield of fire. Will leave them there until French troops come up on left flank. Will move other companies forward dropping them off as needed on left flank until we can get in touch with the 2nd Bn. who I understand are also looking out for flanks."

At Blanc Mont, George W. Hamilton, now a major, led his 1st Battalion, which occupied the left flank of the line, forward against the enemy who were dug in on a hill just before St. Etienne, and successfully overwhelmed the Germans even though his casualties totaled about 85 percent. At the Meuse River crossing, on the night of 10-11, he again led his battalion forward and was again successful in crossing a pontoon bridge under heavy enemy fire, taking up positions on the east bank. He was awarded two Silver Star citations and the Croix de Guerre with Palm.

At 1345 Hamilton told Feland he hadn't been able to make contact with either Messersmith at 2/5 or Larsen at 3/5. He added that he would swing his battalion around to the left, facing the west and northwest: "French have not yet advanced on our left." Feland replied at 1350 that he approved Hamilton's action as far as the French were concerned.

Hamilton sent an update to Feland at 1540 and a sketch of his present position. He added that the French were advancing but had not advanced as far as the Marines. He said he was in contact with 2/5 and that they were having trouble with the enemy to their left. Hamilton was sending stretcher bearers with wounded and "in view of the fact 2nd Bn is watching left flank of Brigade to north, I will not advance North at present."

At 1655 Hamilton sent Feland a message: "Have just located Messersmith. I had previously issued orders to Capt. [DeWitt] Peck [55th Company] to send out an officers patrol to locate him, and will now send location to Peck & tell him to close up. Will replace one of his companies with one of my support companies and will organize strong points on my line and keep enough men in reserve to allow a disposition in depth. My runner has also located Capt. Larsen & 3rd Bn. Will send him a message telling him about Messersmith & aks him to dispose his Bn. so as to give us good support."

By this time Hamilton's 1/5 was facing Germans to their left and were nearly a third of a mile into the French 22d Infantry Division territory. Meanwhile, he was looking for 2/5 to support him.

DeWitt Peck sent Hamilton a request, no time indicated but apparently late afternoon on 3 October, in which he mentioned that two of his companies, 51st and 55th, were occupying trench Passau to the north. He had no connection to his right nor with Messersmith or Feland, and added if Hamilton knew where Feland was to please forward his message. He added that he occupied the position at the request of a French major.

4 October: This was the day of the 5th Regiment Calvary. It wouldn't be until 6 July 1919 that an official report from the then commanding officer, Major LeRoy P. Hunt, would describe the experiences of 1/5 on that fateful day. It is lengthy but accurate and worth being included here in its entirety.

> Maps: TAHURE-ATTIGNY; JUNIVILLE; ST. MARIE-a-PY. 1/20,000.
>
> The night of October 3-4, 1918, found the 1st Battalion, 5th Regiment Marines on BLANC MONT RIDGE in support of the 6th Regiment Marines, after having followed them in support during the entire day's attack. Orders were received for the 5th Regiment to leap—frog the 6th Regiment and start forward again from BLANC MONT RIDGE on the morning of the 4th of October. The plan was for the regiment to attack in column of battalions, with the 1st battalion, the last battalion in column of the regiment. At about 6:00 a.m. the regiment started forward from BLANC MONT RIDGE. At the time of advance, the battalions were not entirely together, but became fairly well straightened out by 7:30 a.m. Stubborn resistance was met all the way and the advance was very slow. The main obstacle was enfilade fire from the left flank, which was entirely exposed for a distance of almost three kilometers.
>
> At about 11 o'clock the 1st battalion had reached a position about a kilometer and a quarter in front of the BLANC MONT RIDGE road; still in support of the other two battalions which were by this time only a hundred yards or so ahead. The pressure from the front and left flank was becoming intense, and the Boche were closing in, endeavoring to cut off the salient thus made by our own advance. The 2nd and 3rd Battalions of the 5th launched a bold attack to the front from the ridge in front of ST. ETIENNE, but suffered such losses that they were forced to withdraw to the cover of the woods on the ridge. The situation became so critical that it demanded immediate and bold action. It was at this point that Major George W. Hamilton, USMC, who com-

manded the 1st battalion at the time, came to the front and showed his wonderful initiative and power of quick decision. The most important thing at the moment was to remove the pressure from the left flank and to extend our line in that direction. Major Hamilton gave orders to form the battalion for attack in a westerly direction and to push west to the ST. ETIENNE–BLANC MONT Road, then to swing northwest up the ridge in front of ST. ETIENNE and hook up with the other two battalions on their left. If possible we were to go on into ST. ETIENNE and take the town. Consequently all four companies of the battalion were placed on a line in a combat formation facing westward between points (260.3-281.7), and (266.3-282.3).

Our path led westward for a kilometer and a quarter and then northwest.

At about noon time the battalion started forward and although the men and officers of the battalion realized the situation to be critical, no one dreamed of what the next few hours were to bring. The battalion had been in every engagement in which the regiment had participated up to this time, but the afternoon of the 4th of October, 1918, was by far the bloodiest and worst day of the entire war.

The moment the battalion started forward, the machine guns opened up and from then on their fire was incessant. To me a counter attack but it was broken up and we pressed on westward down the ravine and into the open until the left of the line finally reached the ST. ETIENNE–BLANC MONT Road. At this point the right of the line held and the two left companies swung around to the right until our line of advance pointed northwest, parallel to the road, the left of the line being just across the road. Then came the crisis. The ridge lay in front of us and as we started forward up the ridge, the Boche, who had infiltrated in our rear and left rear, opened fire on us from that direction.

The fire from the ridge itself was intense. Here we were practically surrounded and receiving a galling fire from three directions. There was nothing to do but to advance on up the hill. The signal was given and the line started up the ridge. No one but those present will ever know or fully appreciate what the battalion went through during the charge up this hill. The rate of casualties was far above anything we had yet experienced, but the men kept on. The crest of the ridge was taken by storm and approximately a hundred prisoners and many machine guns were taken. The crest was in plain view of, and lower than the ridge running parallel to it, and in the rear of, or just north of ST. ETIENNE. We had not been on the hill more than ten or fifteen minutes when direct artillery fire was laid on us, from this ridge, which was very effective and promised to wipe the entire outfit out if something was not done. It was decided to push on down the slope toward the town. This would at least get us out of the line of fire from the rear and left rear. This we started to do, but had not gone more than about two hundred yards when machine gun and direct artillery fire opened up on us from the strongly held enemy nest just southeast of the town of ST. ETIENNE. This fire was so intense and casualties were occurring at such a rate that it meant annihilation to continue the advance with no support and no liaison on either flank. We were absolutely alone and, at this point receiving fire from all four sides. It was imperative to connect up with the rest of the regiment, so we gathered what wounded we could and withdrew to the woods on the on the crest and then pushed through the woods eastward, meeting resistence all the way, until we connected up with the other two battalions of the 5th Regiment at practically the same point from which our attack started (point 266.3-282.1). We arrived back at about 4:30 in the afternoon.

The furthest advance of our main line toward the town of ST. ETIENNE reached a line between points (264.7-282.7) and (265.2-62.7), but a detachment of about thirty men under Lieut. Francis J. Kelly, Jr., USMC, got as far forward as the northern end of the long narrow strip of woods at a point (264.9-283.1), and about 800 yards in front of the town, where they remained until dark before rejoining the battalion, after having gallantly repulsed a local counter-attack launched by a force of 200 Germans from the town.

The battalion dug in with the rest of the regiment, in the vicinity of point (266.4-282.1) with all flanks refused, and remained there the entire night of October 4-5, practically surrounded and under a terrific bombardment. Another heavy counterattack from the left flank was repulsed during the evening and a number of prisoners were taken. It was not until the next day, October 5, that our rear was cleared of the enemy by the 6th Regiment and communication was again established.

To give some idea of the casualties suffered during the day, including men lost from their organizations, the following figures are given, which are absolutely correct as far as my memory goes:

Men present with companies at 6 p.m. on October 4th, 1918.

17th Company	2 Officers	35 Men
49th "	2 "	29 "
66th "	1 "	22 "
67th "	2 "	40 "
Bn. Hdqrs. Group	5 "	30 "
	12 "	156 "

Many deeds of individual heroism and bravery were performed that day, but they are too numerous to mention. All who went through it deserve equal credit.

The work of all the units of the Division was admirable during these terrible days, but although we were unable to hold all the ground we gained during the afternoon, I don't believe any one act of any similar unit helped more towards making the Boche decide to retreat from the Rheims salient than this attack of the 1st Battalion, 5th Regiment Marines, on the afternoon of October 4, 1918.

I was personally present with the battalion on the 4th of October, 1918, and certify that the above account is, to the best of my knowledge, absolutely correct.

LEROY P. HUNT,
Major, U.S.M.C.
Commanding.

It was thus when the 17th company, crashing through the enemy's center of resistance, advanced into the town of St. Etienne only to be forced to fall back because the French forces operating on the left were not equally successful and failed to bring up the flank. Captain LeRoy Hunt, skipper of the 17th, constantly exposed himself to enemy fire while leading his men toward their objective, and was one of eight Marines of 1/5 that were later awarded a Distinguished Service Cross for their actions this day (later also a Navy Cross). Private Karl F. Kness, also of the 17th Company, volunteered to assist a wounded comrade to get to the rear, and although going through an area swept by machine gun and shell fire for a distance of more than a half mile, he managed to get his comrade to the rear, carrying him most of that distance. Displaying extraordinary heroism, coolness and resourcefulness, and utter disregard of personal danger under heavy shell fire, 2d Lt. Eugene West succeeded in stopping a retreat and organized a position of resistance.

Volunteering and leading an attack upon enemy machine gun positions under intense artillery and machine gun fire, and although severely wounded in the leg, 2d Lt. Gillis A. Johnson succeeded in cleaning out several machine gun nests, captured guns and took a number of prisoners. Sergeant Daniel R. Fox volunteered and carried important messages across fire-swept terrain, then returned to report the result of his mission. He was wounded later but remained on duty for four hours, carrying messages across field swept by machine gun fire.

Second Lieutenant Jacob Lienhard led his men in an attack on a strongly held enemy position through heavy machine gun and shell fire, and although severely wounded, continued to lead and encourage his men. Another second lieutenant, Edward E. Lindgren of the

17th, led his men in an attack on a strong enemy position through heavy machine gun and shell fire to support a platoon operating on his left. Although severely wounded, he remained in action until the position was secured. After being severely wounded, Gy. Sgt. Milton R. Scott continued to assist in consolidating the position of his platoon, later placing himself in an exposed position in order to gain good observation for sniping enemy machine gun positions.

With his platoon in a very dangerous position, Sgt. Robert R. Van Deusen volunteered to carry a message from his platoon commander across a machine gun swept field. He was successful but while directing his men to shelter he was severely wounded. He later died of his wounds on 27 October 1918. Showing unusual presence of mind and resourcefulness, 2d Lt. Fred J. Zinner, under terrific machine gun and artillery barrage, rallied men from another company who had become separated from their organization during an attack on a strongly held enemy position. Although severely wounded, he led them to the support of the platoon operating on the left flank, thereby relieving a critical situation.

At 1410 Hamilton was forced to send the following message to Feland: "Absolutely impossible to carry out attack. Machine guns encircling us and reenforcements are needed. It is doubtful if we can hold out here unless machine guns are cleaned out on flanks. Do not send reenforcements straight forward—send down flanks."

Gunnery Sergeant Arthur S. Lyng, of the 49th Company, while engaged in scouting to his company's front, discovered German preparations forming a surprise attack against an unprotected portion of his lines. He quickly formed a sufficient force to destroy the enemy plans and accomplished the capture of ten of the raiding party with 6 of their guns. With the assistance of First Lieutenant Francis J. Kelly, 66th Company, and Sergeant Robert Slover, 49th Company, as well as other non-commissioned officers, Lyng organized a force of thirty men, all that were available in the emergency, and the small band burst from cover with their Springfields, opening fire on the run and howling after the enemy in Comanche fashion. The Germans, whose number was estimated at between 250 and 300, were completely routed, and they left many dead and wounded upon the field, while prisoners and guns were taken by the little force, which became known in the organization as "Lyng's Comanches." Lyng was later promoted to second lieutenant.

Captain Percy Cornell, skipper of the 49th Company, courageously led his company through heavy artillery and machine gun fire in the attack on a strongly defended position. His company held the exposed flank, and later when the battalion withdrew he skillfully covered the other shifting units while exposed to heavy enemy fire. Private Thomas A. O. Miller of the 49th was another who was highly decorated for heroism. He volunteered and carried a message through terrific shell and machine gun fire. In performance of his mission he suffered the loss of a leg from an exploding shell.

First Lieutenant Francis J. Kelly of the 66th was another hero awarded a DSC and later a Navy Cross for his part in action near St. Etienne. Finding himself to be the sole survivor of seven officers of his company, he took command at the beginning of an enemy counterattack. Although greatly outnumbered three to one and having been advised to retire to a better position, he ordered an advance, completely routed the enemy and made prisoners of the survivors. Lyng of the 49th was his second in command, even though the action was labeled "Lyng's Comanches." Hospital Apprentice 1st Eugene H. Tenley, USN, serving with the 49th, earned a DSC and Navy Cross this day when he displayed great bravery and utter disregard for his personal safety. He voluntarily accompanied a small force led by 1st Lt. Kelly into an open attack against an enemy who outnumbered the attacking force ten to one, and rendered valuable medical assistance until he was killed by a shell fragment that day.

Meanwhile, other members of the 66th were busy, like Pvt. John Broxup, who succeeded in bringing a wounded officer back to Allied lines when his company was forced to retire. He was killed in action on 5 November 1918 in the Meuse-Argonne. Murl Corbett, former first sergeant of the 66th, now a second lieutenant of the 49th as battalion intelligence officer, fearlessly exposed himself to enemy fire to secure important information; severely wounded by a bursting shell and incapacitated by gas, he refused aid from comrades in order that the attack might not be delayed. He displayed unusual courage and devotion over and above the call of duty.

Sergeant Harry I. Baker earned a Distinguished Service Cross and Navy Cross for extraordinary heroism. He disregarded his own safety and went out under heavy shell and machine gun fire to carry a wounded comrade to safety. Charles I. Haasis, a corporal in the 66th, gallantly carried an important message through terrific enemy fire. Captain Francis S. Kieran, a platoon leader in the 66th, was awarded two Silver Star citations. For gallantry in action near St. Etienne and for his brilliant leadership while recently commissioned a first lieutenant, Henry L. Hulbert, 66th, already a hero in this war and a Medal of Honor man from the nineteenth century, was killed in action this date, 4 October 1918, earning a Silver Star and a Croix de Guerre with Palm. Another officer wounded that day was 2d Lt. Leonard E. Rea of the 66th, who was decorated for extraordinary heroism in action near Blanc Mont. He retained command of his platoon after receiving a severe wound which rendered him unable to move without assistance, and he would not leave the line until ordered by his commanding officer.

First Lieutenant Henry L. Hulbert, supply officer, 66th Company, 1/5, killed in action at Blanc Mont on 4 October 1918.

There were many other heroes of all four companies on 4 October 1918, many of whom paid the ultimate price. The 1st Battalion was taking a shellacking and needed help badly.

One other company doing good work, and paying the price, was the 67th, commanded by an old hand, Captain Frank Whitehead, who displayed his usual bravery, coolness and devotion to duty near St. Etienne on the 4th. Although severely wounded while attacking an enemy strong point, this officer selected advanced machine gun sites and turned machine guns on the retreating enemy while under very heavy hostile machine gun and artillery fire.

He was replaced by Capt. Felix Beauchamp,

Private Ove Mortensen, of the 66th Company, 1/5 Battalion. At left in Germany, at right home.

who assumed command when Whitehead was evacuated. He was wounded by the same shell but continued in command for awhile. He sent Feland a message: "Prisoner states that there are six or seven companies of about 60 each on ridge on our left but he was taken from right side of ridge occupied by us. Bearer [of this message] helped repel counterattack from our left. Our ridge is swept by heavy machine gun fire from the front."

Beauchamp pushed on with his company even though he was seriously wounded by the same shell. He participated in several minor engagements, and although in great pain, refused to be evacuated until a machine gun wound in the groin put him completely out of action.

Captain Harry K. Cochran replaced Beauchamp, and he survived Blanc Mont only to pay the price next month on 2 November at the Meuse. Other heroes of the company included Cpl. Samuel S. Campbell, who assisted wounded to the first aid station under heavy enemy fire. Another was Cpl. Harry H. Ellis, who assisted the wounded to shelter under heavy enemy bombardment, and Pvt. John F. Hetrick for carrying wounded to the battalion aid station during a heavy enemy bombardment.

Second Lieutenant James E. Foster showed extraordinary heroism and disregard of personal danger as commander of a liaison platoon and platoon commander. By his example of personal bravery and fearlessness until severely wounded, he inspired his men to put forth their best efforts. Private Elmer R. Ingham was decorated for maintaining communications under heavy enemy fire, while PFC Elton E. Mackin was awarded a DSC, later a Navy Cross, for extraordinary heroism. He, as a runner, displayed exceptional courage by carrying messages across shell and machine gun swept terrain, exhibiting singular courage and devotion to duty.

At 1600 Feland sent Hamilton a message that 1/6 and 2/6 were advancing to reinforce lines. He said to send same message to Larsen and Messersmith: "Good work in sticking to your position. We must hold on." Hamilton advised Feland at 1700: "17th reports 2 officers (Hunt and Norstrand) and 35 men present. Kelly has about the same number from the 66th, but the are ahead of the present lines in the woods & I haven't liaison with him. Capt. [Francis] Kieren has 12 men with him and Lieut. [Felix] Beauchamp about 30 (67th Co.) Lt. Norstrand estimates 17th Co. casualties at 75 percent. We will be unable to send details for chow on acc't of so few men. Have you any of the 20 percent available? Can't the carts come down?" He added: "8th Machine Gun company practically wiped out. All platoon commanders and sergeants either killed or wounded."

Hamilton sent Feland a sketch map of the 5th Marines' front and enemy positions. Sometime that day, and it appears to be later, Hamilton sent Feland a message telling him of the situation: "Have entire 67th & 17th companies and parts of the 49th and 66th Cos. Capt. Dirksen has been gassed and evacuated.... None of the regiment is within a kilometer of the objective [St. Etienne].... We need artillery and need it badly. Also food and water. He also mentioned that the left flank was still wide open and that he was in a very precarious position.

5 October: Maj. George W. Hamilton received the following letter from Col. Logan Feland, in command of the 5th Regiment:

> I am very happy to tell you that General Lejeune called me up this morning to ask me about our conditions and can assure you of his appreciation of your good work yesterday and last night.
> He says that General Gouraud had called to assure him that it was the pushing out of this salient and especially our work of holding on last night that has made the Boche take up the big retreat now going on in all this Rheims sector. General Gouraud told General Lejeune that if we had given an inch the Boche would have forced us on, that he was giving us all he had to force us back and so prevent the necessity of his general retreat.
> General Lejeune is proud of you and sincerely sympathizes with us in our losses. I was so happy when I learned that the good work and devotion of you and your men are properly appreciated that I broke down. Let as many as possible of the officers and men know that the higher-ups know the great results gained by their holding last night, and give them full credit for it.
> Yours,
> (Signed) Feland.

He also sent a message at 0630 which mentioned that the French were going to attack and that: "this Reg't will hold and strengthen position, and be prepared to advance if ordered to." At 0750 Hamilton replied. Here in full is his qualified response:

> Your message re French attack on right & left received & forwarded to Bn. Comdrs. 2nd & 3rd Bns. Our forces are so much diminished that we do not extend over to the original left of the sector, nor is it possible to do so unless we move our right. The 17th Company is in these woods with the 45th Company on the left. The remainder of the 67th Company is to the left of the 45th and they hook up with a battalion of the 6th Regt. It would seem impossible to form combat liaison with the French while the 6th is on our left, and we have no battalion large enough to remedy this on account of the wide regimental front.

The other provisions of your message will be complied with.

This battalion will go, or attempt to go, where you order it. You should understand though that your regiment is now much depleted, very disorganized and not in condition to advance as a front line regiment even though the enemy forces in front are found to be small. It is hard to say "can't," but the Division Commander should thoroughly understand the situation and realize that this regiment can't advance as an attacking force. Such advance would sacrifice the regiment.

Hamilton.

Messersmith.

Feland finally realized what Hamilton was expressing and replied to all three battalion commanders at 1120 with a morale-heightening message stating that the 5th should continue reorganization, and "You will await orders from me before advancing in the rear of the 6th Marines."

15 October: Casualty reports consolidated at the close of the engagement in this sector showed the following casualties for the entire regiment:

	Officers	*Enlisted*
Killed in action	6	91
Died of wounds	3	20
Severely wounded	16	209
Slightly wounded	30	484
Missing		151
Gassed	4	83
Shock		21
Sick	2	0
Totals	61	1059

According to the semi-official history of 1/5, there were 53 deaths on the field and 402 lesser casualties in the battalion. The Fifth Regiment, including all three battalions, was in such bad shape, they were pulled back into reserve positions never again to be used during the Blanc Mont campaign.

9 October to 16 October: The organization was relieved from the lines and fell back to Dampierre-au-Temple, where it was billeted until 20 October. At some point, details lacking, replacements were welcomed and blended into the various battalions. An official report from Major George Hamilton to Colonel Logan Feland stated:

17 to 31 October In billets in DAMPIERRE-au-Temple. Rec'd orders at 10:30 a.m. to march to Camp Montpelier as soon as practicable. The battalion under command of Captain Harry K. Cochran cleared DAMPIERRE-au-Temple at 1:30 p.m., October 20, 1918, marching via CUPERLY, LACHEPPE, BUSSY-LE-CHATEAU and SOMME SUIPPE, arriving at CAMP MONTPELIER at 9:00 p.m., Oct. 20, 1918. Troops in billets. Battalion marched at 7:00 a.m. Oct. 21 1918, via PERTHES, TAHURE, AURE and ORFEUIL. Major George W. Hamilton assumed command at AURE. Arrived at point about 3 kilometres S. W. of SEMIDE in woods just west of SEDAN road. Order rec'd here countermanding relief of French Regiment and bivouaced about 12:00 p.m. Remained in place October 22, 1918. Rec'd orders at 2:00 p.m. Oct. 22, 1918, to counter-march to Camp MONTPELIER Oct. 23, 1918, at 8:00 a.m. March begun at 8:00 a.m. Oct. 23rd using paths near SEDAN road to SOMME-PY, thence east thru TAHURE and PERTHES. Arrived at Camp MONTPELIER 6:00 p.m. same day. Troops in barracks. Remained in place Oct. 24th. Rec'd orders to march to junction of SOMME—SUIPPES and SOMME TOURBE roads. Battalion cleared Camp Montpelier at 6:30 a.m., Oct. 25th, arriving at SOMME-SUIPPES, SOMME TOURBE cross roads at 7:30 a.m. Embussed about 8:30 a.m. arriving at LES ISLETTES at 12:30 p.m. same date.

Battalion marched to Camp CABAUD arriving about 3:00 p.m. One company and Bn. Hdqrs. in barracks; three companies bivouaced. Remained in place night of Oct. 25-26th. Cleared Camp CABAUD at 1:00 p.m. Oct. 26th. Arrived in woods 1 kilometre southeast of EXERMONT at 11:00 p.m. Bivouaced. Remained in place October 27, 28 and 29th. Battalion moved by marching at 11:30 p.m. Oct. 30th to woods about 2 kilometres N. E. of EXERMONT, arriving at 3:00 a.m. October 31, 1918. Bivouaced, remaining in place during day of October 31st. Rec'd Regimental order for attack at 5:30 p.m. same date. Moved forward to line at 9:00 p.m. Arrived at line in rear of elements of the 42nd Amer. Division at 12:30 a.m. November 1, 1918.

31 October: A message from Feland to Larsen, sent 1710 stated: "Captain [LeRoy P.] Hunt 1st Bn. [commanding officer, 17th Company] has the official time" of jump-off on 1 November 1918.

Meuse River Campaign

1 November: The First Battalion was designated to carry the assault to the first objective, two and one half kilometers into the enemy's lines. A violent artillery barrage by our guns from 0300 to 0500 was highly effective, and when at the latter hour the First Battalion passed through the lines of a battalion of the 42d Division, the only stubborn resistance offered by the Germans was on the part of isolated machine gun nests which inflicted many casualties before being destroyed.

The attack was entirely successful, and the companies, the 49th and 66th in assault, and the 17th and 67th in support, reached the first objective of the day at 0800 as per schedule. The other battalions of the regiment then carried the attack to the second and third objectives, the First Battalion becoming the reserve of the regimental forces.

Second Lt. Leonard Rea (intelligence officer, 1/5) reported at 0800: "My first line is at first objective. My losses have been Officers—5. Enlisted Few. Several field pieces (77s) captured ... reaching objective without heavy losses." Ten minutes later Hamilton reported to Feland: "Reached objective on time and is now reorganizing. Slight machine gun resistance. We have now taken about 500 prisoners. [Captain Charley] Dunbeck & 2nd Battalion are now passing through our lines.... Cochran [commanding officer, 67th] wounded & Lieutenant [Aaron J.] Ferch [67th] killed. Heavy enemy m.g. fire developing to our left front.... We can see large numbers of Germans to our left front. Our casualties about 5 percent."

At 1520 Hamilton reported to Feland: "Am digging in on ridge just to the north of this ravine [02.8-92.9], with three companies on line and one in support ... both 89th Div. and 6th Regt. believed to have reached 3rd objective.... Men in good spirits but physically weak on acct of diarrhoea. When can we have some good chow?"

Feland complained to Hamilton at 2345 about sending more reports: "Have received only one report from you dated 9:00 a.m. Col. Turrill and Capt. Winans have gone forward to establish P. C. in area northwest of LANDREVILLE ET ST. GEORGES. Locate them and send in to them *frequent reports.*"

2 November: Hamilton sent Feland report at 0850, but didn't say much: "Nothing new to report. A few shells have fallen on us on top of hill, otherwise everything pretty quiet. The 23rd Infantry has not yet passed my lines." Late that day, but no time indicated,

Rea sent this report: "Battalion strength of Cos. 565 men 11 officers Bn. Hdq. 66 men 7 officers."

3 November: The advance was resumed, and practically no resistance was met with from the enemy, which was hastily withdrawing to the east bank of the Meuse River. One/Five assumed second position behind 2/5.

At noon Hamilton let Feland know that Turrill told him it was best for 1/5 to dig in and organize the position if the 9th Infantry had not advanced by 2 p.m. "Is this your wish?" Feland replied at 1615 that when the 3d Brigade advanced, "make every effort to follow closely the advance of the 9th Infantry and keep in supporting distance."

4 November: Hamilton wrote to Feland in anticipation of orders to move forward: "Will I interpret them [orders] to move immediately, or may I wait for my rations.... Hot rations have been cooked and Gunner [William E.] Nice reports them on their way."

Later that day, at 2030, Hamilton wrote Larsen at 3/5 telling him he was going ahead to La Tuilerie Fme, where "the 9th is reported to be." Fifteen minutes later he wrote to Feland telling him the same thing. It appears that Hamilton wasn't pushing his battalion as hard as headquarters would have liked.

5 to 9 November: During this time period, 1/5, like the balance of the Fourth and Third Brigades, were moving towards the Meuse River and by the night of 6 November were on the heights opposite where they would eventually cross that river. The battalion bivouacked in woods south of the Sartelle Farm, and on the night of 10 November it was designated to substitute in an attack across the Meuse for a battalion of the 89th Division which had failed to reach the vicinity.

Lieutenant Rea continued sending intelligence reports that emphasized how heavily the opposite banks of the river were held; the machine gun and artillery fire, etc., but no one in authority paid any attention.

10 November: Feland directed Hamilton at 1815: "Your battalion will be held in readiness to move to the support of the 6th Marines, crossing at Mouzon or the combined force of the 2nd Bn. 5th and one battalion of 89th Div. crossing at the BOIS DE L'HOSPICE. Do not move until you receive orders from C. G. 4th Brigade or from me."

This message was almost as confusing, based on later results, as the following from Lt. Col. Earl Ellis, adjutant, 4th Brigade, to Hamilton at 1930. In it he said that the 89th Division would send two battalions across the Meuse and advance northeast to Bois de Hache Autreville and Hill 252. That would place them very near the town of Moulins. Then he added: "Have your force look out for their troops and get liaison with them as soon as practicable. By command of Major General Neville."

In order to accomplish that, the 5th Marines would have to make plans to cross the Meuse. (To that time I find no orders for the 5th Marines to cross the river at that point, and the following messages from Ellis to the commanding general, or chief of staff, 2d Division, all are frankly confusing.)

At 2310: "They are all across except 1 company and everything looked fine.... Boche were evidently on to it as they had laid down a barrage across the aviation ground(?) That was the upper ground."

On the east side of the river, Corporal William J. Ferguson of the 17th and a companion went out ahead of the line and silenced a machine gun which threatened to hold up the advance of his company. Captain LeRoy Hunt of the 49th Company was awarded two Silver Star citations and a Croix de Guerre, Gilt. The night of 10-11, he found himself called upon to take command of the 1st Battalion crossing, which he successfully did and then pushed his battalion forward, dislodging the enemy machine gun nests, making possible a strong bridgehead.

Fifteen minutes later Ellis wrote to the chief of staff: "The combined detachment reports they all got across the river. They had few casualties. One Marine captain wounded." Ten minutes later he wrote to the chief of staff: "They had forced a crossing at Mouzon. Reports that one of their columns were across and very little difficulty." Where Ellis received this information is beyond me. Mostly, it is wrong, all of it.

This is more general but more accurate. Under heavy machine gun and shell fire from the enemy batteries on the opposite heights, the battalion crossed the Meuse on frail foot bridges which had been thrown across the stream by the 2d Engineers. Major Hamilton directed the combat of both the First and Second Battalions during the operation, while Captain LeRoy P. Hunt commanded the First Battalion and Captain Charley Dunbeck the Second. The losses were horrendous, especially in 1/5. The crossing was accomplished at 2200 and the darkness of the night together with a heavy fog gathered just at that hour aided greatly in the success of the project. The remnants managed to hang on at the eastern bank through the night. Before dawn on 11 November the battalion was dug in barely beyond the east bank of the river and, because the enemy didn't advance, had the situation well in hand. Their casualties were many.

First Lieutenant Ralph M. Wilcox of the 17th Company volunteered and carried out a mission of liaison which called for the highest type of personal bravery. His duties required that he pass through a heavy artillery and machine gun barrage, after which it was necessary to push through the enemy outpost lines. He routed one German outpost and established liaison between the two battalions in time to defeat a hostile attempt to isolate the two units. This was after the crossing of the Meuse River.

With extraordinary heroism Pvt. George W. Budde, entirely upon his own initiative, advanced in front of the line to determine whether a certain machine gun was hostile or friendly, and was killed by a machine gun bullet from that gun.

The following messages were not received until 0650 on the 11th of November. The first is from the combat liaison commander (Hamilton?) to commanding officer, 4th Brigade (Neville).

> 1st and 2nd bns. of the 5th Marines did not complete crossing of Meuse until 11:30 p.m. last night due to heavy shelling, a break in upper bridge and confusion of moving in dark. The Bn. from the 89th Division got lost at the start and at 6:00 a.m. this date had only gathered together some 300 men. Major Hanna was here but has disappeared now. Crossing made under heavy M. G. and Art. fire. The 1st Bn. on the right, ran into a machine gun nest immediately after crossing and had great trouble keeping the men together. The entire bn., numbering approximately 100 men, is now combined as a company and under command of Captain Hunt. The 2nd bn. advanced to the north through Bois des Flaviers but had to hold up movement until daybreak on account of machine gun nests and heavy underbrush. This morning at 6:30 a.m. the 2nd Bn. on the left and the Bn. from the 89th on right advanced toward objective. Sniping and machine guns over-

come and advance going smoothly at present. Enemy Artillery fire heavy. On account of the very small number of men it is going to be difficult to organize this position in depth. Urge that another battalion be sent across river to reinforce us. Message just received from Captain Dunbeck states that advance progressing satisfactory and that he is taking many machine guns. I will connect with the 6th Marines and 89th Division at earliest possible moment.

A message was sent from Shuler (in command of the northern crossing of the 6th Marines and 3/5) at the railroad station where they were assembled for crossing. Shuler said they arrived at this point at 10:30 p.m. They were held up for half an hour because of heavy shelling from Pourron. One battalion commander was there and two others were not. Shuler decided not to sacrifice his command and he removed them from Mouzon, saving his command.

11 November: Shortly before noon, while the battalion was standing by for a further advance, the following order was received from regimental headquarters:

Nov. 11, 1918—9:10 a.m.
 To Major Hamilton:
 All firing will cease at 11 a.m. today. Hold every inch of ground that you have gained, including that gained by patrols. Send in as soon as possible a sketch showing positions of all units at 11 a.m.
 (Signed) Feland.

Three days later the battalion was relieved by a unit of the 77th Division, and hiking into Pouilly, a nearby village, was billeted there until 17 November.

Casualty returns for the operation showed 46 deaths and 448 lesser casualties in the First Battalion from 1 November until the cessation of hostilities.

16 November: The following is a final report by 1/5 commanding officer, George W. Hamilton, giving many more details than the preceding.

DISPOSITION OF OUR TROOPS. 5th Regiment Marines in column of Bns. on right. From head to rear, 1st at, 2nd, 3rd Bns.; 6thReg't. Marines on left. 9th Infantry supporting 5th Marines, 23rd Infantry supporting 6th Marines. 1st Bn. of 9th Infantry acting as combat liaison and moppers up on the right of 5th Marines. 69th Division on right of 2nd Division.
 MAP POSITION (See Sketch #1) Map used. DISPOSITION OF ENEMY TROOPS: See sketch #1.
 After 2 hour preparation by our artillery and machine guns beginning at 3:00 a.m., 10 minutes being allowed for the fire to be pulled back to the wire in front of the enemy trenches, a rolling barrage began at 5:30 a.m. behind which the battalion, with 8th Machine Gun Company, began its advance in the following formation: FIRST LINE, 66th Co. on right, 49th Co. on left. These companies deployed two platoons of front each in the first wave followed by two platoons in support in line of combat groups.
 SECOND LINE, 17th Company on right, 67th company on left. These support companies employed formation of line of groups in the advance. The barrage was followed closely and occasionally resistance in the enemy first lines by machine gun groups was overcome by the use of automatic rifles and hand grenades. The artillery preparation had been so thorough that it had caused a withdrawal of the enemy's main resistance. LANDRES ET ST. GEORGES on our right was found to have been completely reduced by our artillery and gave no resistance. The advance continued and the first objective for the Battalion, a line 01.0-89.4 to 02.0-89.3, was reached on schedule, H & 3 hours; that is 8:00 a.m. Nov. 1, 1918. The battalion halted on a line 01.0 89.4 to 02.0-89.3 and the 2nd Battalion, 5th Regiment passed thru our lines to continue the attack at 8:00 a.m. supported by the 3rd Battalion, 5th Regiment, the 1st Battalion now becoming reserve

and following at about 800 metres distance. The advance continued until 3:20 p.m. November 1, 1918 when the 3rd Battalion having passed through the 2nd Bn. attained the third objective. The 1st Bn. then dug in on the ridge just to the north of the ravine at 02.8-92.9 (BUZANOY SPECIAL 1/50,000) with three companies on line and one in support. Few enemy shells fell on top of ridge, otherwise quiet.

On the morning of November 3rd the 9th Infantry passed thru the lines of the 5th Marines to the attack, 5th Marines following in reserve in column of battalions; 2nd, 1st and 3rd Battalions in order named from head to rear. The advance continued in a N. E. direction until about 12:30 p.m. when the 9th Infantry was held up by heavy machine gun fire. The 1st Bn. then dug in on north side of ravine about 800 metres west of NOUART BELVAL road, the 9th Infantry waiting for artillery support. The 1st Bn. remained in place until 7:00 a.m. November 4th, when the advance was resumed, in support of the 9th Infantry which had overcome enemy machine gun resistance. Advance continued to a point about 500 meters N. E. of BELVAL, when halt was made at 12:30 p.m. upon Regimental order and additional orders for advance were received.

The 9th Infantry, which preceded us, was now reported to have passed thru the BOIS DE BELVAL and other woods to the north, with patrols in the vicinity of BEAUMONT. Upon order from 5th Regiment the 1st Battalion then proceeded about 5:00 p.m. November 4th to a point in woods 307-303.5 (STENAY 1/20,000) arriving at about 1:00 a.m. November 5th where the Battalion bivouaced until 12:30 p.m. the same date, where, upon receipt of further orders it moved to a point in the woods at 308.4-304.5 (STENAY 1/20,000) where it remained in place the nights of November 5th and 6th. The 3rd Battalion 5th Marines was then at a point near 8855 (STENAY 1/20,000). The ridge overlooking POUILLY at this point which was to have been occupied by the 3rd Battalion of 5th Marines was found to be occupied by two battalions of the 89th Division, which had closed in to the left, and was reported to have patrols across the river in the vicinity of POUILLY. The 66th company 1st Battalion, 5th Marines, under Captain Robert Blake had been previously sent out at 2:00 p.m. November 5th to effect combat liaison on our right with the 89th Division which was now found to be unnecessary as elements of the 89th Division and 5th Regiment now overlapped, so returned to the 1st Bn. at point 308.4-304.5. About 3:30 p.m., November 6th, the 1st Battalion, under Regimental order, sent out a patrol of 40 men under 2nd Lieut. Carl J. Norstrand and 2nd Lieut. Leonard C. Rea for the purpose of gaining information of the enemy in the vicinity of POUILLY and whether or not the river (Meuse) was fordable. Patrol returned about 10:00 p.m. with the information that the enemy was holding the east bank of the MEUSE strongly with machine guns and artillery which swept and covered all movement of our troops on the west bank.

Orders were received night of November 6th to proceed to BOIS D'YONCQ the following day. The battalion moved the following morning, November 7th, and while en route to BOIS D'YONCQ received a change of orders; destination, BOIS DES FOUR. The battalion arrived at a point in these woods, 02.8-04.95 (RAUCOURT 1/20,000) at about 2:30 p.m. November 7, 1918, remaining in place that night and night of November 8th. At 1:30 p.m. November 9th the Battalion moved at point 303.5-307.4 (STENAY 1/20,000) S. W. of La Thibaudine Ferme. The Battalion remained in place the night of November 9th and until 5:00 p.m. November 10th, when ordered to Sartelle Ferme, where attack orders for crossing of MEUSE were received. Due to the failure of a battalion of the 89th Division to arrive in position for attack in time, the 1st Battalion, which was to have remained in the woods on the west bank of the MEUSE near Sartelle Ferme, was designated as one of the attacking battalions.

Upon arriving at Sartelle Ferme the order for the attack designated the 1st and 2nd Battalions, 5th Marines, to cooperate with the 89th Division in effecting crossing of the MEUSE at a point 307.3-311.1 (STENAY 1/20,000). The two battalions were placed under command of Major George W. Hamilton, Captain LeRoy P. Hunt taking command of the 1st Bn., 5th Marines. Following an artillery preparation of one hour our troops were to cross on two pontoon bridges to be thrown across the MEUSE at point 307.3-311.1 in time to follow up our rolling barrage at 9:30 p.m.

With the beginning of our artillery preparation the enemy replied with a violent counterbarrage and gas shells on the flats near the river causing heavy casualties. The 1st and 2nd Battalions proceeded to the river, but due to the darkness and fog and the enemy's shelling it was 10:30 p.m. before the 1st battalion had cleared the lower pontoon bridge which had been swung by the 2nd Engineers. The upper bridge parted several times so that the 2nd Battalion did not come up on our left on the east bank until about 11:30 p.m. Both bridges and the east bank of the MEUSE on the flats were raked by enemy machine gun fire causing casualties. By 11:30 p.m. enemy machine gun outposts and patrols were driven from the flats on the east bank and the edge of the woods N. W. of 81 (STENAY 1/20,000). Line was then formed as per sketch (307.6-311 point 0) # 2 attached, with 2nd battalion on left in edge of woods. The 2nd Battalion of the 89th Division which was to have supported us did not get across the river until about 4:00 a.m. The 1st Battalion, 5th Marines remained in place until 6:30 a.m., November 11th. The 2nd Battalion of the 356th Regiment 89th Division passed thru us to attack at this hour. The 1st then moved ahead in support of the 2nd Battalion, 356th Reg' t., to the edge of woods at point 309.1-311.5 arriving at about 11:00 a.m. November 11, 1918. At about 11:45 a runner from 5th Regiment Headquarters brought a message notifying all troops to remain on the ground attained at that hour. The 67th and 49th Companies had already reached the ridge near SENEGAL Ferme running S. W. from about 309.9-311.9 to 309.7-311.4. The 66th company had advanced to the outskirts of MOULIN where they also received news of the armistice and withdrew to above ridge. Sketches were then sent showing the position of each company in the battalion with outposts.

The Battalion remains in place with Headquarters at SENEGAL Ferme November 11, 12 and 13th, being relieved at 11:00 a.m. November 14th by the 2nd Battalion, 308th Regiment, 77th Division. The Battalion then marched to POUILLY November 14th remaining in place November 15, 16th. Troops in billets.

George W. Hamilton
Major, U.S.M.C.
Commanding.

Occupation of Germany

17 November to 15 December: As a unit in the American Army of Occupation, the battalion marched northeast through Moiry toward the Belgian border, which was crossed two days later. Alternately marching and resting in billets, the organization took the following route to the Rhine: Etalle and Arlon, Belgium; Reichlange, Colmar-Berg, Moestrof, and Gilsdorf, Luxemburg; and Holseken, Mertscheid, Olzheim, Stadtkyll, Esche, Antweiler, Ahr Weiler, Oberzissen, Honnigen, and Niederbreitbach, Germany.

The Rhine was crossed at Remagen on 13 December, and the battalion reached its destination, Niederbreitbach, on 15 December, and was billeted in and about the village for the remainder of the year, under the command of Captain Hunt, who relieved Major Hamilton when the latter left the organization 15 December. He was ordered to England to serve on a courts-martial involving a Marine aviation officer who misrepresented his participation while with the Northern Bombing Group. After the trial he was sent to the United States.

16 December 1918 to 16 July 1919: The 66th Company was billeted at Wolfenucker, and later the 17th company moved from Niederbreitbach to Kurtscheid. Athletics, entertainments, and various amusements helped relieve the monotony of the "Watch on the Rhine," keeping all in excellent physical condition, morale and spirit high. A rifle range was built at Niederbreitbach. Frequent maneuvers and parades were held, demonstrating the battalion's fitness for its duty as part of the American Army of Occupation.

Previous to the final presentation of the peace terms at Paris, the battalion, under full combat equipment, moved to Steinen at the perimeter of the Coblenz bridgehead, prepared to move forward farther into Germany if ordered. The troops remained in bivouac until Germany's delegates accepted the terms, whereupon the battalion returned to the Niederbreitbach area to await entraining orders for the return to the United States.

17 July 1919: Departing Niederbreitbach on 17 July and entraining at Niederbieber the same day, the battalion in high spirits left Germany for Brest by way of Cologne, Liege, Arras, Valenciennes and other points in the areas where the Belgians and English had battled the Hun. The First Battalion, as a unit of the 5th Regiment, boarded the *George Washington* on 24 July bound for New York. A battalion of the 6th Regiment was also aboard, together with Major General John A. Lejeune and Brigadier General Wendell C. Neville. The returning Marines were given a joyous and noisy welcome in New York harbor, the troops disembarking at Hoboken and proceeding to Camp Mills on Long Island.

8 August: As a unit of the 2d Division, the First Battalion participated in the parade of the 2d Division in New York City this date, entraining thereafter for Quantico, at which point the Marine units of the 2d Division again came under the jurisdiction of the Navy.

A considerable portion of the men of the battalion were "duration of the war" men, and preparations were made immediately to discharge these men as promptly as possible. In the meantime the First Battalion, as a unit of the Marine Brigade, paraded in Washington, D.C., August 12, being reviewed by President Woodrow Wilson, various cabinet members, Major-General George Barnett, commandant of the Marine Corps, and Major-General John A. Lejeune, who had commanded the 2d Division.

3

Second Battalion, Fifth Marines, 1917–1919

Battalion Headquarters
18th [E] Company
43d [F] Company
51st [G] Company
55th [H] Company

Commanding Officers

From	To	
May 1917	20 June 1918	Major Frederic M. Wise
21 June 1918	25 July 1918	Major Ralph S. Keyser
26 July 1918	August 1918	Lieut Colonel F. M. Wise
August 1918	October 1918	Major Robert E. Messersmith
October 1918	August 1919	Captain Charley Dunbeck

The Second Battalion, Fifth Regiment of Marines, was organized in Philadelphia, Pennsylvania, "about June 1st, 1917" according to its semi-official history. Mainly it was composed of officers and men who had been serving in Haiti or Santo Domingo, and consequently were trained with what was considered as "sufficient skills of the trade." An old hand, Major Frederic "Dopy" [aka "Fritz"] Wise, was to command them.

The companies coming from the tropics were built up with recruits to a total of 200 men with 4 officers. The battalion—comprising the 43rd, 51st and 55th Companies and the 23rd Machine Gun Company—sailed June 9 from Philadelphia. Once in New York Harbor, the battalion was transferred to the USS *Henderson*. They left New York on 14 June and arrived without incident at St. Nazaire, France, on 27 June.

As a part of the First Division, U.S. Army, the battalion commenced intensive training from 27 June to 15 July 1917. This was mostly close order drills and marches. The unit entrained on 15 July and arrived at Menaucourt on the 17th. It was assigned to the veteran French Army 115th Battalion of Chausseurs Alpines for instruction. Training included French methods of company organization, approach and attack, consolidation of captured positions, trench digging, trench warfare, grenades, automatic rifles, bayonet use and battalion maneuvers. This was followed by American style training, including rifle practice on the range, close and extended order, practice marches and athletics.

In mid–September the battalion was in excellent shape and the French received orders for elsewhere. Many of the officers and noncommissioned officers attended French specialist schools during this period. The 23rd Machine Gun Company was dropped as part of the battalion, having been ordered to Gondrecourt for special instruction.

On September 24 the unit entrained for Damblain in the Vosge; they were detached from the First Division and became the core of the new Second Division. Training continued, especially on battalion and regimental attacks, and the battalion worked for a while with the 151st French Infantry. Intensive training continued through the bitter winter. A new unit joined the battalion on January 16—the 18th Company, which had been in Bordeaux with the base detachment of the Fifth Regiment. The battalion trained at St. Ouen for the occupation and relief of a sector, and as spring approached the unit was drilled in regimental and brigade maneuvers.

Orders to leave for the front finally arrived after nine months of this intensive training. The battalion was now one of three in the 5th Regiment. It was part of the 4th Brigade along with the 6th Regiment of Marines and the 6th Machine Gun Battalion. The brigade was part of the Second Division (Regulars), American Expeditionary Forces, the balance of which was composed of old-time U.S. Army soldiers.

Verdun

13 to 27 March: The battalion left Breuvannes on Friday, 13 March. They arrived the next day at Duigny and marched to Camp Nivolette, where they came under a slight bombardment, their first exposure to enemy fire.

They took over front line trenches Montgirmont Sector from 17 to 28 March, carrying out nightly patrols and wiring. The unit experienced intermittent machine gun fire at night and occasional bombardment, especially on rear positions and communicating trenches. The battalion learned much about organizing a position and patrolling in darkness. They also saw and felt the explosion of an immense land mine.

On the morning of 27 March they were relieved and went into reserve near Ancemont. Next they took a reserve position for the Eix-Moulainville-Chatillon sector.

9 to 29 April: During this time the unit was in front line trenches at Chatillon and to the left. Things started out quiet but became more lively as 2/5 patrols got more and more daring. Each company had one platoon in the front line, the others in echelon in the rear.

16 April: Colonel Wendell C. Neville, commanding the 5th Regiment of Marines, sent orders: "2nd Battalion will move machine guns 16 and 17 back to a position in front of BOURBAKI near C. 18. Any additional information will be transmitted by phone in a guarded manner as follows. 'The last requisition of Col. Wise was all right' means that raid is looked for on the right of C. R. CHATILLON."

Each night brought patrols, ambush parties and wiring parties that were sometimes in contact with the enemy. On the night of 19-20 April near Chatillon the 18th Company encountered some of the enemy and suffered two wounded, two missing. The battalion had its first fatality among officers, 2d Lt. August L. Sundvall of the U.S. Army.

The patrol from 18th Company, led by 2d Lt. Fred H. Becker, U.S. Army, and 30 Marines were ordered to place themselves in ambush in the vicinity of Mandre Farm. Sundvall led one section and Becker the other in attempts to capture six Germans also on patrol. Unsuccessful at the ambush, Sundvall ordered a withdrawal. That was when Sundvall was killed and Private Kenneth C. Sands wounded while fixing his jammed pistol. Gunnery Sergeant Elmore Butler and Private Ray H. Azeltine were either killed or wounded, both being missing. Private Sands was brought in by Privates Gerald R. Cortright and Paul J. Warsoki.

Lieutenant Sundvall was carried in by Corporal Wolcott Winchaubaugh. The latter was described as having rescued him from the enemy and half dragging and carrying Sundvall back to their lines "displaying exceptional coolness and courage." He was awarded a Distinguished Service Cross and later a Navy Cross for that action, as well as a Silver Star citation; the French added their ultimate honor, the Croix de Guerre with Palm.

The unit remained in these trenches until April 29, the riflemen, signalmen, Stokes mortar and 37mm gun sections gaining much in experience. After being relieved from the front line, the battalion took up a reserve position in Camp Joffe just to the rear.

8 to 31 May: Via marches and trains, the next weeks took the battalion to Ancemont, Brusson, Merlaut, and Vitry Le Francois, the outskirts of Paris and through the town of Marines. Orders were issued by regiment on 31 May at 0100 for the four units—Headquarters and the 1st, 2d, and 3d Battalions—to go by train to Courcelles on the Gizors–Dangu Road. This was the order to go north to relieve the 1st U.S. Division (that changed but I cannot find an order to that effect). The battalion billeted for a ten day rest at Courcelles. The unit took part in one divisional practice maneuver and settled into a routine of drills and cleaning up.

Belleau Wood

This period was the real baptism of fire for the Americans. The Germans launched a massive fifth attack in 1918, this time leaving the British army alone and giving the French the business in the Chemin des Dames area. It was so huge, so heavy, the French were hysterical and begged Gen John Pershing to send some Americans to bolster their lines before the enemy reached Paris. That, of course, would be more than the French could take, and there were many signs they would most likely fold and throw their hands up should that occur.

Pershing had two divisions in France that his headquarters believed were at the utilization stage: the First Division, which had already been in action, and the Second Division, which had also been in the trenches. The latter had a two week rest period, whereas the prior was waiting to be relieved. Consequently, the Second Division was sent to aid France. They began moving out on 31 May towards Chateau-Thierry and by 1 June were in the area in which they would serve, nobly, for about a month.

Upon their arrival, each unit was assigned to a certain area; the Marine brigade in the north and the Infantry brigade towards the south. The French were still between them and the Germans but continuing to fall back through the American lines. Opposite the Marines' lines were a mass of trees, known locally as Belleau Wood. Meanwhile, at Pyramide Farm, First Lieutenant Elliott Cooke relates what happened to 2/5: "Colonel Wise assembled the company commanders and Captain [Lester S.] Wass returned shortly to say that we would bivouac where we were for the night. We did it all shipshape and by the numbers fall-in—right dress—stack arms—fallout. That was showing Heinie what we thought of him, but I couldn't help wondering what would happen if the German artillery spotted us."[1]

2 June: A report from Neville to Harbord states: "2d Bn. is now moving to designated position. French troops are taking a position on west of road about 200 meters north of Pyramide." A later report dated 18 June stated: "Established a line from Hill 142 to N. E. corner of BOIS DE VEUILLY as a support for the French who were in our front."

Wise's battalion, 2/5, was assigned to cover the brigade's left flank. Lieutenant Cooke made note of a retrograde movement of French Chasseurs, the famous "Blue Devils," at about 1000 that day, and added, "They certainly were blue, in more ways than one. Retreating before the Boche for six days had left them utterly spent." Cooke offered one of them a cigarette, asking how things were going. The French lieutenant's face was one of despair. "My frien' ... lose the gun and the bullet, yes, but save the shovel." Then he was gone. The battalion marched forward, having the entire battlefield to themselves, along with a few Germans, of course.

As 2/5 was moving northward, the enemy started to shell the column. Soon eleven men were down, of whom four would remain still forever. The 18th Company milled about. Captain Lester S. Wass screamed, "Get going. What do you think this is, a kids' game? Move out." That did it. The skipper spoke and everyone scattered. Being a target pleases no one, especially when you can't get back at your tormentor. As Cooke later said, "All we wanted were some Germans in our sights. Just a few lousy Boches to shoot the living guts out of."

Wise and 2/5 had been assigned to a lengthy position to the west of Hill 142 at a place that became well known as Les Mares Farm. It would become one of the most important positions at this entire area. Its defense saved the entire Second Division's successful defense of the road to Paris.

Les Mares Farm was located less than thirty miles from Paris and in 1918 it would be the closest that the Germans would get to that long-sought city. It was also to be the scene of bloody fighting on 3–4 June and forever after would be known as the "Bloody Angle of the AEF." At the farm the battalion companies split up. The 55th remained within the farm enclosures. Captain Charley Dunbeck's 43d Company went next in line to the left. Farther left went Capt. Lester S. Wass and his 18th Company. A gap of approximately a third of a mile separated them from Turrill's 1/5, which was still stationed with the 23d Infantry in the Bois de Veuilly. Captain Lloyd Williams and the 51st Company went to the extreme right flank of the battalion, into the woods, and up a hill. Shortly after, each company prepared their position for what might come. There was now a semblance of order in which to receive any attack the Germans might heave at them, day or night. The only thing they still lacked was the promised machine guns. The guns and operators were coming more slowly than the foot-sloggers.

Meanwhile, the sharpshooters of the 43d were engaged in sniping at Germans, so Lts. Fred H. Becker, USA, the 18th Company's chow hound, and Chester H. Fraser went over

3. Second Battalion, Fifth Marines, 1917–1919   71

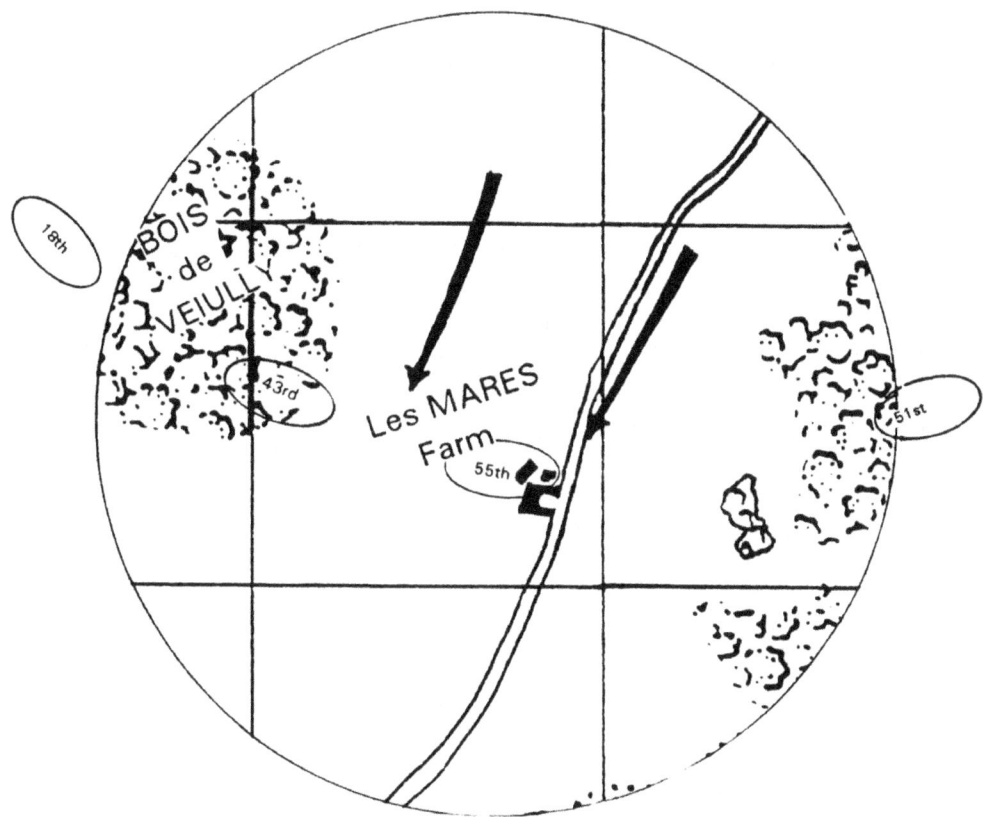

Map showing German advance toward Les Mares farm.

to see. On return Becker acknowledged that though he and Fraser hadn't seen any "Dutchmen," he knew that a few had been nailed by some expert riflemen of the 43d. Williams and the 51st Company were presumed to be on Hill 142, to Wass's right, where the 51st was to connect up with Shearer and 1/6. Williams and the 51st were on the nearest hill to the east, which wasn't Hill 142, although Wise and Williams both thought it was. The maps hadn't changed any; they were still obsolete and so was the map reading.

Sometime during the morning it was decided that 2/5, from Hill 142 to Bois de Vaurichart, was stretched far too thin. Therefore, around noontime, the 82d Company (Capt. Dwight Smith) of 3/6 was ordered there to provide some additional strength and support. When they arrived, they moved to the right of Williams. A memo from 43d Company to battalion headquarters said: "Hit about 12:00 noon by high explosive. Corporal [John F.] LaPointe wounded, Pvt. [Bernard] Werner wounded. Pvt. McCormick slight shell shock. At 3:00 p.m. a Private Bardick accidentally shot himself by shelling on position from 11:30 a.m. to 12:15 p.m. Sergeant Rogers [John W. Rodgers] killed."

According to later official records, Rodgers wasn't killed until 6 June, and there were two Private McCormicks in the 43d Company. Four days later, "Sgt." Bernard Werner was killed in action, earning a Distinguished Service Cross, Navy Cross and Silver Star. there is no record of anyone named Bardick in my records.

Major Wise sent Neville a report with no time indicated: "Part of our line is in front of a battery and I may have to change the line a trifle. The men are all out and it may take me several hours to check everything up. At present Hdqrs. Cemetery N. of Marigny."

Enemy artillery had been working up and down the line all during the night of 2-3 June, but at Les Mares Farm they seemed to be more aggressive than elsewhere. An attack looked inevitable to Capt. John Blanchfield and his subordinates, but it didn't come on 2 June. All five of his officers—1st Lt. Lemuel Shepherd, 2d Lt. Hascall F. Waterhouse, 2d Lt. Lucius Q.C. Lyle, First Lieutenant Tillman, USA, and First Lieutenant Linehan, USA— had their men dug in around the farm or posted inside one of the buildings. Their positions were as strong as they could be, considering their total lack of machine guns and shortage of grenades. Rations weren't getting to 2/5, so the 55th Company took care of their requirements in the time-honored manner. The French refugees had left a calf behind when they fled the farm. That first night the company dined on calf steak and probably other portions as well. There were also rabbits, fowl, chickens and eggs. The garden held vegetables, the wine cave, *vin blanc* and *vin rouge*. The 55th wouldn't go hungry the following night either. Possibly they shared with the three other companies. Food-wise they were in far better shape than many of the other companies in either brigade.

3 June: The earlier report from 2 June continued: "French started withdrawing through our right."

Shearer sent word to Wise at midnight that he was holding a front line "from Hill 142 to Lucy-le-Bocage.... Capt. [George A.] Stowell, 76th Company's left rests on Hill 142." Shearer and Wise had been jockeying about for hours, but it would be many more hours before each found the other. While out scouting the lines, Logan Feland got a report from one of Wise's scouts who had found the location of 2/5's 51st Company and 1/6's 76th Company. They were about a thousand meters apart and that large gap was not soon corrected. Major Shearer told Wise via a message that he could not move any farther to his left than Hill 142. According to his information, that's where Wise's right should be. "I cannot spare men to run line past 142.... The vacancy is yours." Unfortunately, Shearer didn't know he wasn't on Hill 142. Wise thought that Williams was on Hill 142 and evidently so did Williams. The gap was finally partially filled with the arrival of Smith and the 82d Company. Berton W. Sibley, commanding officer of 3/6, later received orders to send more companies to this area.

At 0615 Neville advised Catlin of 6th Marines: "Wise and Shearer [commanding officer, 1/6] are in touch. Wise right company [Williams, 51st Company] has not been able to get in touch with Shearer's left company [Capt. George Stowell's 76th Company]."

The 8th Machine Gun Company recovered quickly from their long walk. A few hours after arriving they had supplied twelve guns to support Wise's left. The 81st Company supplied four more for his right flank. The 15th Company provided another four.

Captain Joseph D. Murray, commanding the 43d Company, sent a report to an unknown person at 0900 which detailed 2/5's current situation: "Companies have all reported dug in. 51st reports enemy advanced considerable distance late p.m. of June 2nd and that French retired to a line just in front of 51st Co. (right of battalion). 55th Co. reported that enemy advanced about two (2) kilometers in a southeasterly direction. 18th Co. casualties 1 killed and 10 wounded June 2nd as per list of names submitted to Regt. Hdqtrs. this a.m. Sent to French dressing station. Liaison agent exchanged with 6th Regt. Capt. [Allen M.] Sumner of 81st Co. with 8 M. G's placed at disposal 51st Co."

The Germans made several major efforts to push through 2/5 at this point, but all were defeated. If they had, the German army would have the 2d Division partially surrounded and certainly cut off from Paris, creating the grave possibility of the war being lost. Later that afternoon, Neville was able to report that Wise had 12 machine guns of 8th Machine Gun Company supporting his left, and 8 machine guns of Sumner's 81st Company, 6th Machine Gun Battalion, on his right.

After another period of heavy shelling, 2/5 was subjected to an intense machine-gun barrage, a signal that the Germans would soon launch an attack on their portion of the line. Some French shells fell too close and set fire to the wheat field to their immediate front, providing a smoke screen for the enemy. The Marines of 2/5 might have wondered whose side the French artillery were on.

While Shepherd and Blanchfield were talking, they noticed that the Germans had stepped up their artillery fire and that a rolling barrage was moving toward the outpost. Shepherd asked to return to his command out front, his skipper agreed. The barrage had already passed the knoll, and when Shepherd and his orderly moved forward they were obliged to walk through a curtain of exploding steel. By the most outrageous fortune, neither was hurt, and soon both dropped into a foxhole on the knoll alongside the occupants.

Looking out of their holes, the group could see the first of the German assault waves advancing toward them. Marine Pvt. Paul Bonner saw his commanding officer, Capt. John Blanchfield, standing at the side of the road: "'The devils are coming on,' he shouted. 'You have been waiting for them for a year; now go get them.' He was shouting in his Irish brogue and his blood was up. He thrilled every one of us."[2]

Marines had spent much time on the rifle range learning just what they were supposed to do at a time like this. Each man did his duty; he choose his target, then squeezed off shots, pull back the bolt and threw another round into the chamber—over and over again. Meticulous training, steadiness, coolness, discipline, and accuracy were soon making a bloody mess of the advancing German line. The Marines were dropping many in the first wave and soon were working over the second. This was a new kind of rifle fire on the Western Front, and the Germans recognized and appreciated it by stopping their forward motion. They hit the ground in a prone position, not to fire, but simply to take cover from those terrible rifles. The Marines were still able to pick off many more.

German machine guns began firing in barrage fashion from the nearby Bois de Mares. Soon the Marines were also taking casualties, especially those in Shepherd's advanced position. Although the Marines were burrowed deeper into their holes, before long the cries of pain from the wounded gave notice that some of the German bullets were also finding their targets. Enemy machine gun fire was so intense that the Marines couldn't raise themselves to respond. Soon after dark, Lieutenant Shepherd gave the order for his detachment to fall back to the main trench line, bringing their wounded with them.

Shepherd and his men made it back to the main line, but the enemy organized an even heavier assault upon the farm itself. At this time the 55th still had no machine guns. A gap of about five hundred yards lay between the left of the 55th and Veuilly Wood, with a wheat field intervening. Part of a platoon from the right wing was placed in the gap. As the gray waves approached again, the Marines lined every window and doorway of the farm buildings and at the breaches created by shells in the walls surrounding the farm. Again, the Marines exhibited their marksmanship. From these positions they aimed and fired as coolly as though they were at practice, and so accurately that not one live German made it to within a hundred yards of the buildings. During this attack Gy. Sgt. Herman "Babe" Tharau exhibited his individual courage. He calmly went up and down along the defensive positions, encouraging his men while pointing out potential targets and somehow avoiding the incoming fire.[3]

Germans made repeated efforts in two waves to penetrate the buildings, but each time, when they came within range of Marine rifles, large numbers of German casualties forced those following to turn aside and re-form. The third line withdrew without attempting to make the assault. German machine guns kept up an intermittent fire until dark and occasionally their bullets found a Marine target.

During the night a detachment from Headquarters Company, with several more machine guns from the 8th, 15th, and 81st, arrived and added greatly to the strength and firepower of the position. It was now the Marines' turn to open up on the German machine guns, forcing them to withdraw out of range. But the German artillery continued to dog the Marines. The company suffered several casualties, and at least one building was set afire by the constant bombardment. That evening the division's 12th Field Artillery was emplaced. They provided a lively fire that silenced the enemy artillery. After nearly thirty-six hours of continuous fighting, the Marines of 2/5 had a chance to rest.

Food constantly on the minds of the Marines in France. For the next few days the Marines in 2/5 would forage and fight, and what cooking was done, often, was while the fighting was still going on. The self-reliant Marines managed to take care of themselves.

On they came again and a young Chauchat gunner next to Cooke began firing away, letting go a full clip. "'Hey, that feels good,' he grinned." Cooke demanded, "Give me a try." As much as the young private, he, too, enjoyed getting even. The area was filled with lead from a few inches off the ground upward, and finally the Germans couldn't take anymore. They withdrew from the field, leaving it entirely to the Marines. German soldiers were lying in heaps across their front. It would be another few hours before they attempted another attack across open ground in the face of something they hadn't seen for years—accurate rifle fire.

The Germans' artillery fire on Les Mares Farm continued most of the day. About a hundred yards in front of the Marines' position, a small knoll offered an excellent field of fire. So, at 1700, Lem Shepherd suggested to Blanchfield that he take ten men and hold that knoll until the artillery fire became too hot for them, and then retire. Shepherd later admitted the offer was phony bravado, believing that his skipper wouldn't take that chance. He was terribly surprised when Blanchfield promptly accepted. Out they went amid falling shells, somehow making their destination without a casualty. After posting his men, Shepherd left a sergeant in charge and returned to Blanchfield to report what he had done.

Captain Lloyd Williams, 51st Co., on extreme right flank, at 1415 reported to Wise: "All French troops on our right have fallen back, leaving a gap on our right. Two platoons from 95th Company have reported to fill the gap. Request that additional men be ordered to fill the gap at once. Pvts. [Earl E.] Naud and [Raphael] Valerio wounded."

Shearer reported to Wise: "Have been trying to connect with your right flank," adding a further description of where his men were and where Wise's men were. Most messages from 2/5 were sent by Murray that afternoon because Wise was with the various companies at the front.

4 June: The official report of 2/5 for the period relates: "Two German attacks on the right in front and to the right of LES MARES FARM, which was repulsed. The same time the French withdrew on our left. For awhile it was rather embarrassing for the new line established. Two companies of the 1st Battalion [17th and 66th] strengthened line on the left. French withdrew from our front. We then held the first line."

At 0430 Captain Charley Dunbeck, commanding officer, 43d Company, asked for an artillery barrage on the enemy occupying the hill east of the woods for a distance of 500 meters east following the crest of the hill. It doesn't make sense because that or those hills are 176 and 142, which were, or should have been, occupied by Marines of 1/6 at that time. At 0800, Dunbeck reported the barrage appeared to be "about 200 yards in width, and between 700 & 800 yds to our front. It appeared to be an excellent barrage and was in the right place, although it could have been much wider extending eastward."

Shortly afterward a couple of companies from 1/5—the 17th and 66th with some machine guns from the 8th Company, which were assigned to support 2/5—were sent to fill the gap between them. The distance was approximately a half mile and this location would continue to dog everyone sent to fill it. The main road between Torcy and Lucy went right through the area making matters worse. Any advance made by German forces south would naturally take this route, the easiest pathway. The entire 4th Brigade's position would be in serious trouble, greatly affecting the 2d Division and thus the entire line, and ultimately the war.

This was the day the Germans tried several unsuccessful efforts to drive through 2/5. All were repulsed by the accurate rifle fire of the Marines, and many German soldiers paid the ultimate price because their leaders didn't know that kind of marksmanship still survived in the war.

Neville wrote to Captain Lester S. Wass, commanding officer, 18th Company, at 0836: "Are you in liaison with French on your left? Also are you in liaison by runner regularly with the 23rd Infantry?" To which Wass responded: "Yes to both questions. My line is now continuous with 23rd Inf; using a platoon of the 66th Co."

In the afternoon, soldiers from the Saxon 26th Jager Battalion crept back through the standing wheat and were heard digging in the field opposite Les Mares Farm. Someone had to go out there and count the number obscured by the wheat field. Corporal Francis I. Dockx volunteered. He took three men with him. After crawling about fifty yards through the wheat, they ran into a German patrol of thirty men and two machine guns. Despite the odds of ten to one against them, the Marines immediately opened up with their automatics and then charged the enemy. From the intensity of the firing, and fearing that the Marines may have gotten into a bad fix, Gy. Sgt. David L. Buford took two more men and went to help. He found Dockx and his comrades fighting off the Germans and hurling back hand grenades. When Buford arrived they had already dropped several Germans. The Germans began to give way with the arrival of more firepower. Buford, an excellent shot with a clear view, took out seven of the Germans with his automatic as they tried to escape. Only the machine guns remained. After a cautious approach, Buford, Dockx, and company rushed the guns. Dockx and one other Marine were killed, but the remaining German gun-crew members were captured. Of that thirty-man raiding group only five Germans escaped to their lines.

This would be the last German attempt to take Les Mares Farm and would be the closest that they would get to their ultimate objective—Paris. A large number of Marines earned some of the highest decorations then awarded by the AEF, but many would get them posthumously. Shepherd had been wounded in the neck on 3 June and would earn the Distinguished Service Cross, and later a Navy Cross, for declining medical treatment while continuing to lead his men. Tharau would get a Croix de Guerre. There were other awards too numerous to cite here.

Sometime that day, Feland, who was Neville's assistant regimental commander, sent a message from "P. C. DUNBECK 43rd Co." to Neville asking for artillery fire "half way between BOIS DE VEUILLY and VEUILLY LA POTERIE. Germans in line along this road."

5 June: At 1130 Neville wrote Wise: "Report desired concerning the liaison between Wise and the French on his left. This must be kept up." The official report indicates that 2/5 was relieved that day by the 116th French Infantry.

6 June: At 0805 Williams reported to Major Turrill, commanding officer, 1/5: "In obedience to orders from Lieut. Colonel Feland, I report with three platoons of 51st Company." Turrill's two-company battalion had been shattered and he was badly in need of help.

At 1845 Feland wrote to Neville: "Williams does not hold small square wood S. E. of Bussiares cross. If attached message is correct it is hardly possible for his left which is refused to a point in the ravine opposite 165 Hill to progress without being in the air. Am awaiting instructions as to progress of first phase since Catlin wounded. Notify Brigade."

This message from Williams at 1957 was possibly to Feland: "So far as can be observed from here, the French have withdrawn from the hill on our left and there is no indication of their activity in that direction." Feland sent that information plus additional information to Harbord at Brigade Headquarters: "Hill referred to is slope east of Hill 165. Then Feland sent Neville: Williams does not hold small square wood S. E. of Bussiares cross [road]." The official report states: "proceeded [from woods northeast of Voie du Chatel] to North and East ends of the woods N. E. of Lucy. Heavily shelled." This was the afternoon in which 3/5 was badly beaten in an attempt to take Belleau Woods.

7 June: The report of Operations, at 0200, dated 18 June:

> 2:00 a.m. proceeded to comply with Brigade Order #83 along LUCY-TORCY road. From reconnaissance patrol found out the Germans held all the ground East of the road and they attacked about 3:30 a.m. They were driven back and I got in connection with the 3rd Battalion, which were holding the high ground on the West of the road. Their positions were lightly held and the enemy were making attempts to get through this point and am convinced that if we had not been there at this critical moment that the line would have been broken. I strengthened the positions of the 3rd Battalion, later on that day received orders to relieve them. That night enemy shelling our whole line. Artillery and Machine Gun fire.

At 0615 Neville reported concerning Lt. Col. Wise and 3 companies located at old command post of 3/5: "Prior to the attack connecting with 6th Regt. on the right and with the 1st Bn. [3d Bn.]5 Regt. Co. M. [47th Co.] on their left. Gen. Harbord intends to withdraw 3rd Bn. 5 M. as soon as Col. Wise takes over the line."

Another report did not identify to or from, nor time: "Has not seen Lt. Col. Wise although Capt. Rockey [1/5] stayed out 5 hours endeavoring to find him. Has connected with left of 3rd Bn. 5th Marines which is evidently badly disorganized and scattered."

An order was telephoned to Lt. Col. Wise about 2000, probably from Harbord: "Take 3 companies of reserve, north on road to Torcy and go into the line on right of Feland between him and the 3rd Bn. 5th Marines. Feland's right is supposed to be about 1K. south of Hill 126. Berry's left near Hill 133. When you arrive approximately in position report by runner to Feland who is on road CHAMPILLON-142-TORCY. Orders will be sent to Feland. 5th Marines. 7 June 18."

From Harbord to Neville, at 2040: "1. Please make the following changes in force that has been operating under Colonel Feland southwest of Torcy: 1st, withdraw company of your 2nd battalion as your Regimental support to some place convenient for the purpose."

8 June: Report of operations: "Heavy shelling during day and night. Line felt out by the enemy during night by machine gun fire, some gas."

9 June: Report of operations: "Heavy shelling during the day and night. Our line felt out at night by machine gun fire."

10 June: Report of operations: "Heavy shelling during the day and night. Our line felt out at night by machine gun fire. Received Field Order #4 with barrage schedule about 10:00 p.m. for the attack against the BOIS DE BELLEAU." From 1st Lt. William R. Matthews, intelligence officer, 2/5, to Neville, at 1320: "Enemy one pounder probably located at Pt. 175.2-262.2. Has been firing into 43rd Co. sector all morning."

Capt. Lester S. Wass, commanding officer, 18th Company, sent to Wise at 1830: "Enemy is registering 77' about 25 or 30 yds in front of our front line." Maj. Frank E. Evans, 5th Regiment adjutant, sent this to Wise at 2315: "Copy message just recd. C.O. 5th to C.O. 6th. My message to you #129 is annulled. 2nd Bn. 5th will attack according to Field Order #4 H.Q. 4th Brig. 10 June 18. The attack progressing from south to north following a rolling barrage."

11 June: Report of operations:

> Attack started as ordered and found quite a few machine gun nests inside of the barrage which gave a great deal of trouble. The whole line received flanking machine guns from both sides, but strongest on the right, which had been reported clear, the men naturally drifted toward it and by 1:00 a.m. all opposition had ceased. That afternoon captured positions were consolidated and I was under the impression that all of my objectives had been obtained. The enemy started to filter in on our left which caused some trouble and I borrowed a company from Major [John A.] Hughes and started to clear them out when I received Regimental Order #134, transmitting instructions from the Brigade Commander, to refuse my left flank, and that the Artillery would attend to it. That night things very quiet. Two companies Engineers reported for consolidating work, and about 150 replacement men.

Wise had real trouble on his right flank. The company from 1/6 assigned to cover Wise's flank wasn't there. The Germans were and concentrated on the 51st Company.

Harbord received this message from Neville by telephone at 0550: "Message from Lieutenant Colonel Wise, Commanding the 2d Bn. 5th Regiment: Firing has begun again. I can hear nothing but the fire of my automatic rifles." Wise sent this to Harbord by telephone, received at 0553: "Machine gun fire begins and stops again." From Capt. Charley Dunbeck, commanding officer, 43d Company, to Harbord, by phone and received at 0611: "All objectives reached and am mopping up with machine guns."

Capt. Lloyd Williams, commanding officer, 51st Company, sent this message by phone to Harbord and received at 0650: "Holding everything. Machine guns are causing damage on our right rear. Request company be sent in." From Wise through Neville to Harbord, sent at 0855, received at 0945: "Barrage needed in front of us, point 176.1-262.5-176.7-262.7 as it is reported that the Germans are massing in front, Captain Williams wounded. Casualties quite heavy as the barrage did not clean things up. We have the situation in hand but the 6th has not come up on right. The barrage is badly needed and artillery officer could be used as we have spotted a nest of enemy artillery."

When the 2d Battalion went into Belleau Wood in the same opening that ruined 3/5 on 6 June, they expected their right flank to be covered by 1/6, which went into the southern portion of the woods on 10 June. In fact they expected the 76th Company, 1st Lt. Macon Overton, to cover Williams' 51st Company's right. Overton missed the boat and the 51st was slaughtered on the way into the woods.

Neville sent to Harbord this message by telephone, received at 1015: "From Wise at 9:25 a.m. This is our position from report sketch we are sending down. Four machine guns are in and the machine gun officer is sending four more. Please send prisoner chasers back as I am short handed. The 6th Regiment is not up on our right. All reports full of confidence. Artillery barrage and officer badly needed." From Wise via Gy. Sgt. Cook, 43d Company, to Harbord, by phone and received at 1015: "All companies have obtained their objectives and losses have been so heavy that we are only able to hold one line. We need barrage at once." From Wise to Harbord, by phone, received at 1045: "Counter battery work is needed as well as a barrage as we are being shelled regularly and it is coming from those in touch with 6th Regiment. If I can get the artillery I am satisfied."

From Wass at 18th Company to Harbord through Wise, received at 1045: "Have obtained our objective. The enemy are preparing counter-attack on our left flank. We need barrage immediately along Bouresches-Belleau Road, the northwest along our front." From Wise to Harbord "relayed," time received at 1250: "Artillery officer arrived and will be a great help. Positions are now organized; in perfect touch with the 6th. I will shortly inspect and can then give an idea of losses. Think we can get more prisoners as lots of them are hiding afraid to give up, so with German speaking men we are going to comb them out. We have lost quite a few officers."

From Wise to Harbord, sent at 1125 and received at 1318: "I think my left flank is rather weak. The Germans are massing in our front I can hardly spare any men. They could very easily filter through tonight for counter-attack. Nothing new to report except increased artillery activity." From Harbord to Wise, sent through Neville at 1145: "The Division Commander is at Brigade Headquarters and sends hearty congratulations to you and your gallant men. He says the task could not have been performed any better. The objectives of the Brigade have been attained everywhere after days of fighting which the Division Commander has never known to be excelled. To this I add my warm personal greetings and congratulations."

From "43" Dunbeck to Wise, at 1300: "Artillery is falling short. Could be raised about 200 yds, or more. Recommend an observer be sent here several small woods in front should be" (message incomplete). From Capt. Shuler, regiment adjutant, to Harbord, received at 1340 by telephone: "At 12:02 p.m. troops still reported massing on our front in the direction of Belleau and Torcy and think counterattack is on foot. Companies 43rd, 51st and 18th have about 30 men each lost and 55th about 83. I hardly believe the latter. Increased shelling."

The 55th was the company that wasn't covered by 1/6 and they did lose a load of men, including their skipper, Lloyd Williams. I'm sure Shuler found out the real facts, not his assumptions, later that day.

Harbord received this phone message from Wise at 1350: "Prisoner states a Division at Belleau." Harbord sent to Lt. Col. Wise, at 1400, No. 4: "Artillery very watchful on your left flank, you need have no fear for it. Use your engineers to consolidate your front as rapidly as possible. Refuse your left flank slightly, along ravine or higher up along edge of woods.

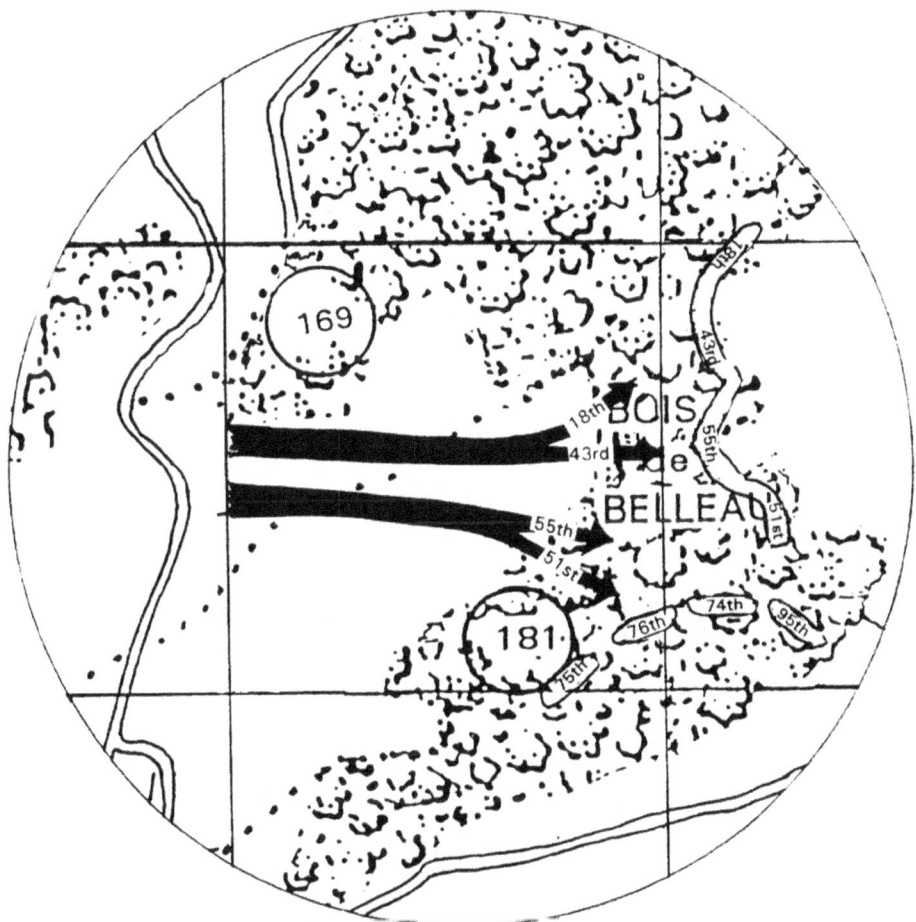

The attack by 2/5 launched on 11 June 1918 including the final positions occupied that night.

Let us know your losses as accurately as you can give them. What are your capture of machine guns. Your affair today was certainly well handled and is the biggest thing in prisoners that the A. E. F. has yet pulled off. We are delighted. Approximately 1000 replacements arriving for the Brigade today."

12 June: Report of operations: "Enemy in position on my left and gave some trouble, and received some permission to drive them out and after an Artillery preparation we attacked on their left flank at 5:00 p.m. and were successful, but too much ground had to be occupied and they filtered in again and we received the heaviest bombardment that I have heard in France that night."

Wise sent to Harbord at 1000: "Men in fine shape and line is holding but getting thinner. Heavy shelling and some gas. About out of officers. Request barrage immediately. Are getting hell shelled out of us now." Neville received this from Wise at 4th Brigade headquarters at 1630: "The artillery officer states that barrage was entirely light and from 3:30 to 3:40 it entirely stopped and then the Germans pushed up their guns expecting us to come across. I request that it be increased and kept up for another hour. The artillery officer could do very little spotting. I am afraid we are going to have a bit of trouble. Area to be looked out for entirely too large for the number of guns assigned to us."

Harbord received this from Neville at 1815: "So far no reports, but machine gun fire has now ceased. We intended to use V. B.'s if held up. Trench mortars were in woods also. I am positive that everything is going along all right. There is heavy artillery fire on our entire position." Captain Wass, 18th Company, sent to Colonel Wise: "Have reached my objective and am holding it. No connection on left yet. Am trying to connect with 51st (Co) and machine guns on right. Need guns and send non to fill gap between me and 51st. I think other companies are too far to N. E."

From Wise to Harbord, sent at 1815, received at 1938: "All objectives reached and we are consolidating. From prisoners we hear that one battalion of 500 men were in there. Dunbeck and [Capt. Gilder D.] Jackson wounded. Very short of men. Quite a heavy bombardment on P.C. and the whole woods. Still think the line rather thin as our losses are heavy. Enclosed is Wass' report. Gas dropped also. Enclosed Wass' report, but when Engineers arrive the line will be in better shape."

From Wise to Neville, received at 4th Brigade Headquarters, at 2040: "I know positively all positions attained and linked up. We have only two wounded Germans as they got away. Lost a great many men. We are getting a devil of a shelling, and quite accurate. Quite a few machine guns captured. They should be dug in well before dark. Everything running smooth and men in fine shape, but as I put in my report I am afraid of the reaction. P.S.—This is a different outfit from the one of yesterday." In other words, Wise was telling his boss that he was in serious trouble and needed help. From Wise to Neville to Harbord by telephone, at 1845: "Think all objectives have been reached but expect a counter-attack. Line rather lightly held. No reports except from walking wounded."

Brigade headquarters received this from 2d Lt. Drinkard B. Milner of the 43rd Company at 2255: "We reached our objective and returned from the crossroads to the left at 175.8-262.5. We are in touch with the 55th Co. on our left but have not gotten in touch with the 18th Co. Captain Dunbeck wounded at the start but not serious. Losses were heavy."

Second Lieutenant Drinkard B. Milner, a minister's son, assumed command of the 43d Co. after Dunbeck was wounded, and he did a great job.

From Wass to Wise, at 1935: "Have part 1/2 platoon of the 55th Co. and this line has now about 2 squads of 18th Company. Line is thin and we should get more men right away. Also a machine gun and Chauchat machine gun ammunition, Request barrage immediately, also Very pistols, signals. Are getting hell shelled out of us now." From Wise to Harbord, received at 1945: "The two prisoners that we have came from 1st Company, 2d Bn. 461st [German] Regiment. They were on outpost and came and gave up when fire came down; thus confirming order of battle."

Wise sent this message to Neville at 2015: "Line holding but getting thinner. Heavy shelling and some gas. Think I am entirely too weak. Do not expect any trouble before dark. Men in fine shape." That last comment didn't make any sense. Wise's message of 2115 told to Neville: "German officer captured states that they intended to attack." From Wise to Harbord, received at 2300: "Hughes [commanding officer, 1/6] sent me notice at 8 p.m. that he was going to take over the rear line. Captain of Engineer Corps just reported that he has not. Sent out again to find out. Things known but no support as I had to use everybody. Shelling has been very heavy. Very hard to get up supplies. About out of officers."

Second Lt. Milner sent to Lt. Col. Wise: "A prisoner says that a Division was going to attack us tonight from the north. Why cannot we have a barrage put in front of us tonight?" From Wise to Harbord, received at 2307: "A dying German officer states that a fresh Division is in and the plan was to attack tonight. Would like artillery up on my front during night. We are in full spirits. Have not 350 old men left and 7 officers. They are shelling very heavy."

13 June: Report of operations by Wise: "Was convinced that we did not hold entire north and eastern edge of woods and that the enemy still had re-occupied some strong positions, but did not have sufficient men to drive them out, and received Brigade Field Order #5 in which the 2nd Battalion, 6th Marines were to relieve me. Major Holcomb arrived that afternoon and he agreed to give me a fresh company to attack the north and western edge of the woods at 4:00 a.m. June 14th, whole area heavily shelled."

From Lt. Colonel Wise, relayed by Colonel Neville, to Harbord, received 0510: "The lines appear to be holding. Terrific barrage from my P.O. forward. And it was a real barrage, Losses must be very heavy. So far no counter attack. If reinforcements are available they could be used. Irritating gas giving a lot of trouble, Detail requested to bring our rations as all of mine are fighting. So far have been very hard up to get runners through. Some have never returned. Morale excellent but everybody about all in." From Lt. Col. John A. Hughes, commanding officer, 1/6, to Neville, relayed by Harbord, at 0504: "Have had terrific bombardment and attack. I have every man except a few odd ones in tow now. We have not broken contact and have held. Request two companies at least for myself and two companies for Colonel Wise."

Neville received this at Brigade Headquarters at 0835, from Wise:

> Things quiet at present. Getting supplies up to the front line. Have one replacement officer per company left and about 300 men not including replacements. Engineers are getting well dug in. As all these woods are ranged to the yard they are absolutely torn to pieces. When this is going on it is absolutely impossible to get men or supplies up to the front, Captain [Joseph D.] Murray

has been out for some time making reconnaissance of the whole line and then can give a more full report. Not having officers makes it hard to get detailed information promptly. My idea is that attack will come from the N. W. All company commanders request men.

14 June: Report of operations:

2nd Battalion, 6th Marines, were badly gassed and instead of arriving night 13-14 with about 800 men only 325 effectives arrived, so the attack could not be delivered, and I did not consider that they were sufficient to relieve me and remained in position. I had received orders to stay in the sector with Major Holcomb until the enemy were cleared out but Major Holcomb brought me word that I could be relieved, but did not consider it safe to do so. Lt. Colonel Feland arrived and assumed command of the 2nd Battalion, 5th Marines and 1st and 2nd Battalions, 6th Marines. Lines re-established and the whole position put in a much safer condition.

From Wise through Colonel Neville to 4th Brigade Headquarters, sent at 0605:

[Lt. Col. Thomas] Holcomb arrived with 1¾ companies at 3 a.m. and other two companies badly broken up, from shells and gas. About 150 of these have showed up. My men physically unable to make another attack. Have just made another reconnaissance of the line and consider my present line unsafe unless whole woods are in our possession and not enough troops on hand and if those woods are taken there must be enough troops to hold them, or it will be the same story again; that is they will filter in. The woods are larger than shown. I request permission to withdraw slightly to make the line safer and that Holcomb be given more men as many of them here have had gas. Some gas here.

Wise was describing what bad condition not only 2/5 but also 2/6 were in; they had been badly hurt by gas, and was in no condition to relieve anyone. Nobody seemed to be paying attention.

From Lt. Col. Lee, commanding officer, 6th Regiment, to Wise and Sibley, commanding officer, 3/6, by runner at 1925: "Movement of enemy troops by foot and auto from N. W. to S. E. towards north end of BOIS DE BELLEAU was reported this evening. Take precaution."

15 June: Report of operations: "Conditions remained the same and received Brigade Field. Order #8 in which the 7th U.S. Infantry were to relieve us. Shelling brisk."

16 June: Second Battalion of the 5th Regiment was relieved by the 1st Battalion, 7th U.S. Infantry in the early morning and proceeded to Mery for rest and recuperation. Wise and 2/5 had effectively reduced the German presence in Belleau Wood when they were relieved. The enemy was barely holding on to the top portion of the woods. That would change.

20 June: Harbord sent the commanding officer of 3/7 a message of congratulations for their good work in "occupying and holding the ravine to crossroads without loss." He suggested they send out patrols to ascertain if the enemy occupied Hill 126, located to the south east of Torcy. It appears that 3/7 was the most successful of the 3 battalions of the 7th Infantry.

On the night of 20-21 June, Wise and 2/5 returned from their short rest period and were sent to the Bois Gros Jean as division reserve.

21 June: Headquarters 4th Brigade sent Field Order No. 7 which described how the 4th Brigade units were to relieve the various 7th Infantry units: "The 2nd Bn. 5th Marines to relieve the 3rd Bn., 7th Inf., night of June 23-24." Further down, the report described movements of the 4th Brigade preliminary to relief of the 7th Infantry: "2nd Bn. 5th

3. Second Battalion, Fifth Marines, 1917–1919   83

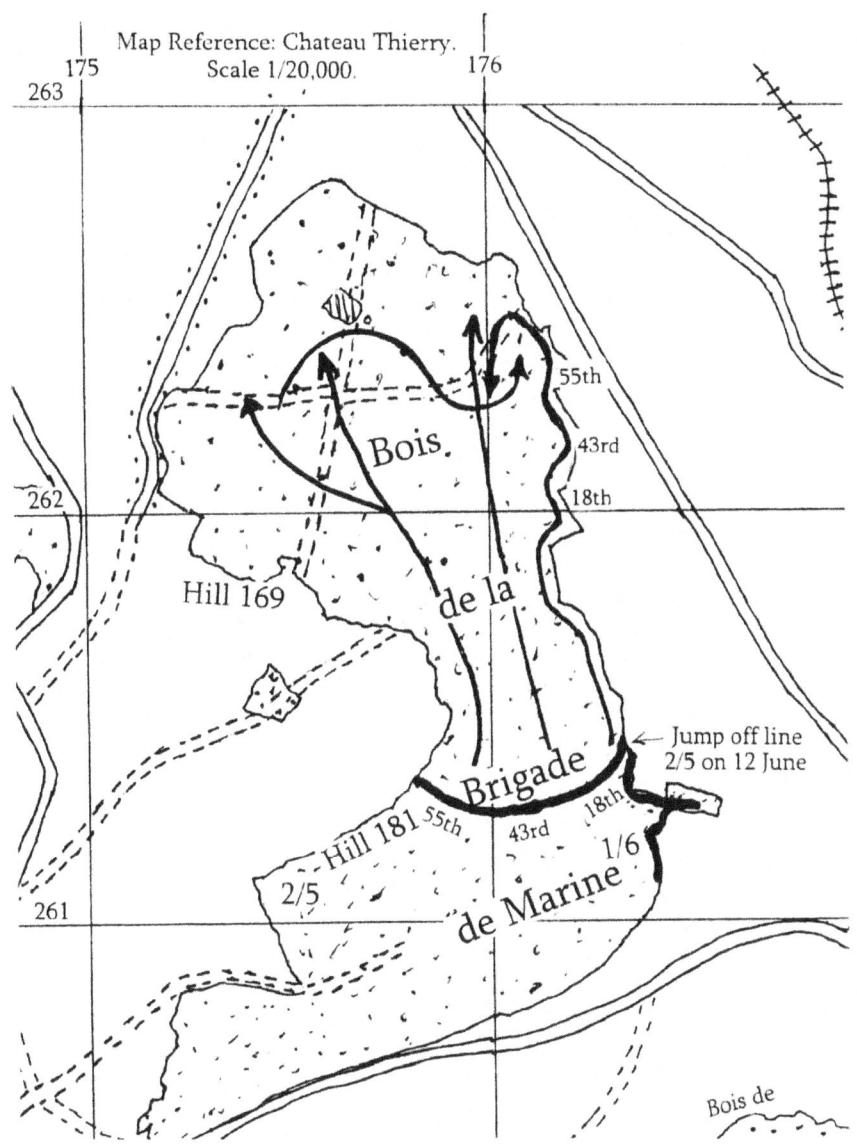

Last positions of 2/5 in Belleau Wood.

Marines to BOIS GROS JEAN as Division Reserve night of June 21-22; to wood n. w. of LUCY-LE-BOCAGE as Brigade Reserve, night of June 22-23."

23 June: From Capt. Joseph D. Murray, adjutant, 2/5, to all platoon leaders of 2/5, at 1340:

> The battalion commander (Wise) insists on immediate attention to the following: (1) Camouflaging worst openings in the woods which would permit enemy observation; (2) Collection of arms, equipment, etc., scattered through the sector which will be turned in at Batt. Hdqtrs. each time any carrying parties make a trip; (3) stringing of low trip wires in front of each platoon, and (4) absolute prohibition of use of paths for trails which are not completely concealed both overhead and toward the front. Cans, paper and all other material which cannot be used or sal-

vaged will be buried at once, Tools, ammunition and fireworks are available and are being distributed. Put in for what you really need and will try to get it for you.

From Lt. Col. Lee, commanding officer, 6th Marines, to Wise, at 1920 by motorcycle: "When tonight in accordance with Field Order No. 7, Hdqrs 4th Brigade, you will have relieved the 3rd Bn. 7th Inf. please report the fact to this P.C. (call 'Form F-1') over the phone by the words 'In positions.' Thereafter make frequent reports of events either by runner or phone. If the latter method is used be most guarded in your language not speaking in such plain language as to give any information to the enemy who is sure to be listening in. Keep yourself and this office informed of conditions in your front by use of small patrols during the night. Particularly be watchful On your right over the roads leading from the north." Why Lee would be ordering Wise (or is it now Keyser?) to perform services is beyond me. I can find nothing that indicates that 2/5 should report to Lee.

24 June: From Harbord to Wise, through Lee, sent at 1200:

1. The position turned over to your battalion is not exactly as reported by the 3rd Bn, 7th Inf., in that it does not run out to 175.2-262.6 where their right was supposed to be. They occupied a line of individual pits, of which there are believed to be two rows near each other. I desire your line to be advanced tonight to the road with the double row of trees which runs just west of the BOIS DE BELLEAU, and dug in, so as to conform approximately to sketch sent you herewith. This will very greatly facilitate operations in the BOIS.
2. You are cautioned, that two companies are considered enough for your entire front lines and that your support (2 Cos.) should be back in the woods where it will be well in hand near your PLC, if needed.
3. It is expected that you will push patrols out tonight and get some identifications of what is in front of you if enemy is still there. Send picked men in groups of two or three and find out definitely where the enemy's lines are, The artillery will not fire west of the double row of trees on road near BOIS nor south of TORCY unless requested by you.
Copy for C.O. 5th.
C.O. 6th.

Wise sent to Lee at 1300: "Enemy showing great activity in trench east of road running N.E.–S.W. along edge of BOIS DE BELLEAU—This trench faces west, it is just west of point 133—Coordinates 175.5-262.8—. Some shelling at 173.7-262.6. Enemy seems to be moving from top of hill 133 & woods to trench and road west of 133 at about 175.5-262.8. 7 Planes seen over enemy lines at 8:40."

At some point, Lt. Col. Wise was relieved (various other words were used to describe the action) by Brig. Gen. Harbord after an altercation. Harbord complained that Wise had misled him in various reports, and Wise asked why Harbord hadn't come to where Wise was to determine what was really happening. Wise was eventually, after a brief leave, sent to some school at Langres. Also note that from here on, the brigade commander and battalion commanding officer are communicating directly, eliminating the regimental commanding officer, hardly a satisfactory arrangement.

From Major Ralph S. Keyser, the new commanding officer of 2/5, to Harbord, no time indicated: "Battalion carried out relief at 1245 a.m. without incident. 1 casualty. Unless otherwise instructed by you will have 55th Co. [1st Lt. Elliott D. Cooke, USA] patrol to north until contact with enemy is obtained and the same for 18th Co. [Wass] to the N. E. tonight.

The 51st Co. [Capt. William O. Corbin] will also reconnoitre the field and woods to the front of its present position. Have plenty of new 1/50,000 maps of BOIS DE BELLEAU but only one of our sector."

25 June: From Harbord to Keyser, through Lee, at 0145:

Your message of 10:20 p.m. [24 June] received. The clump of trees mentioned as containing machine guns was occupied by the 7th Infantry night before last and visited yesterday. It is in your right rear according to our understanding of your position, and should have been under the observation of your line ever since you went in. I do not credit the theory of the motion of the wheat being seen hundreds of yards at night by the light of the flares if enemy has been able to reoccupy that clump of trees under eyes of your line. Make it certain that it is now occupied by machine guns by sending out patrol that will go close enough to be sure. If it is occupied we will clean it out by artillery today. It is already too late for you to carry out your orders tonight. I want your patrols to dominate that whole region day and night, and it ought not to be necessary to specify the separate clumps of woods, or even to tell you to keep patrols out. That is elementary. Give me an accurate statement of where the right of your line ends, and an estimate of the time needed to extend it by digging to the road mentioned in your orders today, in case you cannot extend it in any other way. Let me reiterate that your occupation includes necessary patrolling to the enemy in your front, and flanks and that the small clump of woods ought certainly to have been included without specification from here, which if done would not have lost us this whole night as matters now are.

Keyser sent the following to Harbord at 0230 by runner: "My line is now held continuously from the French (174 Reg) on hill 142 to double row of trees, road opposite bald spot in Bois de Belleau with the exception of about 75 yds. running from right of strong point at cross roads of LUCY-TORCY road. I am not in touch with [Maurice] Shearer [commanding officer, 3/5] and have nothing to indicate position of his left in BELLEAU woods. I have sent one platoon to connect up with the left of 16 Co."

From Harbord to Maj. Gen. Bundy at 2d Division, sent at 1330:

Message received from C.O. 2nd Bn. 5th Marines; The Adjutant said that when he last saw the plane (German aeroplane) it was descending in flames at an angle of about 45 degrees in the direction of the road running north of the road which runs east and west through LUCY. This plane was being closely followed by a second plane which, however, flew away. This second plane was closely followed by a third plane, presumably a French machine.

Message from C.O. 5th Marines: About an hour ago an enemy airplane shot down, apparently by French aviator, at point 75.80-62.70, northeastern part of BELLEAU. Burst into flames just before striking ground, probably landing within enemy lines.

From Harbord to Keyser, through Lee, at 1545:

1. With reference to your No. 7, the artillery have been requested to fire on the edges of the Bois de Belleau in the part where you think there may be machine guns between the double tree road and the Bois. A short time before dark I will have artillery fire put on the old line of German trenches which runs out slightly to the N. W. from the BOIS DE BELLEAU, and after dark believe you will have no trouble in advancing your line according to our conversation this morning. From a study of the ground from the trenches of the 43rd Co., near the clump of woods that you had reconnoitered last night, it appears to me that the swale in which you have your other two companies from your left, passes the crossroad and extends up near enough to the double-tree road so that if your line followed that it would be on the reverse side of a slope almost to the double-tree road and not open to anything but an indirect fire, unless, as you suggest, there are some machine guns along the edge of the woods. If Major Shearer occupies the north edge as we expect

this evening, he will refuse his left flank along the edge of the woods pending your line coming up approximately abreast of him. I do not believe that when he has accomplished this and the artillery has played on the edge of the wood for the afternoon that there will be any machine guns there, but you are authorized to send a platoon around to your right when you make your advance to cover the ground between the road and the edge of the Bois, if you still deem it necessary.

If you have not already thought of it, I suggest you should take with you the Officers who are to go forward on your right and go to the position to which Captain Murray took me this morning, near the little clump of woods, so that you can indicate to them in daylight the probable point which will mark their advance. When you do that you will notice that the swale referred to curves around between the clump of woods and the double-tree road.

For C.O. 6th.

For some reason, which I cannot find any reference to, at this point in time Lt. Col. Lee began giving Keyser orders and it appears that Harbord must have ordered Keyser to report to Lee.

From Plan A-1 (Neville?) to Harbord, sent at 1750, by motorcycle: "Cook, 55th Co., reports heavy artillery shelling French on our left at 173.9-263.4. They pay no attention to light signals. Artillery should lengthen its fire at least 400 yds making petit post untenable" (Should be "Cooke"). Keyser (A-7) sent this to Lt. Col. Lee at 1900 by phone: "O. P. reports that the Germans sent up four rockets on Hill 193 with four green stars. Need 400 sand bags. Must receive them before 10:00 p.m. if sent tonight. If not send tomorrow. Phone back from this."

Harbord sent to Keyser, through Lee, at 2310: "In moving your line forward it is important that you send a platoon to clean up in the edge of the Bois, parallel to the double tree road. The 16th Co. [Capt. Robert Yowell] in trying to come out to position on that side of the road is meeting some resistance. Send your platoon by your right rear to come up now on the left and help clean it out. I do not believe the remainder of your line will meet with much resistance."

At 2320, Harbord sent this to Neville:

Our Shearer Battalion [3/5] has done splendid work. I have no fear of a counter attack by the Germans tonight. You are in charge of the BOIS DE BELLEAU and can divert such part of Major Sibley's Battalion [3/6] as you think best. His front is practically wired in. In connection with the movement of Keyser's Battalion [2/5] to connect up with the west side of BOIS DE BELLEAU, I have ordered him to send a platoon by his right rear to come up on the left of the 16th Company and help clean that edge of the woods. It is very important that Shearer be told of this in order that the 16th Company may not, in the dark, confuse that platoon with the enemy.

Artillery are trying to neutralize some of the enemy artillery.

J. G. H.

From Harbord to Neville, no time indicated: "Contingent upon Major Shearer obtaining his objective orders were this afternoon sent Major Keyser to advance his line tonight and bring the right of the line on the double tree road just west of Bois de Belleau. This will begin shortly after dark, Please notify Major Shearer that the movement is going to take place so that in the dark he will not confuse it with a possible counter attack. Keyser's movement will be preceded by considirable artillery firing on the old trenches which run north west from Bois do Belleau."

26 June: Keyser sent to Lee at 0145: "My new line to double-tree road opposite bald spot in Belleau woods connected up and digging in, about half completed. Intermittent M.G. fire heard near upper North corner of bald spot, but none directed on us. The platoon sent to assistance of 16th Co. was instructed by me not to enter wood until he got in touch with left of 16th Co. Have no news of them since they left here."

Lee replied to Keyser at 0400: "Have tried to get information from 5th as to location Shearer's left, but they have no definite dope. They sent out message to have liaison runners report your P.C. and say two (2) went over, Shearer has sent in 60 prisoners through here & more through 5th. Brigade reports that prisoners attempting to surrender in numbers were shot down by own M.G's. Lot going through do not stack up much in size or Kultur. If you get in touch with Shearer have message telephoned in 'Have hooked up on my right.'" Sender was F. E. Evans, adjutant.

From A-7 (Keyser) to Form-F (?) at 0518: "In regard to picks and shovels. Have them gotten to P. C. & inform A-7 when we have them. Awaiting further instructions as to sending them out during the day. At 6:25 sentry reported that 4 prisoners went through P. C. at 3:30 a.m. & were given guide to Brig. Hqrs. This makes total of 64 reported."

Lee received from Keyser at 0549:

> Am back at P. C. My new line is well dug in & men have had the cooked meal sent them. As I was leaving 43 Co. I met a man from the platoon of the 51st Co. that was sent to touch up and assist 16th Co. who reported that he and one other from his Plt. were trying to bring in 2 wounded and were coming to get assistance. I got the information from him that the patrol sent out by the plat. Commander to get liaison with left of 16th Co. was successful and the plat. while moving into the woods at the point about 200 yds in rear of my right was shelled and the plat. badly scattered. This information I consider vague & not much to be relied on as the man was a recruit & excited.
>
> Intermittent M.G. fire now still to be heard in the Bois when I left at 4:15 and an occasional flare sent up from the high point well to the east of 43 Co. PC. The north end of Bois de B. was quiet. Received 5:49 a.m. by C.J.C. [1st Lt. Charles J. Churchman].

From Lee to Keyser, sent at 0835, by runner: "The Brigade directs that you establish and maintain close liaison with Shearer's Bn. on your right as quickly as possible. Take all precautions for security and information. Am notifying Shearer of this." And from Lee to Keyser, sent at 0835 by runner: "Please furnish the Brigade through this office a sketch on map if you have one, showing your exact position and the distribution of your command by companies from left to right, and the elements in depth—show them as such platoon, such Co., etc. Let me have this as soon as possible."

At 1405 Harbord sent to Keyser through Lee: "Make your preparations and as soon as possible after dark tonight swing your line forward so that it will run approximately straight from the cross-roads south of Torcy (174.75-263.1) to the double tree road, at 175.4-262.7. I will have the artillery keep down any fire from the trenches running northwest. from the BOIS DE BELLEAU, between 10 and 12 p.m." Copy to Major Shearer through commanding officer, 5th Marines. Delivered to A-l at 3:00 p.m. by runner.

27 June: From Lee to Keyser, at 1150:

> Please let me have the sketch showing your dispositions and Co. designations asked for early this morning. Keep in constant communication with your O.P's. and report immediately all enemy

movement of troops or vehicles irrespective of numbers and report each movement observed in time for battery preparation and action.

Push out small patrols to your front to ascertain if the enemy are in TORCY and CHATEAU BELLEAU by night. This may necessitate their going as far as the BELLEAU-TORCY-BUSSIARES road. Confine your patrolling to your own front, limited by the two-tree road running S. W. from BELLEAU to LUCY on the East and the line 174 on the west. Notify adjoining sectors on your right and left of the presence of your patrols in time. Keep in close touch with Holcomb on right and French on left.

Keyser replied to Lee at 1330, sent by runner: "Was talking to Sig. corps Captain about connecting up new front line by phone. Strongly recommend it and request your approval. Patrols will be put out as ordered and also Will send sketch showing position & disposition Bn as soon as return from Belleau."

From Lee to Keyser, sent at 2030 by runner:

Please make to me each morning, not later than noon a full report of the work of your patrols. They must be given specific missions before starting out, and made thoroughly ready for the work—relieved of all matters such as papers and other identifying matter, properly clothed, armed, equipped and inspected before starting out. The prime object should be to get contact with the enemy and discover his disposition, strength, etc. and report instantly the number of men or vehicles, their direction of movement and the map coordinates at which observed. Effort should be made when he is seen at work to ascertain the nature of the work and its locations stated. The reports should be made to me by your Int. Officer & Scout Officer under your supervision.

From Harbord to Keyser through Lee, no time indicated: "Orders have been given Major Holcomb [2/6] to direct two Platoons of the 51st Company to return to their Battalion after dark. I am very much pleased with the success in advancing your line in the way you did last night. Please let Captain Wass [18th Company] and your other officers know that it was a good piece of work."

28 June: From Lee to Keyser, sent at 1435 by runner: "Please send in by phone upon receipt this message, the positive points upon which you think it advisable to have artillery fire for tonight. The normal barrage over your front now is 173.8-264.1 to 175.8-263.4. Any change in this normal barrage take in consideration your order for movement from Gen. Harbord which accompanies this message." Sent by F. E. Evans, adjutant, by order. From Lee to Keyser, sent at 1755 by runner: "Please observe your instructions as to patrolling of yesterday adding effort to collect anything that may be of value to make identification—any materials or if possible the capture of a sentinel or member of a hostile patrol if such should be encountered. Verify any information obtained last night by your patrols as to location and strength of enemy and nature and progress of work executed by him."

29 June: From Lee to Keyser, sent at 0945 by runner: "Brigade Commander directs that you submit to Brigade via these Hdq. your present correct battle position, showing location of all your units and those on your left as soon as practicable." Keyser sent back to Lee, at 1255, by runner: "Enclosed is a sketch for Brig. showing new dispositions. Sorry for delay but Int. Officer was taken sick in woods and I have just heard from him. This will show you new disposition after relief last night. The changes I believe improve things. If you can't take what you want from Brigs Map I will send you separate sketch. Phone me if you need it."

From an unknown person to Capt. Joseph D. Murray, adjutant, 2/5, sent at 1530: "Capt.

Spencer informs me that the sales commissary is in his district. Should any of the officers or men in your company desire to purchase supplies, please furnish me with a list of the articles desired & the money. I will forward same by runner to Capt. Spencer. Runner leaves Bn. P. C. daily at 7 a.m. Furnish you today with form for daily strength reports. Please fill out on each day to this P.C. by 6 a.m." From Lee to Keyser, at 1710 by runner: "Please conduct your patrolling tonight with the same objects in view as were indicated in your instructions of yesterday. Bearss [Lt. Col. Hiram I.] has something on hand for tonight and I presume that he has told you of it. You must time and govern your patrolling accordingly. Make the primary object of your patrols identifications[,] prisoners are the best."

Keyser sent to Lee at 1745 by runner:

> Col. Bearss is here and I am giving him every assistance. My patrols will conform and go out as directed. Wass & Cook[e] think it advisable to connect at rifle pits that men are now in and run communication trench from rear of 1st Plat of 51st Co. to woods where 51 P.C. is located. If you approve will start work tonight. Give answer "O.K." over phone. Am investigating the mysterious cutting of O.P. phone line three different times. The last this a.m., one strand only of wire was cut, and the three times in same place. Am making careful investigation and taking steps to catch the "bird" and protect ourselves against prowlers. Will report detail later.

Lieutenant Colonel Hiram I. Bearss, then associated with the 6th Regiment, had a varied and distinguished career as a Marine prior to the American Expeditionary Forces and interesting part in the development of the 5th Regiment. He was the officer in command of the 5th Replacement Battalion, which arrived in France in July 1917. He replaced Col. Doyen as the commanding officer of the 5th Regiment, when that officer assumed command of the newly created 4th Marine Brigade. Then, when Doyen assumed command of the 2d Division, Bearss assumed command of the 4th Brigade. When Col. Neville arrived in late December 1917, he replaced Bearss in command of the 5th Regiment and Hiram was allowed to become a drifter because there was no unit in the Marine Brigade for him to command. Later, in late June 1918, he returned and was sort of a wandering "uncle" who tried to find work. He did, in command of a U.S. Army regiment and later a brigade with which he earned a Distinguished Service Cross in combat.[4]

Keyser sent to Capt. Joseph D. Murray, at "6:50" by runner (whether "a.m." or "p.m." is not indicated on original of this message. It is assumed that the hour should be "p.m."): "Send out tonight two patrols of the same strength and with the same mission as the patrols sent out last night. They will, however, leave about 10:30 p.m. instead of midnight and remain out until about 3 a.m. unless their mission is accomplished sooner. Identification of enemy units is especially desired. A combat patrol for the capture of Prisoners is being sent out by 51st Co. to confine their activities to west of LUCY-TORCY road. Artillery have been informed of this."

30 June: From Harbord to Keyser, at 1100: "The 2d Battalion 5th Marines will be relieved as soon as possible after dark tonight by the 1st Battalion, 5th Marines, Reconnaissance by Battalion and Company Commanders during the day of June 30th. The 2d Battalion 5th Marines will take station in woods northwest of LUCY."

Keyser sent the following to Murray, no time indicated, by runner: "This Batt. will be relieved tonight as soon as possible after dark by the 1st Batt., 5th Marines. The four guides from each company, one for each platoon, will be at Batt. P.C. by 9:30. The 51st & 43rd Companies will send their guides to report to Batt. P.O. early as possible to do so with safety. This Batt. will take station in woods N. W. of Lucy vacated by the relieving Batt, tonight as soon as it is dark enough to work with safety start connecting up the rifle pits with the idea of making a continuous trench line. Be certain to provide for traverses and a latrine."

And from Lee to Turrill, 1/5, sent at 1130 by runner: "Am inclosing your orders and five copies of the map of the sector. Upon completion of relief please furnish this office with detailed sketch of your dispositions by company units. Get in touch with Keyser as soon as possible for your reconnaissance, as indicated in the order. Let me know anything that this office may do for you and keep me advised constantly of events."

3 July: From Lee to Keyser, sent at 1810 by runner: "Inclosing orders from your Regt. Hdq. They have advised that you will drop off guides at this P.C. on the way out, as follows: 1. from Bn, Hdq., 1 from each Co., 1 from each platoon to show the strangers in."

The following was part of Lt. Col. Wise's report for 16 June but was a comprehensive description of what all Americans encountered while fighting Germans in the war.

> We were continually fighting for two weeks and during that time the men did not have even a hot cup of coffee and lived entirely on cold food, and at times water was scarce, and from June 11th were without packs. I have never seen such a spirit as existed in the men in regard to every task that was given them and their losses seem to inspire fresh courage, and at all times were eager for the attack, and such a record may have been equalled during this war, but never surpassed. We had lost rather heavily before the attack on the BOIS DE BELLEAU and only had about 700 effectives that morning and attacked on a front and depth of a kilometer. The following points were observed:
>
> (a) That the maps used were incorrect and orders were not received in sufficient time to make a ground reconnaissance.
> (b) That in wood fighting it is very difficult to determine that you are in the right position and especially so when the underbrush was very heavy.
> (c) The enemy gives no trouble at all after you are at bayonet range, and is only too willing to surrender.
> (d) That it is much cheaper in life to have German's surrender instead of killing all in sight and that German-speaking men were used very successfully this way.
> (e) That Germans were very helpless when there were no officers or noncommissioned officers around and machine gun crews were much braver than the infantry.
> (f) That it is a safe method to bayonet all men on the ground as some are not wounded.
> (g) That machine guns were exceedingly well camouflaged and look out especially for brush heaps and wood piles also in trees, and that they generally develop one gun at a time and after that is taken a flanking one will open up.
> (h) All men should have a working knowledge of German machine guns which are very simple and when captured can be used as there is always plenty of ammunition around.
> (i) The majority of Germans captured and well treated were more than willing to tell everything they know and in fact to assist you, as the ones I saw were dead tired of the war.
> (k) When prisoners are taken, the machine guns in their vicinity should be brought out by them, unless you are absolutely certain you are going to consolidate that certain spot. If this cannot be done a pistol bullet in the breech and water cooler casing will put them out of action and they cannot be then used again. In wood fighting it is very easy for men to conceal themselves and after you have run over them to come back again, so a gun should never be left intact.

- (l) Automatic and rifle fire from the hip was the only kind that could be used in thick cover and it was found very effective.
- (m) In open warfare and when the lines are under 1000 yards sniping was very successful as they had no idea we could kill at that range.
- (n) In thick cover and when machine gun nests were run into if prisoners were available one in front of a man secured many machine guns as they would not shoot on their own men.
- (o) All attacks must have good mopping up parties as the German who is willing to surrender at the time of the attack is a different man several hours afterwards when in hands of an officer. All Germans captured were very much surprised that we did not immediately kill them as they were told that was our practice.
- (p) The six or seven officers taken were very easily handled.
- (q) Intelligence section should have experts near P.C. so that all information from prisoners can be used at once. A novice gets very little out of a prisoner and during an attack the small staff of a Battalion Commander are absolutely necessary for other things under our present organization. It is most important that this data be gotten first hand.
- (r) That staff officers be on hand immediately after an attack to see that all orders have been carried out and that they make a daily inspection of the lines, as a great many officers are casualties and you don't get correct reports from the inexperienced ones left and a clear mind of that kind from one who knows exactly what the higher command desires would be invaluable and I personnally can say that towards the end of our stay in the sector from excessive work that I was not at my best in giving clear reports, and I was over my positions at least once a day.
- (s) Rifle and hand grenades were found very useful against machine gun nests also a Stokes Mortar when the nest is located.
- (t) The enemy used very effectively 37 and 47 mm guns and 77's point blank against our consolidated positions.
- (u) Machine gun nests and troops cannot be driven out of woods by artillery when they desire to remain and it takes the personal contact of the bayonet to do it.
- (v) The enemy have a very irritating substance in their high explosives which a mask won't stop. It is not dangerous but makes you get out of a small dugout, as the gas causes a sore throat, sneezing and eye irritation.
- (w) It is not desirable to have replacements take place in the lines as the men never have a chance to get oriented and it has a bad effect on them as they don't know even their leaders and it is most essential that teamwork must exist to be successful.

In ending this report I wish it to be clearly understood that I am giving what information I consider might be of value and most of it comes from personal observations as most of my officers were casualties and I have not the benefit of their views. All of my losses were caused by rifle or shell fire as we had no gas with the exception of 12 cases, and I left COURCELLES with 965 effective men and 26 officers in the companies and lost 815 men and 19 officers. I am convinced that at times we were all over the BOIS DE BELLEAU but from lack of men the stopping infiltration was impossible. All prisoners and machine guns taken on June 11th and 12th were entirely due to the efforts of this Battalion and we occupied part of the sector assigned to 1st Battalion, 6th Marines. Heavy casualties among my best officers was one cause of not obtaining the whole woods as the youngsters left in command did not size up the military value of ground promptly. I understand over 450 prisoners including 5 officers were taken and I personally know that over 500 machine guns were taken or destroyed; also 2 each large and small mortars. I can also state with pride that we may have overrun ground, but not one inch of it that was ever taken up, was given up after consolidation.

F. M. Wise
Lt.-Colonel, M. C."

Soissons

Major Ralph Keyser was now commanding[5] 2/5, which embused at Crouttes at 1900 on 16 July and arrived at Brassaire at 1100 on 17 July and debused. The other two battalions (1/5 and 3/5) left several hours later and all wound up in the Foret de Retz near Keyser's positions.

The 1st and 2d Battalions of the 5th were selected to lead, with 3/5 to remain in support. The position of each company of was, left to right, 55th (Cooke), liaison with the 66th, 43d (Joseph D. Murray), and 18th (Wass) and the 51st (William O. Corbin) as liaison with the 9th Infantry. The 5th Marines were aided by about thirty, some say fifty-four, French St.-Chamond heavy tanks.

First Lt. Elliott D. Cooke, U.S. Army, commanding the 55th Company, told of his difficulty in seeing the one map that the battalion adjutant, 2d Lt. James H. Legendre, had carried from French headquarters. Major Ralph Keyser, the battalion commander, gathered his officers in a circle on the ground and gave them instructions for each company.... Lastly he said, "The Fifty-fifth Company will maintain contact with the First Battalion. One officer and twenty men from each company will be left behind." Cooke asked, "I only have a hundred sixty men now, Major. Why leave any behind?" The answer curdled his blood. "They will be needed as a nucleus to build new companies on, after the attack," Keyser said, not looking up from the map. Probably he was too distressed to let his juniors know what he expected. Cooke wrote, "Well, I got what I asked for and I wished I'd kept my mouth shut. So did everybody else."

The French guides who were supposed to lead the advance weren't at their designated posts when 1/5 and 2/5 arrived. Those for 1/5 never showed up. Only enough guides showed up for two companies in 2/5, the 43d and 55th, and according to the official histories, they led those companies to a position north of the Paris-Maubeuge Highway. The 43d discovered the error in time and managed to relocate themselves to almost cover their designated sector. Though lost during the move to the jump-off line, the 55th finally reached 2/5 before they were even missed, according to Cooke. Other records say otherwise. There is no question but that Cooke and his lads were up to their hip boots in Germans all day, but mostly they were in Moroccan territory while so engaged.[6]

18 July 1918: A message from Colonel Feland, no addressee, was dated 5:45 a.m. "The runner thinks he must have made a mistake, It was dated later than that. Turrill and Keyser were in place for the attack, Keyser being a few minutes late. No telephone line from Brigade but they will be in in a few minutes. Trying to establish liaison. Found neither regimental commanders on right or left. SIGNED FELAND."

Keyser's 2/5 wasn't having it any easier than was 1/5 moving toward the attack positions. Cooke's company was last in line. The group they were following, possibly the 51st, stopped the line. One Marine was putting on his leggings and the entire line stopped behind him until he was finished. By the time Cooke and the 55th were underway again they were distracted by the new skipper of the 51st, Capt. William Corbin, Williams's replacement.[7] Corbin just had his men sit on the roadside while Murray and Wass continued somewhere up ahead. In the darkness Cooke couldn't tell where they had gone. Since he hadn't heard all of Keyser's instructions, or gotten a look at the map, he was quickly getting into trouble. His was supposed to be to the right of Crabbe's 66th Company of 1/5 and to the left of Murray. After catching up, Keyser provided a French soldier to guide them forward to find the two officers. Cooke knew he had to be in position when the attack started, so he started to run. He and his runner ran forward while his company followed. All the while the Frenchman protested, "*Mon Dieu*, the front line, she is approached with caution! *N'est-ce pas?*"

Then the big bang exploded. The 10th Army's artillery opened up and all hell seemed to break loose. Cooke's company followed rapidly to everyone's great surprise, they soon found themselves swarming over the Germans' front lines. After an exchange of grenade tosses and rifle fire, the Germans realized their predicament. *Kamerad!* was their common reaction. They were anxious to surrender and get to the rear out of range of everything. So much so that when they were told off under guard they began running for cover. The Marines sent to propel them back for collection were forced to fire over their heads to slow them down.

The 9th Infantry—with a longer distance to go and with their left flank in the air and the 5th Marines not being up yet—advanced a half mile to near the Verte Feuille Farm, where they began taking enemy fire. By that point the 9th was already out of their bounds. Keyser, at Verte Feuille Ferme, sent to Feland at 6:10 a.m.:

> Have established P.C. as above. Sent runner to get contact with companies. We went well to the first objective and I just saw lines. They were on the way to the 2nd objective, which was about 30 minutes ago.
>
> Aeroplane made signals at 6:00 a.m. indicating troops forming for counter-attack southwest. Enemy aeroplane forced to land, in front of my P.C.
>
> Indications are that we have many prisoners and small losses. The 9th Infantry runner came in with a message and reported that they were on Turrill's left. A wounded infantryman from the 23rd Infantry also reports his regiment there. Have no news from CORBIN, who should be in liaison with them.

Some of 2/5 came up and both regiments put the kibosh on the Germans holding the farm. The actual seizure was carried out by the 18th and 43d Companies. Now, both the 5th and the 9th had "an awkward change of direction to make," a partial right turn. The 5th Marines had a large front to cover and as they moved forward and spread northward, it became even larger. This change was to create extensive problems for the 9th and 5th.

Corbin's 51st Company was last to reach its post and had some difficulty making contact with the 9th Infantry, which was quickly moving forward. Nevertheless, the 51st had Pvt. James H. Roberts, who more than made up for the company's delay in getting into action. Armed with a Chauchat, Roberts crawled through barbed wire and disabled one machine gun with a hand grenade and forced the crew of a second gun to surrender. Because of this action, his company's advance was nearly casualty free.[8]

Back where the 51st was sitting by the roadside, the 55th, as the division history states, "diverged to the north." As the 5th Marines passed the Translon Farm, instead turning to the right they continued straight forward for some considerable distance, taking them well into the Moroccans' territory. The Moroccans were to take the Bois du Quesnoy, just outside the 5th Marines' northern boundary. They planned a flank movement against it but they were slower than the Americans. Thus the Germans were still firing on the flanks of the 5th Marines. The 55th Company, which was way out of sync with where it was supposed to be, attacked them in a northerly direction in response. After that, never changing direction, they remained in the Moroccans' sector most of the day.

The Marines weren't the only ones going wrong. Where the division's boundaries made a gradual turn and, shortly afterward, a sharp turn southward, some units followed one turn, and some didn't. Those who didn't continued onward and partially covered the Moroccans' zone. In fact, elements of the 1st Battalion, 9th Infantry, also continued in that direction. Soon the units became entangled with each other, Marines and soldiers. Captain Charles E. Speer, leading 1/9,[9] continued onward northeast and came upon Maison Neuve Farm, which his unit took with the help of Cooke's 55th Company.[10] The Moroccan Division had some of the best American infantrymen fighting their battle, which was a good thing, because the Moroccans, for all their vaunted reputation, were having a difficult time keeping apace with the Americans.

At 11:30 a.m. this message was sent from the 4th Brigade (Neville) to the 2nd Division (Harbord): "Major Keyser, 2nd Battalion, Marines. We need Water and ambulances badly. If you send them they can go into the field in front of my P.C. and pickup wounded with safety. Can you have an ammunition dump located here, and hot food for men at noon today. They will have gone 48 hour's without anything hot. 51st Company has called for reinforcements and I have asked the 3rd battalion for two Platoons. No positive news yet from Companies. KEYSER."

The rest of 1/5 had pushed ahead with 2/5 on its right. Resistance increased as the Marines went forward and communication between their own units became more difficult. Capt. Joseph Murray was wounded shortly after the advance resumed. His company joined the 18th and passed under the command of Capt. Lester Wass. Most of the other officers of the 43d were also down. Gunnery Sergeant Herman "Babe" Tharau of the 55th, whom we've already met at Les Mares Farm, went out ahead with some others from his company to establish liaison with the company on his right. He found a machine gun and captured it while killing its crew. That Buffalo, New York, native was killed in action in the relatively soft Marbache Sector in August.

Major Ralph Keyser told in a later report what had happened to 2/5. His writing was based upon reports from the company lieutenants, not the skippers, since all except Corbin were down. He wrote Corbin's 51st was the only company that did not reach the first objective. He explained about Cooke and his company—where they had split, some "going northeast toward Maison Neuve Farm and the remainder going to southeast." This was where the division's boundary had changed direction.

In his memoir, Cooke described in word and diagram where he and his company had gone, although it isn't always completely clear. They were north of the division's left boundary, having been unintentionally led astray by their one French guide. Still lost, Cooke aided the 9th Infantry at Maison Neuve and then traveled further to a point just west of Chaudun.

Seeing a village occupied by Marines, and without a verification of any kind, he reported that Vierzy had been captured. He soon learned it was Hunt and the 17th Company at Chaudun. Hunt was also lost. Cooke's erroneous report, combined with a lack of information on events up front, confused the division, both brigades, and all regiments. The 4th Brigade lines were in a terribly agitated state, though they maintained reasonable liaison with the

3d's right flank and continued fighting. Marines and soldiers of every stripe and shape were mixed up and spread northward well into the sector of the Moroccans.

Germans held the eastern side of Chancy and kept a constant artillery and machine-gun barrage upon the western edge. It was almost impossible for 2/5 to scale the opposite slope, it being that steep. Keyser sat for a spell trying to decide how best to continue forward without losing his entire command. The staff of the 3d Brigade made the decision.

Cooke's 55th finally came back within division boundaries. He was to have been at the left flank of 2/5, with liaison to the 66th Company led by William Crabbe. According to Cooke, he moved south until he and Crabbe made contact. Crabbe didn't know where he was, so the two skippers readjusted their formations to adapt to the fouled up situation. Cooke's narrative said that neither Crabbe nor he had any idea where they were nor where anyone else was. Cooke suggested they maintain liaison as ordered but move forward in a different direction. As Cooke said: "'Bill,' I tried to grin, 'it looks as if we've got to take on the whole German army by ourselves.' 'Fair enough,' Crabb [sic] hitched up his belt, 'you knock 'em down and I'll count them.' Taking out my notes on the attack order, I suggested that we make a change in direction before going any farther. Bill agreed with a shrug. He wasn't any brass hat. Whether we fought Germans at eighty degrees or at a hundred and sixty was all the same to Captain Bill Crabb."[11]

The two skippers blew their whistles, waved their arms, and ran up and down to change the men's direction from right to forward. Several men from the 9th Infantry, without arms, were with the 55th; Cooke learned that they had been captured by the Germans and when the Marines came along and ran over them the soldiers naturally tagged along. They were scrounging through some material the enemy had left lying, and when he inquired he learned that they were looking for their Springfields that the Germans had taken from them. As Cooke said, they learned that "we were not alone on the battlefield. Other people were present—if we could only find them." Crabbe nearly walked into German artillery hidden in a shallow ravine just to their front. Though caught by surprise, the Germans recovered quickly and began sending big rounds toward the Marines. The heavy artillery fire soon fell upon the 55th and that company scattered. "It certainly seemed as if our god of Luck had paid his lodge dues and was in good standing," Cooke wrote. The Marine casualties were relatively light.

The two companies soon overtook the guns and gunners. Some Marines stopped long enough to collect souvenirs from the deceased foe. As the two companies came out of the ravine they saw the 18th and 43d Companies approaching over the rise; from which direction Cooke doesn't tell. About this time that the Moroccans were finally seen advancing on the left. About this time Corbin's 51st, which had been hugging the left flank of the 9th Infantry most of the day, joined the 18th and 43d Companies in the ravine northwest of Vierzy. Cooke and his lads joined the support line of 2/5, in a ravine northwest of Vierzy. Shortly afterward Cooke, the last of the "old-timers" of 2/5, got nailed. His wound was serious and it took him out of the battle.[12]

The original plan was modified: 2/5, located in the ravine northwest of Vierzy, would now advance with the 9th Infantry and help take that town. Major Keyser hurried to the proper location with the 18th, 43d, and 51st Companies and sent a runner to the 55th to inform them of the proposed attack. The message was delivered but the 55th, way off in the distance without their skipper, could not arrive in time. Therefore only the three companies would advance—in two waves with a five-hundred-meter front to cover.

Finally, after nearly a two-hour delay, the attack jumped off at 1900. Two/Nine held the left with 1/9 and 3/9 in support and 2/5 on their left flank. Although Col. LeRoy Upton of 1/9 and his men were initially held up by severe machine gun fire, they still made five hundred meters' progress in short order. But because the Moroccans still weren't keeping up, the left flank was again wide open. The 9th Infantry and 2/5 soon cleaned up the obstacles before them and continued onward. Corbin's 51st Company made an advance of a half mile despite intense machine gun resistance. Meanwhile, the 9th Infantry continued their advance, taking a part of the 18th with them. Six French tanks were just returning from a previous attack and moved through the advancing infantry units. German guns focused on the metal monsters as they retired, resulting in heavy casualties to the advancing infantry. Capt. Lester E. Wass, skipper of the 18th, was mortally wounded. Four of the six tanks were also destroyed. It was also at this time that 2d Lt. Fred H. Becker, U.S. Army, the renowned "Chowhound" of the 18th, earned his awards the hard way. Going forward in advance of his platoon, Becker destroyed a machine-gun nest. This prevented many more deaths or serious injuries among his men. He was killed as he was finishing the job.

Keyser and his battalion seemed to be surrounded by machine guns in the tall and dense wheat. He and his runner were temporarily separated from his command and had to crawl in a ditch to avoid exposure, but they eventually made it back to the battalion. The location of the 9th Infantry wasn't apparent, so Keyser saw no reason to go forward since both his flanks were in the air and it was now dark—or as he later said, "I deemed it advisable to attempt to clear the ground." He then ordered his command to retire to the position where they had been located at 1900, which they managed to reach by dusk. In Keyser's report he stated (see following) that he had no grenades to attack the machine gun hidden in the wheat fields, so he stayed put for the night. Without consulting his commanding officer, Maj. Gen. Hanson Ely of the 3d Brigade, Keyser decided that to go forward in the dark would just inflict unnecessary casualties upon his already decimated battalion.[13]

Brig. Gen. Albert J. Bowley, commanding officer, 2d Field Artillery Brigade, sent this to Harbord at 1550:

> C.O. 2nd Battl 5th Marines states normal line of our objective is lightly held by French Moroccans (2:00 p.m. from our North Division line to point south east edge of Vierzy. C.O. 2nd Battl. 5th saw this himself at 2 p.m. He put 100 men into this line & ordered 50 more to west line. From point 65.74 (300 meters west of 149) 18th and 213 and 23rd Inf. have built line of rifle pits extending north east for a distance of 1 Kilometer (saw only one company). Vierzy is not occupied by Boche. A few Moroccans or Colonials were in Vierzy. Saw Americans (heard they were Marines & 9th Inf) (confirmed later) in line just South of Vierzy in combat group—& skirmish line standing up. (About 2 p.m. Heard some machine guns fire south of Vierzy 2 p.m. C.O. 2nd Battl. 5th Marines says there will be little opposition in an advance to Soissons Chateau-Thierry road especially if tanks precede them. These tanks were 3 kilometers southeast of Vierzy 2 p.m.
>
> 3:55 Some tanks (about 10) are here now. Some reported headed South East across field.
> A.J.B.

Keyser added detail about Wass's company in his later report: "As all of the officers of this company [the 18th] are casualties, the information regarding it is meager." The single-page description for the 18th Company in its semiofficial history declares, "It seemed impossible for us to go through another attack that day, but that's what we did just before dusk that evening—advanced five more kilometers over the wheat fields and ravines to the left of Vierzy.... This company had the center of the attack. The advance was made in the face of frontal and flank machine-gun fire and heavy artillery fire; men dropped like flies.... Finally the tanks came up and helped us through the last few hundred meters of the push. What was left of our outfit dug in and held overnight [in a ravine] and through the next day and night." Second Lt. Joseph B. Carhart was cited for extraordinary heroism. He and a small detachment of men from the 18th charged German machine guns, killing the crews and capturing the three guns, which they immediately turned on their enemies to open a path for the company's advance, which had been held up by the enemy's fire. The advance made little progress and contributed little of importance to the overall situation of the 18th Company. But they did try.

Later that evening, at 2200, at Oulchy-le-Chateau Keyser sent a message to Col. Logan Feland, commanding officer, 5th Marines, explaining what he and 2/5 had accomplished and where they were:

> Will you please communicate C.G. 3rd Brigade, under whom I am operating that I am occupying old trench line with about 120 men who were my Battalion support in operation of this afternoon. We were delayed in going forward with advanced companies by heavy shelling controlled from Aeroplane and prevented from continuing our advance by M.G.'s that the forward companies failed to locate. I deemed it inadvisable to go around them and leave them and found it impossible to destroy them with rifle fire in growing darkness and without grenades.
>
> I have just received word from my left company [55th] that it was unable to proceed further than a few hundred yards beyond my position so I have ordered them to retire here. My right company [51st] I have no news of. They continued to advance when my left was held up. I have heard nothing from them other than this. We have had no tank support or grenades, and I consider it highly impracticable to clean out M.G. from wheat or Woods without at least one of these weapons.
>
> I shall remain here holding line until further orders.
>
> My whole Battalion is utterly exhausted, having had no hot food or drink for 60 hours.
>
> (signed) Keyser.

Keyser added that he had no grenades or tank support and he believed it impractical to attempt to eliminate the many machine guns before him this way. Nothing ever changed. No food, no rest, nothing.

Sometime during the night the 55th Company had some close contacts with the enemy. Corporal Joseph L. Hopta ran out in front of the company and took a machine gun and its crew single-handedly, under a heavy concentration of machine-gun fire. Private Frank J. Barczykowski displayed extraordinary heroism in charging three machine-gun nests with the aid of a few of his comrades, killing the crews and capturing all the guns. They then turned the guns upon the Germans, freeing up his company from the enemy fire. He and his comrades who were awarded the Distinguished Service Cross and Navy Cross included 2d Lt. Joseph B. Carhart, Cpl. John Doody, Pvt. William A. Justensen, Pvt. Albert Barrows and Pvt. Paul T. Hurley. Meanwhile, four more Marines of the 55th, Pvt. William McIntyre, Pvt. Elias I. Messinger and Pvt. Dolph Wood, allied by Cpl. Bernard W. Montag, fearlessly exposed themselves to the accurate fire from a machine gun. Even though all four were wounded, down went the gun and its German crew. All in all, this listing constitutes a bevy of American names from a variety of origins.[14]

This was the final activity of 2/5 at Soissons, the 5th Regiment being relieved the following morning.

Marbache

Marbache was, technically, a quiet sector. Lieutenant Colonel Fritz Wise was back in command of 2/5 and led it from Nancy to their new position in the Pont-a-Mousson Sector. Within a very few hours they were engaged with the enemy as described in the following report.

7–8 August: Report of Attack from commanding officer of 2/5 to Col. Logan Feland.

1. At 1:58 a.m. a patrol from E Company [18th] was in ambush at point 3771-2361, they heard a noise and immediately afterwards saw about 12 Germans N. W. of them and at about 100 yards distance almost immediately a large explosion took place among the Germans which caused a great deal of confusion and they asked for a barrage, which continued for over an hour and was quite heavy.
2. Just upon daybreak a patrol was sent out to the place where the explosion took place and one wounded and one unwounded prisoner secured and from them it was found out that the Germans seen were a raiding party, the explosion was from a loaded pipe, which they intended to use to blow up our wire.
3. The premature explosion caused a panic, the leader requested a barrage, and everybody scattered and the raid abandoned and no Infantry attack attempted, as the Machine Guns from S. P. Respaut opened upon them also. It apparently was a large party as the carrying part of it consisted of 24 men from the prisoners report.
4. Two Machine Guns at Respaut fired N. W. and W. by N. of their position during the barrage.
5. Eight men were killed and wounded from shell fire, and one ammunition dump at Vin Sans Eau blown up. The shelling was rather heavy, and including 77's, 105's, 155's and 210's.
6. Tracing from Mousson map 1/10000 showing different positions enclosed [not included]. F.M. Wise.

Wise was still in command but upon promotion to full colonel on 1 July would be too senior for command of a battalion and would be relieved by Major Harold L. Parsons. For some reason, the companies were being described by their alpha designation rather than the numeric. This continued at least for 2/5 until the end of the war.

9 August: The commanding officer of the 5th Regiment, Col. Logan Feland, sent the following message to Maj. Gen. John A. Lejeune, commanding officer, 2d Division:

1. I propose to send the following patrols out on the nights of August 9-10 and 10-11, 1918, one of (8) eight men from E [18th] Company, F [43d] Company and H [55th] Company respectively for the purpose of observation and ambush. These patrols will go out in front of their respective companies.

G-3 Notify the Arty [artillery]

(Sgd) LOGAN FELAND
Logan Feland

Eventually, the so-called rest period at Marbache ended and the 2d Division was called upon to join with many U.S. and French Divisions to dissolve the St. Mihiel salient which had been in the possession of the Germans since 1914. The division would make its way northeast to a town named Limey, arriving on the night of 11 September 1918.

St. Mihiel

12 September: Feland sent Messersmith, commanding officer of 2/5, a message at 0635: "I shall order the leading Bns. forward about 6:45 a.m. Watch their progress as they clear space south of French front lines move over and follow at 500 or 600 yards. Continue to advance as they advance. When you get on line of advance try to locate my P. C. I shall move approximately in center of our sector."

Feland continued to send messages to the three battalion commanders as the 3d Brigade, which was leading the advance, continued to take various small villages in their path. He kept insisting that the 5th "press forward so that our leading Bn is in touch with the rear of the 9th Inf. He reported that "2nd Batt had had five men slightly wounded by our artillery falling short." At 1900 the 55th Co. was reporting that "our artillery is shooting all around us." Later, at 2100 on 13 September, Col. Joseph R. Davis, commanding officer, 15th Field Artillery, sent Captain DeWitt Peck, commanding officer, 55th Company, a message that he located the unit firing short rounds. It was, according to him, Battery E, 20th FA, 5th Division, that was the culprit.

14 September: From commanding officer of Company F (Dunbeck, 43d Company) to Messersmith at 0845: "Very quiet during the night. Few shells dropped in Bois du Fey. No casualties. About 10,000 Boche grenades stored north of my P. C. Battery of Boche 6" just west of my P. C. Dunbeck. P.S. Ammunition dump in 6th Marine sector exploded at 2:00 a.m."

That afternoon at 13:05 (?) Messersmith sent Feland a message asking for food: "Men have not had food for some time. Yesterday's food supply very meager."

17 September: Major Robert E. Messersmith, commanding officer of 2/5, gave a report of operations.

> Assumed command of the 2nd Battalion, 5th Regiment, relieving Major [Harold L.] Parsons, at about 1:00 p.m. Sept. 11th. Battalion moved from Bois-des-Hayes by way of 2nd Division Headquarters, Bois-Montjoye to Lironville to P.O. of the battalion of the 89th Division holding the Front line along Limey, one company taking over the trenches at the west of Limey, the 18th Company taking over the trenches east of Limey, the 55th Company occupying Limey, the 43rd Company relieving part of the 90th Division in trenches Le Haricot. The 51st Company was stationed in the Bois-du-Buchot.
>
> This Battalion jumped off from these position. At 11:50 the night of Sept. 11th, 350 replacements were brought to my P.O. in trench between Lironville and Limey, impossible to distribute these to their companies. Barrage opened at 1:00 a.m. Sept. 12th and 7:05 a.m. this battalion moved towards the Front, being the third battalion in line. We advanced by bounds as ordered in regimental order, and bivouacked for the night of the 12th and 13th on the south slope of the ridge immediately north of the Bois-d'Heiche. Two men wounded on this date.
>
> Sept. 13th—Remained in bivouac until 5:00 p.m. when we relieved the 3rd Battalion, 9th Infantry in the support positions. Relief completed at 7:10. Bombarded by own Artillery and had three men wounded. All quiet during the night.
>
> Sept. 14th—Manned support positions. Bombarded during day, one man killed and five men

wounded. The 55th Company claims to have brought down enemy aeroplane by rifle fire. Plane landed in our lines.

Sept. 15th—Manned reserve position, bombarded during day and had three men killed and eight men wounded.

Sept. 16th—Withdrew from lines and went to rear.

(Sgd) R. E. Messersmith

After St. Mihiel, the Second Division was assigned to the command of the French Army and directed to the area known as Blanc Mont. The Germans had conquered that ridge in 1914 and had it well developed by now. Concrete bunkers spread over the entire area, on the top of the ridge and the flat ground going to the north. The French army had been trying to retake this important location and had failed miserably with huge losses. They asked Gen. Pershing for three U.S. divisions. He gave them one, then later added a brand new division, the 36th "Cowboy" Division from Oklahoma and Texas. They would arrive later and without artillery. Like the 2d Division, they too would be slaughtered.

The men of the division made their way to the Champagne sector, arriving on 1 October.

Blanc Mont

1 October: Feland sent a message to Messersmith at 1400: "We will enter the lines tonight. Have everything ready to leave at a moment's notice. Draw ammunition, pyrotechnics, guns, etc."

1–8 October: From the commanding officer, 2/5, to Col. Logan Feland, operations report:

1. The night of October 1st, 2nd, marched from Bois-de-la- Cote and relieved (3) three companies of 219th Regiment French, and (2) two companies of 265th Regiment, French, with (4) four companies of Battalion: the 23rd M.G. Company attached to Battalion, relieving the French M.G. Company; in trenches around point 268.8-277.0 along railroad South of Somme-Py. Relief completed about 4:00 a.m. October 2nd, 1918. Sketch appended, marked "A" [not included]. Relief held up by the impossibility of a reconnaissance prior to relief being made, and nonappearance of guides for companies.

October 2nd, spent in trenches, a few casualties.

On the morning of October 3rd, Battalion moved to left along railroad between points 268.4-276.85 on right, and 267.0-373.7 on left, the 4th Brigade limits for the advance. Jumped off about 6:55 a.m. with (18th) "E"—(51st) "G" companies in line supported by (55th) "H"—(43rd) "F" companies, the 23rd M.G. Companies in rear of center of these companies....

Advance made by combat groups. The 2nd Battalion of 5th being support Battalion of 5th Regiment. The 6th Regiment leading in the attack.

The advance was made difficult by the French not advancing on left flank. Our flank was thus exposed to flank fire and casualties resulted. Another difficulty was the passing over of M.G. nests, which later opened on us.

The final objective was attained by 6th Marines. The 2nd Battalion then received orders to protect their left flank and after consultation with Major [Ernest C.] Williams of 2nd Battalion of 6th Regiment, I moved the Battalion to his left flank, entrenching along line 265.75-280.8-265.95-280.1 where we joined with a company of French troops.

At 7:20 p.m. October 3rd, 1918, received orders to occupy line 265.6-280.75 to 287.3-281.0

and be ready to attack with 3rd Battalion leading 1st in support and 2nd in reserve. We finally were able to leave for attack at 6:00 a.m. the objective being ridge South East of St. Etienne 264.8-283.2 to 266.2-283.8. Moved towards objective under heavy machine gun fire and artillery fire until about 2:30 p.m. October 4th. This heavy flank fire was caused by French not advancing and 23rd Infantry on right not attaining its objective.

We were forced to retire but held about 4:00 p.m. and dug in and consolidated new position with 23rd Infantry on right and left flank open.

October 5th remained in position. French advanced about 10:00 a.m. on left flank. Late afternoon part of 6th Regiment passed thru us.

October 6th in same position. Moved to rear, jump off place about 8:00 p.m.

October 7th, in position.

October 8th, 5:15 a.m. 142nd Regiment advanced to attack.

R. E. Messersmith.

	Killed	Wounded	Missing	Gassed	Sick
E Company	8	60	11	6	7
F Company	3	47	6	1	3
G Company	12	63	44	0	0
H Company	7	21	46	0	4
Total	30	191	107	7	14

What Messersmith didn't add to his report was the fact that the 2d Battalion was so badly hit on 4 October that they started to panic and ran from what was later titled the "Box." His reputation suffered greatly when Major George Hamilton sent in a report telling what happened. He was relieved soon after and spent the balance of the war as a non-person. It ruined whatever career he might have had in the corps. Later, Major Larsen of 3/5 reported that many men of 2/5 were huddled in 3/5's bunker. Later, on the night of 10-11 November, 2/5 would make up for any deficiencies at Blanc Mont by their superbly courageous crossing of the Meuse River under terrifying enemy artillery and machine gun fire.

In the semi-official history of the 5th Regiment of Marines, on page 27, the author said, "October 4th was the bitterest single day of fighting that the Fifth Regiment experienced during the whole war." John W. Thomason, who was there in 1/5, commented later, "The war wasn't any fun after the Champagne."

Soon after numerous replacements filled the badly depleted ranks of the regiment, as well as the 6th Marines, the Second Division was on its way west to help Pershing in his so-far disastrous Meuse-Argonne Campaign. Pershing needed every first-class outfit he had, and the Second Division was the best.

Incidentally, after Messersmith was relieved, Captain Charley Dunbeck assumed command of 2/5. With him, they did their job.

17–31 October: Report of Operations, 2nd Battalion, 5th Regiment Marine Corps.

Oct. 17th, 18th, 19th and 20th billeted at Camp Carriere.

20th departed from Came Carriere, arriving at Camp Montpelier same date, billeted at Camp Montpelier night of 20th-21st.

21st departed from Camp Montpelier arriving at Semide same date. 21st and 22nd at Semide. 23rd returned to Camp Montpelier. 24th billeted at Camp Montpelier.

25th departed from Camp Montpelier debussing at Les Islettes same date. From there we marched to Camp Brune in Southern edge of Argonne Forest and billeted for the night. 26th we marched Northward through Argonne Forest to woods one kilometer Southeast of Exermont where we remained bivouaced until October 30th. From this point we marched Northeast to woods north of Le Neuville Cante.

On the night of 31st we marched North to a jumping off position on a road one-half kilometer East of Sommerance and took up position for the attack. (Rav du Grasfaux).

31 October: Message from Feland to Larsen (commanding officer, 3/5), time 1410: "Am enclosing barrage map. Be sure that [Captain Charley] Dunbeck [commanding officer, 2/5] sees it. Division order here. No material change. Day and hour not yet known." Feland sent to Captain John R. Foster, commanding officer, 18th Company, at 1450: "Major [George] Stowell has command of the combat liaison on the left flank of the Brigade sector and has nothing to do with your work on our right flank."

Meuse-Argonne

1 November: Report of operations by Charley Dunbeck, commanding officer, 2/5, at 0530: "We moved forward to the attack in support of 1st Battalion of 5th Regiment, and the companies were disposed as follows: Company "G"—Left forward company. Company "F"—Supporting Company. Company "E"—Right liaison company, with 89th Division." Message from Foster to Feland at 0815: "Have Liaison with 23rd Inf. Assault wave going good."

Second Lieutenant Henry P. Glendinning, intelligence officer, 2/5, to regimental intelligence officer, at 0820: "2nd Batt. of 5th Reg. just passed through 1st Batt. Assaulting wave in front of Landreville—everything going nicely. Have liaison with 18th Co. which is connected with 23 Inf on right—Sixth Reg. on left." Foster sent Feland this message at 0920: "18th Co. is in liaison with 89th Division on our Rt. flank." Most of those fighting men kept the messages limited to necessary text.

Dunbeck, also known as "Slap A-1," sent Slap (Feland) this message at 1130: "Objective reached. 6th U.S.M.C. is not on left. Enemy laying down slight barrage. Casualties very slight (1 percent). 89th Div—on right." Later that afternoon, at 1420, Hamilton of 1/5 sent Feland a message that the 3/5 was on the 3d objective with 2/5 in close support. At 1530 Dunbeck let Feland know: "Casualties—Wounded—1 officer and 12 men. Prisoners taken—130."

At no time indicated but probably mid-afternoon, Dunbeck sent a message with no addressee named:

Material captured by this battalion between 1st and 2nd objective
   2—8 in Field Art[illery]
   12—3 and 6 *in*[ch]
   Several Minenwerfers and *number* of M.G's on 1 Nov. 1918

Report of operations:

At "H" Hour, plus three, at a point one Kilometer South of Landreville Farm, the 2nd Battalion leap-frogged the 1st, (Line east and went through Northern point of Bois L'Epasse) the 1st Battalion having reached their objective. The position of the Companies were unchanged when we became the assault Battalion. From this point Northward to our objective we followed the barrage very closely, meeting strong rearguard resistance, artillery and machine guns on right flank. We advanced to our objective, arriving on time as per attack order. The heaviest fighting took place in the capture of Landreville where enemy had machine guns placed in windows throughout the village. In one section of the town, Geneva Red Cross flag was hanging over window of Chateau and a machine gun firing through this window. Approximately 100 prisoners were taken from this Chateau. In woods one and one-fourth kilometre East of Bayonville, it became necessary to despatch one company (Company "H") to execute a flanking movement and surround the woods (Hill 299) before the advance could be continued. In these woods and vicinity Northwestward toward deep ravine we captured approximately 30 machine guns, one battery of 8" and about 12 6". It is roughly estimated that there were about 30 artillery officers and Non-commissioned Officers found at their guns either killed or wounded. They had continued to fire until our Infantry advanced and captured the pieces. Noticeably among them were several Captains. Our objective being the deep ravine just Northeast of Bayonville this Battalion came to a halt and was leap-frogged by the 3rd Battalion, this at "H" Hour plus 6:20.

At "H" Hour plus 7 we followed in support of 3rd Battalion continuing the advance to a point near Hill 300 where we organized a support position and entrenched for the night. The right Liaison Company ("E" Company) took up position on Corps objective line, right of 3rd Battalion, forming Liaison with 89th Division.

2 November: At 0700 Dunbeck reported to Feland: "All quiet during the night. Co. 'E' has completed mission and will rejoin the battalion this a.m. (Slight shelling at present from the enemy right). Will send in morning report, report of casualties, etc. this a.m." Dunbeck also wrote in his operations report that "This Battalion rested in place."

3 November: Operations report: "At 6:00 a.m. we leap-frogged the 3rd and moved forward in support of 9th Infantry to a position Southeast of Le Champy Haut, where we remained in support until about 3:00 a.m. November 4th when we continued our advance Northward still supporting the 9th Infantry."

4–7 November: Operations report:

The route taken was through town of Belval to La Forge Farm, thence to a position 500 Yards South of La Tuilerie Farm where the undersigned reported to Colonel [Robert O.] Van Horn, [9th Infantry] at that time commanding the troops in front line. This position was held from 8:15 a.m. to 9:00 p.m. day of Nov. 4th. During this time we were under extremely heavy artillery and machine gun fire. In the afternoon we were forced to wear gas masks for approximately 4 hours, the enemy continuing to bombard our positions heavily with artillery.

At 9:00 p.m. same date we moved our position to La Belle Tour Farm. At this place we took up front line position forming liaison between 9th Infantry and 89th Division, facing Northeastward towards Pouilly. Strong patrols were sent to river bank and in direction of Bois de Jaulnay. This position was held day of 5th and on morning of 6th we moved eastward to point 308.4-304.5 and remained until November 7th. (Reserve Position).

8–9 November: Operations report: "We next moved to Bois de Murets again taking a reserve position and remaining until afternoon of 9th. Our next move was to Bois de Fond de Limon remaining there night of the 9th."

10 November: Operations report:

At 8:00 p.m. we moved to Northeastern edge of Bois de Hospice, preparatory to crossing the Meuse. At this point we crossed the River about 9:00 p.m. on foot bridge laid down by 2nd Engineers. This crossing was made under withering fire from Machine Guns and extremely heavy artillery fire.

The following dispositions and orders were given to Companies of this Battalion:
Disposition of "H" Company

Two unidentified members of the 5th Regiment on guard duty in Germany in 1919.

"We are to attack the enemy at "H" Hour"

You will march your company across foot bridge at time to be announced later. Your mission is to screen the bridge while other units pass over. After all units have passed you will, send two platoons to Bellefontaine Farm, seize the place and connect with 6th Marines who are operating North of this Farm. One platoon will remain at Bridge as Bridge Guard. One platoon will be at the disposal of Battalion Commander.

Mission of "F" Company.

Have your Company cross the river before "H" Hour. Advance Northeastward along woods thence to National Highway. Capture the Stone quarry, Senegal Farm and mop up Bois des Flaviers.

Mission for "G" Company.

You will follow in close support of Company "F" passing through their line, which extend from the Stone Quarry to Senegal Farm, advance Eastward and capture Moulins. Connect up with 89th Division on your right.

Mission for "E" Company.

You will take up position about 1000 yards South of Bellefontaine Farm and at "H" Hour advance Eastward towards National Highway, thence towards Vaux, occupying Hill 341 and Folie Farm, thence push forward and capture Vaux and connect with 6th Marines operating in that vicinity. At starting of this movement my P.C. will be near the bridge on opposite side and later on if circumstances permit I will move to Bellefontaine Farm thence along national highway towards Moulins.

Objectives were taken with the exception of Vaux and Moulins. We were on outskirts of Moulins and advancing on Vaux when we received word of signing of armistice. Immediately thereafter the Battalion halted and organized positions with line extending along National Highway.

Nov. 14th we were relieved by a Battalion of the 77th Division.

The 5th Regiment marching in Washington, D.C., in August 1919.

Throughout the eleven days of almost constant fighting, the Officers and men of this Battalion never faltered in an advance, always pressing forward seemingly imbued with a victorious spirit.

The undersigned considers it worthy of note to record the fact that with the exception of one day this Battalion was supplied with hot food from our Galleys.

C. Dunbeck,
Captain, U.S.M.C.
Commanding 2nd Battalion.

Following the armistice on 11 November, the entire Second Division rested for a few days. It wasn't until 17 November 1918 when the 4th Brigade led the division in its march towards and into Germany and occupation. The latter has already been described in other parts of this book, as has the return to the United States during July–August 1919; after parades the 4th Marine Brigade was disbanded on 13 August 1919.

4

Third Battalion, Fifth Marines, 1917–1919

Battalion Headquarters
16th [I] Company
20th [K] Company
45th [L] Company
47th [M] Company

Commanding Officers

From	To	
May 1917	25 March 1918	Major Charles T. Westcott
26 March 1918	30 April 1918	Major Edward W. Sturdevant
1 May 1918	6 June 1918	Major Benjamin S. Berry
7 June 1918	8 June 1918	Captain Henry Larsen (temporary)
9 June 1918	28 September 1918	Major Maurice Shearer
29 September 1918	August 1919	Major Henry L. Larsen

The Beginnings

On 6 April 1917, the United States formally declared war upon Germany. Marine Major General Commandant George Barnett immediately offered a regiment of Marines for service with the American Expeditionary Forces (AEF), the official title of the military force being assembled for duty in France. In a somewhat convoluted manner the offer was accepted.

In Philadelphia during May 1917 Major Charles T. Westcott, USMC, was busy creating what was to become the 3d Battalion, Fifth Regiment, of Marines from a group of companies just recently recalled from duty in Santo Domingo and Haiti. They were the 8th (Capt. Holland McT. Smith), 16th (Capt. Edward W. Sturdevant), 45th (Capt. Benjamin S. Berry) and 47th (Capt. Frederick A. Barker) Companies.

On 8 June the 3d Battalion moved by rail from Philadelphia to New York. Headquarters, together with the 8th (briefly with 3/5) and 16th Companies, embarked on board the USS *Seattle* and the 45th and 47th Companies aboard the USS *Charleston*, which lay off St. George, at Staten Island. On 13 June the entirety transshipped to the USS *Henderson*.

On 14 June, three ships, carrying the entire regiment, weighed anchor and departed that day for France. Quarters on all three ships were crowded but the newness of the voyage to many of the new men was sufficient distraction. Marine gun crews were organized and much time was spent in target practice on the way over. Details of company and battalion organization were perfected and each unit had plenty of opportunity to become acquainted with their fellow Marines in the other units before the two week voyage was completed.

Although the *Henderson* arrived at St. Nazaire, France, on 27 June, it would be 3 July before the 3d Battalion would disembark. By that night the battalion was ashore and slept under canvas nearby.

On 13 July the 3d Battalion was temporarily split up. The 45th Company was detailed as a deck guard and moved into billets in the town, while the 47th Company was sent as a guard for Permanent Camp No. 1 at St. Nazaire, under command of Major Westcott. The 47th also supplied the guard for the remount station and a provost guard for the town itself. The 16th Company was shipped to Nevers, where it also performed provost duty and in addition supplied the guard for the medical depot there.

At tent camp close order drill and practice marches were the order of the day. On 15 July the 8th Company along with the 1st and 2d Battalions and regimental headquarters company entrained for their training camp, Menaucourt near the Meuse River. While the main portion of the 5th Regiment was in training it was reviewed twice by Gen Pershing and his staff and once by Gen Petain. It was the consensus of opinion that the 5th Regiment "was the finest body of men under our command."

All the while that the 3d Battalion was not with the regiment, elsewhere many changes took place, some of which affected the 3d Battalion directly or indirectly. Lieutenant Colonel Hiram I. Bearss succeeded Colonel Doyen as the temporary regimental commander in early November 1917. The 8th Company had been dispatched to St. Nazaire in August as permanent camp guard for Camp No. 1, Base Section No. 1.

In January 1918, the 8th Company received a commendation from the commander of Base Section No.1 for doing its duty so well. Captain John H. Fay became its commander, relieving Capt. Holland M. Smith, who went to an Army school. On 9 January the 8th Company with the 45th and 47th Companies entrained at St. Nazaire, and on 11 January 1918 arrived at Colombey-les-Choiseul. It was here that the 8th Company was detached from the 3d Battalion and designated the Regimental Machine Gun Company. Meanwhile, the 16th Company arrived from Nevers and the recently arrived 20th Company both joined the 45th and 47th to finally complete the 3d Battalion.

With a modicum of battalion training the 3d entrained at Breuvannes on 15 March for Ancemont for additional training under live shell fire. On each cloudy day, until 28 March, the battalion continued its regular drill schedule when not engaged with the artillery experience. The regiment had been sent to this quiet sub-sector of Verdun for a 30 day period of training where a maximum could be learned with a minimum of human loss. In addition to being subjected to artillery fire, at night the regiment also learned patrolling and barbed wire repair. Especially good training was in unit organization and organizing positions. Here the regiment learned about having one battalion on line with two in reserve and the problems inherent in relieving units on the front lines. On 26 March, Maj. Westcott was assigned to an Army school and was relieved of command of the 3d Battalion by Maj. Edward W. Sturdevant.

Verdun

In the early hours of 31 March the 1st and 3d Battalions of the Fifth Regiment along with the 8th Machine Gun Company relieved the 14th French Regiment at Eix-Moulainville-Chatillon sub-sector of Sector Verdun. On 9 April the 2d Battalion relieved the 3d, which then marched to Camp Chiffoure. While there the battalion working parties were sent out each night to dig reserve trenches. On 20 April the 3d Battalion relieved the 1st Battalion. It was on this night that the Germans made a raid on the trench section occupied by the 45th Company. Trench mortars and one pounders assisted the company to repulse the attack where the Germans lost two officers and one NCO dead, with one private so seriously wounded that he died on the way to the ambulance.

19–20 April: Report of operations:

Captain [Benjamin S.] Berry commanded the 45th Co in which two men were killed and 10 wounded and that the 16th Co also had casualties of one killed and two wounded.

During the night of April 19-20th the 3d Bn relieved the 1st Bn, Fifth Regiment in subsector MOULAINVILLE. New order of companies, north to south is as follows: 45th Co., 16th Co., 20th Co., 47th Co.

At 4:15 a.m. the enemy made a raid on the Post of Command at ST. PRIVAT. A heavy barrage of shells of big caliber was thrown in between our first line and line of support. They attack our first line in force and were driven out without having gained a foothold in any place. One German officer and two men were found dead in our trenches, one German wounded was captured. Observatory reports that a number of Germans were seen being carried back to their lines. Our losses are two men killed, twelve wounded, one badly, no missing. The trenches and dugouts are badly damaged.

CHATILLON reports that a patrol from the 18th Co encountered some of the enemy, our casualties, two wounded, two missing.

On the same night of 20-21 April, 1/5 was relieved by 3/5. The 45th Company of 3/5 occupied the trench line through the town of Eix and connected with the 16th Company to their right flank, which was also in part of the town. They in turn connected with the 20th Company at Moulinville-la-Bas, which in turn met with the 47th Company on the extreme right flank of the line. Between 0400 and 0500 hours on 21 April, the Germans laid down a barrage upon 45th Company. A raiding party followed but was repulsed before it got much beyond the first line of wire. Three men in the battalion were killed and eleven were wounded.

The Germans seemed to have fared better—they lost two officers and two enlisted men killed or who later died of wounds. Reports indicate that several German ambulances were seen going to the rear, which seems to signify that many more Germans sustained losses than previously reported. In fact, their casualties may have been quite heavy. Captain Benjamin S. Berry, then in command of the 45th Company, along with 2d Lts. F. E. Conroy and Edward B. Hope, plus nine enlisted men, were awarded the Croix de Guerre for their courageous actions during the raid.

The Supply Company of the 5th Marines was shelled on the night of 22 April. Two men killed and three wounded; losses in horses and mules were very heavy. The next night the Germans again shelled the same company killing another Marine and wounding two more. Stables were destroyed along with two more horses and thirteen mules. Two U.S. Navy men, Dental Surgeon Alexander G. Lyle and Pharmacist Mate 1st Class Tony Sommer, were cited in General Orders No. 35 for acts of bravery.

20–21 April: The usual reliefs took place for several weeks and all was quiet until two companies—the 45th of 3/5 under Maj. Benjamin Berry, and the 84th Company, 3/6—became the subject of intense German attention. A platoon of the 45th, commanded by 2d Lt. Edward B. Hope, which had just finished relieving 1/5 at Eix at night, were on the extreme left of the divisional and corps sector on a commanding ridge. The Germans desired that ridge and after a severe bombardment launched a massive, well-planned raid on that section of the line. The specially trained raiding party left behind two officers and two enlisted hanging on the wire after the Marines were finished with them. The enemy carried a large number of Germans back with them when they retired, according to observers. Hope's losses were three Marines killed and eleven wounded. The brigade diary entry, signed by Neville, gave the date as the night of 19-20 April, but most sources agree on 20-21 as the correct night. The French awarded the Croix de Guerre to a number of the officers and men who participated. Their French liaison officer, Lieutenant Viaud, reported to command that U.S. troops behaved admirably. The 84th had a similar experience. A raiding party, loosely identified as the "Hindenburg Circus," invaded their trenches with flamethrowers and grenades the same night. The raid was repulsed with rifle fire and grenades. No Marine casualties were reported. German losses, if any, weren't noted.

During these few nights an inordinate amount of activity was reported by Neville to division. One such bears an adequate exposure because of the modest failures and the overall learning experience it reflected.

25 April 1918: From Capt. George K. Shuler, adjutant, 5th Regiment, to (now) Maj. Benjamin S. Berry, commanding officer, 3d Battalion, at 1940: "1. Machine guns Nos. 3 & 4, will be placed for tonight on positions further to the rear, the same as done previously. Tomorrow Captain [Louis R.] de Roode [77th Machine Gun Company, 6th Machine Gun Battalion] and yourself will locate these guns permanently on positions in rear of the first line. Inform this office the location of the new positions."

During this period in the trenches, in a letter written by Sgt. Merwin Silverthorn of the 16th Company, to no one named, he complained about the living in "utter darkness," about the hordes of rats, especially the great "big field rats." He went on, "I have never experienced such foul air as when I slept in dugouts when I was with the French" and added, "They just lay down in their regular clothes. It was the foulest smelling air."

On the evening of 12 May the 277th French Regiment of Infantry relieved the Fifth Marines and by 14 May the 3d Battalion proceeded to Heiltz-l'Eveque, under the command, according to the official history, since 1 May, of Maj. Benjamin S. Berry. Berry was actually in command, or perhaps was assistant commander, at least as early as the 20th of April.

The regiment only remained at their location until 19 May when they entrained and detrained at their new training area in the District of Oise, just north of Paris. The 3d Bat-

Marines of the 6th in April 1918, at their dugout at Verdun.

talion was billeted at Vandancourt. This was remembered as the most pleasant location in the history of the regiment in France. Intensive training didn't dampen the spirits of the men, who soon learned the words of the song "Parlez-vous" and created a whole section of stanzas of their own. But their idyllic situation was going to change drastically and very soon.

Belleau Wood

31 May to 1 June: The Second Division was scheduled to relieve the First Division which had gallantly driven off a German attack at Cantigny and then had successfully counterattacked the enemy 27–28 May 1918. They were about fifty-five miles northeast of Paris, but fate was to deny the Second Division possible obscurity. The German Army launched another, the third, major attack in 1918 against the Allied lines on 27 May, this time across the Chemin des Dames toward, mainly, a French force trying to recover from several bad batterings already received from the Germans.

On 29 May the French high command ordered the Fourth Brigade to the Beauvais area, several days' march northward. It was scheduled to start on 31 May. Instead the Second Division moved on to help stop the massive German forces headed toward the ancient town of Chateau-Thierry. They left on camions and wheeled rapidly, 31 May to 1 June, through the countryside before arriving near their intended target, the Germans who were by now at or near Belleau Wood.

1 June: Neville sent this to Major Berry at 1600: "Proceed at once with your battalion to Pyramide, ready for action. Place your Battalion in rear of 2d Bn. in column of route on left of road and await orders."

2 June: Neville to Berry at 0900: "Move your command to position in south edge of wood west of PYRAMIDE FARM—Your right and Bn. Hdqts. at Stone Pile" (as brigade reserve).

That morning, Maj. Benjamin S. Berry and 3/5 were assigned as brigade reserve and that afternoon were reassigned to corps reserve. Ben Berry and 3/5 became corps reserve and were positioned just to the rear of the junction of the 6th Marines and the 9th Infantry, the weakest part of the division line. Harbord directly passed along those orders as he did those to Maj. Julius Turrill later, when he placed 1/5 in reserve. All during the action in June, it was common for Harbord to bypass his regimental commanders and send orders from his command post to nearly every lower level: to battalion and occasionally even down to company level. Harbord to Neville at 1630: "Berry's 3d Bn now Corps Reserve."

Ben Berry's 3/5, which had been serving as corps reserve, was returned to brigade control and now, as brigade reserve, relocated to the woods southwest of Marigny. The 5th Marines front was still held generally by Lieutenant Colonel Wise's 2/5, but they were supported by some reinforcements from 1/5 and the regimental Headquarters Company. The 6th Marines remained as they were, clustered about Triangle, with Lucy to their left and facing toward Bouresches.

4 June: Berry sent a message to Neville at 1250: "Third Batt. now in woods 150 yds west of a point about 1 1/3 kilometers south of MARIGNY (western end). I have a liaison post on the road leading south from western end of MARIGNY. The post is at southern edge of newly plowed field about 1½ kilometers south of MARIGNY."

5 June: Harbord to Neville and Catlin, no time indicated: "1. As soon as practicable after dark tonight, the following changes will be made: (a) The 3rd Bn. 5th Marines will relieve the 1st Bn. 6th Marines.... The sector to be held by the 3rd Bn., 5th Marines will be from the brook 173.8-262.7 on the west to LUCY-LE-BOCAGE–TORCY Road 174.8-261.0, inclusive." Berry and 3/5 would take up a position running from just east of Hill 142 southeast to a point north of Lucy-le-Bocage. In other words, facing Belleau Wood along the Torcy-Lucy road. At 2225 Harbord sent Field Order No. 1: "3. (b) The 3rd Bn., 5th Marines, will advance its left along the brook which rises 1 kilometer N. E. of CHAMPILLON to conform to the progress made by the 1st Bn. [1/5], in its attack."

6 June: Berry to Neville, at 1200, sent by runner: "If Turrill is not in the area bounded by the below named points the area should be shelled as after personal observation at 10:30 a.m., I believe it occupied by enemy machine guns and troops. A 45th Co Platoon is 150 yards south of the" (message incomplete). Berry sent by runner to Neville at 1235: "Capt. [Peter] Conachy on my left received orders from me at 10.30 a.m. to occupy as far north as practicable the ravine leading up to point 173.9-263.3 and to connect with Turrill right, Have had nothing further from him as yet.

Berry to Neville, at 0130: "I am for tonight at Mairie building in LUCY [le Bocage].

Relief not yet completed." Then at 0245: "Relief completed. I occupy sector as indicated in Brigade order this date." And at 0720: "At 6:05 a.m. one platoon of my left company established itself at 174.4-262.7. Ravine of creek will be occupied as soon as Major Turrill has gained his objective [Hill 142]. Following casualties so far reported: Lt. E.[dward] A. [B.] Hope wounded, leg. [45th Company], Pvt. Crowder, 118103 William A., killed. [45th Company]."

Harbord sent to Neville at 0900: "I congratulate you and 1st Bn. and the 3d Bn. on doing so well what we all knew they would do." To Neville from Turrill, at 0900, in which he mentions 3d Bn.: "Berry is fighting in woods on my right. Woods not shown on map." The position was just at the bottom of Hill 142 and between that and northwestern edge of Belleau Wood. Captain George W. Hamilton, commanding officer of the 49th Company, requested, among other things, that the recipient of his message "Push Berry up to our right."

Neville to Harbord, time received 0950:

> Just heard from [Maj. Henry L.] Larsen [3/5 adjutant] on the end of the line. Last seen of Berry was when he went up with 4 runners to find out where his line was. The battalion started to advance across the open square. The line advanced about half way across. Machine guns got busy. Larsen says he does not think many of them left. Nothing has been seen or heard of Berry since that incident. He is trying to locate the 47th Co. [Capt. Raymond E. Knapp] which was the right company and they did not have to go across. The objective was not gained and he doubted whether they got to the edge of the woods and without further support they must attempt to withdraw what few of them there are out there, Had no report for the 47th Co.

I believe it was remnants of German troops driven off Hill 142 by Turrill's men that Berry's men noticed, but the Marines of 1/5 were very close and most likely if any shelling had occurred they would have taken casualties. After the battalions' morning assault just two companies were left, the 49th and 67th, though by this time of the morning the 66th and 1 battalion'ss had arrived to support 1/5.

Berry sent a message to Neville at 1235: "Capt. Conachy [45th Company] on my left received orders from me at 10:30 a.m. to occupy as far north as practicable the ravine leading up to point 173.9-263.3 and to connect with Turrill's right. Have had nothing further from him as yet."

At 1240 Turrill sent Neville a message that stated, "Unless Berry comes up to my right I will have to fall back, there is nothing on my right between the front and way back to where we started from, as far as I can find out." Conachy was not where he was supposed to be, although he must have tried his best to so be. I believe he never made it to protect Turrill's right flank. A half hour later Turrill was still looking for Berry's men. "As I said before a strong attack on our right would finish us off."

Berry to Neville at 1345: "Order of Battle 3d Batt. Front line, right 47th Co. [Capt. Philip T. Case] 174.8-261.0 to 174.8-261.9 inclusive. Center 20th Co. [Capt. Richard N. Platt], around edge of wood from left flank of 47th Co. to 174.4-262.4 left. 45th Co. [Capt. Peter Conachy] from last mentioned point, along edge of wood to 173.8-262.3 incl." If Conachy was where Berry had sent him, he would have been at Turrill's headquarters, according to the next message. The 16th Company, Captain Robert Yowell, would constitute the reserve.

From the assistant regimental commander, Lt. Col. Logan Feland, to Berry at 1527: "Have commander of your left company [Conachy, 45th] meet me at Turrill's headquarters on road at point 173.7-262.9 at 4:00 p.m. today." Neville to Berry at 1547: "All officers that can possibly be spared will report to Col. Feland at P.C. Turrill immediately. P.C. Turrill 173.6-262.95." Berry to Neville, no time listed, but prior to 1700: "16 Co. in reserve less one plat. which is on line with 20th Co. Each co. has a platoon in reserve."

At 1700 the 3d Bn jumped off with an almost perfect skirmish line. The 16th Company was kept in reserve plus a platoon from each of the three other companies. On the left was the 45th Company, in the center was the 20th and then the 47th on the right flank.

Deadly machine gun fire from the woods was encountered in crossing the open country west of the northern half of Belleau Wood. Then fire from three points, before them, to their left and right.

Colonel Albertus Catlin, commanding officer, 6th Marines, in overall charge of the

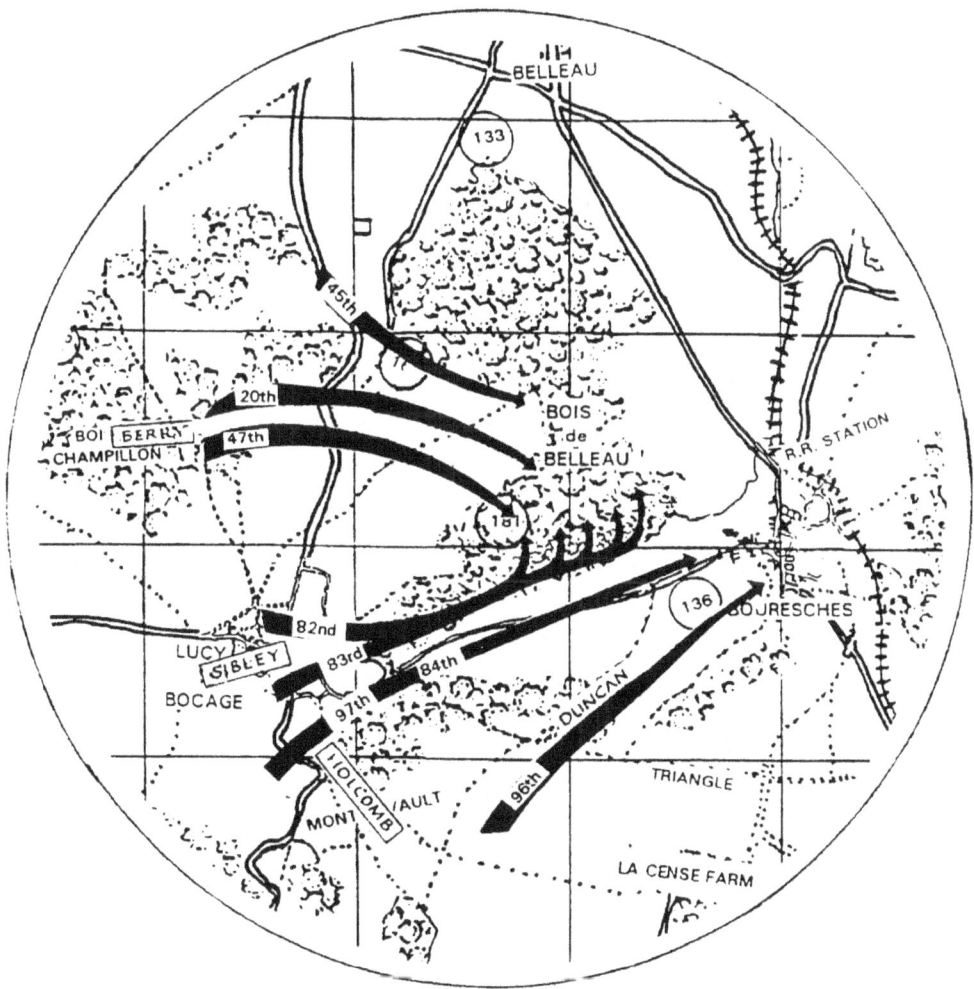

The attack as launched by 3/5 and 3/6 on 6 June 1918.

attack, was badly wounded within a few minutes. Berry was in even worse shape himself, losing much of his right arm, and his command was devastated. It was then that Captain Henry L. Larsen, his adjutant, assumed command. The 3d Battalion "retired" in some disorder, with additional losses, to where their jump-off point had been. The two battalions of the 6th Marines were also badly handled by the Germans but 2/6, Maj. Holcomb, made it to Bouresches and for all intents and purposes, held that town for the next twenty days. Sibley's battalion, 3/6, sustained heavy losses at the southern edge of Belleau Wood.

Col. W. C. Neville states he believes this message was sent by Maj. Berry immediately following the attack on Bois de Belleau, June 6, 1918: "Following information is all available re position companies. 2 platoons 47th Co. reformed and attempting to protect left flank of adjoining organization on right. 20th Co. reforming on similar mission. Nine men only reported returned of 3 platoons of 45th that went over the top. Yowell has two platoons of 16th with him to northward have no report from lines other two platoons holding."

Neville to Harbord, received at 1810: "What is left of battalion is in woods close by. Do not know whether will be able to stand or not. Increase artillery range."

Larsen sent the following, time not noted, and the first page is missing; it begins: "to my immediate front to report what is there. Three of my companies average about two platoons each and not over 25 men present with 47th Co. Am getting them rounded up as best I can. What men we have at present are standing by for orders. M. G. Co. attached has 38 casualties. 23d Inf. are again in our sector and facing westward. M. G. fire just reported sweeping up the road on which our P.C. is located (fire from front). Just got word from 20th Co. patrol M.G. fire opened up on them one km [kilometer] to their front."

From Capt. Henry Larsen, adjutant, 3/5, to Capt. Charles C. Gill, 4th Brigade Headquarters; received there at 1951: "From 3d Bn., 5th: Three platoons 45th Co. went over [the top]. Only a few returned. Captain Conachy familiar with the circumstances." It seems odd that 3/5 would bypass headquarters of the 5th to correspond directly with brigade. But this also happened with several battalions, several times, during the following months. There were a number of times when I couldn't "find" Neville during much of the Belleau Wood period. Control of the regiment, most of that time, seemed to be in the hands of Lt. Col. Logan Feland, his assistant. After the battle in early July, Neville was taken to a hospital for nervous exhaustion.

Neville to Brigade, time received 2150:

> Just heard from Larsen on the end of the 3d Bn. line. Last seen of Berry was when he went up with 4 runners to find out where his line was. The battalion started to advance across the open square. The line advanced about half way across. [German] Machine guns got busy. Larsen says he does not think many of them [3/5] left. Nothing has been seen or heard of Berry since that incident. He is trying to locate the 47th Co. which was the right company and they did not have to go across. The objective was not gained and he doubted whether they got to the edge of the woods and without further support they must attempt to withdraw what few of them there are out there. Had no report for the 47th Co.

Somehow a few Marines from both the 20th and 47th Companies on the right flank had not only managed to survive but got into the woods, remaining there at least until the 8 of June, possibly longer. In a message to his headquarters, Maj. Berton W. Sibley, commanding officer of 3/6, at 1220 a.m. 7 June, stated, "Still unable to get in touch with Berry's battalion on left." Which meant, I suppose, that the few 3/5 men left were scattered about and probably hiding from the Germans.

7 June: From Captain Charles C. Gill, intelligence officer, 4th Brigade, to 4th Brigade Headquarters, received at 0215:

> Message from Larsen to Neville—Following information available reference position of companies: 2 platoons 47th Co. reformed and attempting to protect the left flank of adjoining organization on right 20th Co. [3/6] reforming on similar mission. 9 men only reported reformed from 3 platoons of 45th who went over the top. Yowell has two platoons of 16th Co. with him to N.W. Have no report from him. Other two platoons hold sector and covering machine gun positions there. Western edge of BOIS DE BELLEAU filled with enemy machine guns, making advance over open [ground] impossible with[out] further preparation.

Larsen to Neville, at about 0230: "1st Sgt. 16th Co., reports heavy artillery shelling in woods back of old position 3d Bn. 5th. Front line under serious machine gun barrage. Request artillery fire on western edge of BOIS DE BELLEAU, from 262 to point 133. It seems front line of old position cut off." Neville received this from Larsen, adjutant, 3/5, at 0300 at Brigade Hdqs: "Front only under machine gun barrage."

Several messages follow, some from Turrill to Neville in which he describes what Captain Peter Conachy was doing at 0710:

> Conachy with one plat of his co & two platoons of engineers was attacking woods to right of our right ravine. The attack started about 4 a.m. No reports of how attack progresses. At 7:40 a.m. Capt. Conachy Comdg. 45 Co. is on left of 3d Bn., 5th Regt. Is in touch with 17th Co., of Turrill's Bn. on Conachy's right he is in touch with the 16th Co. Conachy has with him the portion that is left of the 1st & 2nd Platoon. 2 Plat. Engineers 65 men each and 30 men of the 16th Co. 3 Lieuts. with him and the men are reporting to him in small bodies.
>
> At 8 a.m. Sent [1st] Lt. [Walter H.] Galliford & one man to locate Conachy & his men. At 9:18 a.m. Capt. [William A.] Snow 2d Eng. showed me a note from Lt. Hathaway 2d Eng. Co. E., in which it was stated that C.O. 45th Marines withdrew from open ground on our right rear, at 3:45 a.m. on account of the refusal of units on his left to attack.

Harbord to Neville, at 1230: "If the remnant of the 3d Bn. your regiment, has not already been directed on the wood between MARIGNY and here, please direct it on MON BLANCHE, S.W. of LUCY about one kilometer N.E. of LA FERME PARIS. It will be easier supplied at that point, equally safe, and more accessible if needed again. The point designated this morning is now outside Division area. Once it clears LUCY it can go up the stream GOBERT without being under observation from the enemy." I've wondered how Harbord could even consider that 3/5 would be useful until heavily showered with replacements. The battalion was shattered.

Larsen sent this to an unknown destination at 1415: "2 Plats, 47 Co. reformed & attempting to protect left flank of adjoining organization on right [3/6]. 20 Co. reforming on similar mission." From brigade to division, at 1515: "Captain Larsen, 3d Battalion, 5th Marines, reports to Col. Neville, German shells bursting in our front lines pouring a black smoke. Heavy stream of black smoke also behind the German line." Harbord to Neville, at 2040: "Please make the following changes in force that has been operating under Colonel

Feland southwest of Torcy: 2nd, send the company of the 3rd Bn. to Mon Blanche to join the remainder of the battalion."

This is probably from Larsen, but no time, nor addressee, is given: "2 Plat 16 Co. to N.W., other 3 platoons hold the sector and are covering the M.G. position of enemy at N.W. edge of BOIS DE BELLEAU. 45 Co. consisting of about 9 men relieved west of 147.7-262.3 20 Co. little more than one platoon organized at 275.6-61.2. 47 Co. organizing at same place. Left of right wing very weak against movement from north. 7 June 18."

Larsen to Neville, no time indicated: "Have delivered message to Col. [Frederick M.] Wise [commanding officer, 2/5] as ordered. Have established liaison with Maj. Turrill on my left. Col. Wise and I occupy the same P.C. (LUCY) until you are notified of change. Am now verifying continuous line connecting 16th Co. with Bn. of 6th Reg't on my right." Larsen to Neville again, no time indicated: "Col. Wise expects to be able to begin relief at about 3:00 p.m. Will report casualties as soon as possible. Will report immediately upon being relieved and upon arrival at camp."

Larsen, 3d Battalion at Lucy, sent this to Feland at Headquarters, 5th Marines, no time given:

> [1st] Lt. [William A.] Duckham commanding 2 platoons of 16th Co. occupies old line of trenches held by 3d Bn. 5th yesterday morning. He reports repelling enemy attack on his center this morning also that Col. Wise with 2nd Bn. also occupied the same trenches since early this a.m.
>
> Duckham is attempting to get in liaison with Yowell, supposed to be on his left front.
>
> Duckham is now ordered to maintain liaison with Col. Wise, 47th Co., and what is left of 20th Co. was ordered to take position and protect left flank of organization on our right [3/6] from enemy on our north of that position. C.O. 47th Co. also ordered to establish liaison with Bn. on his right at about 11:00 p.m. last night. Few men that are left of the 45th Co. have joined 16th in old position of 3d Bn. [and a little later].
>
> 2 platoon 16th Co. have fallen back to original position. 45 Co. consisting of about 9 men relieved west of 174.7-262.3. 20 Co. little more than one platoon organized at 275.6-61.2 [can't locate those coordinates on available maps]. 47 Co. organizing at same place. Left of right wing very weak against movement from north.

From Capt. Larsen, commanding officer, 3/5, to Neville, at La Voie du Chatel, no time indicated: "Have delivered message to Col. Wise as ordered. Have established liaison with Maj. Turrill on my left. Col. Wise & I occupy same P.C. (Lucy) until you are notified of change. An now verifying continuous line connecting 16th Co. with Bn. of 6th Reg't on my right." From ? to ?, no time indicated. Probably to Neville: "2 Platoon 16 Co. have fallen back to original position. 45 Co. consisting of about 9 men relieved west of 174.7-262.3. 20 Co. little more than one platoon organized at 275.6-261.2. 47 Co. organizing at same place. Left of right wing very weak against movement from north. 7 June 18."

Sometime after this message was sent, Maj. Maurice Shearer, who had been serving with 1/6, relieved Larsen of battalion command on the evening of 7 June 1918. Shearer immediately commenced to reorganize the shattered battalion. The official history of the 5th Marines says it lost "25 percent of it's effectives." That, I believe is a very modest and incorrect statement of the numbers. Some of the companies were down from 250 or so to twenty or thirty officers and men.

Message from ? (probably Larsen) to ? (probably Neville), no time indicated, but probably in the morning: "7:40 a.m. Capt. Conachy Comdg. 45 Co. is on left of 3rd Bn, 5th Regt. is in touch with 17th Co., of Turrill's Bn. on Conachy's right he is in touch with the 16th Co. Conachy has with him the portion that is left of the 1st & 2nd Platoon. 2 Plat. Eng. 65 men each and 30 men of the 16th. Co. 3 Lieuts. with him and the men are reporting to him in small bodies. 7 June 1918."

This one involves possibly same people as above: "At 5:35 Lieut. [James F.] Robertson [commanding officer, 96th Company, 2/6] reported that Major Turrill, Comdg. 1st Bn. 5 Marines has not moved from the position held prior to attack afternoon 6 June 18. Has not seen Lt. Col. Wise although Capt. [Keller E.] Rockey [adjutant, 1/5] stayed out 5 hours endeavoring to find him. Has connected with left of 3rd Bn. 5th Marines which is evidently badly disorganized and scattered."

8 June: From Harbord to Maj. Shearer, then still with the 6th Regiment, sent at 2152: "I desire you to go over early tomorrow morning and familiarize yourself with the line he [Holcomb, 2/6] is holding, including the town of Bouresches. It is the present intention that your battalion will relieve his tomorrow night and I want you to be familiar with the situation as the town of Bouresches and the line to Triangle Farm is considered to be very important. As soon as you have familiarized yourself with it, join your battalion and the other orders for the relief will be made later." Though they had received a few replacements, 3/5 was in very bad condition, and for Harbord to have them take over that extremely important village at this time was questionable.

9 June: To Commanding Officer Maurice Shearer, 3d Battalion, 5th Marines, from Harbord, time 1442: "As soon as it is dark tonight send one company of your battalion to the wood S. E. of LUCY as regimental support for the 6th Marines. Take the other three companies and relieve the three companies of the 2nd Bn. 6th Regiment now holding BOURESCHES-TRIANGLE FARM." This is seemingly a strange message; ordering a very badly depleted battalion to support another regiment, and bypassing the commander of the 5th Regiment in so doing. Replacements were received the night of 7-8 June but it is not known how many were sent to 3/5. We also have a record that Harbord advised Wise on 11 June 1918 that "1,000 replacements arriving for the Brigade today."

10 June: From N-1 (Shearer) to N-7 (? Shuler or have no idea), at 1215: "Confirmation telephone message. Relief completed 2:30 a.m. 10th. Please send message to farm 174.7-259.5 on crooked road running south from LUCY. They will be relayed or telephoned to me from there. everything O.K. Our heavy artillery [17th Field Artillery] fired into BOURESCHES last night. Reported Same. Captain George K. Shuler's name on reverse side of message."

11 June: From Shearer to Harbord, received by telephone at 0555: "Germans along railway tracks. Request barrage closer." From Shearer to Harbord, by telephone, received at 0600: "Germans attacking with machine guns and infantry."

12 June: From Lt. Col. Lee, 6th Marines to Larsen at 2120, message No. 47: "Copy message #14 from C.O. 23rd Inf. Same patrols to our front tonight as last night. Notify your right company of their presence. Please comply."

13 June: Message from Adjutant Larsen to headquarters, 5th, sent 0410: "Maj. Shearer by runner, that enemy has taken town of BOURESCHES. Barrage in town. Enemy still advancing. [Maj. Thomas] Holcomb [commanding officer, 2/6] in woods."

From Capt. David Jackson, adjutant, 3/5 to unknown, sent 0445: "MONTGIVRAULT Farm, 6/13/18. PLAN. A. 1. Requests barrage be lengthened 300 meters. It is falling on his own men. Maj. Hughes [commanding officer, 1/6] requests reinforcements as soon as possible. This was received by me over phone from LUCY." Captain Gilder Davis Jackson was listed as the adjutant of 3/5 at that time, whereas David was not, but this was sent and signed by David.

This message was from Major Edmund C. Waddill, 23d Infantry at P.C. Triangle, 0430, to Shearer: "Are your companies still in BOURESCHES or have they evacuated?" The reply came at 0605: "Our men are still holding town. Am getting details as to number of Germans who got in. Will send you word. Shearer."

From 5th Regiment Adjutant Captain George K. Shuler to Brigade Headquarters, time received 1745: "Shearer in BOURESCHES. Has not given up one inch of ground. Casualties: Captain [John F.] Burn[es], [commanding officer] 74th Co, wounded in both legs. Lieutenant [Edgar Allan] Poe [Jr., 74th Company, platoon leader], severe wound in back. Captain [Edward C.] Fuller, [CO] 75th Co , killed. Burnes died; Poe, nephew of the famous poet came back; Fuller was the son of Col. Ben H. Fuller, future commandant.

Lt. Col. Harry Lee, now commanding officer 6th Marines, to Shearer at Bouresches, sent at 1810: "Enclosed is a copy of Field Order No. 5 which I am sending for your information. You must burn it as soon as soon as you finish with it. Be careful to observe Par. 3 (b) … Section (b) as soon as darkness permits, tonight June 13th; 3d Bn. 5th Marines to woods northwest of LUCY as Brigade reserve. Relief was reported completed at 0330 on 14 June."

14 June: From ? to ? telephoned and received at 0500: "'APPOMATOX' telephoned at 3 :30 a.m. from Shearer at H.Q. 6th. Gas in BOURESCHES." Shearer was incapacitated and wouldn't join 3/5 until after the relief of the 7th Infantry later that month. Message from Maj. Ralph S. Keyser, 2d in command, 3d Battalion, 5th Regiment, to Brigade Headquarters, received at 0900: "Officers and men are exhausted. They are doing good work but on their nerve only; physically they are all in. Maj. Shearer is in care of the 6th Regiment Surgeon suffering from temporary exhaustion. On 19 June, Keyser was in command of 2/5."

21 June: From Harbord to Shearer through Neville, at 0235:

1. It is believed that by judicious use of sharpshooting snipers you can reduce the German positions without much expenditure of men. These men should be provided with canteens of water, with some rations and crawl out toward the German positions exerting every effort, exercising the patience of Indians and waiting for shots without exposing themselves. Pairs to be sent in from all sides. Additional pairs to be sent in at night along the west side of the BOIS from both north and south. These will stop any infiltration if any has taken place. Some should be sent in where the tree boarded road which runs from LUCY toward CHATEAU BELLEAU touches the BOIS DE BELLEAU (175.2-262.3 approximately) to scout up the road watching for a chance to snipe.
2. The wiring up on the east and the north of the BOIS must proceed. Just as soon as it is completed the line can be held with comparatively few men and remainder dug in support and out of shell fire.
3. It is not practicable to withdraw again and give further artillery preparation. With the sniping which should worry the enemy you should be endeavoring to get the machine gun nests surrounded so you can rush them when ready and put an end to them.

4. The 3d Bn. 7th Infantry holds the ravine from 174.0-263.4 to crossroads 174.8-263.0 and tonight will extend that line to the east to vicinity of 175.3-262.5. That will enable you to control any approach of Germans down that road from LUCY toward CHATEAU BELLEAU.

It appears strange that the brigade commander would be giving directions to a battalion commander of a nature of which it would seem as though the battalion commanding officer would already be well aware and would do naturally without special prompting. Incidentally, the 7th Infantry of the 3d Division (Regular) had been sent in to relieve units of the 4th Brigade on or about 16 June. Both Marine regimental commanders, Neville and Lee, remained in command of those 7th Infantry units that relieved the various Marine units, with their own commanders reporting to either Neville, 5th, or Lee, 6th. Needless to say, the 7th had no combat experience whatsoever and understandably did poorly at Belleau Wood, in some cases losing ground already won. When the Marines returned they were furious at having "to go and do it again." As in the following, Harbord continued to bypass the regimental commanding officers.

Field Order No. 7 came from Harbord to everyone at noon: "2. (a) The 3rd Bn., 5th Marines to relieve the 1st Bn. 7th Infantry night of June 21-22." Lt. Col. John P. Adams, commanding officer, 1/7, sent this to Shearer, commanding officer of 3/5, at 1125: "Attack this morning failed. At the hour of attack the enemy put down a barrage of great intensity on line of Co. B. (Approx. east and west on X line 262.) When the barrage lifted the attack again started but M. G. fire stopped further advance. Losses 170 officers and men. Cos. C and D occupy former positions."

From Harbord through Neville to Shearer at 1435:

2. The wiring up on the east and north of the BOIS must proceed. Just as soon as it is completed the line can be held with comparatively few men and remainder dug-in support and out of shell fire.
3. It is not practicable to withdraw again and give further artillery preparation. With the sniping which should worry the enemy you should be endeavoring to get the machine gun nests surrounded so you can rush them when ready and put an end to them.
4. The 3rd. Bn. 7th Infantry holds the ravine from 174.0-263.4 to crossroads 174.8-163.0 and tonight will extend that line to the east to vicinity of 175.3-262.5, That will enable you to control any approach of Germans down that road from LUCY toward CHATEAU BELLEAU.

These were more directions of a basic sort to a man who should have known all that he was told beforehand.

Harbord sent this to commanding officers, 3d Battalion, 5th; 2d Battalion, 7th Infantry; and 3d Battalion, 7th Infantry, at 1445: "Push out patrols in front of your positions each night and secure identifications, if possible of live or dead Germans. This is most important for your saftey against surprise and to give information on which action of higher authority can be based. Stealthy patrols of two or three men are what is desired."

22 June: From Col. Lee to Shearer at 0930 by runner: "Have the commander of your right company meet the representative of the 23d. Inf at TRIANGLE Farm at 10 p.m. tonight to arrange for the relief of his company by a company of the 23d Inf. Relief to take place tomorrow night. Copy for Col. Malone."

23 June: From Col. Lee to Neville at 1720 sent by motorcycle: "Just had a verbal message from Shearer that he had operation on for tonight and wanted battalion on his left to understand. He is trying to get in liaison with that Bn. Think he intends message for you." I believe it was the 1st Battalion, 7th Infantry, which had not yet been relieved. Message from Shearer to Brigade, at 2000: "Making progress slowly. Little shelling on front line companies."

24 June: Message from Neville to Harbord at 0105: "Things are rather bad. One company [20th] almost wiped out." Message from Shuler, adjutant, 5th to Brigade, received at 0131: "Platt's [20th] losses were light. He was held where he was but would take another crack in the morning." From Lt. Villaret, 23d Infantry, to Malone, 23d Infantry, at 1920, by runner: "Am informed that liaison has been established between Marines and 3rd Bn., 23rd Inf, These two Marine runners (bearers of this note) are sent as *additional* liaison agents to operate between your P.C. and 3rd Bn, 5th Marines, P.C. All is quiet here."

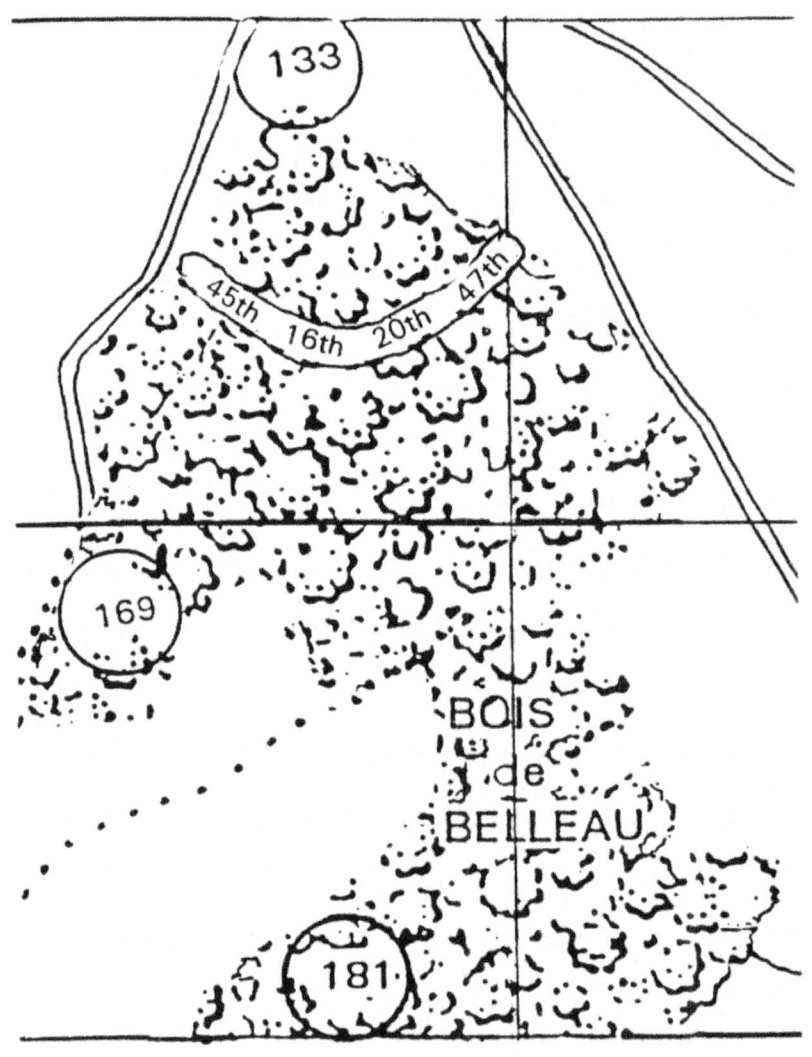

The positions held by 3/5 prior to their first attack on 23 June 1918.

23–24 June: Diary, written by Major Keyser, received at 4th Brigade Headquarters at 1100:

The attack started by 16 and 20 Cos. at 7 p.m. June 23rd. The 16th Co. sent out combat groups ahead of the line. These groups encountered several M. G. positions (Number not definate yet) which enemy abandoned on being bomb with grenades. The enemy took out guns, light type, and casualties, but left much ammunition. They apprently fell back to alternate positions as their fire did not seem to slacken. Men of 16th Co. report that they saw several enemy hit but no prisoners were taken and no bodies available for identification.

This co. [16th] advanced to position on attached map [no map present] when M. G. fire became so heavy as to hold them up; also they lost with 20 Co. on right as that Co. was not able to advance to keep connection.

The casualties became so heavy (estimated, 1 officer, 75 men) that Capt. [Robert] Yowell had to withdraw to his original position to get cover. In was not possible to dig in under the heavy M.G. fire that every movement brought down. Two artillery barrages [enemy] were put over but practically all casualties were from M.Gs.

The 16th Co. now holds position indicated on map [no map present].

From reconnaissance in person this a.m. and reports, I am of opinion that Capt. Yowell's withdrawal was justified under circumstances. He could not now re-occupy his advanced position of last night without repeating the attack of last night and there is no reason to believe the circumstances would not be the same. Two platoons, 83d Co., 6th [Capt. Albert R. Sutherland], were sent forward to reinforce Yowell arriving on old line about [undecipherable] a.m. They were held there by Yowell as he was then withdrawing to old line. It was not a question of number of men in his advanced line but their inability to dig cover under M. G. fire. The M. Gs. supporting Yowell's line remained in place ready to advance on establishing new line.

Men and officers showed good discipline and advance and withdrawal were made without confusion. The M.G. officers operating with 16th Co. reports (estimated) 16 heavy M. Gs. and 35 light type to front of 16th Co.

The 20th Co. [Capt. Richard Platt] sent out combat groups at 7 p.m. and were immediately under heavy M.G. fire. These groups cleared out about 3 enemy gun positions. Enemy withdrew guns and injured as in case of 16th Co. No prisoners or bodies available for identifications. The attacking line has been moved from it's dug in position before the attack to a jumping off position. Three attempts were made to advance from this position, each time being driven back by heavy enfilade M. G. fire and 1 pdrs [pounders].

The farthest advance made by line was about 20 yards (i.e. to top of rocks near hook sector). This position was immediately made untenable by fire from M. Gs.

This Co. gained no ground to front that could be held and are now in original position.

Three outposts have been established to front of old position. Sniping from these positions is being successfully carried on.

The discipline was good and no confusion during action. Difficulty was caused by carrying party for grenades getting lost in woods. Sufficient V.B.'s and grenades were later gotten forward but could have been used to advantage earlier.

Under the circumstances I am of the opinion that Capt. Platt did everything he could to put over the attack successfully but could not get through the machine gun fire. 20th Co. casualties (estimated) 26 men—7 killed.

The 47th Co. [Capt. Philip T. Case], less one platoon operating with the 20th Co, crossed in to their left as 20th Co. cleared old line as per plan. They were under shell fire several times. Casualties (estimated) 1 officer [and] five men.

The 45th Co. [Capt. Peter Conachy] less 50 men with 16th Co closed in on right of 47th Co. as per plan. Also were under shell fire. Casualties (estimated) 1 officer, 28 men.

Total estimated casualties 3 officers, 134 men. This does not include casualties of 2 platoons of 83d Co 6th and probably of 47 and 45 Co men operating with 16–20 Co Correct lists will be sent in as soon as possible.

The enemy seems to have unlimited alternate gun positions and many guns. Each gun position covered by others. I know of no other way of attacking these positions with chance of success than the one attempted and am of opinion that infantry alone cannot dislodge enemy guns. Water is difficult to obtain and rations scarce. Men and officers very tired but retain their spirit.

From Capt. Phil Case to Maj. Shearer at 1144:

I have to report the following named men killed and wounded by enemy 1 Pounders at short range, at about 10:40 a.m.

Killed	Wounded
Baier, Ernest H.	Muncey, Alton E.
Skidmore, Van Reusuler	Fagan, Clarence
Joyce, Thomas H.	Robinson, Andrew F.
Brown, Joseph B.	

My officers and men are showing the effects of being constantly on the alert and under frequent shell fire. Lieut. [Jacob H.] Heckman is slightly shell-shocked but I think he will be all right in a little while.

    This is not included in attack report.   M.E.S.[hearer]

The positions held by the 4th Platoon (Heckman) [Jacob H.] and 3d Platoon (Stallings) [Laurence T.] are catching hell from whiz-bang firing, which in many cases caves in the parapet of the trenches owing to the nature of the soil in which they are constructed. In many cases the enemy seems to be able to enfilade the above mentioned positions with his whiz-bangs.

    G.[AINES] MOSELEY [Acting commanding officer 47th Company]

From Harbord to everyone in 4th Brigade, no time indicated:

The 3d Bn., 5th Marines will be withdrawn from its present position to the X line 262 before three o'clock tomorrow morning, June 25th. The artillery will be free to fire from that hour anywhere north of the line 262 as far east as the railroad and as far west as the road with the double row of trees which runs just west of the BOIS DE BELLEAU. It is desired that the fire be intense enough from 3 o'clock on to prevent the entrance of any Germans and that for a period of about an hour before 5 p.m. June 25th, it be made of maximum intensity. It will be the intention to follow the artillery preparation by an attack with the 3d Bn. at 5 p.m. on the 25th. The rate of advance of the infantry will not exceed 100 meters each three minutes. The objective of the advance is the north edge of the BOIS DE BELLEAU.

25 June: From Capt. Shuler to Harbord, time received 1955: "5:55 p.m. from Shearer: Attack started O.K. at 5 p.m. Heavy firing on us just before we jumped off. Several casualties. Very little machine gun fire. Telephone line out. Runner reported 7 prisoners and one captain also prisoner, carrying back wounded. The two left platoons 16th Company reported grenades and Sniper working on them. No report from companies yet. Will go through if humanly possible." At 2040 Shearer sent to Harbord:

47th Co. gained objective—20t'h and 47th digging in. 45th still in reserve but will occupy positions just as soon as things settle. 16th still working into position. Estimated 150 prisoners, by 20 and 47th companies. No report of 16th as to prisoners. More prisoners just coming in too numerous to count. I am making prisoners dig and carry wounded. Every one doing fine work; Yowell 16th, meeting resistance, Will send him help. Will need all my company to hold new line. Can't Keyser [2/5] send me two platoons. Just reported counterattacks on 47th. Am sending two platoons 45th to help.

    Report capture of some of the [men] 47th Co.— Our casualties will make help necessary Please keep artillery and machine guns going to stop reinforcements of enemy.

Shearer to Harbord, time received 2245: *Holding.* "The 16th Co. still meeting resistance. 47th and 20th have got objectives and dug in. The 47th Co. say they have about 100 Germans trying to give themselves up but their own people fire on them when they try to do so. Need reinforcements badly. Have got to have reinforcements to hold on. Counter attack will be bad."

Shearer through Neville, to Harbord, sent 2130, received 2312:

20th and 47th are in position. 47th apparently too far east but am trying to rectify the same. 16th has not made position yet and reports machine guns still in their front. They are forward of last advance position held during last attack. They are still trying to work forward to objective. Reported about 100 enemy on 47th Co. left who want to surrender but Boche machine gun shoots them as they try to come out. Companies may have passed some enemy. Our casualties so heavy can't spare men to patrol to rear. Any counterattack by enemy would be fatal to us in present condition. Can't some force come in east and west line advancing north and clean up woods and thicken our lines? We must not lose what we have now. Enemy shelling woods continually. Please get heavy counter battery work on them. Estimate 150 prisoners. Impossible estimate enemy casualties. Heavy though. Sending prisoners back to Sibley [3/6] to send in. Had to use Reserve Co. in line so Sibley is filling up gap on right of 20th Co. east side woods and Sibley's left. *We have taken practically all of woods but do need help to clean it up and hold it. Do we get it?*

From Harbord to Neville, sent at 2320:

Your Shearer Battalion has done splendid work. I have no fear of a counter attack by the Germans tonight. You are in charge of the BOIS DE BELLEAU and can divert such part of Major Sibley's Battalion as you think best. His front is practically wired in. In connection with the movement of Keyser's Battalion to connect up with the west side of BOIS DE BELLEAU, I have ordered him to send a platoon by his right rear to come up on the left of the 16th Company and help clean that edge of the woods. It is very important that Shearer be told of this in order that the 16th Company may not, in the dark, confuse that platoon with the enemy.

Artillery are trying to neutralize some of the enemy artillery.

J. G. H.

From Harbord to Neville, no time indicated: "Contingent upon Major Shearer obtaining his objective orders were this afternoon sent Major Keyser to advance his line tonight and bring the right of the line on the double tree road just west of Bois de Belleau. This will begin shortly after dark, Please notify Major Shearer that the movement is going to take place so that in the dark he will not confuse it with a possible counter attack. Keyser's movement will be preceded by considerable artillery firing on the old trenches which run north west from Bois de Belleau."

26 June: Shearer advised brigade early in the morning, but no time indicated: "Woods now United States Marine Corps entirely."

From Capt. Shuler to Harbord, received 0310: "Regimental Aid Station states that all patients are from Shearer and none from Keyser. About 90 being treated." Then from Lt. Col. Lee by F. E. Evans, adjutant, to Keyser, at 0400: "Have tried to get information from 5th as to location Shearer's left, but they have no definite dope. They sent out message to have liaison runners report your P.C. and say two (2) went over, Shearer has sent in 60 prisoners through here & more through 5th. Brigade reports that prisoners attempting to surrender in numbers were shot down by own M.G's. Lot going through do not stack up much in size or Kultur. If you get in touch with Shearer have message telephoned in 'Have hooked up on my right.'"

From Harbord to every unit in 4th Brigade, sent at 0815: "1. The Second Battalion,

Sixth Regiment, Marines, as soon as possible, tonight, June 26-27, will relieve the 3d Battalion, 5th Regiment, Marines in the North end of the Bois de Belleau. Battalion and Company Commanders will make reconnaissance today. The Third Battalion, Fifth Marines, when relieved will take station in the Bois Gros Jean. Command Passes when relief is completed."

Lee sent this to Keyser at 0835 by runner: "The Brigade directs that you establish and maintain close liaison with Shearer's Bn. on your right as quickly as possible. Take all precautions for security and information. Am notifying Shearer of this." Harbord sent to Keyser through Lee, at 1405: "Make your preparations and as soon as possible after dark tonight swing your line forward so that it will run approximately straight from the cross-roads south of Torcy (174.75-263.1) to the double tree road, at 175.4-262.7. I will have the artillery keep down any fire from the trenches running northwest. from the BOIS DE BELLEAU, between 10 and 12 p.m. Copy to Major Shearer through C.O. 5th Marines. Delivered to A-1 at 3:00 p.m. by runner."

Harbord advised Keyser, and nearly everyone else, that 2/5 would relieve 3/5 the night of 26-27 June in the north end of Bois de Belleau. Shearer and battalion would retire to the Bois Gros Jean for a much needed rest.

The total dead casualties, officers and men of 3/5, for the period 6 June 1918 through 26 June 1918, were as follows:

16th Co	37	20th Co	68
45th Co	54	47th Co	60

The 3d Battalion suffered three additional dead between 1 June and 5 June. Their total dead far exceeded any other battalion, in either regiment, during the period.

30 June: Harbord to Shearer and Sibley, sent at 1200: "In accordance with Field Orders No. 9, Headquarters 2d Division, 30 June 1918 (Note: this order has to do with a contemplated attack by the 3d Brigade) the 3d Battalion 5th Marines and 3d Battalion 6th Marines, are placed at the disposal of the Division Commander. These Battalions will remain in the Bois Gros Jean until further orders and maintain a liaison officer at Division Headquarters from and after the receipt of this order."

The 2d Division was relieved by the 26th "YD" Division and the 4th Brigade was withdrawn to support lines. On 5 July the 3d Battalion left their positions near Gros des Jeans and bivouacked that night in Bois de Chamoust. The next day the battalion arrived at Crouttes and billeted. They were soon joined by Headquarters, Headquarters Company, and the 8th Machine Gun Company. The division remained in the area until 16 July when word was passed to "stand by for camions." This was the end of their exertions at Belleau Wood.

Soissons

The Second Division was chosen to take part in French General Mangin's great counterattack against the Germans at Soissons. The attack was to also include the U.S. First Division and the famed First Moroccan Division. The plan was for the 1st to take the left flank, the Moroccans the center and the Second Division the right flank. The 1st and 2nd Battalions, Fifth Marines, were selected to lead the assault with the 3d Battalion in reserve.

The 3d Battalion boarded camions at Citry at 2000 on 16 July and arrived at Morienval at 0900 on 17 July. From there it marched to the Bois de Foret Domiale. The march up to the line that night was made under the greatest of difficulties. The men were exhausted at the outset. The night was pitch dark and the roads, soaked with rain, were slippery clay. The mass confusion of men crossing through marching ranks from other units contributed to a near disaster. In the dark men were mixed up with those from other outfits and it would be hours before they finally reached their jumping-off point. All were exhausted from the night's strain and it was only sheer luck and courage that allowed a massive victory in the morning.

Maurice Shearer and 3/5 had a relatively easy time of it compared with 1/5 and 2/5. Yet, the men and officers of 3/5 had been severely taxed by their movement forward and about daybreak had rested at the location of the divisional ration dump. After a rest of about ten minutes, Capt. Thomas Quigley, skipper of the 45th Company, received word that the line was broken and that 3/5 had moved forward. In fact only a few men had. The others were so tired and sleepy from their great exertions that morning they hadn't heard the orders when the word was passed and consequently didn't fall in. Quigley sent runners back to the 16th and 47th Companies, both of which were in the rear of the 45th, to get their companies in motion. Quigley led the battalion forward and they were just a few minutes late arriving at their allotted place in line. At 1000 Major Shearer sent Quigley's second, Capt. Raymond E. Knapp, with the 45th Company to reinforce the 55th Company in a front line position west of Vierzy. Knapp, with apparent utter disregard for his own safety, inspired his men to greater efforts, and through a withering machine gun and heavy artillery fire they went, for a distance of at least a mile and a half. So the 45th Company was rendering support to 2/5 and as already seen the 16th and 20th Companies were aiding Turrill and 1/5.[1] As Shearer later reported, 3/5 mostly just followed the other two battalions that first day, adding support where needed. That report wasn't completely accurate. Several officers of the 47th Company. were out, as the company had been knocked around a bit, so Sgt. Frank Sockel was cited for his "brilliant leadership of his platoon" as well as his own gallantry in action. Poor man would only survive this final day, being killed in action on 19 July 1918.

21 July: Report of operations:

> This battalion left camions in a.m. 17 July 18 near MORIENVAL and moved into woods of RETZ. At about 5:30 p.m. we advanced into woods about 5 kil. At 9:00 p.m. the battalion advanced to attack with 1st and 2nd Bn s of 5th Marines arriving at CRE. DE MONTGOBERT about 4:30 a.m. 18 July 18.
>
> This Bn. advanced as a reserve and occupied the French trenches in rear of jumping off line.
>
> Later moved to advance line of trenches. At request of C.O. 2nd Bn., 45th Co. (less 10 men) [Capt. Thomas Quigley] was sent in to re-inforce 55th Co. [Capt. Elliott Cooke, USA] at about 8 a.m. After reconnaissance the 20th Co. [Capt. Richard N. Platt] and 16th Co. [Capt. Robert Yowell] were sent to support the 1st Bn. At order of Div. Commander a provost guard of 30 men, 2 officers was established at CRE-DE-MONTGOBERT from 47th Co [Case]. The balance of 47th Co. was used to escort prisoners to rear and bring ammunition forward.
>
> The Bn. P.C. was then moved to VERTE FEUILLE FME. with orders to Bn. C.O. to prevent all straggling to the rear and collect and forward all men to front line. This duty continued till 3 a.m. 20 July 18 when division was withdrawn from line. This Bn. joined 5th Regt. in position in woods at Cre. FOURNEAUX.
>
> signed M.E. SHEARER.

Following the attack launched by the 5th Marines on 18 July, the balance of the fighting was left for the 6th Marines on the 19th of July.

Marbache

In the month of August and through early September, the 2d Division would be in a rather quiet place for rest and replacements. Little if any contact with the enemy took place until 12 September. Few if any messages originated by 3/5 during this period.

St. Mihiel

12 September 1918: Message from Feland, commanding officer, 5th Marines, to Shearer, commanding officer, 3d Battalion]: "Commander of tanks reports that he reported to you & you stated that you had received no instructions regarding tanks. You will see that when tanks report to you as ordered you will issue the necessary instructions to them and direct the pioneers who are detailed to your Bn. to assist tanks. Send in position report every half hour." At 1230 Feland sent orders to the three battalion commanders to "Close up on 3d Brigade."

It appears that Shearer had "lost" the two companies. Earlier the commanding officer of the 23d Infantry had requested two companies, which were the 45th and 47th. Shearer sent a message to Feland at 1340: "When tank officer reported I told him I had no instructions for him at that time as I was in French trenches. I detailed a liaison man for him and turned him over the pioneers detailed. He has no complaint. He failed to send his liaison man to me as agreed. If my 47 [Moseley] & 45 [Quigley] cos. can be located please send them up. My battalion had marched when I returned from your P.C."

Feland again sent to his three battalion CO's a message, no time given: "THIAUCOURT has been taken and 3d Brig. is now making 2nd day attack. This regt must move." At 1555 Feland again sent the three "recalcitrants" another message: "The 9th Infantry have taken JAULNY. It is imperative that we press forward so our leading Bn is in touch with the 9th Inf." At 1605 he even brought Neville, now brigade commanding officer, into the fray: "Enclosed copy of order sent to Bns. Will do all possible to get them closed up and as soon as possible will let you know disposition from the new P.C."

An hour later he was able to advise Neville that "regiment beginning to come up to these positions." Then at 1725: "In view of Turrill's report that the 9th Inf. occupy the BOIS DU FEY and are digging in, I have ordered the 3rd Batt. to occupy ravine just on the south edge of the woods." Message from Feland to Neville, sent 2015: "Two companies of the 3d Batt have been sent the Colonel of the 23d Inf who had just requested them of Maj. Shearer. These were the two companies that Shearer had in the ravine south of BOIS DU FEY."

A corrected message was sent 2040: "I enclose herewith message just received from Maj. Shearer which corrects my message in regard to supporting the Infantry with two companies. Shearer has sent all that he has with him south of BOIS DU FEY."

This message was from "Sister" [Neville] to "Surprise" [Lejeune?] at 2130: "CO 5th reports that his leading battalion the 3d has at the urgent request of the CO 9th Infantry, sent two companies and machine gun company to support left flank of 9th. His other two companies are not definately located at present time."

Message from Shearer to Feland, no hour. "Whereabouts of 45th and 47th Cos. still unknown. Col. of 9th *urgently* requested support of 2 Cos. and M.G. to enable him to hold his present line. Account emergency 16th and 20th and part M.G. Co have been sent forward to reinforce his left flank."

13 September: Message from Shearer to Feland, sent 0845, "Enclosing casualty report. Am getting coordinates of Co 20–16 location plotted and will forward same at once. Have officer looking up C.O. 9 Inf to learn when he will be able to release my Cos. No news yet of 45–47 Co. Searching parties out. 16–20 Cos. are with left flank of 9 Inf. Capt. Yowell's report enclosed. Will report to you in person as soon as I can get some information in." Message from Shearer to Feland, sent at 5:05 p.m.: "20 & 16 Cos. in reserve positions. 45 & 47 Cos. not arrived yet. Have reported to C.O. 9th and taken over command of reserves. Colonel Stuart has moved his P.C. to place selected for you by Lt. Col. Turrill this a.m. There is plenty of vacant room left."

I have been unable to determine just what happened to the 45th and 47th Companies and how Shearer could have misplaced them. At any rate I believe it was the main cause for his eventual transfer to an Army school at Langres.

Message from Yowell, 16th Company, to Shearer, no time. "Everything quite here. Would it be possible to hurry our kitchens forward. A hot cup of coffee would put new life in every-body. Platt [20th] and I are going out to look the lines over now and will let you know if anything happens. Have you found the 45th or 47th?"

14 September: Captain Richard N. Platt, commanding officer, 20th Company, sent to Shearer, no time: "Have gotten Co. into woods & am digging in behind Capt. Moseley [47th]. More news later."

Captain Thomas Quigley, commander of the 45th Company, sent several messages to Shearer describing what his company was doing. Apparently, and it isn't clear from the messages, they were afraid that 3/5 might fire upon them. Another report—from L.W.T. Waller, Jr., commanding the 6th Machine Gun Battalion, with no time nor date but assumed to be on the 14th—stated "3d Bn. 5th Marines occupy woods to the west of JAULNY. 45 and 16 Cos. on right of river and 47 and 20th on left of river in woods Bois du Rupt."

15 September: Message from Feland to Neville, time 0210, "The enclosed messages from C.O. 45th Co 3d Bn. and [Lt.] Col. Turrill [assistant brigade commanding officer] explain themselves. Will continue to forard reports as fast as received here." Message from Turrill to Feland, time 0615: "Shearer left JAULNY about 5:15 a.m. he went on EAST side of river. Platt on the West side of the river, both have disappeared toward front, there has been no rifle fired heard here only intermittent M.G. fire on the west side of the river. About a little west of JAULNY has been heavy shelling around here. Valley is full of smoke."

Message from Shearer to Feland, from Post of Command 365.0-243.3, at 0620: "45th Co. along E and W ridge 365.0—E236.6 243.5. 16 Co. in support position 365.0-243.3. Woods patrolled. No enemy found. Outposts along line directed will be immediately established. 16th Co. & 45th Co. kitchens, rations and watercarts can be sent to present P.C. cover darkness. (Previously sent in) 47th Co. 2 a.m. Sept. 15, reported woods clear and liaison established with 6th Inf. [5th U.S. Division] but expects to regain same this a.m. Telephone line being established. 2 (two) platoons 49th Co will hold outpost positions along line held by 45th Co. Exact location outposts will be sent in when established. Forwarded LAT."

Shearer sent to Feland, at 1915, "The Co. of relieving Bn. was directed by me here to go to 1st Bn. P.C. JAULNY where he could men who could take him to 20–47 Cos. It was the understanding that he would arrange with Captains of Cos direct to arrange for guides for tonight. I will have a guide from 20 & 47 Co. at 1st Bn. P.C. JAULNY to take him in. He seemed to want me to furnish guides to bring him from his present position to the front line. Obviously I could not do that as my men know no more of the route than he does. I am handicapped in making arrangements as we have no details. Orders state relief tonight and permissable roads only."

Message from Lt. Oliver B. Cunningham, 15th Field Artillery, at 3d Battalion Post of Command, to commanding officer 2d Battalion (5th Marines?) at 1930:

> 3d Bn., 5th Regt. will be relieved tonight by 309th Infantry ... [78th Division] 1st Bn. position unchanged.
>
> Enemy observed loading motor trucks in REMBERCOURT at 5:30 p.m. This town may be visited by advancing patrols after tonights relief. Battery in BOIS DE LA PERRIERE Cal. 150 continues increasingly active firing on JAULNY RIVER Valley north of JAULNY and BOIS DE LA MONTAGNE steadily between 6 and 7 p.m.—Causing losses in our infantry. C.O. 1st and 3d Bns., 5th Regt. request maximum amount of harrasing fire on heights north of REMBERCOURT and MON PLAISIR FARM, and German positions north thereof during period of relief.

16 September: Message from "SLAP" (Feland) to "Sister" (Neville) at 1845 p.m. "3D BN. RELIEVED BY 2ND BN. 309TH INF. 1ST BN. RELIEVED BY 3D BN. OF 309TH INF. IN BOIS D'HEICHE."

17 September: Report of operations:

> On Sept. 11 at 8:30 p.m. the 3d Bn left BOIS DE LA RAPPE and marched to a communication trench at LIRONVILLE, then to a support position along the road east of LIMEY, this position was reached at 5:00 a.m. Sept. 12, 18 this battalion being the leading battalion of the 5th Regiment. About 6:00 a.m. received an order to advance to the old French line trenches, and then to advance and continue to advance until the battalion was 600 yds in rear of the rear element of the 9th Inf. This position was reached about 6:00 p.m. Sept. 12, 1918 at BOIS DU FEY east of THIAUCOURT, where the battalion bivouaced. About 3:00 a.m. Sept. 13 sent the 16th and 20th cos to reenforce the left wing of the 9th Inf. those companies reporting back at 9:00 p.m. same date. At 7:30 p.m. Sept 14 the 45th and 47th Cos were ordered on patrol duty and to establish outposts. The 45th Co. patrolled the BOIS DE HAILBAT, the 47th Co patrolled the BOIS DU RUPT. At 11:00 p.m. Sept. 14, 1918 the 16th and 20th cos were ordered into a support position in rear of the 1st Bn. 5th Marines in expectation of a counter attack, no attack materialized and the 16th Co was ordered up to support the 45th Co. in BOIS DE HAILBAT and the 20th in support of the 47th in BOIS DE LA MONTAGNE. On Sept. 15 at about 5:30 a.m. the Battalion consolidated its position during the day and the following morning Sept. 16 at 10:00 a.m. the relief was complete and Headquarters moved out to BOIS DE L'HEICHE, being relieved by the 309th Inf. [78th Infantry Division]. The Battalion was all assembled & marched to BOIS DU MINORVILLE arriving about 9:00 p.m. By order of Maj. Shearer,
>
> (sgd) J.[ames] J. Brennan, 2nd Lt. M.C. Adjutant

29 September: Report of operations: "At 6:00 p.m. the 3d Bn in command of Capt. H.[enry] L. Larsen left its billets COURTISOLS and embarked in camions about 7:17 p.m. same date, disembarking at 1 a.m. September 30, 1918, two kilometers south of SUIPPES, and marched to a point four (4) kilometers east of SUIPPES where we bivouaced. The Battalion marched from the above mentioned point at 7:30 p.m. October 1st, 1918, to BRAAQUE where we took a reserve position relieving a battalion of the 219 French Infantry and one battalion of the 255 French Infantry."

Maurice Shearer left the battalion on 28 September, after the end of the 4th Brigade's commitment at St. Mihiel. I can find no written record of his relief but because he ran into a great deal of difficulty in maintaining control over his four companies and knowing where they were, plus the fact that he and Feland had a disagreement over the "tank incident," this seems to suggest that he was persona non grata. The change-over probably came and Brennan was temporarily in charge. Captain Larsen again assumed command and appears to have done as well as could be expected during the next two bloody periods to come.

Blanc Mont

The 2d Division was next called upon to support the French Army at a very troublesome place. It is know as Blanc Mont and although the division's casualties were again too high for the ground they bought with their lives, Petain himself claimed that the "taking of Blanc Mont is the single greatest achievement of the 1918 campaign [in the] Battle of Liberation." And since he was one of the three finest military men in the French Army he should know. Foch and Mangin were the others.

1 October 1918: Message from Feland to Larsen, time 0200. Same message sent to all three battalion commanders: "We enter the lines tonight. Have everything ready to leave on a moments notice. Draw ammunition, pyrotechnics, etc."

2 October: Message from Larsen, Post of Command Baraque, to Feland, time 0500, "Have relieved reserve Bn. of left regiment and now awaiting word from two companies relieving reserve Bn. 265th Regt. [French] on our right. 77th Co. M.G. have also relieved their unit in this sector (left). Am now establishing relay courier services between French Regtal Hdqts in SOMME PY and Brigade Hdqts. at 268.3-274.5. Will communicate immediately I hear from two companies on right. My P.C. at 268.2-275.3."

Message from Larsen to Feland, time 0655, "All O.K. Relief completed about 4:00 a.m. but unable to get from relief of regiment on right until now. Here with is rough sketch of positions of companies" (sketch not available).

Message from Larsen to Feland, time 0735. "As near as we can determine the companies are located as shown on accompanying sketch. I just heard from the 17th & 49th [1/5] so have not been able to report a satisfactory relief until now. Capt. [Frank] Whitehead [67th, also 1/5] reports that he is very much exposed & has to sit tight. Has been sniped at. So has intelligence officer, who met Frenchmen returning from front lines who said Germans had left Tr.[ench] d'Essen on left of main road from SOMME-PY. French Maj. has left. Relief satisfactory but liaison poor."

Message from Larsen to Maj. Robert E. Messersmith, commanding officer of 2/5, time 0735: "Have had my runners sent to Regtal since 2:30 a.m. Have trached them and believe they have located his present P.C. I have not seen anything of your doctors. I am sending you rough disposition of my companies in trenches with fairly good shelter from shell fire. Please forward to [Captain Alphonse] De Carre [commanding officer, Headquarters Company, 5th Regiment] for me. Tell them I am trenches & re shelter. [On reverse side] Doctors have been with us since 6:30 a.m.—[1st Lt] G.[eorge] A. Plambeck, Adjutant, 3d Bn."

Message from Feland to Larsen, no time listed: "Have you any 37 m.m. guns with you? If so have them work up this way. My P.C. is in tunnel under railroad track at 269.4-277.2." Message from Larsen to Feland, at 0845: "Have no 37 m.m. with Bn. now. He did not stay with us on march last night. I am trying to locate them now, and will send them forward as soon as possible and notify you. The right of 45 Co. is resting on road leading S.E. from SOMME-PY (right of Bn.). Our phone should be connected in a few minutes."

Message to all three Bn Co's from Feland at 1900: "Unless countermanded the attack will take place at 6:30 a.m. Oct. 3, 1918 in accordance with verbal instructions and the tentative plan given you. The attack will probably be preceeded by an artillery preparation of twenty minutes. This regiment supporting the 6th Marines in the attack." Message from Larsen to Capt. John H. Fay, commanding officer, 8th Machine Gun Company, at 2020: "Have received 100 picks, 100 shovels, 100 wire cutters for 5th Regt. What disposition will be made of same? All C.O.'s received rations & overcoats at dusk."

Second Lt. Timon J. Torkelson, battalion intelligence officer, sent this to De Carre, regiment intelligence officer, at 2100: "The companies of this Battalion will take up positions as indicated on attached sketch [not included] at 5:00 a.m., Oct. 3, 1918. The Battalion P.C. will be at 267.5-275.5 and will proceed up communication trench leading aproximately north thru this point. The first jump to companies will be to railroad embarkment thru points 267.0-276.7 and 268.0-276.75. Please transmit this information to higher authorities for Capt. Larsen."

Sometime during that day an order was issued from the 5th Regiment to itself describing what would happen on the following day. The regiment would attack in a column of battalions with 1st Battalion leading followed by the 2d Battalion and with the 3d Battalion in reserve, all following the 6th Marines. The objective of the brigade was Blanc Mont–Schwaben-Py Lone–Medeah Ferme.

3 October: Message from Feland to Larsen, at 0430: "H Hour has been fixed at 5:50 a.m. preceded by 5 minutes artillery preparation. If we allow only 1500 meters head of the 6th Regt. to head of 5th Regt. Messersmith [2/5] will cross the Trench ESSEN the jumping off place of the 6th Regt. at 6:50 a.m. about. This may guide you a little in advance. Be careful of interfering with advance of reserve battalion of 6th Regt. which is now on your left and perhaps a little in your rear. Get in liaison with any French troops on your left in the advance. Other instructions unchanged. This P.C. will not move *before* 7:30 a.m."

Larsen, at Post of Command Dusseldorf Trench, sent to Feland at 0615: "3d Bn, 6th Reg't just leaving this trench at 6:15 a.m. I am in position to move forward with proper interval when 6th has advanced." Torkelson sent to De Carre, at 0730: "Batt. P.C. moved forward to 268.0-276.8 on south side of R.R. track. The whole battalion is on south bank of track. The 20th Co. is on the left of the line with their left rests on 266.7-276.3. The 16th Co. is on their right. 45 Co. on right of 16th. 47 Co. on right of 45th. All companies are on south side of track. As soon as Batt. moves forward the 20th Co. will get behind the 16th whose left is now at 266.8-276.3." Larsen sent to Feland at 0750: "Am advancing from R.R. Embankment to trenches in our front. Have just seen message from 3d of 6th who are 1500 yds in front of Tr. ESSEN. (Reported in message) from 3d 6th."

Message from 1st Lt. Fred Thomas, acting commanding officer of the 45th Company:

> STRIKE OUT ANYTHING NOT APPLICABLE AND SEND TO NEXT HIGHER HQ. AT ONCE.
> For use of Company, Platoon and Patrol Commanders.
> SITUATION REPORT
> From "L" [45th] Co, Fifth Regiment.
> Map Reference App. Coord. 267.9E-277.N
> My company is now at trench line ELBE.
> Our casualties about ½ percent.
> Enemy's artillery is firing on Trench ELBE from northwest.
> I am in touch on my right with 2nd Batt. who are at Trench ELBE. On my left with 47th Co. who are at same trench.
> I intend to remain here until 2nd Bn moves forward.
> Hour (9) Nine Mins (10) a.m.

Fred Thomas hopefully wasn't always so loquacious, otherwise he would never have had time to earn two Distinguished Service Crosses, one at Belleau Wood and another at Blanc Mont, and a Navy Distinguished Service Medal. His award at Blanc Mont indicates that he was with the 16th Company. The message could be confused, which wasn't unusual since the materials were compiled a number of years after the event.

Message from Torkelson to De Carre, time 0950: "Batt. P.C. is up BOYAU DE LAND-SHUT at 267.7-277.3. The 16th and 45th Co. are leading elements of 3d Bn. advance. The 20th Co. behind the 16th & 47th is behind the 45th. The 16th and 20th are aproximately ⅛ Kilo to south of Tr. DE PACHA in the trench. Have information that 2nd Bn. P.C. is in Tr. D'ESSEN. Please transmit to higher authority for Capt. Larsen."

Message from Feland to Larsen, time 1120: "Please forward these two messages to C.O. 2nd Bn. [Messersmith] immediately. *This is very important* [emphasis in original]." Larsen replied to Feland, time 12:30 p.m.: "Have forwarded message to C.O. 2nd Bn. re-filling gap to left of 6th joining with French. My battalion is following 2nd Bn. about 300 yds. and will support him. When we stop I will dispose companies in depth for flank protection if exposed. Companies are now advancing and are about 1/2 way up in BOIS SOMME PY. Casualties about 2 percent."

Torkelson sent a message to De Carre at 1300: "20th Co. in edge of BOIS SOMME PY where BOYAU DE PASSAU enters the woods.

16th is in BOYAU DE PASSAU. The head rests at junction of PASSAU with the woods, 45th right resting on 267.8-279.7. 47th is advancing up PASSAU trench about one Kilo to rear of 16th. The 47th is only aproximate. Have received no report from 47th as yet. Will send sketch of position as soon as we get set. (Supplement to report) Report from 47th that it is with 16th." And another at 1420: "On the east side BOIS DE SOMME PY sketch accompaynying [not available]. A French skirmish line is just passing westward thru the wood, possibly to attack on the west side of our objective to the south of BOIS DE SOMME PY. (Supplemental message) P.C. of Batt. changed from 267.25-279.4 to dugout at 267.4-279.55. The French referred to in main message & who are attacking to our west are 3d Reg. French Chasseurs."

Larsen sent this to Maj. George W. Hamilton, commanding officer of 1/5, at 1430: "Am returning your message re 37 mm. 2nd is evidently connecting up 6th Reg't. with French on our left. I am supporting him. Attached is a rough sketch of my disposition and above is my P.C., about. French are moving westward in my rear between these woods and Trench ESSEN. Please forward this note & my disposition to C.O. 5th."

Larsen sent to Feland at 1555:

> No more casualities reported. Will guide my ration carts to my P.C. at dusk. Batty of 75s moved to ravine to our south about 400 yds.
>
> French are attacking westward and are using BOY PASSAU as jum off or support position. 20th Co. is in same trench as 16 at present while French are jammed in Trench PASSAU but 20th will move into PASSAU as soon as congestion is relieved by French. 20th will face westward. 16th has 4 M.G. in position on their left flank covering exposure to N.W. at which point Boche are reported still holding. 20th has another platoon of M.G. covering flank. 45th covers right half of original sector facing northward. 47 is in BOYAU AUGSBURG facing east. 45th has 4 M.G. Established liaison with French on left at 11: a.m.

Message from Larsen to Feland, at 2240: "Have been [in] position since ½ hour after leaving you. Have not been able to connect up with 1st Bn. Capt. [Frank] Whitehead [67th] is behind me but does not know where any other Co. of Bn. or his Bn. P.C. is. Have scouts out in all directions trying to connect up with 1st. Will advance immediately. I know they are in position."

Each battalion and the individual companies of the 5th Marines were having location problems because each unit had to turn leftward to engage the Germans on that flank. Orders were given to tie in with the 6th Marines on the right and the French on the left. The French weren't there, but plenty of Germans were. Consequently the left flank would continue to be a burden for both regiments for several days to come. Because of the ensuing disaster, reportedly Lejeune proclaimed that he would never serve in liaison with French units anywhere or anytime afterward.

4 October: Message from Larsen at post of command of 2/6, to Feland, time 0315: "Hamilton has located 67th giving him 1 Co. and two one halfs from two companies total. Messersmith has 1¾ Companies. We will move forward at 6:00 a.m. If they not located any more men the two outfits of them will form one battalion in my rear. They seem to be having trouble finding their men. My front line is lying back of front line of 6th about 10 yds." Message from Larsen to Feland, time 0600: "Have started advance at 6:00 a.m. 51st and 55th joined Messersmith at 5:45 a.m. At same time Boche artillery started shelling our front lines quite heavily. Have no report of casualties yet. My first phase is in position wherever we connect up with 23d Inf. From there we will attempt to make objective."

The formation of the advance of the Fifth Regiment was as follows: Larsen 3/5 first, with Messersmith 2/5 next and last, Hamilton's 1/5. Feland sent to Larsen, time 0615: "Brigade orders that we dig in. 6th Marines are coming up now. Get this to Messersmith and Hamilton."

The situation was beginning to heat up for the 5th Marines. An extract from a message to Feland by Messersmith at 0805 partly describes it: "3d Bn. has gone ahead but we are being fired upon from right & left by M.G. On left here is a field piece with direct fire upon us. Have seen a number of casualties. Our left flank is exposed. Plenty of Hun planes, no allied. We had no food last night."

At 0600 3/5 led off with an attack up the road toward St. Étienne, two companies abreast, with the 47th Company (Moseley) leading on left and the 16th (Yowell) on the right. The 45th Company (Quigley) was on the left and 20th (Capt. Gilder D. Jackson) the right in the second line. Message from Larsen to Feland, time 0825:

> My companies appear to have lost liaison with one another. I cannot trace 45th Co my right front. Quigley and his second in command evacuated. 47th just passes forward of me on right and 20th is on my left now. Some of 16 is forward of 20th on left. Have not found Yowell. My P.C. is at 266.1-282.1.
>
> We are being shelled quite heavily by short range artillery from N.W. and we are flanked by machine guns from all sides. Need help to protect flanks from batt. in support. Am requesting that from him now but have no information of his P.C. [Hamilton, 1/5].
>
> Have not been able to connect up with battalion of 3d Brig. on my right. Yowell just reports connecting with one company of 23d about 200 yds to my front. Verifying that now.

A few minutes later Messersmith sent a message to Maj. Ernest (Bull) C. Williams, commanding officer, 2/6, in which he states: "20th Co held up by heavy fire on left of sector along road. The company needs assistance and I have none to send. What can you do for us? About 265.4-281.5."

The 5th Marines were in what was later referred to as a "box." The French were still south of Blanc Mont Ridge and the Germans were still there, on top and around it. Therefore the 5th Marines had enemy fire coming from front, sides, and rear. It doesn't get any worse than that.

Feland sent a message to the battalion commanding officers at 1040: "When leading Bn. reaches line between point 266.7-283.6 and pt 264.5-283.2 [just before the town of St. Etienne], take good position. Get up stragglers and straggling units, by sending small patrols under energetic officers or N.[on] C.[ommissioned] officers to get them up. Each Bn. must help the other in this. Send in more frequent reports."

Message from Larsen to Feland, time 1102: "Am in liaison with 1st Bn. 23d who now occupy trenches about 266.6-282.0. Maj. Cole [commanding officer, 1/23] though he had gained objective but I convinced him of his position. He has orders for left of his sector to travel up ST. ETIENNE Road about our center. I have connected up with him. My battalion will advance to objective immediately. Shelling us. Just reported heavy reserves (no estimate given) moving into wood to our left. Have informed 1st and 2nd Bn. and asked for support of that flank."

Message from Larsen to probably Feland, time 1215: "Order re left of 3d Brig. just received. Am sending out patrol of one platoon under officer to travel eastward to far side of narrow guage [railroad] and then northward cautiously to establish combat liaison."

Torkelson sent to De Carre at 1230: "Woods ahead of us are filled with machine guns. Large trenches in front & running east & west are being filled with Boche. The seem to be approaching trenches in skirmish lines. As yet it has not been determined if these skirmish lines are going past trenches. Not much shelling today; but snipers are picking off a few of our men."

Message from Larsen to Hamilton, time 1300: "I cannot hold front longer. 1st or second must come up to take over or assist." Then Larsen to Feland, time 1300: "Cannot hold front line longer; that is, my position S.E. from position as indicated for 23d Inf. this morning. Have evacuated three company commanders and many officers—Having hard time to hold men together. Am sending this request to 1st and 2nd Bn. to help hold. Am being shelled heavily and m.g. fire from 270 degree of compass. Situation is critical. I sent word back with your liaison officer that Boche was preparing for counter attack from our left front."

At the same time Larsen sent Messersmith the same message as to Hamilton underlining "*Urgent*." He also sent a message but not known to whom. In it he gives his coordinates: "266.1-282.3 & 265.2-281.7. Our danger lies in being cut off from left rear. I think 6th Reg't. *must* come up to protect left flank. (Casualties estimated by officers 60 percent)."

The situation was becoming intolerable but no one in charge made a move to stop the slaughter of the Fifth Marines.

Message from Larsen to Feland, time 1405: "I am not in position or condition to make attack as per Div. order this p.m. Good stunt will be for artillery to give them hell from 300 yds in advance of 266.3-282.1 & 265.1-282.0 and to our left flank. Boche occupies trenches our objective and more coming in. M. guns flanked us from both flanks. No Co. officers with 45th so my Adjutant [1st Lt. Thurston J. Davies] is now in command."

At 1424 Feland reported to Major General John A. Lejeune, commanding officer, 2d Division: "They have been badly shot up [the regiment] and had very heavy casualties. 3 company commanders evacuated and one battalion commander." The commander is unknown—must be an error because Hamilton, Messersmith and Larsen were still with their respective battalions. Feland didn't say that they have their location but he got word back that it is almost impossible for them to hold on; must be Larsen he is referring to. His opinion was that they could not advance under the conditions. "The whole woods were full of machine guns. Getting artillery and machine gun fire from the flank."

Message from Messersmith to Feland re: 3/5, sent 1500: "The 3d Bn. are all intermixed and thoroughly disorganized. Some companies reduced to 10 or 30 men, so reported by those in command. All my captains have been wounded or killed. All my present Bn. Staff wounded except one. Am having hard time holding men in line where no officers are. Have not attained objective. Before anything can be done reinforcements must be had and must cover ground on both flanks, cleaning out Machine Gun nests especially so on left flank. We are doing our best to hold ground gained." I have included Messersmith's entire message because it affects all three battalions and best explains at this juncture just how bad things were going for the regiment.

Larsen sent the following to Feland at 1530: "Holding positions 266.3-282.1 & 284.2-281.5 and trying to organize in depth. Have not heard of H hour but Messersmith has told me he has information that it was 2:30 p.m. but [2d Lt. Frederick] Israel was going back to try to stop it. Had liaison with 23d Inf. all morning but his runner is now missing." Israel was a former enlisted man with Headquarters Company who earned a DSC, Navy Cross, Silver Star and Croix de Guerre for his work at Blanc Mont.

At 4:00 p.m. Feland sent a message to Hamilton that help from the 6th Marines was on its way and "good work in sticking to your position. We must hold on." Larsen then sent to Feland, time 1700:

> Front line advanced to positions about 400 yds of objective and there flanked on all sides by M.G.'s and suffered such casualties they had to withdraw. It would have been absolutely fatal to have tried to go further so we withdrew to no. edge of woods and stopped. Boche counter attacked and was repulsed. They shelled us out of woods and we were obliged to retire to our first position *where I found some 2nd Bn. men occupying our shelters* [emphasis added].
>
> 45 formed line to their rear a few yds and when they passed thru the men in pits began to fall back to S.W. All Bn. Hdqts were utilized to stop men and organize on present line where men are pretty much mixed. Boche attempted another counter here from left and a little N. but was repulsed. We have many casualties from snipers flanking positions. Aproximate strength 16th 3 ½ platoons, 20th about 3 platoons, 45—1 platoon, 47—1 platoon. [Supplemental message on reverse side] Will give you report from patrols I have sent about 1000 yds to our front to get dope on enemy or friendly troops on flanks that may be there.

Hamilton also sent a report to Feland about the near rout which Larsen touches on above. He accused Messersmith of leading his battalion in a very hasty retreat, which Messersmith later denied, saying it was anything but a rout. The above message sort of puts the finishing touch on what was happening to the 2nd Battalion at that time.

Message from Torkelson to De Carre, time 1810: "The enemy are shelling us with a very heavy bombardment of everything they have. A company of 6th has just arrived to help situation. What we need is an artillery barrage. Have been in touch with liaison officer of the 12th Field Artillery. Casualties are heavy." Message from Feland to Larsen, at 1815: "Brigade orders that we dig in. 6th Marines are coming up now. Get this to Messersmith and Hamilton."

And while these movements and messages were circulating around, Colonel Stone, commanding officer of the 23d Infantry, sent Larsen a message that his regiment and the 9th Infantry were under orders to fall back to "yesterday's position at 7:00 p.m." This meant that Larsen's right flank would be wide open, just like his left.

Message from Larsen to "Slap" (Feland), sent at 1945:

> 16th Co. patrol reports Boche (some) absolutely 250 yds from his left flank as indicated on last sketch (W) [not available].
>
> Have no report of 74 [1/6, 1st Lt. Leo D. Hermle] being able to get into position. I had given them guide and they had started for position when I sent last sketch but from reports they met opposition before they got very far to West. We are in serious situation now with two flanks exposed. 23d just reported withdrawing. Now shall we attempt to cover original front of sector occupying trenches to right[?] 55th Co. is in those trenches now. None except 74 of 6th are in touch with us as far as I can determine. Am using M.G's to protect flanks and cover front with cross fire. Boche have our P.C. and lines spotted for shelling.

Message from "Slap 1" to probably Lejeune at 2135:

> A 16th Co. patrol reports Boche 1250 yards from left flank. Have no report of 74th Co. 6th Regiment being able to get into position. I have sent them guides and they have started for position but have not reached position yet. They met opposition before they got very far to the west. We are in a serious condition with both flanks exposed. The 23d just reported that they were withdrawing. Now shall we attempt to cover the original front of sector by occupying trenches to the

right. The 55th Co is in those trenches now. None except 74th Co. 6th Regiment are in touch with us as far as I can determine. I am using machine guns to protect flank.

Message from Feland to Larsen, time 2150:

The whole situation has been laid before Gen. Lejeune. The order is that the 5th Regiment must hold. The 3d Brigade line only withdrew the troops north of us to position opposite our right. All artillery protection possible will be given. Give me any targets you want fired on or any information you can regarding accuracy of our artillery fire. The left of the 3d Bn. is approximately at 267.2-282.4 at present marked MEDEAH-WEICHE near position of narrow guage road. We must get in liaison with them and fill if possible any considerable gap. The 6th Regiment will be again ordered to support us. [Maj. George K.] Shuler [commanding officer, 3/6] will attack the machine gun nest, on our left flank to-morrow morning. We must stay where we are. Get this to Hamilton and Messersmith.

Unusual message and somewhat convoluted. How Lejeune expected that a regiment down to about 400 effectives would be able to stave off a German attack that night isn't explained. No further explanation is available.

5 October: Message from Larsen to Feland, time 1215:

Order re left of 3d Brig just received, am sending out patrol of one platoon under officer to travel eastward to far side of narrow guage and then northward cautiously to establish combat liaison. They will then occupy trenches running N.W. SE just to west of 3d Brig on right of our sector. Platoons will then send scouts back by direct route to rest of 18th Co. [Capt. John R. Foster] and conduct the remaining platoons to the trenches where they will form strong point and connect with 3d Brig on right. We will connect with 18th Co. with troops we have now on right of road to protect our right flank tonight. All these changes of position will be made under cover of darkness if possible to complete same as M.G. Snipers work all day and artillery must have good observation. With our outfit connected with 3d Brig on right and 6th Reg't to clean up or protect our left flank, we can hold. It is difficult to give definate or locate definate targets but I have already indicated on sketch by [not available] where I know German troops are holding fast with strong M.G. positions for flanking fire. They have been giving us hell with artillery all day too as well as the worst M.G. I have ever seen. Will give you sketch of my line as soon as located.

Message from Larsen to Feland, time 0545:

Patrol sent to reported left flank of 3d Brig. and patrol reports running into Hdqts 23 Inf. who informed the Lieut. in charge that left flank of 23 Inf advanced and that they did not know where it was. We have just received word of expected German attack from MEDEAH FME. at daybreak and as it is just about that time we are sending 18 Co. to trenches as originally planned—organize a strong point and from there locate and connect with left flank of 23d. A Lieut. of 23 Inf–3d Bn. reported at 3:00 a.m. that their left flank was about at a point 600 yds. W. of r.r. junction and that they were in connection with 5th Reg't on their left. He reported to Messersmith at this P.C. but the fact of connection with 5th has not been verified by any of the companies of the 2nd or 3d as yet. Early last evening, about 20 hours our own light arty. was firing on us and about midnight our heavy stuff hit us but evidentaly by continual Very signals and thru arty liaison officer the fire was stopped as we have received no more reports of friendly arty. hitting us. Just received report from 45th Co. that just on his right is a small mixed detachment of companies of other battalions and they are connected up with 23d Inf. who are now in trenches again at 266.3-282.5.

We are using extra machine guns from companies of support battalion to strengthen flank and think we can hold without doubt. 23d seems to run up trenches indicated and bend down railroad toward junction.

At 0945 Lejeune sent Feland a lengthy memo in which he lauded the activities of the 5th Regiment, and it appears that it finally got through to him in what bad shape the regiment was. He commented, "Our casualties have been pretty heavy, but we think when we count up it wont be quite as heavy as we think now." He was wrong.

6 October: Message from Torkelson to De Carre, time 0804: "We are still holding. Heavy artillery fire still continues. Have lost contact, temporarily, with the 23d on our right but will try an re-establish liaison as soon as possible. Some American unit is advancing on our right. Six enemy avions went south over our position this morning at 8:00. Casualties are still coming in due to enemy artillery fire last night. Our own artillery seems to have the range better now; for we see no rockets going up lately. No Allied planes have been seen as yet. The unit advancing on our right is the 23d. They are encountering heavy machine gun fire."

Torkelson sent this to De Carre at 1105: "Intermittent enemy artillery fire continues. About 20 allied planes seen going north. Machine gun sniping comes from our right. There are also enemy batteries in this locality. If there was an artillery observation post on our hill they could do some effective firing although the target is out of our sector & to the right. It is passed around that the 6th and 23d have reached their objective and are straightening out the line. Am sending back maps captured in a dugout near our dressing station."

Report of operations: "We marched to a trench two (2) kilometers south of relieving point where we bivouaced until 8 p.m. October 9th, when we marched to a point 2 kilometers south of SOUIAN, arriving there at 2 a.m. October 10th, 1918, continuing the march about 10:00 a.m. October 10th, 1918, to Camp Coutes, where we arrived about 1 p.m. October 10th, 1918, and billeted. HENRY L. LARSEN."

For the next couple of days the 5th Marines were in no condition to do anything more at Blanc Mont. It seems that the French Army finally got to where the 4th Brigade was stalled and the 16th Company was assigned to be liaison with their division. Otherwise the regiment was finished.

12 October: Report of operations:

1. About 8:00 p.m. on the evening of October 1, 1918, the Third Bn left woods about 4 kilometers north and 2 kilometers east of SUIPPES, position of Army Reserve, and marched via SOUAIN to trenches [coordinates given] east of road, relieving battalion of 219th French Infantry, and battalion of adjoining regiment on the right reserve position of front line regiments. Relief completed at 3:30 a.m., October 2, 1918.
2. At 5:00 a.m., October 3, companies took positions in trenches as indicated in attached sketch marked A [no sketch available].
    (a) This Battalion was second line battalion of supporting regiment during the attack, which started at 5:50 a.m., following the Second Bn of the Fifth at about 500 yards. Advances were made by bounds until position aproximately 279.5 [no map] was reached. At this position orders were received for the Fifth Regiment to pass through the Sixth, and continue the attack, Third Bn being in the front line in this attack, and objective being line of trenches about 600 yards southeast of ST. ETIENNE.
    (b) The terrain over which this operation was executed is of a gently rolling nature, and covered with several small woods, affording good cover for enemy and machine gun nests.
    (c) During the time the Battalion was in support and moving forward the formation of platoon columns was adopted, two companies in front line and two in support.
    (d) This formation was found very suitable for protection against the artillery resistance

which the enemy was offering, but owing to constant machine gun fire from our left flank which was exposed, companies took formation in communicating trenches, affording best cover during our advance. Enemy was entirely cleared from territory in our advance as supporting battalion, and there was no mopping up necessary.

When halt was made at about 279.5, position was taken as indicated in sketch B. This position was necessary to protect exposed flanks. Liaison on the left rear was established with the assaulting battalion of the 69th French Infantry, the Commanding Officer of which informed me that he had met strong opposition in woods at 265.7-278.6, and his advance was held up.

(e) At about 6:30 p.m. this battalion was ordered to position about 267.4-281.1 and 266.0-280.3, and attack as soon as First Bn was in position for my support. At 7:30 p.m. this Battalion was reported in position ready for attack, two companies in front line in one line of skirmishers, with two companies in support. Owing to the difficulty in organizing battalions in support, advance could not be made until 6:00 a.m., October 4th, the time agreed upon among Battalion commanders as zero hour.

At 6:00 a.m. advance was made, the Third Bn in above indicated formation, the flank platoons of support companies taking a position in column of half platoons for cover-up flanks. Owing to the wide front to be covered in advance, practically two kilometers, and also to the fact that our flanks were exposed, this formation was most feasible. The advance was made with little resistance from the front, but terrible machine gun fire from the flanks. The Battalion advanced to position aproximately 266.4-282.5 and 265.1-282.2, where liaison was established with First Bn , 23d Infantry on our right. The undersigned personally visited the Commanding Officer of the First Battalion, 23d, and was informed by him that he [was] under the impression that his objective had been gained, and that the 23d would not advance further without orders. The undersigned also verified the fact that part of the 23d Infantry was in our sector, owing to the fact that the road running northwest-southeast, practically up the center of our sector, and almost parallel to our advance, was designated as the left of their sector. While in this last position as indicated above, the Battalion was organized in the same formation as for first advance, 47th Co right front, 16th Co left front, and advance continued about noon.

Advance was made under heavy machine gun fire from front and flanks, to position aproximately 266.2-283., and 264.7-282.8, when heavy machine gun fire from flanks, both of which were entirely exposed, and direct artillery barrage from heights north of ST. ETIENNE, made further advance impossible, whereupon orders were issued to withdraw to position left about noon (see sketch C) with 23d Infantry on our right, and only the left flank exposed. 20th Co in support of our left front company formed [a] skirmish line facing west, right of line connecting with the left of 16th Co.

During the afternoon about 350 enemy attempted to counter attack from left front and were repulsed. Later it was verified that a hundred dead Boche lay in position of their first wave. At about 8:00 p.m. about 300 enemy were reported at 265.7-281.5 and 265.3-281.4, approaching in waves, generally in a northeasterly direction from our rear. Next morning much enemy equipment and some machine guns were found as deserted by the enemy.

On the night of the 6th one battalion of the Sixth Regiment passed through our front line, leaving us in support.

(f) The 37m/m gun [1 pounder] was used effectively on the afternoon of October 4th against the machine gun nest at 266.1-283.2. Our positions were constantly under enemy shell-fire and sniping from enemy machine gun nests.

(g) The attack was made without artillery support, and no support was called for by this Battalion during operations in attack. On two occasions on [the] night of October

5th it was necessary to relay information to the rear that friendly artillery fire was falling short in 23d Infantry's and 6th Marine's front line, causing them to fall back.
(h) While the Battalion was in support, there were no obstacles to pass in our sector, as the attacking regiment throughly cleared all resistance in our sector. During our attack, all enemy resistance to our Battalion was cleared during our progress until the furthest point of the advance was reached, when enemy machine gun fire from concealed positions on our flanks made further advance impossible.
(i) No difficulty was encountered in passing through leading elements when this Battalion leapfrogged 2nd Bn of the Sixth.
(j) Machine gun encounters as described above.
(k) Fighting in intermediate zone consisted in combat with strong rear-guard action, largest number encountered in one unit being aproximately 75 or 100 men.
(l) Immediately that line was established, strong patrols were sent forward and to flanks to verify enemy positions.
(m) Messages were sent direct to destination rather than being relayed, and proved very satisfactory except for distance to Regimental Headquarters, which required too much time.

    Henry L. Larsen, Captain, U.S.M.C.

The report on K [20th] Company was prepared by 1st Lt. Thurston J. Davies of the 45th Company, but commanding the 20th Company at the close of operations.

On October 2nd and 3d, the Company [20th] carried out all orders received from Battalion and Regimental Headquarters. After moving up into the trenches, in readiness, orders were received to attack at 6:00 a.m., October 4th. K Co was in support 400 meters in rear of our company [45th]. The advance was made in four wave formation, the four platoons in line, the first two waves as skirmishers, the others in line of combat groups. The platoon of the 77th Machine Gun Co [6th Machine Gun Battalion] was attached to K Co, and took position on the left flank. The bearing for the advance was 343 degrees. Advance was made without opposition to about 800 meters beyond the railroad track. At this point it was noted that the advance of I Co [16th] had stopped. Enemy machine gun fire was notable from front and left flank. Three patrols were sent to gain liaison with M Co [47th] on the right but were unsuccessful. Two machine guns were posted to guard the left flank, and 15 men of the 4th Platoon under Lieutenant [Earl T.] Martineau took position near them. Contact with the enemy was gained by the detachment. To lessen chances of enemy observation the lines were moved to the right into a small patch of woods, and after fifteen minutes under heavy shell and machine gun fire, the company was moved into a ravine where it remained under verbal instructions from the Battalion Commander [Maj. Henry L. Larsen]. At noon moving to the left of the road an advance was made behind I Co with a bearing of 343 degrees, where heavy machine gun and shell fire from three sides held up the progress of both companies. At this point Captain [David T.] Jackson was wounded, and the company was moved to the left and formed line to cover the left flank. Under verbal orders of the battalion Commander withdrawal was made to the ravine previously held. At 6:00 p.m. a counter attack was threatened. The enemy was observed moving toward the ravine from the left, but patrols reported that they withdrew at once. The company was held in readiness until five outposts of five men each were established for the night, two directly in front of the ravine, two in the rear, and one on the left flank, when the rest of the company was distributed in depth. No change was made in the disposition of the company of October 5th, and it remained in the ravine under heavy shell-fire until the evening of October 6th, when under orders it took position in the trenches [in the rear]. From this time and the close of the operation all orders of the battalion Commander were carried out. The company withdrew from the line on the night of October 9th, beginning at 8:00 p.m.

The total casualties of K Co during operations so far reported are as follows: Killed, 3, Wounded, Officers 2, men 34.

During the operation patrols were sent out as follows:
(a) Contact patrol of 1 N.C.O. and 4 men, October 4th, at 4:45 p.m. to south of ravine, to determine nature of troops advancing from west (see above). Reported enemy troops numbering about 50 advancing in westerly direction.
(b) Combat patrol, Lieutenant [Robert C.] Babcock, and 10 men, October 4th, 6:15 p.m. sent to gain contact with the enemy. Reported enemy withdrawn.
(c) 4 Patrols, each consisting of one N.C.O. and 4 men were sent out from ravine October 5th, 9:00 a.m. to learn position of any friendly troops, and observe as far forward as possible. All patrols advanced with a 345 degree bearing. It was reported by all that enemy machine guns were in the woods directly to the north of the ravine, enemy movement noted along road running East and West in front of ST. ETIENNE, and enemy taking positions in trenches in front of road. The 43d Co was reported 340 yards directly north of the ravine, and the patrol on the right gained contact with the 23d Infantry at aproximately [map coordinates given, no map available].
(d) Two patrols, one N.C.O. and 4 men each, sent out 1:00 a.m. and 2:00 a.m. October 6th, to learn position of friendly troops to the north. Both reported the 43d Co 300 yards to the north and the 2nd Bn of the 6th Regiment holding the line [map coordinates given, no map available]. THURSTON J. DAVIES, 1st Lt. USMC.

The total casualties for the 5th Marines at Blanc Mont came to 1,120 officers and men, of which one hundred eleven died and one hundred fifty-one were missing, the balance being wounded or gassed. Most of that total came on 4 October 1918.

17 October–19 October: Diary—billets—3d Battalion: "CAMP TOMBEAU DES SARAZINS."

20 October: Report of operations: "Entire regiment marched to CAMPS MONTPELIER and des SOUCHES."

21 October: Diary—billets—3d Battalion: "SCAY FARM."

23 October: Report of operations: "Orders received countermanding the relief of the French, thereupon the regiment returned to CAMP MONTPELIER and CAMP DES SOUCHES."

25 October: Report of operations: "Regiment boarded camions at 8:30 a.m. at SOMME-SUIPPES and SOMME TOURBE cross-roads and arrived at LES ISLETTES at 12:30 p.m. Marched to CAMP CABAUD arriving at 3:00 p.m."

26 October: Report of operations: "At 1:30 p.m. regiment marched to woods 1 kilometer southeast of EXERMONT arriving at 11:00 p.m. Bivouaced in these woods," remaining through 29 October.

27 October: Message from Feland to Larsen, noon: "You or your 2nd in command and each company commander or his 2nd in command will report to these headquarters at 1:15 [p.m.] this date to go to the line for reconnaissance." Message from Larsen to Yowell, 16th Co., at 1435: "Regiment will not move tonight. I will be back late tonight. Notify 77th M.G. Co." (Captain Louis de Roode).

On 30 October, at 0800, 1st Lt. Timon J. Torkelson, 3d Battalion intelligence officer, sent a report to Captain Alphonse De Carre, regiment intelligence officer, concerning his reconnoiter of the position held on Hill 263 by the 165th Regiment (the old 69th New York), 42d Division. Torkelson made the report as exciting as he could but nothing of substance appears to have had any impact on the 3d Battalion, 5th Marines.

Later that same date, at 1830, Feland sent each battalion commanding officer the same message when they arrived at new positions "the command passes to the C.G. 42nd Div."

30 October: Report of operations: "At 11:30 p.m. regiment moved to woods 2 kilometers northeast of EXERMONT arriving at 3:00 a.m. October 31st."

31 October: Report of operations: "At 9:00 p.m. regiment moved up in rear of the line held by the 42nd Division [U.S.] or the jump-off line."

The Second Division was barely recovered, somewhat, with some replacements, after the shellacking they took at Blanc Mont, and General Pershing rushed them into another maelstrom farther east.

Meuse Argonne

31 October: Message from Feland to commanding officers, 3d and 2d Battalions, time 2110. A slightly different message went to Hamilton, commanding officer of 1/5. "For carrying out operations ordered in F.[ield] O.[rder] #49 2nd Div, the following has been fixed. D Day Nov. 1, 1918. H Hour 5:30 a.m. (5:30 hours). Move up and take preliminary position by 2:00 a.m. Nov. 1st. M.P. will take prisoners of war north of SOMMERANCE on the SOMMERANCE-LANDRES ET ST. GEORGES ROAD. This order is being sent you in duplicate with all your runners. Acknowledge receipt by one runner. Send the others back when you are in preliminary position for attack with report. Time of Hunt's watch was two (2) minutes too fast."

Message from Larsen to Feland, no time shown: "I understand that 6th Reg't maintains 1000 meters between successive battalions while we keep 500 meters. This might result seriously in case of mopping up and they were not with us. We should sychronize watches."

1 November: Torkelson sent De Carre a message dated 1 Nov. and the time as 0615 in which he included a small sketch of the positions of the 3d Battalion. Unfortunately, the sketch is based upon an entirely different map than is being used in this book. Basically the battalion was moving in a double column of companies, 20th and 45th leading, left to right, followed by the 16th and 47th, same order. He also comments, "Prisoners are coming in continually now. Companies are being held well in hand."

At 0800 Hamilton, whose battalion was leading the attack, followed by the 3d Battalion, sent a message to an unknown person that he had reached his first objective and had lost 5 officers but "few enlisted." A message, no time, was sent to Captain John H. Fay, 8th Machine Gun Company, from Dr. (Lt. Comdr.) Robert J. Lawler, "Can you direct Chief Phar. Mate [Forest T.] Medkirk to 3d Bn or possibly you may have a runner with whom he can go?" At 0815 Torkelson sent another message to De Carre in which he included yet another sketch based upon another map. It simply stated that 3/5 was doing what they were paid to do; also sending prisoners back and "no enemy artillery lately."

Message from "Slap P1," Larsen, to Feland at 1153: "Now at second objective and will go over the top at 12:20 [p.m.] Have met very little resistance to the present but the Boche are firing some small artillery piece from woods Cote [Hill] 300. There are some enemy there too but we do not anticipate any resistance that cannot be overcome casualties one officer and two men wounded. I have liaison with 89th on my right but 6th seems to be behind."

Reports from both the 1st and 3d Battalions were very good. Hamilton had reached his 2d objective, had small losses (5 percent) and he had captured upwards of 500 Germans. At 1420 he advised Feland that the 3d Battalion was "apparently on the objective with 2nd Bn in close support." The 6th was still being reported as being behind the 5th.

Message from Larsen to Feland, at 1430 from Cote 300: "*Gained objective (3d).* Am pushing strong patrols to front to Exploitation line—meeting no opposition, except our own artillery falling short. Enemy artillery is very weak. 6th and 89th are advancing with me on flanks. Will send sketch immediately line is established. Casualties about one percent—captured six pieces of artillery and about 100 prisoners. P.C. still on move. Can you have my rations sent to BAYONVILLE ET CHENNERY. I'll have guide meet."

Larsen sent another message to Feland at 1607: "I am at hill 300 coordinates 294.2-303.5. Request artillery fire on; In front of 3d Objective. I am in need of rockets for artillery falling short. My losses have been: Officers 10 percent Enlisted 5 percent. Prisoner just taken says enemy is massed to our front for counter—he thinks—have no report from patrol. We ran into a hell of a snag of M.G's. & one pounder just on objective. [2d] Lieut. [Robert C.] Babcock killed reported [20th Company]. Front line not yet established because 47th eased off too far to the right, to connect with 89th Div. They are moving to left & 18th Co. will fill gap until 89th takes over."

This message went from Feland to Larsen, time 1900: "Send out strong patrols in conjunction with the 6th Marines to the following areas. Along the edges of the woods to the north and northwest of the junction of the 5th & 6th Marines. The area around Cote 313. The area around MAGENTA FME. Be on your guard against the enemy filtering in your lines. Kitchen will be up tonight." Message from Feland to Neville, no time: "The 3d Bn reached 3d Objective at 2:30 p.m. Larsen is pushing strong patrols to exploitation line. He captured 6 pieces of artillery and 100 prisoners. He reports that 6th and 89th Div. advanced up with him."

Report of operations: "The 3d Bn leap-frogged the 2nd Bn at 11:50 a.m. During this advance the battalion was deployed as follows: 20th and 45th Companies leading, each being deployed in two waves, each platoon having it's own support. The 16th and 47th Companies followed at about 150 meters, deployed in a staggered line. The Corp and 3d Objective was reached [noted as a line running from 03.3-95.4 and 04.9-94.8, Remonville map, not included]. At that point the 2nd Bn advanced to a point behind the 3d Bn's line, to a point near Hill 300 where it entrenched. That day the entire regiment dug in and remained until 3 November."

2 November: Message from Larsen to Feland, time 1205:

18th Co. reports that left element of 89th Div. moved up to about 150 yds. N.E. of my extreme right and dug in for the night. Coordinates 04.8-94.5. Right flank of 6th Reg't at 03.2-95.4 connecting with my left. This latter information received late this evening & no dope on change received. I have been unable to get runners back from 89th Div. If I get any further information I will forward immediately. It is terribly foggy and runners are coming in here from all outfits Bns & Reg'ts. lost in the darkness. We are still receiving machine gun fire from our front but probably from only two or three light m. guns. I understand that 23d Inf. has orders to *march* up main road three kilometers. No one has passed through me to my knowledge. Just received memo about advance tomorrow. If I am required to keep in liaison with the 9th Inf. Hdqts. information is requested of their present P.C.

Runner from the 2nd Bn. 6th (Front Line) saying that there is no change in his line & that no one has passed through him yet but believes that the 23d is coming up. C.O. 18th Co. reported that the right of 89th Div. was moving forward this evening but that left was held up by M.G. fire and dug in. If the left has moved forward I do not know of it and runners have evidentaly been lost in darkness.

Message from Larsen to Feland, at 0800:

Line established on 3d objective. In going around obstacles our lines became seperated to some extent and all four companies had some elements on line. I am reorganizing however now and am in good shape. Reports from patrols on right state enemy lines about 200 yds to their front and that they forced them [Germans] to retire. The heard voices down in the ravine to their front in considerable numbers. I see what appears to be enemy on ridge on sky line of Hill 315, N.E. of our right flank. 89th Div. & I have liaison but they do not know where their front line companies are.

These people on sky line are about 150 strong in sight and are digging in. I would not like to ask for artillery on them inasmuch as the possiblity the 89th Div. may have one company run up there. They should verify this. Patrols from left companies report Boche 400 strong about 400 yds to their front. Our patrols are holding them by line of outposts. Boche had strong patrols out last night getting into contact with our people right up to our line. They killed one of our men and we got several of theirs. The 46th Co. [must have meant the 47th; there was no 46th] just sent in word that he has two strong patrols out to Exploitation line with orders to reach & hold that line. Have not heard from them yet. Enemey artillery from N. has been very active all night. Captured 112 prisoners and 6 M.G's. who were holding our objective just before we got there. The man from Regimental [?] is here and have sent out for guides—we captured a battery just going into position yesterday, killed some of the personnel of the Batty & got (7) seven of his horses. Our casualties not over 3 percent estimated. If they are planning on giving the 23d Inf. a barrage please let me know and I'll get back my patrols. Also in Bn. Comdr. will report to me I'll give all the dope I have about the front & best way of bringing companies up. They should come up in extended order, on account of shelling. I could meet him personally on the south slope of Hill 300 & give him every assistance. You have runners who could conduct Bn. Comdr. to my P.C. My left & right of 6th are in close touch resting on road W. of Hill 313. Foster with 18th Co. just reports that 89th are on 3d objective—Their left is not far enough to the westward by several hundred yds. but we are covering it. Everything is O.K. Would appreciate blanket rolls and chow.

Message from Torkelson to De Carre, time 0900: "The enemy seems to be concentrating a little to our front center. Considerable movement is noticed here. Will give exact location next message. A battery of enemy artillery is off our left front and firing continous harrasing fire. We are dug in and are holding."

Feland sent the three battalion commanding officers a message which described a system he was implementing in order to move messages to him and to them from him in a better organized fashion. He said a "line of relay posts from P.C. of 1st Bn. [then in reserve] to this P.C. is to be established." That would be the place all messages went before being dispersed to their ultimate destination.

This message was from Feland to Larsen, time 1030: "Withdraw at once all your patrols on your front to the line of 3d objective. Report immediately their return to your lines."

Feland to Larsen again, time 1830: "The 3d Brigade passes thru our lines tonight and advances to the exploitation line. This regiment stands fast till further orders. Co. "E" [18th] Capt. Foster commanding has been ordered to take position in rear of your right on left of 89th Div. to maintain liaison."

3 November: Report of operations: "At 6:00 a.m. the 2nd Bn passed through the positions held by the 3d Bn . The 1st and 3d Bn s followed in that order, and bivouaced one/half kilometer northwest of NOUART."

Message from Larsen to Feland, time 1122:

> Following up 1st Bn. at about 600 yds. My formation is:
> Co. I [16th] left front   Co. L [45th] right front
> Co. K [20th] left rear   Co. M [47th] right rear
> I am in liaison with 17th & 67th Cos. of the 1st Bn. Casualties about ½ of 1 percent so far today.

At 1635 Feland sent the following message to all three battalion commanding officers: "3d Brig. attacks at 2:45 p.m. this date pushing to northern edge of BOIS DE BELVAL ... make every effort to follow closely the advance of 9th Infantry ... battalions will move in present order," i.e., 1st, 2nd and 3d. At 8:15 p.m. he sent another message: "When 3d Brig. advances to northern edge of forest on our front, this regiment as part of Division reserve will move up to today's objective ... without further orders."

4 November: At 0420, Feland advised the three Battalion commanders, "9th is moving up.... Second Bn. will keep in close liaison with the 9th Inf."

Several times during the afternoon, Torkelson, who was out on a reconnaissance, sent messages back to Larsen describing conditions, mainly that roads "are muddy but the wagons can pass over them if necessary." The report of operations stated: " The 3d Bn moved to a point 307.0-305.0 (BUZANCY)."

5 November: Message from Larsen to Feland, at 0800: "Arrived as per position sketch at 11:30 p.m. [4 November]. Came to road not shown on map and halted for the night sending out strong patrols in all directions. Connected with 1st & 2nd Bn. (5th) and 2nd Bn. 6th. Have patrol forward now and will move into position as soon as they return. We are proceeding cautiously although I do not believe there are any Boche in these woods as they were shelled by the enemy last night. By evening I will try to give you some dope on bridgehead. Casualty report and position sketch enclosed."

For the next few hours the 3d Battalion was leading the regiment, followed by 1/5. By 1240 Turrill was reporting that 3/5 had "moved toward the heights south of POUILLY in FORET DE JAULNY and 1st Bn. to ridge where Larsen was to have gone."

Larsen sent the following to Feland at 1345:

> 89th Div. is advancing northward with it's left about 400 yds east of my present P.C. I am moving forward connecting up with the 89th. They are in our sector but if I can cover bridge first I'll send message immediately. There appears to be no Boche this side of the river but is shelling weakly. Will send out vigorous patrols at once we are set, and attempt to connect up with some of 2nd Div. on my left also. Men should have chow—only two cooked meals in five days. Their blankets are still at LANDREVILLE. Not much pep but are willing to go to Hell if we say so. They will shell us if we get outside of N. edge of woods and possibly M.G. us as it appears now my line will be about 309.9-305.8 & 309.5-306.6. Have had no casualties so far this morning.

Message from Larsen to Feland, at 1445: "356 Regt. beat me to it. Their first wave went over at 10:00 a.m. and had M. guns covering bridge before we arrived in place. This Bn. of 89th covers exactly the same section as assigned us and has same mission. I have taken up position as per sketch. We have reconnoitering parties to front and will keep connected up O.K. Sorry they beat us to it. Enemy positons freshly dug cover front lines on northern slope and I have best available cover and am in close support."

Report of operations: "The 3d Bn moved to FORET DE JAULNAY at about 310.2-385.7 (BUZANCY) and operated with the 89th [U.S. Infantry] Division. Strong detachments were sent to mop up the northeastern half of the woods and officer patrols were sent to PROUILLY FME [farm] and CARRE near INOR. Patrol was sent to reconnoiter bridge and town of POUILLY."

6 November: Message from Larsen to Feland, time 1000: "Patrol from N.E. reports from 312.0-307.0 that they have encountered no enemy. [2d] Lt. Floyd W.] Bennett in charge reports that 89th Div. patrols have reconnoitered POUILL FME & CARRE & found nothing. Bennett continues to carry out his orders. He says that 89th Div. patrol was able to get across river into INOR last night. Am sending out patrol to WAME FME. & will transmit all dope gained as it is received. If we can get across river we will as soon as men have fed."

An hour later Torkelson was telling De Carre that Pouilly and its environs were clear of enemy and that "men can pass along in the open just across the river from POUILLY without being fired on." At 1210 Larsen sent to Feland:

Lt. Bennett has returned from mopping up N.E. 1/2 of BOIS JAULNY. Reports seeing no enemy this side of river. Reconnoitered POUILL FME & CARRE—both deserted and being shelled by enemy constantly. Enemy seen walking along side of hill across river N-W of POUILLY FME. Enemy have dug in positions along hillside from quarry, & NE from narrow guage road & unimproved road running NE & SW over knoll. A little artillery in this area would make them keep their heads down or get out possibly. I have given our artillery liaison officer the dope. If we get out in open under observation they snipe at us. Bennett reports about 100 yds of double guage railroad torn up near POUILLY FME. River is about 100 feet wide there and apparently quite deep. Report from other patrol to WAME FME. states that place is deserted and enemy is shelling same. When our patrol gets in open enemy snipes with 77 or 37 MM. They have been unable so far to locate a ford or get any information about same. The patrol is proceeding NE toward POUILLY FME and will attempt to locate crossing and M.G. position to cover same. 3d Bn. of 356th is reconnoitering for crossing also. Enemy planes are working overhead quite low unmolested.

Feland responded two hours later, "Recall those patrols (intelligence and otherwise) immediately and you will come up to this P.C." He followed that up with a 1430 message to Col. Allen of the 356th Infantry: "In accordance with instructions received, I am moving my 3d Bn. which is to the left of your front line to about 1 kilometer south of FME DE LA FNE AUX FRESNES (8.3-3.8)."

Second Lt. James S. Withington, 47th Company, sent this to Larsen, time 1520: "Reconnaissance patrol of 20 men from 47th Co. went N.E. from 305.8-310 to edge of wood opposite FME DE LA WAME. Three men then reconnoitered farm and found it uninhabited. The entire patrol then went N.E. along & inside edge of woods to about 306.8-310. From here I went on with one man in a N.E. a N.E. direction parallel to R.R. to about 307.3-311. I then rejoined patrol and came back to starting point. Secured information as to position of 89th

Division. Also that bridge across river at POUILLY, tho blown up was passable by one man at a time. No fords or other means of crossing river had been discovered."

Message from 2d Lt. John T. Foster, 16th Company, to Larsen, no time indicated:

> Upon receipt of order for patrol from Bn. Hdqs. I started out. I took a course through woods until I arrived at railroad (coordinates 309.7-306.8 Stenay Sector map). I followed railroad until reaching road leading to bridge. I crossed canal and 1st bridge and reconnoitered second bridge of river. The bridge over canal is blown up but men can cross on locks. The first bridge over river is partly blown up but men can cross without assistance. The foundation of both bridges are almost intact. The town is held lightly by enemy outposts, and machine guns in rear of town.
>
> I saw the enemy flares come from town and heard machine gun fire. I did not enter town because 89th Div. were withdrawing their patrols and support to edge of the woods south of bridge which would have left me without any support. It would take one platoon almost an hour to cross the canal and both rivers. I returned by road at north edge of woods.

Report of operations: "3d Bn moved to FORET DE DIEULET to a point 08.5-04.0 (BUZANCY)."

7 November: At 0830 Dr. Lawlor, 5th Regiment surgeon, sent a message to Dr. Herbert H. Thatcher at the 3d Bn. in which he advised that he was sending Medkirk, chief pharmacist's mate, back where "he and Beaum [John, pharmacist mate 1st] can work on examinations until after this pinch." That day 2d Lt. Leonard E. Rea, 1/5 intelligence officer, advised De Carre that he had been advised by Foster what to expect when 1/5 took over the 3/5 position.

The regiment moved to Bois de Four, arriving at 2:30 p.m. and taking position at point 02.8-04.95 (Raucourt 1/20,000) and remained there through 8 November.

8 November: At 1150 Feland advised each battalion commanding officer to "make reconnaissance of trails leading thru the woods in a direction magnetic SOUTH. This is in order that we may avoid the roads, in case we are lucky enough to get the order to march SOUTH ... have your kitchens arrived?"

Larsen to Feland, time 1342: "Kitchens are right here with me and we are feeding well for the present. Capt. [Raymond E.] Knapp [43d Co.] is reconnoitering trails leading *south*. Capt. [Thomas] Quigley is my second in command. Capt. Ducham [William A. Duckham] assigned to 47th Co. and Lieut. [Oliver D.] Bernier assigned to the 16th Co. All our M.G. carts and transportation for M.G. Co. are here and ready to move SOUTH anytime."

On 8 November at 1635 Feland sent a message to all battalion commanders that "regiment will remain in place for the present ... make reconnaissance tomorrow so that if ordered, the move ordered tonight may be carried out easily." Everybody wanted to be out of the lines and were showing it.

9 November: Report of operations: "The 3d and 2nd Bn s moved to the BOIS DE MURETS."

10 November: Report of operations: "The 3d Bn was ordered to join the 6th Marines in the FORET DE LIMON southwest of YONQ arriving in these woods at 5:00 p.m. Having been ordered to support the 1st Bn [Maj. Frederick A. Barker] of the 6th Marines in crossing the MEUSE, this battalion left the woods at 8:00 p.m. and marched to the MEUSE RIVER to a point 2 1/2 kilometers north of MOUZON. As the 6th Marines did not cross the river the 3d Bn returned to the BOIS DE LIMON at 8:00 a.m. November 11th." Feland added a personal warning to Larsen in his message, which does not appear in the diary. "The Sixth Marines are so reduced in number that your assignment to that regiment becomes a neccessity."

While not part of this history, what happened to 1/5 on the night of 10-11 November was simply that they were shattered once again. Results were that about 100 officers and men were still on their feet the next morning. Two/Five fared a bit better. Three/Five was assigned to the 6th Marines who were to cross the river at Mouzon, a town a few miles north. However, they were in luck, the bridges pushed across the Meuse were destroyed by the Germans before anyone tried to cross and the crossing was called off.

11 November: Report of operations: "The 3d Bn crossed the MEUSE at 1800 and relieved the 1st Bn of the 9th Infantry in a support position in FORET DE ALMA GISORS."

12 November: Report of operations: "The 16th and 45th Companies of the 3d Bn relieved the 2nd Bn of the 356th Infantry [89th Division] at the north and eastern edge of FORET D'ALMS GISORS. The 20th and 47th Companies remained in the FORET DE ALMA GISORS."

13 November: Report of operations: "The regiment remained in position, except that 45th Co of the 3d Bn moved to LA SARTELLE FME.

14 November: Report of operations: "Regiment was relieved by the 308th Regiment [77th U.S. Infantry Division] at 11:00 a.m. 1st and 2nd Bn s marched to POUILLY and 3d Bn marched to LETANNE."

19 November: Diary—it was a recapitulation of the Fifth Marines part in the Meuse-Argonne battle.

1. In accordance with Memorandum 2nd Division dated 20 September 1918, the following report is submitted.
    (a) The Fifth Regiment Marines attacked on about a two kilometer front on November 1st, being deployed in a three battalion depth. The Third Bn was third line battalion for the first objective, the second line of support battalion for second objective, and attacking battalion for third objective or day's objective.
    (b) The terrain was of gently rolling nature, having a few small patches of woods, and three somewhat prominent hills, affording strong points to the enemy.
    (c) During the advance, while this battalion was in reserve and support, the formation was of a staggered line of combat groups in a single file. While attacking the battalion was deployed two companies in front line, each company being deployed in two waves, each platoon having it's own support. The two supporting companies, followed at about 150 meters distance, were deployed in staggered line of combat groups. The machine gun company attached was disposed of as follows: one platoon to each of the front line companies, the third platoon accompanying Battalion Headquarters as reserve.
    (d) The formations adopted as indicated above were found satisfactory in light of subsequent events.
    (e) No remarks.
    (f) The plan of having one platoon of the machine gun company with Battalion Headquarters was found very satisfactory. This platoon was used very effectively in capturing, destroying or putting to rout a hostile battery of 105's reported moving into position by our combat liaison group on the right during the advance. It was also used for the purpose of replacing guns of the front line as they were put out of action.
        At our jump-off or the second objective, our artillery barrage was very weak and

irregular, and it became necessary to use a machine gun barrage to cover our advance over a wide clear valley, which was commanded to our front containing enemy. Upon reaching objective machine guns were used to cover our flanks and cover our front by cross-fire, each of these positions being supported by automatic rifles.

Hand grenades were not needed. Rifle grenades were used very effectively at one point when our advance was held up by enemy machine guns from a strong position at our front. Rifle grenades were here used from a flank position, neutralizing the enemy machine gun fire, while a detachment was encircling the enemy to their rear.

The 37m/m gun did not accompany us in moving from our reserve position October 31st to our original jump-off position at 5:30 a.m., November 1st, owing to the fact that our orders to move were received so late that the battalion had to march to it's jump-off position faster than the one pounder could follow.

(g) No artillery accompanied the battalion during the attack. The artillery support was very effective almost to the position of our second objective, after which it was very irregular and weak, probably owing to the rapidity and depth of the advance. Heavy artillery was falling short in our lines continually during the 30 minute rest on the second objective. Every available flare indicating friendly artillery falling short was used in vain. During our advance from second to third objective also artillery was falling short. After reaching objective no barrage was called for.

(h) While in reserve and support positions the battalion mopped up all obstacles which the attacking battalion had passed around according to orders. While this battalion was attacking, just before reaching our objective some wooded hills containing enemy were encountered; these were passed by the two leading companies on either flank, and mopped up by supporting companies who advanced to objective connecting up the two original front line companies.

(i) No difficulty was encountered by this battalion in passing through the lines of the battalion in advance.

(j) Machine gun nests and strong points were overcome by employing sufficient holding force to their front, and sending detachments around flanks and to their rear, after which the enemy was easily destroyed or captured.

(k) Subordinate commanders used initiative and good judgement in overcoming isolated groups of enemy encountered.

(l) Upon reaching objective strong patrols kept contact with the enemy while line was organized generally following edge of woods about 5 meters back from clearing with two-men outposts about two to three hundred yards to the front.

(m) Throughout engagement perfect liaison was maintained with battalion on our left and also with corresponding unit of 89th Division on our right, by means of E [18th] Co [Captain John R. Foster], which had been detailed for liaison.

HENRY L. LARSEN

5

First Battalion, Sixth Marines, 1917–1919

BATTALION HEADQUARTERS
74th [A] Company
75th [B] Company
76th [C] Company
95th [D] Company

COMMANDING OFFICERS

From	To	
August 1917	14 October 1917	Major John A. Hughes
15 October 1917	25 April 1918	Captain Robert E. Adams
26 April 1918	8 June 1918	Major Maurice E. Shearer
8 June 1918	9 June 1918	Capt. George A. Stowell
9 June 1918	August 1918	Major John A. Hughes
August 1918	August 1919	Major Frederick Barker

On 4 August 1917, in accordance with directions issued by the president, the secretary of the Navy directed the major general commandant "to organize a force of Marines, to be known as the Sixth Regiment of Marines, for service with the Army in France," and the regiment was organized as directed.

According to the "official history," "By the middle of August the regiment had attained approximately three quarters of its enlisted personnel strength." There were some delays due to the necessity of having barracks completed at Quantico before they could be inhabited by the new men arriving. It was necessary to regulate the induction of new companies mainly because there were few officers trained to take command of newly formed companies. The training time allocated for these new officers, many who had not any training at all, was scheduled for three months. The training began on 30 July and consequently would not turn out the first officers until 31 October.

Meanwhile, at the end of August enough new recruits had been shipped up from Parris Island and elsewhere to make up the 95th, 96th, and 97th Companies. Consequently, three battalions were organized. The First Battalion, to be commanded by Major John A. Hughes, was composed of the 74th, 75th, 76th, and the 95th Companies.

Major John (Johnny the Hard) Hughes and his battalion left Quantico by train early on Sunday morning, 16 September 1917, for League Island, Philadelphia, where they were to board ship for transport to France. The morning was dark and it was raining as the men boarded one of the two long trains awaiting them. The post band played, and as the trains pulled away from the station the battalion was given a rousing cheer by the fellows left behind. That night the battalion embarked on the USS *Henderson* and on the following morning the transport sailed for New York. Taking one day to make the trip, the ship arrived in New York harbor and there rested for five days. On 23 September 1917, at 2230 hours, the battalion sailed on the *Henderson* from New York. The trip was uneventful. General quarters and abandon ship drill filled in some of the time while guard details, to spy for submarines, took up some more. The ship was darkened at sunset and no smoking or lights of any kind were allowed. Two companies were quartered below decks and two had above deck accommodations. A few lucky men received hammocks, whereas most of the others slept on the deck. The battalion survived the dull trip and landed at St. Nazaire, France, on 5 October 1917.

The First was assigned to a large French camp with wooden barracks just outside town. The barracks weren't in the best of condition but as always Marines must adapt to any and all conditions, even those that aren't of their making. Like the Fifth Regiment, the Sixth spent several months performing undesirable duties along the line of communications. The battalion was assigned to guard duty at the camp and to longshoremen's tasks on the docks. In addition, a large working party of upwards of two hundred men was assigned to help build a dam, near the camp, under the direct supervision the 17th Engineers.

Major Hughes and twelve other officers on 15 October left St. Nazaire for Gondrecourt, where the 1st Corps school was held. Captain [later Major] Robert E. Adams was in command of the battalion during part of this absence.

Beginning on 7 November the battalion was assigned many laboring tasks. The 95th Company was sent to do guard duty at Brest and La Harve, two platoons going to each of those locations. On 13 December the company was reassembled and took over the barracks at Camp Pontenezen from the French. Later these barracks would become infamous and Colonel Smedley D. Butler would, after using some Marine organizational skills, make them famous. One platoon from the 76th Company and thirty men from the 74th were sent on 17 December to St. Nazaire for duty as military police and dock guards at Nantes. The rest of the battalion remained at St. Nazaire until 6 January 1918 when the 74th, 75th and 76th Companies entrained at St. Nazaire for Damblain, in the Voges mountains. That was the area designated for training the Marine brigade. The 95th Company rejoined the battalion there on 28 January 1918.

On 12 January 1918, Colonel Albertus W. Catlin established headquarters of the Sixth Regiment at Blevaincourt in the Bourmont training area. The Third Battalion arrived on the same day; the First Battalion arrived later during the month, and finally the late-coming Second Battalion on 10 February. By that date the entire 4th Brigade was together, except the 67th Company, 1/5, which was assigned to duty in England, in the training area for the 1st time. Major General Omar Bundy, USA, commanded the division and Brigadier General Charles A. Doyen, USMC, commanded the brigade. Training was begun immediately and because of the severity of the weather and the strenuous schedule it was grueling, but it soon hardened everyone to what could be expected in war in France. Hikes, close order drill, bayonet practice plus rifle and grenade throwing were the order of the day, as was trench storming, taking strong points, and of course gas attacks.

About 1 March rumors had it that the regiment would be going into the lines. Equipment like trench boots, trench knives and extra clothing was also appearing, lending credence to those rumors. On 12 March the sea-bags were packed and stored. Beginning on 14 March the regiment was moved by rail to the Toulon Sector and by 16 March headquarters was established at Camp Boues. The 1st Battalion was last to leave and its move began on 17 March by train. It detrained on 18 March at Lommes and marched 18 kilometers to Sommedieue, where it was stationed in reserve behind the French 10th Army Corps.

Verdun

[None of the three battalions of the 6th Regiment wrote any substantive messages during the entire period they were stationed in the Toulon Sector. Each day they wrote, "Nothing of importance to report." Consequently, this portion of their history is very weak. One noticeable situation regarding 1/6 was that for at least the first two campaigns, Verdun and Belleau Wood, though many men were heroes, not many awards beyond a USA Silver Star citation or Croix de Guerre were given.]

The sector was considered to be a quiet one but evidently the German gunners were trying to impress the new occupants of the line. The German artillery increased its activity and it gave the 6th Regiment a daily dose of effective shell fire. On 6 April the enemy tried to make a trench raid against the 74th Company, which was posted in the town of Tresevaux, but they were repulsed, leaving four dead behind. The 74th lost one dead (Cpl. Charles K. Toth) and three men wounded.

On the night of 6-7 April, three officers and twenty-five enlisted men of the 95th Company went on patrol with a French officer and thirty soldiers. They actually left their trenches early on the morning of the 7th and sections were dispatched at several points, both French and Americans. At 0210 an enemy patrol of an estimated thirty men was discovered, which immediately ran for cover. Next came a German artillery barrage supported by machine gun fire. The French and Americans had a few men wounded and Corporal Toth (see above) was missing. It was later assumed that Toth was killed and not discovered. First Lieutenant Carleton Burr led the Americans assisted by 1st Lieutenants Joseph F. Gargan and Frederick C. Wheeler.

The company was less lucky on 12 April. The Germans launched a deadly gas attack against the positions held by that company early one morning, catching most of the men and officers in quarters without their masks. All officers were evacuated in serious condition and two hundred twenty men were also affected. Forty of those died later as a result of that attack. On 25 April, Major Adams was assigned to detached duty, later appearing as the 3rd Battalion commander of the 38th U.S. Infantry, 3rd Division. Major Maurice E. Shearer assumed command on a temporary basis.

25 April 1918: Message from 1st Lt. Arthur H. Turner, adjutant, 1/6, to Col. Albertus

W. Catlin, sent after 1830: "6:30 tonight one gas shell fell just off right front line. Also more gas shells falling on hill to right of our front line."

30 May: From Col. Albertus W. Catlin to every person of importance in the regiment: "Advance information official received that this Regiment will move at 10:00 p.m. 30 May by bus to new area. All trains shall be loaded at once and arrangements hastened. Orders will follow. Wagons when loaded will move to SERANS to form train." Everyone believed that they were going to move northeastward to relieve the 1st U.S. Infantry Division at Cantigny. Little did they know at that time what their real destination would be.

Belleau Wood

Corporal Martin Gulberg of the 75th Company tells us that the 6th had arrived at Montreuil about 0600 and stayed until 1300. During that period they ate anything and everything that wasn't nailed down. Gulberg remarked that a French officer had told them to help themselves to anything they wanted, because the Germans would get everything eventually. He also said he heard one of the boys remark, "Gee, that Frog officer ain't got much confidence in us, has he?" Gulberg wrote, "We visited the wine cellars and helped ourselves to the choicest wines: raided rabbit and chicken coops and feasted royally. We didn't leave much for Fritz in case he should get through." He described one Marine coming down the street with a squealing pig under his arms yelling, "Pork Chops." Although many of the Marines took away many of the dressed and prepared animals, most never had the chance to actually eat their prizes.[1]

1 June: Major Maurice "Mud" Shearer, temporarily in command of the 1st Battalion of the 6th Regiment while Maj. John A. Hughes was away at school, led his force northward off the highway and marched up behind the machine gunners. Continuing on the road, they reached the town of Lucy-le-Bocage, as German shells began falling in a field close by. The battalion extended its line northward on the road to Torcy, sheltering in the St. Martin Woods.

Harbord sent to Major General Omar Bundy, 2d Division, at 1705 hours: "1st Bn. 6th Marines going into line from LUCY through Hill 142. 3rd Bn. in support at LA VOIE DU CHATEL which is also P.C. of the 6th Marines. 6th Machine Gun Bn. distributed at line. No instructions as to the evacuation of the wounded. From Shearer to Catlin, sent at 2015: "1st B., 6th marines in assigned position 7:30 p.m. Have sent out a man to establish liaison with unit on our left."

Harbord began getting a bit testy with Catlin when he harangued him for not sending the desired liaison man to brigade and to report every fifteen minutes no matter what. "Please give these matters your attention at once."

2 June: Shearer to Catlin, at 0700: "Liaison with the Bn. on our right was accomplished properly last night and our runner to the Bn. on our left (French) went over to their P.C. last night, guided by a French soldier, but no runner from this French Bn. has as yet reported to us. One Engineer company reported this a.m. Shall we dig?"

As the morning proceeded, the Germans stepped up their artillery attacks and just after noon began to hammer the various 4th Brigade positions, and 1/6 was a target. One/Six, still located in St. Martin's Woods, opposite Belleau Wood, were the major victims. Gulberg describes what happened to the 75th Company's first casualty. Private Warren F. Hoyle "stuck his head out and as he did so a shell took his head off." Three additional men of the 75th were wounded or shell shocked. Captain Oscar R. Cauldwell of the 95th Company was shot through the leg, which took him out of the lines. "There were a few French soldiers in this wood walking around with rosary beads saying prayers." So Gulberg and Riley Brennan, his foxhole mate, just dug deeper. During that afternoon the Germans launched at least two attacks along the right of the brigade's line. Catlin had been informed that a German attack was in the offing, so his men were reasonably prepared. Each attack was repulsed, principally, by machine-gun fire. According to reports, "dead Germans piled the slopes."

In the meantime Harbord sent Catlin a message that indicated an expected German "attack in the direction of BOIS DE VEUILLY from around HAUTEVESNES. Everybody, including French Headquarters, expressing confidence in you, Holcomb and Shearer." He also had to tell Catlin that there were "no large scale maps, have requested division for them."

Harbord sent a memo to Catlin at 1443 hours: "Note the statement that Shearer's Battalion has its left 1,000 meters S. E. of Hill 142. Is this true? Please note also that Feland says that there is a Battalion of French troops on the right of Wise and that Wise is at 142. I am speaking of 142 as shown on the map, not any hill in the vicinity; the actual figures where the left of Shearer's Battalion is supposed to be. Are the troops that you put in to fill the gap between Shearer's Battalion and 142, or between 142 and Wise's right?"

At 1500 hours Harbord was back at Catlin again: "We have had nothing from you since the telephone went out. You have runners and are expected to use them every fifteen minutes to send messages." Harbord to Catlin at 1520: "Send reliable officer to 142 to find out if Shearer left rests there and report facts to me as soon as possible."

Shearer sent to Frank Evans, adjutant, 6th Marines, time 1545: "Infantry Col. Comdg. Sector [French] sends me word that in his sector red lights call for barrage. White lights called for lengthening. No difference as to number of stars. Any light will do. This does not seem O.K. but is his dope. He loaned me about 20 pistol lights accordingly. He asks that this be transmitted to all USMC."

Shearer to Catlin, time 2230: "French colonel 152nd RI [Infantry Regiment] holding TORCY-BELLEAU has been forced back., his left retiring towards our left at 142. At his request am furnishing him two platoons from reserve co. to close line ¼ km. north of 142. No telephone installed here yet.

Shearer to Lt. Col. Frederic W. Wise, commanding officer, 2/5, at midnight: "1st Bn., 6th Marines now holding line from Hill 142 to LUCY inclusive as front line. Capt. [George A.] Stowell's 76th Co's left rest on Hill 142. French orders #77 states 2nd Bn. 152nd Regt Infantry will reform N. of road VOIE DU CHATEL."

One young officer, 2d Lt. Morgan R. Mills, Jr., assumed command of his company, the 95th, after his "skipper," 1st Lt. Clarence W. Smith, was wounded and out of the picture. He directed the 95th with rare judgment during the night of the 2d and 3d, and the attackers were beaten back. Because of this a splendid morale was sustained within the company through his untiring efforts. He was aided greatly by Gy. Sgt. Peter Morgan of his company, who ably assisted in maintaining superior fire power against the oncoming enemy. Morgan was later promoted to second lieutenant.

This was going on while the Fourth Brigade was still trying to "sort itself out" after their trying period while getting to the area in bits and pieces. The 5th and 6th Regiments were still scattered around and it would be another day before most units would be realigned with their fellows in their own regiment. Fortunately for everyone the Germans didn't know what was going on, or if they did they were too tired to try anything. All that would change soon enough.

3 June: At midnight Shearer notified Wise at 2/5 that he was holding a front line from Hill 142 to Lucy-le-Bocage. Capt. George A. Stowell's 76th Company's left rests on Hill 142." Shearer and Wise had been jockeying about for hours, neither ever quite making their units meet. It would be many more hours before they found each other.

Logan Feland had received a report from one of Wise's scouts who had located both 2/5's 51st Company and 1/6's 76th Company. They were about a thousand meters apart. Neither battalion commander decided to change the situation and that large gap was not soon corrected. Major Shearer sent a message to Wise that he was not able to move any farther to his left than Hill 142. According to his information, that was where Wise's right should be. Unfortunately, Shearer didn't know he wasn't on Hill 142. Apparently Wise was suffering from the same problems, because he thought that Williams was on Hill 142 and evidently so did Williams. When Smith and the 82d Company arrived, the gap was partially filled. Later Sibley received orders to send more companies.

The commanding general of the French 152nd Division issued orders that the Americans would sit tight while the French launched an attack on 3 June. Under no circumstances were the doughboys nor Marines to fall back from the positions they occupied, *"at all costs."*

Message from Stowell to unknown at 0157: "Capt. Stowell reports 2nd Bat. right rests on road CHAMPILLON-BUSSAIRES 1 k. north of CHAMPILLON and not 142. All [Captain Oscar R.] Cauldwell's men [95th Co.] used, Engineers as reserve. French reported to be where they were approximately [message incomplete]."

From Col. Wendell Neville, commanding officer, 5th Marines, to Catlin, at 0615: "Wise and Shearer are in touch but Wise reports his right company [Captain Lloyd Williams, commanding officer, 51st Company, 2/5] has not been able to get in touch with Shearer's left company [Stowell's 76th?]. Wise has gone this morning to his right to establish this liaison. He thinks there is a gap of some extent between Hill 142 and your left. Have directed him to find where your left is and to extend to the right if he finds that any gap exists. Wise will send a guide with this who can indicate our right." At least at this time, 1/6 was farther to the left than Hill 142, as indicated by Stowell's report, if that was accurate.

Shearer to Wise at 1245 but not received until 1605: "Have been trying to connect with your right flank. My left flank is on 142. Liaison man states your right rests on CHAMPILLON-BUSSIARES about 1 kilometer north of CHAMPILLON. My line runs from 142 S. E. to LUCY, so if the above is true the vacancy is yours. I am trying to extend to reach your right. Please advise exactly where your right is as I cannot spare men to run line past 142 as I understand your Bn. line runs from 142 to VEUILLY." Wise and 2/5 were then located at Les Mares Farm.

Meanwhile, on the front of the 75th Company, sometime shortly before noon, as Gulberg said: "They [the Germans] made a few calls.... They came out of the wood opposite our position [Belleau Wood] in close formation. They came on as steadily as if they were on parade. We opened up on them with a slashing barrage of rifles, automatics, and machine guns. They halted, withdrew a space, then came on again. They had a good artillery barrage in front of them, but it didn't keep us down. Three times they tried to break through, but our fire was too accurate and too heavy for them. It was terrible in its effectiveness. They fell by the scores, there among the poppies and the wheat."[2]

Shearer sent to Catlin at 2140: "956 bandoleers and 10,000 rds Chauchat going to 82 & 83 Cos. by carriers now."

4 June: Shearer to Catlin, time 0750: "74 Co. less 1 plat. Capt. Burn[e]s, 4 lts [lieutenants], relieved French Bn. at 3:30 a.m. 3rd June, taking up position in support of the French M.G.'s as indicated on sketch in three positions [no sketch available] one platoon each position."

Recently returned Captain Harold D. Shannon, having been hospitalized because of gas poisoning at Verdun, distinguished himself by his coolness and initiative. Regardless of his personal safety, he led his men of the 75th Company, out of an area under bombardment, even though he was wounded. Shannon would be a hero in a later war when he, commanding the Marine Defense Battalion at Midway Island, defended it successfully against efforts by Japan to conquer the island.

5 June: As the official history of the regiment for the 5th stated: "Conditions continued much the same as on the previous day. The day was spent in digging and strengthening the positions. During the early morning hours the enemy launched an attack but was repulsed without serious loss to this regiment." First Lt. Frederick C. Wheeler, of the 95th Company, was conspicuous for his bravery in remaining in action, although twice wounded, refusing to be evacuated until wounded a third time, and then endeavoring to return to his command.

Harbord sent orders to 5th and 6th Marine commanding officers: "1/6 to proceed to 170.0-259.0 as Corps Reserve, 21st French Corps."

Sometime that day Major John Hughes returned to 1/6 and resumed command. Shearer returned to Regimental Headquarters for a little more than a day after which he would relieve Larsen at 3/5. Somehow and for some reason, Major Franklin B. Garrett commanded 1/6 the following day at 2015.

6 June: Hughes to Catlin, 0730: "Missing platoons 74th and 95th Cos. reported. Lt. Smith [must be Clarence W., 95th Company] reports enemy attempted to pull off small raid during relief. Driven off. 2 Pvts. 95th Killed. Need rations."

At Belleau Wood on 6 June, Gy. Sgt. John J. Nagazyna of the 95th Company was in command of his platoon at 3:45 a.m. while a relief was in progress. The relief had been barely accomplished when a terrific machine gun and artillery barrage was laid down on their position at the edge of the woods. The enemy was then seen advancing behind the barrage in small columns 500 yards from his position. He immediately placed his platoon back on the line and by his energetic efforts contributed materially to the repulse of the attempted attack, which was so well frustrated that losses were held to a minimum.

Garrett to Harbord at 2145: "Message for Colonel Catlin from Holcomb. [First] Lieutenant [James F.] Robertson is in BOURESCHES with 2½ platoons. Captain [Donald F.] Duncan killed. No information for 3d battalion. Have you any orders or information?"

This was the day that the famous, or rather infamous, attack upon Belleau Wood and the town of Bouresches took place, at 1700 hours to be exact. Somehow, a few members of the 96th Company (2½ platoons of the 96th and 1 platoon of the 79th) made it into that town and held it. The only battalion in the 6th Regiment to be excluded that day was 1/6. The other two battalions of the 6th Marines were subjected to almost as much punishment as 3/5.

However, when 1/6 was busy trying to complete a relief, the Germans attacked with a terrific machine gun and artillery barrage, and they could be seen advancing behind the barrage. Gunnery Sergeant Forrest J. Ashwood of the 95th Company immediately placed his platoon back on line and energetically contributed materially to the repulse of the enemy. Consequently, his losses were minimal and the relief was completed in excellent order. Ashwood was promoted to second lieutenant.

7 June: Major Hughes was back with 1/6 and asked Lt. Col. Lee, now commanding officer, 6th Marines: "Request Lt. Merou be relieved from duty this Batt. Utterly useless to me and a decided nuisance. Spends all his time with the French and could not establish proper liaison with them. Did so my self aided by [2d Lt. Brewster] Reamey."

That day the regiment issued a casualty report. Losses to 1/6 were negligible compared to the other two battalions: one man in the 74th Company, two in the 75th, and two in the 95th Company, with no loss to the 76th.

8 June: Harbord to Hughes, time 1820 hours: "By order of the Corps commander your battalion is relieved from duty as Corps Reserve and will proceed tonight to a point S. E. of LUCY to relieve the 3rd Bn. of the Regiment. The Regimental Commander has arranged to have guides meet you at the bridge crossing over the GOBERT brook. It is desired that you start at such an hour that your march will not be apparent to ballon observation of the enemy. You should be amply provided with ammunition, rations, etc."

At 2140 Harbord sent to Hughes: "I desire you to reconnoiter tonight the wood directly S. E. of LUCY where the 80th Co. [2/6] is stationed. After ... put in there tonight as many of your companies as you think safe, at least one. Those companies for which there is no room there will be put in the north-eastern end of Mon Blanche Wood S. W. of LUCY. You should have your own P. C. with the portion of the battalion that is in the wood S. E. of LUCY. It is understood that Colonel Lee has withdrawn the 80th Co. to the wood S. E. of LUCY."

Hughes left Stowell, senior company commander, in command of the battalion while Hughes conferred with Harbord. Confusion reigned. The French guides weren't where they were supposed to be and two companies at the end of the column were diverted to the north when they should have marched east. They were finally located by Stowell, but the time lost caused the battalion to stray into the open and German artillery laid it in on them. Stowell moved the battalion into some woods but they were unable to move out again during daylight hours and reach the position Harbord had assigned for them. Hughes was furious and relieved Stowell of command of the 76th Company, replacing him with 1st Lt. Macon Over-

Houses at Triangle Farms after being subjected to German artillery fire.

ton. Consequently the relief of 3/6 as conceived was off temporarily. Harbord had Hughes send in one company to where 3/6 had been and Sibley left the 80th Company behind since it was his only company which had not been chewed up. Hughes was to remain in the wood southeast of Lucy as originally ordained. Just after midnight Hughes arrived at his new quarters, located about where 260 and 175 intersect on the map.

9 June: From Lee to Harbord at 1215: "Major Hughes Battalion (1st, 6th) is located in the woods just west of point 205 on North side of the road LA VOIE DU CHATEL–LUCY LE BOCAGE. Hughes has just reported here with this information and I am waiting for the side-car to send him to you to explain the results of his reconnaissance of the woods occupied by the Regimental reserve."

Major John A. Hughes, Company 1/6, in Germany.

Harbord to Hughes, at 1440: "As soon as dark tonight be prepared to move your battalion into a position for an attack which will be outlined in field orders which you will receive later today." Field Order No. 3 issued by Harbord at 1830 gave as the objective the southern edge of Bois de Belleau with X line at 261.7, with eastern coordinates at 176.5-261.0 and western at 175.6. In other words the southern half of the woods. The attack would begin at 0430 on 10 June by Hughes' 1/6.

10 June: Hughes to Harbord, at 0245: "In position." Lee also sent a message at 0350 telling Harbord that Hughes reports O.K. in position and ready to carry out any orders. Hughes sent to Harbord at 0451: "Artillery barrage working beautifully. 3 or 4 casualties in the 74th Co. coming in. Otherwise all o.k. Kindly have artillery fire on [the] machine guns firing down the line we have to cross."

Harbord's plan was that 1/6 would move into the southern portion of Belleau Wood in the morning and later on the following day Wise's 2/5 would move into the woods from a left angle, about where Berry's 3/5 had gone in on 6 June. Hughes would advance at the same time as the right flank to 2/5. Both would go northward in the woods.

From 2d Lt. Bradford Perrin to Harbord, sent at 0620: "The line advanced [1/6] obtaining objective without opposition. One trench mortar (a large Minnenwerfer on wheels) quite intact. Will try to find C.O. [Hughes]. About the same time [Captain Edward C.] Fuller, of the 75th Co., was reported to have reached his objective." (Nothing more is known about Perrin other than he was liaison officer with the 6th Marines but not his own regiment.)

The 6th Marines' intelligence officer, 1st Lt. William E. Moore, reported to Harbord at 0650: "Captain Fuller, 75th Company, reports that at 5:12 a.m. he had reached his objective. No indication of the enemy." Eight minutes later Moore reported: "Have run into nest of three machine guns approximately 176.1-262.3. Fuller is cleaning them out with help from Cole [commanding officer, 6th Machine Gun Battalion]." Lee advised Harbord at 0710: "3

5. *First Battalion, Sixth Marines, 1917–1919* 159

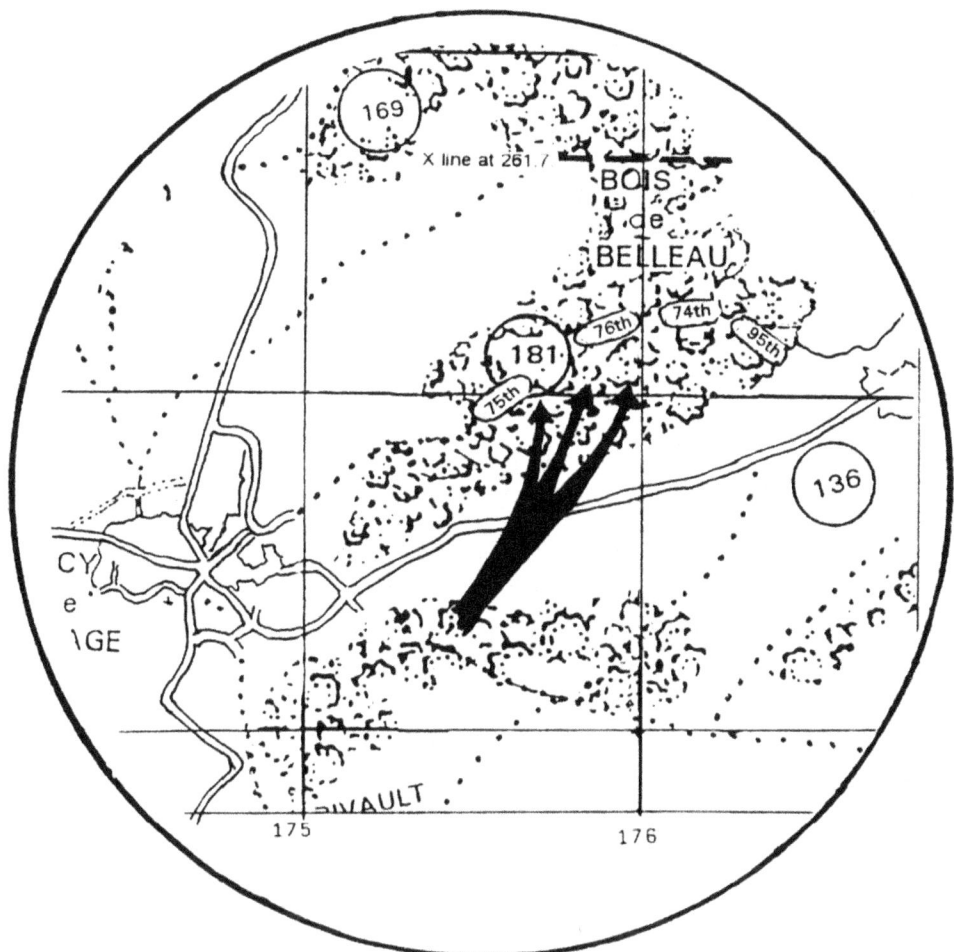

The attack launched by 1/6 on 10 June 1918. Note the X-Line objective and the actual final positions.

machine guns still active at point 100 yards north of second 'e' in word 'BELLEAU.' Hughes making dispositions for their capture. Also one company going up from Regimental Reserve."

Hughes to Harbord, time 0712: "Everything going nicely. No losses coming across. Have received no word from companies, but there is practically no firing. Artillery has the BOIS DE BELLEAU to mince meat." Not quite: editorial comment. Hughes to Harbord, at 0754: "Everything O.K. now except nest of Machine Guns previously mentioned. Am sending Fuller two Stokes Mortars and have instructed him to await their arrival before attempting to take them [machine guns]. 2 privates of the 75th Co. killed. Have identified two of three dead Marines in trenches. One is 2nd Lt. Clarence Dennis and the other Private Robert A. Kirk, 3rd one blown to pieces." Both were in the 80th Company; Kirk's middle initial was B.

At 0756 Hughes advised brigade, through Lee, that Major Edward B. Cole, commanding officer, 6th Machine Gun Battalion, had been badly wounded in face and hand by machine gun fire and that he had brought up the 74th Company. Cole died of his wounds

18 June. During this horrendous day, Hospital Apprentice 1st Class James L. Weddington aided Pharmacist Mate 1st Class Percy V. Templeton carrying wounded Marines out of the woods to safety, thereby saving many lives that might have been lost. Templeton became an even greater hero at Blanc Mont later in October. Another pair of corpsman heroes were Pharmacist Mate 3d John R. Litchfield of the 74th Company and Pharmacist Mate 2d Martin W. Spence of the 76th Company. After the capture of numerous machine gun nests these men rendered conspicuous service. The 74th Company was subjected to a heavy artillery bombardment every half hour for 48 hours in which numerous casualties were sustained. Both day and night Litchfield and Spence worked unceasingly, and due to their efforts the casualty rate was kept to a lower figure than would otherwise have been possible.

Harbord sent to Hughes, time 1002:

> Very important that you give me your judgement on what is north of you in the BOIS DE BELLEAU. Push your reconnaissance and let me know at the earliest possible moment whether you think it possible to take wood north of your present position.
> Let me know:
> 1st: Whether you think it will be practicable to take the part of the BOIS DE BELLEAU north of your present position with your force as it now stands.
> 2nd: How much further artillery preparation should there be on that part of the wood.
> 3rd: If you think your forces are not equal to it with artillery preparation, give me your opinion on the forces necessary.
> All this on the assumption that machine gun fire along the railroad will be kept down by our artillery and that Wise can advance on the left of the BOIS DE BELLEAU.

Field Order No. 4, issued at 1745 by Harbord, gave as the objective (a) Northeastern edge of Bois de Belleau; Hill 133. Coordinates eastern: 175.4-261.7 to 176.3-262.3; western: 175.0-261.9 to 175.5-263.0. The attack would be made by the 2d Battalion, 5th Marines. (b) When objective was attained, liaison would be established on the right with the 1st Battalion, 6th Marines, which was to advance its left to conform to the progress of the attack. The attack would begin at 4:30 a.m.

11 June: Hughes to Harbord at 0700: "Everything is O. K. and in good shape. I have liaison men with men and am getting reports from them. The machine gun nest kept up harassing fire on me all night."

Harbord gave this report to Bundy relative to the attack of 10 June, time sent 0800:

> 3:30 a.m. the 1st Bn., 6th Marines, under command of Major Hughes following an extensive artillery preparation, took the southern half of BOIS DE BELLEAU; rectified our line across the narrow part of the wood about 261.7, with liaison with the Marines on right and left. There remains a nest of machine guns in the eastern edge of the south half of the BOIS DE BELLEAU, about 176.3-261.3. Our line after crossing the narrow part of the BOIS DE BELLEAU as stated bends backwards to the S. W. then roughly to the S. E. to the corner of the wood, containing this nest of machine guns.

Hughes to Harbord, time 0705: "Lieutenant Overton reports that Wise is held up by constant machine gun fire. 3 platoons 76th Company in connection with them. Machine gun nest on my right front partly neutralized by use of mortars [Stokes] and rifle fire. Have had nothing direct from Wise since attack began. Am getting pretty heavy shrapnel fire around my P.C. and have asked for retaliation."

There is a bit more to the story than briefly mentioned above. Wise's 2/5, especially his right flank, was badly shot up by German machine guns as they went into the woods and turned left. One story, by Fritz Wise, tells us that he learned several days after the attack that Hughes had never received orders to advance with Wise, which doesn't sound creditable. Another story, told by Elliott Cooke, commanding officer, 55th Company, states that an unnamed lieutenant of the 6th was embarrassed to find that he had missed the 51st Company, right flank of 2/5's advance, in the dark and mist, and consequently the 51st was shot to pieces by German machine guns. That officer would have been Overton, then in command of the 76th Company. A different version is told by Millett in *Many a Strife: The Story of Jerry Thomas*, then a sergeant in 1/6; Wise complained that Overton wasn't on his flank and Thomas replied to Hughes that he was and that Macon was fighting hard and well. Cooke, a U.S. Army officer, with little direct interest in the outcome, was probably the most objective, and also, he was on the scene at the time. Whatever the true story, Macon Overton redeemed himself many times over before he was killed in action at the Meuse-Argonne.

From Major Frank E. Evans, adjutant, 6th Marines, to Lee, 1015: "Message just received from Brigade. 'Tell Col. Lee to get word to Hughes that Wise passed 2 or 3 M.G.'s on his [Wise's] right. Have Hughes connect up on his left with Wise's right and leave no gaps for M. G.'s to work into rear. Believe are few M.G.'s now in position to fire on our rear. Have Hughes use cover and guard against shell fire.'" The same message was sent to Hughes by Evans.

At 1020 Maj. F. E. Evans, regiment adjutant, sent Hughes an order from brigade: "Connect on left with Wise right.... General wants no gap left for M. G's to get through." From Lee to Harbord, re: message from Hughes, sent at 1348: "Overton just beat off Boche counter-attack. Just sent two platoons to Wise as he said enemy were on his left. Have men in good spirits."

Harbord sent to Hughes at 1405:

Was the nest of machine guns which Lieutenant Overton cleaned out, the main one? Are there any now to prevent your line from straightening out on the east edge of the BOIS DE BELLEAU? In liaison with Shearer on right and Wise on left? If not, what is your exact position now? If machine gun nest still there suggest some German speaking Marine call to them that over 400 of their comrades have surrendered this morning in the north end of the Bois, and are now safe and well fed [better than the Marines?], and ask them to surrender. If nest of machine guns is still there, is it possible to connect your line up on the east edge, with them behind you? What are your losses? What are your captures? Approximately 1,000 replacements arriving for Brigade this p.m.

Diary:

In the south half of BOIS DE BELLEAU, the 1st Bn. 6th Marines, under Major Hughes, has cleaned out the nest of machine guns which has held it up from getting to the other side yesterday. The 76th Company under Lieutenant [Macon C.] Overton, attacked the machine gun nest and carried it. Number of machine gun nests captured not known, but one platoon captured seven. A number of others are presumed to have been captured. Loss in this attack on machine gun nest: 18 wounded, 3 killed, 3 shell shock. Prisoners taken by Major Hughes' battalion turned in and no count kept. Reported as 60. Presumed to be in the estimated total of 400.

Liaison established between BOURESCHES, Major Hughes in the S.E. corner of the BOIS DE BELLEAU and with Lt. Col. Wise's battalion [2/5] to the northwest corner of the Bois near 133, his left flank being slightly refused.

For several days, the 10th through the 13th, 1st Lt. Charles A. Etheridge of the 75th Company performed his duties at the highest level. With combined skill and disregard for danger, Etheridge made repeated reconnaissance in Belleau Wood that proved invaluable to Major Hughes. On the night of the 12th he posted himself and 8 members of the 2d Engineers in a gap in the lines and killed or captured twelve enemy soldiers attempting to get through that gap. He would continue his brave actions throughout the war.

12 June: Message from Hughes to Lee, time sent 0125: "All holding. No other definite information for you yet. Do we get that hot coffee and food before morning? And, can you get some cans of water up to me as far as my P.C.? Advise coming up just S. of ravine. No idea as to casualties." From Lee to Hughes, sent at 1327: "Just as soon that time permits gather up all arms and ammunition and other abandoned property in the sector occupied by your command. Let me know where you assemble them on the W. side of the wood in order that they may be collected and brought to the rear." Lee again to Hughes, time 1351: "Your ammunition and pyrotechnics will be at the dump at or about 9:00 p.m. Please have party report to Lieut. [John I.] Conroy."

Captain John F. Burnes, a 35 year old former Marine gunner, was badly wounded this date but continued placing his men of the 74th Company while under a violent artillery and machine gun fire. His serious injuries caused his death on the 14th.

Hughes to Lee, received at brigade at 2000 hours: "Am being shelled. Front line companies support and reserves on the job. Am attempting to relieve Wise's 51st Company [the skipper, Lloyd W. Williams, had been killed the previous day] on the line, as he needs the men."

Hughes to Wise, sent at 2000 hours: "Am relieving that company of the right but that leaves me only our one company in support and Colonel Lee's orders are that I keep that." Hughes to Lee, sent at 2200 hours: "If it is humanly possible please get a rolling kitchen to P.C. Cole tonight to make hot *strong* coffee for entire Bn. Also please establish relay runner post at same place. Everything quiet and everyone on their toes. Approximately 50 casualties today so far including Lieut. [Edgar Allan] Poe [Jr]. He was wounded in his back. Please send at least two flashlights by bearer. Am sending ammunition carrying party to LUCY dump tonight. Please make Q.M. get me up hot rations by pack animals according to agreed plan, soon as possible. GOBERT practically impassable."

13 June: From Hughes to Harbord, time sent 0050, received at 0315: "All holding. Nothing definite for you as yet. No idea of losses." Lee then sent through Evans, time 0325: "Your message received at 2:48. Impossible to get you hot coffee or water before tonight. I will not be out this morning."

Lt. Col. John A. Hughes, commanding officer, 1/6, to Neville, relayed by Harbord, at 0504: "Have had terrific bombardment and attack. I have every man except a few odd ones in low now. We have not broken contact and have held. Request two companies at least for myself and two companies for Colonel Wise."

In a phone message at 0417 Harbord sent Bundy word that a runner had passed along word that the Germans were attacking Bourseches, and all along the line; that Major Hughes has been under a tremendous strain for a long time, but I don't feel like crediting that information as very reliable. There were several messages received by Harbord that the Germans had taken Bourseches, including one from the 23rd Infantry. But that story was quickly put to rest, the Marines still held the town. A message from Hughes early that morning stated, "Attacking along lines with fresh troops." This could only have meant that the enemy were those attacking since they were the only group that might have had fresh troops. Hughes certainly didn't.

While Hughes was very much in control of his battalion during this period, his adjutant, Capt. Arthur H. Turner, was at all times in the forefront of operations against the enemy. Under all types of hazards, shelling, both gas and shrapnel, Turner exerted control over the many facets of the battalion while in action at Belleau Wood, especially during the period 10 to 13 June.

Another message, from the adjutant, 5th Marines, told of Captain Burns [sic], 74th Company, wounded in both legs (he lost both at the knees). Captain Fuller, 75th Company, was killed. Burnes would die of his wounds on 14 June.

Harbord advised Bundy at 0555 that he had word from Hughes who was doing O.K., "Condition and conduct of men—MAGNIFICENT."

Hughes sent the following to Neville, 5th Marines, and also to brigade at 0504: "Have had terrific bombardment and attack. I have every man, except a few odd ones in tow now. We have not broken contact and have held. Request at least two companies for myself and two companies for Col. Wise."

Hughes to Lee, at 0505: "Everything O.K. now. Men digging in again. Trenches mostly obliterated by shell fire. Estimate casualties at under 20 percent including Capt. Fuller killed and Capt. Burns wounded. If a support Bn. is sent, would like to put it in the line and pull my men out. The evening's barrage was terrific. The conduct of everyone magnificent. Can't you get hot coffee and water to me by using prisoners? As far as I can find out Wise is O.K." Burnes died of his wounds that day.

Hughes to Evans, at 0745: "I am assured a constant stream of coffee from the cook at P.C. Cole. Can't you even give me Boche prisoners to carry it? Have them report to cook." Hughes to Lee, at 1000: "Everything quiet on my front. Wise just asked for a 15 minute barrage on his front. Casualties since yesterday are: Killed 16, wounded 74, missing 12. Includes officers. Available now 15 officers, 700 men."

From Hughes to Lee, no time indicated, but late in day:

1. According to Brigade Commander's orders yesterday I had a conference with Lieut. Col. Wise taking my Intelligence Officer with me. I showed him exactly where the machine gun nests were. The conference as usual resulted in nothing.
   B. I went over my whole line taking with me [2d] Lieut. [R. H.] Loughberry [Loughborough, USA], 51st Company [commanding], agreed with me that his right and my left were almost exactly where they showed on the map. We went back to see Col. Wise and found everybody shooting. I stayed there 15 minutes but Col. Wise wouldn't notice me. There was great confusion and a heavy bombardment going on.
2. Between 7:00 and 8:30 p.m. last night, I got a message from Col. Wise who wanted to know whether I ever intended to relieve his right company. I sent two platoons of the 95th Company under [1st] Lieut. [Morgan R.] Mills [Jr.] to relieve the 51st Company which was only half strength and to tell Lieut Loughberry [sic] to report to Col. Wise. Lieut. Mills sent back word that Loughberry refused to be relieved, claiming that he had no orders. Lieut. Mills stayed there entrenching himself on the left of the 76th Company, where he had been ordered to go and he is still there. At 8:00 a.m. I got another note from Col. Wise

stating that Lieut. Loughberry reported that he had not been relieved. I wrote back that I had relieved him at 9:00 p.m. and that he had refused to go.

3. I wish to report that at 4:30 p.m. this date, a German aeroplane flew twice over my battalion, very low, firing machine guns on it.

Loughborough was the last officer standing on 11 June and assumed command of the 51st Company. Obviously, Wise and Hughes had not been getting along.

14 June: From Hughes to Harbord at 0520: "Front line being gassed. Major Holcomb's other two companies being checked both sides. Lieutenant Colonel [Hiram I.] Bearss going to investigate." Message from Hughes to Lee at 0530: "Fairly heavy gas shell fire on all my companies. CO. reports o.k. are in masks."

This was the period in which the Germans had plastered the entire 4th Brigade with gas shelling for hours. The 2nd Battalion, 6th Marines, caught it worst of all with 378 Marines evacuated, while Hughes' battalion lost 165 Marines for the same reason. The other members of the brigade had fewer casualties but all losses were significant. Late in the day Evans was reporting to Harbord that the men of the 6th Marines had been wearing their masks at least six hours, which of course, in addition to being very uncomfortable, impeded their effectiveness greatly. Later in the day, at about 1645, the regimental gas officer, 1st Lt. Henry E. Chandler, reported that Hughes was suffering from gas himself and when Chandler suggested that he move his post of command to higher ground, Hughes responded, "My orders are to stick." Harbord ordered Hughes to move his post of command and battalion to the west and higher ground the following morning.

At some point in time 1/6 was assigned to the 5th Marines and Hughes was made responsible to Neville. Lee sent an order to 2d Lt. John I. Conroy, Headquarters Company, stating that 5th wanted wiring for Hughes' battalion begun immediately. A few minutes later, at 1145, Lee sent Hughes a message telling him: "Col. Neville wants wiring for your Bn. begun immediately.... Could not get you by phone. Coffee for 75th goes to LUCY in 5 minutes by King ambulance." Lee sent to Hughes at 1210: "I should like to do all you ask and am as ever much interested in you and the 1st, but you are now under the 5th Regt. and should ask these things of the 5th Hdqrs. Am sure that they will comply. We wish and *will do anything* permitted by the 5th. Congratulations on your fine work."

Conroy advised someone, possibly Lee, at 1250 hours that he had no wire nor stakes and if they were wanted, then they will have to be gotten at the engineer dump at Ferme de Paris. He continued: "Please let me know when they start [installing wire] and I will send some good men over to assist in the work." Hughes to Lee, sent at 1440:

> Can't start wiring until Conroy supplys me with wire and stakes. Do not believe it will be possible to begin wiring until after dark as slightest movement in front line draws heavy shelling. In view of this shall I start immediately upon receipt of wire, mauls and stakes, or shall I wait until dark? Please answer at once. Your message received at 12:45 p.m. Sent an officer at once to observe [Brigadier General Manus] McCloskey's [commanding officer, 2nd Field Artillery Brigade] firing. Presume he will be too late. Please let me know if I shall recall him. Relative to coffee request; Conroy have ordered that no ration or carrying parties enter LUCY by daylight. GOBERT trench and woods full of Mustard Gas.

Hughes still asked Lee to direct him. It was evident he didn't think much of the order to wire his front.

Evans sent to Hughes at 1445:

Am sending Lt. C.[lyde] P. Matteson, Hdqrs Co., Comdg. 1 pds Plat. & 2nd Lt. F.[rederick] J. Scheld, Inf. USR to you. Matteson is a bearcat, strong, fearless & made good at BOURSECHES with Holcomb. Sibley in BOIS DE BELLEAU. You can have absolute confidence in him. Scheld is Infy. Officer by training, was formerly in 82nd Co. before being detached as instructor in 32nd Div. So far as I know he's good. Make any changes in re to officers to Cos. you want to. Will have wire out tonight and hot coffee. Believe you can string wire on trees. Have no stakes. Expect to change back to P.C. CHATEL tonight. Wire will go out at dusk. The artillery dropped fifteen in a cluster on supposed enemy battery. Sorry I had to send message as phone was out. Managed by luck to get observation through [1st Lt. William A.] Eddy [regiment intelligence officer]. Am sending for samples by bearers that I hope will help. Glad to know that all is quiet in the Bois. Have told Walker about your signal bunch.

At 1440 hours, in a message to the commanding officer, 23rd Infantry, Colonel Malone, the unit's liaison officer with the 6th Marines reported the following information: "Sketch gives position of the troops in the Center of Resist. on the immediate left of the 23rd Infantry. This force is the 1st Bn., 6th Marines, to be under the command of *C.O. Fifth Marines* from this date."

Lee advised Adjutant Evans at 1605: "Regt. Surgeon [Lt. Cmdr Wrey G. Farwell] just reported ... he has evacuated 150 from 1st Bn. 6th & that woods are being gassed."

Harbord sent this to Neville at 1700: "Because of mustard gas in the south half of BOIS DE BELLEAU, leave not to exceed one company of the 1st Bn. 6th on the east edge of the BOIS DE BELLEAU. These men with care can get far enough into the open to strike sunlight and be out of the gas which remains in the woods." Evans sent to Harbord at 1737: "Regt. Gas Officer left Hughes P. C. 4:45 p.m. Gas shells being dropped rear Bn. P. C.... Hughes showing effects. Regtl. Surgeon reports 185 evacuations 1st Bn."

For the balance of that day reports kept coming in that the enemy were bringing up troops via cars, trucks, etc., and Lee ordered vigilance. Sometime that day Hughes, having been gassed and thoroughly incapacitated, was relieved by Maj. Franklin B. Garrett. Garrett was not an officer who was considered for anything but relief roles and administrative kinds of duty. As Millett stated at the moment, "However, the 1st Battalion did not need a heroic leader. It needed rest." Hughes was out of the war.

15 June: From Garrett to Lee, sent at 1350: "New coordinates are 175.7-261.1. Have 15 officers and 633 men." Evans duly passed that information on to Maj. Harry Lay at 4th Brigade.

At 2000 hours the regimental surgeon, Commander Wrey G. Farwell, sent an order to Dr. White, surgeon, 2nd Battalion: "Send Gates, your new Ch. P. Mate to Reg. Aid Sta so he can be sent to 1st Bat. [6th]. [Lieut. Francis E.] Locy and [Ch.P. Mate Maclyn E.] Dent evacuated." The navy was also having their troubles.

16 June: Harbord sent a message to Neville at 1630:

On the arrival of the 2nd Bn., 7th Infantry [3d U.S. Division] please relieve with it the 1st Bn., 6th Marines in the south half of the BOIS DE BELLEAU. The 1st Bn., 6th Marines, when relieved will proceed by marching to the vicinity of MONTREUIL where it will take trucks and proceed to near MERY to the station vacated by the 2nd Bn., 7th Infantry. The battalions will exchange temporarily their transportation, rolling kitchens, ration and water carts, etc. Details of this temporary change will be arranged by battalion commanders. Command passed when relief is completed.

The actual relief of 1/6 didn't take place until the night of 18-19 June. They were the last and down to less than half strength. And so the time had come for the Marine Brigade to obtain some slight relief from the rigors they had lived with for nearly seventeen days. Quiet, hot meals, water to bathe in and delousing too, probably, and of course hot coffee. The trouble was that the 7th Infantry, though classed as regulars, was an untrained unit.

Harbord, who was still in command of the sector wrote to the commanding officer, 1st Battalion, 7th Infantry: "Your battalion will be relieved tomorrow night [21st June]. Tomorrow morning is its only chance to redeem the failure made this morning. If you clear the northern half of the BOIS DE BELLEAU the credit will belong to the 1st Bn., 7th Infantry and will be freely given. The battalion can not afford to fail again." Clearly not a very responsible message to send to men who were trying. The Marines had been shattered going up against that wood and how Harbord expected untrained troops to do better is beyond me.

One/Six was back in the Belleau Wood area beginning on the night of 23-24 June, when they were placed in the Bois Gros Jean as division reserve.

26 June: Harbord to Garrett at 0830: "At dark tonight move your battalion to the woods northwest of LUCY as Brigade Reserve. Your battalion will furnish a detail, daily or nightly, of approximately 200 men for work on the support trenches in that sector. Lieut. Wyman, 2nd Engrs., has the supervision of this work."

Except for moderate participation during the balance of the campaign to take the woods, it was mostly a 3/5 show for the rest of the period and 1/6 had a very small part. On 28 June, 1/6 relieved 3/6 in the southeast corner of Bois de Belleau. There and then that battalion was given, by Harbord, the entire defense of the woods with support from the 6th Machine Gun Battalion. For all intents and purposes, even though 1/6 and 2/5 didn't take entire control of the woods, they were the two battalions which broke the back of the German defensive by killing more of them than anyone or anything else, except for the artillery.

28 June: From Harbord to Neville, Turrill [1/5], Lee, Hughes [1/6], Sibley [3/6], at 2200: "The 1st Bn. 6th Marines will relieve the 3d Bn, 6th Marines in the BOIS DE BELLEAU as soon as practicable after dark, night of June 29-30. Reconnaissance by Battalion and Company Commanders during the day June 29th. 3d Bn. 6th Marines to BOIS GROS JEAN south of PARIS-METZ Road as Division Reserve. 1st Bn. 5th Marines to woods N.W. of LUCY night of June 29-30 as Brigade Reserve."

30 June: From Harbord to Neville, Lee, Waller [6th Machine Gun Battalion], Hughes, and Holcomb [2/6], sent at 1640.

> When the 2d Bn. 6th Marines is withdrawn from the Bois de Belleau it will not be replaced. The 1st Bn. 6th Marines will hold the Bois alone. The wiring must be completed without delay. Positions selected as strong points should have the rifle pits connected for occupation by squads or platoons according to their location, field of fire, etc. The C.O. 1st Bn, 6th Marines will consult with the C.O. 5th Marines and the C.O., 6th Machine Gun Bn. in making the plans for taking over the defense of the entire Bois. The present intention is to relieve the 2d Bn. on the night of the 2d-3d. of July.

The 26th U.S. "Yankee Division" was their replacement unit. On 4 July the 104th Infantry, later to be commanded by that fighting Marine Hiking Hiram Bearss, arrived and 1/6 went into virtual retirement, at least for a few days, anyway. They did the same things all the other members of the 2d Division did; they went swimming in the Marne River, bought up all movable products found in French shops and slept to their hearts' content.

5 July: Lee to Garrett at 0955: "Your relief is in the same woods as your P. C., and I hope you will find it easy. Immediately upon completion of your relief notify me by phone 'The mail has arrived.'"

6 July: At 1945 Lee sent Garrett a message: "Obtain 30 picks and 30 shovels for use in construction of pits for the shelter of your command in the position now occupied by it."

8 July: Message from Lee to Garrett, at 1540: "You will at 6 p.m. this date relieve with your Bn. the 3rd Bn. of this regiment, who will turn over to you his new sub-sector, which has been extended to the westward to included the BOIS DES ESSERTIS, connecting with the 1st Bn. 23rd Inf. You will arrange the details for this relief with the C.O. 3rd Bn."

On 11 July Harbord had been promoted to major general and command of the division, and Neville to command of the 4th Marine Brigade. Harbord went on five days' leave and a worn-out Neville was taken to a hospital. Lieutenant Colonel Harry Lee assumed command of the brigade during that period of time. Both Harbord and Neville returned in time to participate in the Aisne-Marne Offensive, more commonly known as Soissons.

Soissons

The 6th Regiment had a tough time getting to the assignment, just south of the city of Soissons, just as had the 5th Marines on 18 July. The latter, of course, with the 9th and 23d Infantry Regiments, rolled forward and drove the Germans back many kilometers nearly to the city of Tigny on the Soissons–Chateau-Thierry Road. They suffered numerous casualties but were generally considered very successful. The following day was just the 6th Marines and no one else, and they paid an awful price for the "honor." On 16 July Major John A. Hughes returned to his battalion to reassume command.

19 July 1918: The attack lineup of the 6th was as follows: One/Six on the right; 2/6 on the left with 3/6 in the support line. Hughes still commanded 1/6; Thomas Holcomb, recently promoted to lieutenant colonel and assistant to Lee, at his own request had within hours resumed command of 2/6 from Maj. Robert L. Denig, and Sibley still had 3/6. All were capable but, under the circumstances, could do nothing to abort what was going to happen to them and their battalions that day.

At 0730 the regiment moved forward from their place of repose. Two battalions went into their first line at Vierzy. Hughes' battalion, 1/6, moved to the right flank and Holcomb's 2/6 the left flank. Sibley's 3/6 would support the first line. Hughes had gone forward and settled his men in an open wheat field, somewhat exposed to artillery and Maxims. Most of Holcomb's men were inside a walled cemetery that initially provided some protection. Several hours before the 6th Marines were to jump off, the artillery had already fired their rolling barrage. Hence, when the 6th took off from their positions at 0830, in and about Vierzy, there was no rolling barrage for them. Worse, the Germans were ready for them. The only artillery fire they witnessed was incoming and dropping on them. The regiment had to cross

Top: The 6th Regiment advancing at Soissons on 19 July. *Bottom:* The champion 6th Marines baseball team in 1919.

Unidentified members of the 74th Company, 1/6, resting between voyages while on the Rhine duty.

over two miles to their target. Most wouldn't make it. Hughes sent very few messages this day. His battalion was badly handled.

An outstanding Marine, Gy. Sgt. John J. Nagazyna, of the 95th, was awarded a Distinguished Service Cross, later a Navy Cross, a Silver Star citation, and the top French award, their equivalent to our Medal of Honor, a Medaille Militaire plus 3 Croix de Guerre, a Palm, a Gilt, and a Bronze. During a critical time in the assault against Tigny, when his company had suffered heavy losses, he set such an example of personal bravery and determination as to inspire his men to success. At a time when it seemed impossible to advance any further, his fearlessness in moving up and down his lines to steady his men encouraged them to go forward against heavy odds and take and hold their objective. Sergeant Oliver C. Farrant, of the 95th Company, led his platoon with remarkable coolness in the advance under heavy fire of machine guns & artillery. He was severely wounded but continued to advance, thereby setting such an inspiring example to the men of his section that they routed the enemy. He died of his wounds on July 22, 1918. For extraordinary heroism he was awarded a Distinguished Service Cross, Navy Cross, two Silver Stars, and a Croix de Guerre.

Corporal William H. Skaggs, of the 76th Company, was awarded a Navy Cross and a Silver Star citation for extraordinary heroism. Although seriously wounded in action, he carried a wounded comrade six kilometers to a dressing station through terrific enemy fire.

Hughes sent the following message to Col. Lee at 1015: "P.C/ 1 kilometer due east of TIGNY. My Bn. held up 300 yards W. of TIGNY. No troops on right. None on left. Tanks all out of action. Request immediate reinforcements. Dr. Mack only Dr. with me. Need doctors and some means to evacuate badly wounded. Request counter battery work at once.

Remnants of Bn. clear of TIGNY to west. Have about 200 men left. Lt. [Clifton B.] Cates 96th Co. reports 20 survivors." Hughes must have meant one kilometer west of Tigny; east would have placed him and his command behind the German lines.

With a small detachment 2d Lt. Scott M. Johnston of the 76th charged a machine gun which was inflicting severe losses on the American lines. Although seriously wounded, he stayed with his men until ordered to a dressing station by his company commander. He died of his wounds on 15 August 1918. There were many heroes on this date.

Later, at 1235, Hughes notified someone: "Germans entering Parcy-Tigny in strong numbers. Thinks they will counter-attack." At 1545 Lee sent the following message to all three battalion commanders: "The Division Commander directs us to dig in and hold our present line at all costs. No further advance will be made, for the present. He congratulates the command on its gallant conduct in the face of severe casualties. Let me make a sketch of your position and disposition. Ammunition at crossroads 122 southeast of Vierzy."

Corporal William H. Faga, of the 76th Co., received a Distinguished Service Cross at Soissons on 19 July for attacking and capturing a machine gun that was inflicting heavy losses on the American lines. In addition, he volunteered and successfully carried messages of great importance to his battalion commander through a machine gun and artillery barrage. He would be awarded a second DSC, with Oak Leaf Cluster, and a Navy Cross at the Meuse-Argonne.

Later that night the French relieved the 6th Marines, who began a retreat backwards for several days. While in bivouac near Translon Farm on 20 July, German artillery cut through the heavy old trees and in cutting the branches, wounded several men.

One/Six lost several officers, including Captain John Kearns of the 95th Company, 2d Lt. Carleton Burr of the 74th Company, and 1st Lt. David A. Redford of the 75th. While at Soissons Captain Arthur H. Turner of the Battalion Headquarters and seven unidentified lieutenants were wounded.

On 31 July the regiment entrained for the Toul Sector and detrained the following day at Nancy. For the next few days the regiment was cleaned up, rested and fed.

Marbache

No official reports, messages, or diaries mention 1/6 during this period, except for one brief entry for 24 August.

The semi-official history of the 6th Regiment stated that on 7 August, 2/6 occupied trenches at Pont-a-Mousson relieving the 347th French Infantry Regiment, with the 1st and 3d Battalions in reserve. On 16 August, Holcomb was assigned to duty as second in command of the regiment. On 17 August, 1/6 was moved to Harmonville and billeted on 19 August.

24 August: Memorandum from Capt. Walter H. Sitz, Regt. Adjutant, to Lt. Col. Thomas Holcomb, now assistant regimental commander, stated: "The 1st Battalion will leave Harmonville at five o'clock p.m. tomorrow afternoon for Camp Bois de l'Eveque." The balance of the message concerns 3/6.

From this sector the Second Division was moved, beginning on 22 August, to assist in the 1st U.S. Army's attack upon the St. Mihiel Salient. They arrived in place before the town of Limey on 11 September. On that date a number of replacements arrived bringing the regiment almost to full complement, according to the semi-official history.

St. Mihiel

On 11 September the 73d Machine Gun Company was assigned to 1/6 for the St. Mihiel campaign. Several entries of that company are included here.

12 September: The first entry was from Major Frederick Barker, commanding officer, 1/6, to Lee at 1930: "Batt. P.C. at R.R. Station in north-west part of town. The Batt. holds a line along the VERDUN and NANCY road from 362.-326.8."

13 September: The 73d Machine Gun Company was assigned duty with 1/6. Captain George Shuler, commanding officer, sent a message to Lee at 0800 describing the disposition of his company: "Company distributed as follows: 1st Platoon with 74th Company ½ kilo north of town of THIAUCOURT. 2nd Platoon with 75th Company. 3rd Platoon with 76th Company. One gun mounted Ant-Aviation. Our guns fired occasionally during night at enemy working parties. Have sent for company train to come to THIAUCOURT. Casualties to 8:00 a.m. today, one man, [Private] Benjamin D. Middleman 120234 slightly wounded, not evacuated. Going strong."

Barker wrote to Lee at 2045: "This battalion has relieved the 3rd Battalion of the 23rd Inf. Relief completed at 8:00 p.m. Battalion holds support line along Beney-Thiaucourt Road 361.0-362.5 except 3 platoons of 74th Co. which is 400 yds. north of the road. Order of companies right to left 74th Co., 76th Co. 75th and 95th Co. in rear of 74th & 76th South of road. Battalion P.C. at R.R. station 362.8-241.4."

14 September: Shuler, at 1/6's post of command, wrote to Lee at 0900: "Report up to 5:30 a.m. this date—killed none, wounded two slightly, both returned to duty. Missing in action—none. AWOL 1 sergeant, 1 private. Sick—three privates."

Shuler, still with 1/6, wrote at 1915 to Lee: "Have sent 1st platoon with 74th Co. 3rd platoon with 76th Company. 2nd platoon remains in place with 75th Co. I am at Railroad station same place as today. Telephone in working order. Captain [George] Stowell, Senior Officer of 1st Batn. is with me."

15 September: From Barker to Lee at 1205 that morning: "74th Co. has taken up outpost positions and is in liaison with the 47th Co. [3/5] on right. 76th Co. in reserve protecting the left flank. Enemey artilley in wood to the left approximately on hill 363.4-244.9. Am reconnoitering to left front now. No resistance. One casualty."

The best entry for 1/6 is the operations report written by Major Frederick A. Barker, the commanding officer of 1/6. No time is mentioned, but it covers 12 to 15 September:

> Par. 1: In compliance with field order #27, Headquarters Second Division, A.E.F., Sept. 10th, 1918, and Field Orders #57, Headquarters 23rd Infantry, A.E.F., Sept. 11th, 1918 this battalion plus 73rd Machine Gun Company, Regimental Machine Gun Company, 6th Reg't. maintained liaison between the 2nd Division, A.E.F. and 89th Division, A.E.F., having been placed under the command of the Regimental Commander of the 23rd Infantry during the attack and capture of Thiaucourt Sept. 12th, 1918. During the advance very little resistance was encountered, 13 prisoners

were captured. Upon arrival at Thiaucourt this battalion was placed in reserve along the Beney-Thiaucourt Road. This battalion suffered very few casualties during the attack.

Par. 2: On Sept. 13th, 1918, at about 8:00 a.m. orders were received from Regimental Headquarters, detailing the first battalion as relief for the 3rd Battalion, 23rd Infantry who were holding the line 200 yds north of Thiaucourt-Beney Road. This relief was completed at 6 p.m. same date.

Par. 4: At 4:30 p.m. Sept. 14th, 1918, orders were received from Regimental Headquarters to have in readiness at short notice two companies prepared to leave on reconnaissance duty to the north of Thiaucourt to discover the exact location of the line of resistance established by the enemy. At 6:30 p.m. orders were received to move the two companies to the north and establish an outpost line on the northern edge of the Bois de la Montagne. At 7:30 p.m. I moved out to the north with the 74th and 76th Companies and two platoons of the 73rd Machine Gun Company. We entered the Bois de la Montagne at a point approximately 363.9 to 44.1 (Map Hageville 1 to 10000). Outposts were established by the 74th Company at 384.9 to 244.7 (Map Hageville 1 to 10000). Liaison was established with outpost of 47th Company, 5th Regiment on our right. The 76th Company was held in reserve to protect our left flank. Combat patrols were sent out from this company along the Rupt Ravine. I was informed that the 89th Division was to make a raid on Charey at 11:40 p.m. I did not establish outposts to the west of the Rupt Ravine, so as not to get caught in the barrage preceding the raid. The 89th Division did not execute the above raid. We met with no resistance except the woods occupied by us was heavily shelled during the night.

Par. 5: At 4:30 a.m. Captain George Shuler arrived with the remaining platoon of the 73rd Company and the 75th and 95th Companies of the First Battalion. Captain Shuler informed me that Major Williams [commanding officer, 2/6] was on his way to join the First Battalion with orders to occupy a position in reserve along the north edge of the Bois de La Montagne. Also at this time 45th Company, 5th Regiment joined us on the right. Major Williams did not communicate with me upon his arrival and entered the Bois de la Montagne to the west of the position occupied by my battalion at this time. I issued orders to Captain Stowell commanding 75th Company to establish outposts to the west of the 74th Company along northern edge of the Bois de la Montagne. I directed the 95th Company to take up a support position in rear of the 75th Company. Before the 75th Company and 95th Company had time to advance and take up positions assigned them the 2nd Battalion had advanced, towards north part of the Bois de la Montagne and had engaged the enemy. The 2nd Battalion advanced to the north end of the woods and continued to attack the enemy but were compelled to fall back to the north edge of the Bois de la Montagne, due to the heavy Machine Gun fire from Machine Guns located at the Mon Plaisir Farm and the Grande Fountain and also fire from their front. The enemy then attempted a counter attack, which was repulsed. The 75th Company, 95th Company, the 2nd Battalion, 74th Company, 6th Regiment and the 45th and 47th Companies, 5th Regiment in order named dug in and held positions on north edge of wood. I ordered all organizations to hold what they had and not to advance in accordance with my original orders to establish a line of outposts on northern edge of Bois de la Montagne. The positions occupied by the First and Second Battalions were continually shelled during the day. At about 6 p.m. Major Williams reported to me that the enemy was about to make another attack on the positions held by us. I requested a barrage and this attack was quickly repulsed. At about 4 p.m. we received orders that we would be relieved by the first battalion 310th Regiment, 78th Division. All preparations were made to execute this relief which was completed at 2:30 a.m. Sept. 16th, 1918. At 8:00 p.m. orders were received, that the Division on our left had not advanced and established outposts on left of our line and that it would be necessary to send out covering detachments to cover our left flank. The 78th Company furnished the covering detachments for the left flank.

Par. 6: The 2nd Battalion suffered heavy casualties during the attack made by them in the morning. This battalion suffered the following casualties: 2 officers, 64 men. The prisoners captured during the day were taken by the 2nd Battalion.

F. A. BARKER, Major,
   Commanding 1st Bn.,
      6th Regt. USMC.

Following this campaign the Second Division was reassigned to the command of the French Army with instructions to head for their lines just west of the Argonne Forest. On or about 30 September most of the Second Division arrived in the area of Suippe, located at the foot of the Blanc Mont Massif. There they spread out, the 3d Brigade moving to the eastern side of the Bois de la Vipère and the 4th to the western side.

Blanc Mont

30 September: Major Barker advised Col. Lee at 1700 that he was holding aside the following officers from the various companies of his battalion:

74th	75th	95th
2nd Lt. Wilbur Eickelberg	2nd Lt. John R. Hardin	1st Lt. John N. Popham, Jr.
2nd Lt. [?] Thames	2nd Lt. Roger B. Kirkbridge	2nd Lt. Raymond F. Murphy
2nd Lt. Wilbur Summerlus [Summerlin]	2nd Lt. Forrest J. Ashwood	2nd Lt. George Belmont
		2nd Lt. Stephen Elliott

76th
2nd Lt. William H. Busby

[I could not find any mention of anyone with a name similar to Thames in the entire Marine Corps of that period. Could he have been a U.S. Army officer left over or newly appointed to the 4th Brigade?]

There were two Murphys in the 95th, Lewis J. and Raymond F., both former enlisted Marines.

At no time indicated, Barker had a sketch sent to Lee showing his various companies' location: "1st Batt. in trench facing N. on West side of SUIPPES-SOUAIN Road 2½ kilometers north of SUIPPES. Order of companies from road to west 76, 95, 75 and 74. Batt. P.C. at P.C. Bordeaux."

1 October: Barker sent Lee a correction to the first message: "2nd Lt. Tom E. Wicks, 75th Co. is one of the officers that are to stay behind instead of 2nd Lt. F. Ashwood as per memorandum of Sept. 30."

2 October: From Barker to Lee at 0445: "Relief completed at 4:45 a.m. with one casualty, Gy. Sgt. Berdleman 73rd Co. This battalion has taken up its position against the railroad bank between the following coordinates: 268.5-276.8–267.3-276.6, in the following order: Companies from left to right: 75, 74, 76, 95." Barker sent to Maj. Ernest Williams, commanding officer, 2/6, at 0815: "The 1st Bn. P.C. is in a tunnel running under railroad track at point 268.3-276.6." At the same moment Barker sent to Lee: "One Captain and one lieutenant of the 2nd Bn. 23rd Inf. made a reconnaissance at 8:00 a.m. this date, but the battalion has not moved into position yet."

At 0920 Col. Lee sent the following message to all three battalion commanders:

On "D" day and "H" hour I have warning that this regiment will advance in three echelons to the North and West against the positions held by the enemy in our immediate front in trenches Pacha and d' Essen, then a little West of north to include BLANC MONT. In this event, 2nd Battalion leading with two front companies in its front line and 2 in local support will be followed by, the 1st and 3rd., respectively at about 800 to 1,000 meters, similarly disposed and during the advance guarding carefully our left flank for the entire advance to BLANC MONT. Precautions must be taken in each Bn. for combat liaison with the battalions on their right "of the 5th Regiment." It will be well if in each Bn. as many maps are marked to show the regimental sector and as much consideration of the maps be had as is possible before "H" hour.

The boundaries of the regimental sectors will be as follows;
Western
from 266.9-277.0 North to 277.7 then Northwest to 265.8-280.8.
Eastern
from 260.0-277.0 to 267.2-280.1.

It is thought the order might make this the final objective where possibly the 3rd Brigade will leap-frog to exploitation. Until orders are received make this your plan and be prepared to move to its execution before noon. Packs should be left at the jumping-off point under charge of one man from each platoon. In case of shortage of grenade should be made for supply in the sectors you now occupy. Impress all men with the fact that musketry is still KING and they have but to sit tight and shoot straight insuring superiority of fire and guaranteeing success.

(signed) Lee

The last part of that order has surely spawned reactions of surprise and amusement for the past nearly 100 years.

A later message from Lee to 1st and 2d Battalion leaders at 1045 said: "Attack is postponed for twenty four hours." At 1830 Barker sent a strange message to Lee: "Co. G. 2nd Bn., 23rd Inf. has withdrawn 4 kilos. to the S.E. leaving our left flank open for a kilo. We have no information regarding this withdrawal: can this information be given us at once." This seems strange because the 3d Brigade had its own positions to the right of the 4th Brigade with the Bois de la Vipère between them. I've checked the records of the 23d Infantry and can find nothing to explain this stated situation. Yet mention of a battalion of the 23d continued on that date.

3 October: Lee sent to all three battalion commanders the following message at 0350: "'H' hour for the attack is at 5:50 a.m. October 3, 1918. Artillery preparation starts at 5:45 a.m. No other change except that a battalion of the 5th Regiment will take of hook in trench ESSEN to our left. Detailed orders will be sent to you as soon as orders received." The 17th Company, 1/5, was selected to take out the Essen Hook. They did and turned it over to the French army unit to their left, which allowed the Germans to retake it that afternoon.

At 0500 Lee sent a highly detailed message to all three battalion commanding officers describing their actions at 0550. Essentially it said that the 6th Regiment would lead, followed by the 5th Regiment in a column of battalions, with a distance of 1,000 yards between them. There would be a 5 minute artillery preparation and at zero hour a rolling barrage would begin and precede the infantry by 100 yards. French tanks were assigned: 12 tanks to the leading battalion "in the usual front line attack formation" while the next battalion would have 12 tanks following them to repel possible enemy counterattacks. All troops would be in position two hours before "H" hour (i.e., at 0345). What he didn't mention was the actual formation. The first unit was 2/6 with the 81st Machine Gun Company, 6th Machine Gun

Battalion, followed by 1/6, Barker and the 73d Machine Gun Company, 6th Regiment, and last by 3/6, with the 15th Machine Gun Company. Barker advised Lee at 0720: "Held up by M.G. fire on right flank B. Somme-Py. No troops on right flank at all."

Private Wilfred J. Serpas, of the 76th, on this date guided and placed four tanks into the most advantageous positions under terrific machine gun, anti-tank, and one pounder gun fire. He was awarded two Silver Star citations and a Croix de Guerre, Silver.

At 0730 Lee told Barker: "Well done. Bn. of 5th should be on your left flank. Think it is there. Try to get contact with them. Don't hesitate to ask for artillery barrage when it is needed. Likewise state your own position. Always state time." At 0800 Maj. Williams, 2/6, sent Barker a query: "Are you in contact with any one on your right."

Evidently, Williams was expecting some unit, perhaps from the 3d Brigade, to be in the Bois de la Vipère. There were a few Germans left, but not too many; most had retreated up to the ridge under orders when the Second Division appeared.

Barker gave Lee an update of his location and situation at 1000: "Gained objective at 9:45 a.m. now consolidating line. 23rd Inf. on our right, 2nd Batt. on our left. Have seen nothing of the 5th Marines, our left flank is exposed, we expect a counter attack on our left, preparing for it. Col. of 23rd Inf. is going to send a Batt. to help protect left flank."

At 1010 Major George K. Shuler, now commanding 3/6, sent Lee a message that "1st Btn. has passed through 2nd Btn. and holds objective." Barker and 1/6 were on Blanc Mont Ridge but there were numerous Germans buried in caves within that would have to be removed in a day or two. Barker sent 3/6 a message at 1130: "Have reached our objective and consolidating line. 2nd Batt. on our left, 23rd Inf. on right. Left flank exposed. Expect counter-attack. Have you seen Fifth Marines? Let us know your exact location of P.C. and your companies."

Shuler sent Barker a message at 1210 telling him his post of command location and that he had a message from Williams of 2/6, "Enemy were circling left and [Williams was] asking for help." At 1240 Barker replied to Shuler: "1st and 2nd Batt. on front line with no support. In need of support line. Can you help us out." Then at 1325 Williams sent Barker a message: "Messersmith [78th Co.] has orders to extend my left flank and connect up with French on left. Will not assist in strengthening front line. Battalion from 23rd has not started yet. We need the 95th Company, at least until Bn. of 23rd appears."

At 1331 Shuler sent Barker a message which indicated that 3/6 was "about 800 meters in your rear" and if Barker wanted him closer, "Give me an idea where you would like my line." At 1415 Barker advised both the commanding officer of the 23d Infantry and Col. Lee of the current situation: "It is reported that a great amount of artillery coming in on our left flank along the road running W. at 266.3-282.3."

Lee sent a message to both 1/6 and 3/6 at 1445 telling them that "the French division on our left has advanced. Our division will move forward at 4:00 p.m. and occupy the ridge to the eastward and southeastward of ST. ETIENNE." He also mentioned that the 5th Marines would pass through the 6th and the new objective. When that happened the reorganized 6th would follow the 5th "in the order—Barker, Williams, Shuler, and would assure the protection of the left flank."

Five minutes later Lee told both Barker and Williams that a captured German major had told him that there were "twenty pieces of artillery" located about 1 kilometer north of "Mont Blanc" [*sic*] and that they were to make a careful reconnaissance to verify his statement, and if correct to make plans to capture them.

First Lieutenant Leo D. Hermle, commanding officer, 74th Company, sent Williams, 2/6, a message at 1555: "The two platoons of the 74th Co. on your left were relieved by the 43rd Co. 5th Reg. and the gap is now closed. Our two platoons have drawn back to the support. Is this all right." Barker sent Shuler a message at 1915: "As far as I know we will remain here tonight. Have just received a message from Regt. Commander that kitchens, water carts etc. will be up tonight. You will send a continuous patrol all night on your left flank and front. I will send out a patrol to our rear and left to connect with yours at the edge of the woods."

4 October: Barker sent Shuler a message at 0220: "Information received that Boche will attack on our left about 4:00 a.m. Our left flank is still exposed. Can you move your battalion so that two companies join our left flank and face West. At least two companies are necessary. Whole battalion if possible. Fresh division facing us."

Barker sent the commanding officer of an unnamed battalion of the 9th Infantry a message at what looks like 0322. He told of expecting a German attack and said: "Our left flank is badly exposed and we would appreciate any help you could give us." Then he added, "Would you help our left flank if the attack develops by taking up a position along the road running north and south (app) at 266.4-280.0 from this point to the south along this road." These various messages are confusing since the 3d Brigade was to the right flank of the 4th Brigade. It would mean that the 3d Brigade would have to move far to their left to be on the 4th Brigade's left.

Lee sent a message to all at 0750, advising them that the "French 2nd Division attacks on our left ... leading French elements will jump off from a position abreast of Shuler Bn. at 9:50 a.m." First Lieutenant Alfred H. Noble, commanding officer, 83d Company, 3/6, sent message to Shuler telling him that "Objective has been reached by 1st Batt ... 1st Batt. is on front line. 2nd Batt. halted on first ridge. 1st Batt. went on thru."

The problem that faced the 5th Marines began early afternoon and Lee indicated this when he sent a message to Shuler at 1255: "Rear element of the 5th Regiment [1/5] is at approximately 281.7 and is being subjected to heavy M.G. fire from left flank and right and left rear. Get in touch with Barker and tell him to move forward to relieve the 5th of this fire, both on the left flank and from the right and left rear. Your Bn. and the 2nd Bn. will stand fast, for the present. The "H" hour for today is 2:30. Inform the other two to that affect. You will understand that the regiment is not to move forward as a whole, but only Barker, who has a special mission to perform." Moments later Shuler sent Barker the information.

Lee phoned a message to "Sister II" (someone at Brigade, possibly Lt. Col. Earl H. Ellis) at 1445 that he had just gotten word that "Barker has not moved. He has gone down to visit Shuler." However, at 1500 Shuler told Lee that "Barker and Williams had already moved forward."

Barker sent a message to Shuler at 1550: "Are you in liaison with the French division on our left, if so please give us their extreme north and eastern limits, as they have not arrived at our lines yet, and we are receiving severe machine gun fire from our left rear. Answer at once." Colonel Logan Feland, commanding officer of the 5th Regiment, sent Barker a message at 1625: "Request that you support our line as soon as possible, in accordance with orders which the Brigade says have been given you, also to the 2nd Bn. of the 6th."

That afternoon the Fifth Marines were literally destroyed, especially 1/5, and had fallen back to more defendable positions along the Suippe–St. Etienne Road. Lee sent Barker and Williams an order at 1900 for both to "take up position in support of 5th Regt. and dig in. There will be no further advance tonight." At 2310 Lee notified Barker: "Brigade directs that you place your two advanced companies in a position in rear of the 5th Regt. to support it in case it is attacked."

Earlier that evening, at 2030, Barker had sent Lee a message, which didn't arrive until 2330, telling him that he had already taken up positions supporting the 5th Regiment, setting the 74th and 95th Companies on their left flank and the 76th and 75th remaining in the main line of resistance. He also mentioned that the 74th Company was attacked by the German infantry "while taking up their new positions."

Second Lieutenant William J. Mosher, of the 74th Company, was conspicuous for bravery, coolness and good judgment on the evening of 4 October, when he took command of two platoons, placing them on the exposed left flanks of the front line, thereby saving the company to his right.

On 4 October, 2d Lt. Edwin J. Davenport was commended for remarkable skill and courage in leading his platoon from a support position to a place in line in the face of a strong artillery barrage. Because of his skill and coolness in forming a skirmish line and directing a steady rifle fire, an attempted enemy counter attack failed.

5 October: Lee sent several messages early that morning to Barker and Williams about artillery firing upon German machine nests between 0515 and 0615 and for the troops to be out of the line of fire. Lee sent all three battalion commanders the following message at 0815: "This regiment will at once be organized and be prepared to pass through the 5th Marines and continue the advance when ordered. Usual formation—order of battalions, head to rear, Williams [2/6], Shuler [3/6] and Barker [1/6]."

In a phone conversation at 0920 Lee asked Barker the following: "How is everything? Is everything getting straightened out? (Answer: Yes) Orders are out to you by Mr. [2d Lt. Joseph D.] Broderick ... he will also give you information about chow and water etc. I am going to get them out to you right away. Where do you want the water and the kitchens and the carts? (Answer: at the P.C.) What do you know about the 5th? You send word to Williams about the water and the chow."

Lee sent all three commanders a message at 1205 telling that "the French Division on our left has advanced to the ST. PIERRE–ST. ETIENNE road and have met little opposition. This regiment will advance at once conforming to the French Division on our left and in liaison with them and the 3rd Brigade on our right, etc." Further directions to Barker and Williams stated that they were not to go beyond St. Etienne.

Barker sent Williams a message at 1710: "I will remain here till further orders. Please send me your position and the time you arrived there." Barker doesn't say where his post of command was located. And a message to Maj. Shuler, 3/6, at 1800: "Please send as soon a s possible a guide from each company and one from Batt. Hdq. to guide this batt. to the positions occupied by you."

Lee reinforced that message by directions to all three commanders at 1820 that 1/6 would relieve 3/6 in second line, then 3/6 would relieve 2/6, which would then become the third line. At 1950 in a phone conversation, "with Site [Lee]" possibly with "Sister," who I believe was still Neville, asked how many effectives: Barker had 21 officers and 568 men.

6 October: Williams sent Barker a query at 1220: "Have been informed that 23rd Inf. has retreated down the SOMME-PY ROAD. Do you know anything about this?" To which Barker responded: "Have not heard anything about this. Did you receive order about the expected counter attack."

First Lt. Fred W. Maack, of the 75th, obtained sketches on neighboring units for his battalion commander during the advance near Blanc Mont while exposed to heavy artillery and machine gun fire.

Lee advised all three Battalion commanders that they would provide his headquarters with a guide for each platoon to serve as guides for the incoming 141st Regiment, 36th National Guard Division.

7 October: Barker notified Lee, at 0730: "Relief completed at 6:50 a.m. this date by the 1st Bn., 142 Inf. Both battalions are well dug in and are improving their position. 1st Bn. 6th Marines no casualties during relief. The 1st Bn. 142 Inf. 2 casualties (wounded)."

Private William O. Schnur, of Headquarters Company, 1st Battalion, successfully guided the company through a heavy barrage to aid and strengthen a position ahead of the line.

Barker notified Shuler of a message he had from a French Lt. Beleu, which describes the French losing St. Etienne then recovering the town. At 1315 he sent Shuler another message which said: "The attached note received from Regt. P.C. 6th is intended to be forwarded to the French P.C. in St. Etienne." At 1900 Lee advised Barker, Williams and Shuler that the French notified him that the enemy was forming at the northeast of St. Etienne in order to attack and try to recapture the town.

8 October: The 6th Regiment was still in position on the Blanc Mont plain. At 0615 Barker sent Lee a message: "3 small French tanks on left near road motionless south of town. Six tanks advancing through cemetery. Being sniped at continually by M.G. on right flank. Large fire about 800 yds N.E. of town. U.S. infantry entering wood on our extreme right in very thin lines. Two platoons of 76th Co. advancing on left of town. M.G. platoon following. Some of our Infantry coming over behind us. Have seen no prisoners. Seems to be very little opposition on the left. Right going well. Very little German shell fire. Troops seem to be about half way up slope of hill beyond the town."

About an hour later Lee requested "your last message in writing. The one you were trying to send over the phone about the 76th being held up by M.G. fire." About the same time, Barker sent Lee a message at 0750: "The 75th Company is held up by heavy machine gun fire at the N.E. of St. Etienne. Lts [Henry E.] Chandler, [Edward F.] Durk [*sic* Dunk] and [Charles F.] Dalton are wounded. I am trying to get aid to the 75th."

Barker to Lee at 0825: "74th and 75th Co's are held up on a line approximately 264.5-283.5 by heavy M.G. fire from left flank and by artillery fire. Infantry held up on hill 266.6-284.0 by heavy M.G. fire from these positions. Request artillery action immediately."

Lee replied to Barker's message, time 0825: "I would advise you hold your forces and observe machine gun positions in your front, sniping as much as possible to clean out personnel. Would not attempt to rush the positions. Give us the location of these machine gun nests by coordinates and we will make an effort to get artillery fire on them. State clearly what positions you request artillery fire on, if your men are too close to get under the fire."

First Lieutenant Fred W. Maack of the 75th Company sent 6th Regiment Intelligence Officer Lt. Joseph D. Broderick a message at about 0900: "Hill 265.2-285.1 seems to be giving trouble. One tank approaching it and line slightly held up there. 1st Batt. and M-guns in ST. ETIENNE and line of infantry on left at 263-285 seems doing well. Town heavily shelled by Germans. Tanks advancing well. German M.Guns firing on hill at O.P. from N.E. Fire and smoke on side of hill 1 Kilo. N.W. of ST. ETIENNE. Infantry now beyond observation until clouds lift. Casualties seem light. Visibility poor."

Major George Stowell, commanding officer, 75th Company, sent Barker following message at 1410:

> Am with 75th Company and have been trying to round them up but can find one sergeant, two corporals and ten privates. All officers wounded but I have not seen any of them. Am situated about 150 yards to left of 142nd Inf. Cannot reach front line now on account of concentrated machine gun and artillery fire which breaks up all formations. 142nd Infantry appears to have many stragglers. Request that relief be sent down for 75th. but if this is done a barrage (Standing Barrage) will be required. Have no map so cannot give you position of front line. We need artillery fire from our own guns, as enemy machine guns and artillery are practically unmolested. Please ask for fire on enemy front line and also counter-battery fire and lots of it. Please send me map by return runner. My P.C. is in an old German Machine Gun Nest about 300 east of cemetery and 150 yards south of it. Have not been able to get in liaison with either 142 Inf. or 76th Co. but will try to do so.

Barker sent Stowell's message to Lee at 1510. Then, at 1830, he ordered from Broderick red flares and illuminating flares.

Barker advised Lee at 1900 that he had a message from 1st Lt. Macon Overton, commanding officer of the 76th Company: "He just repelled a strong counter attack on his right. He is in liaison with French on his left & with 142 Inf. on his right but doubts if line on his right is very strongly held. He has requested to have his right strengthened and when the Engineers arrive it can be done. Shuler and I are picking up stragglers from 142 Inf. and placing them in line to connect with Shuler's position on the right."

A U.S. Army officer, First Lieutenant Frederick W. Wagoner of the 76th Company, displayed unusual leadership, courage and fearlessness in the fighting about St. Etienne. He was foremost in all the heavy fighting, and when the counterattack of the enemy was launched his platoon withstood the brunt of it. He had his men so completely under control that not a shot was fired until he gave the order.

At 2100, 1st Lt. Maack sent 2d Lt. Broderick another message: "10—155's and heavy M. Guns near 268.2-286.8 in small woods on hill. Mustard gas in hollow at 265.0-282.5 now disappearing. At 1.p.m. German planes dropped 5 or 10 bombs near 1st Bat. P.C. Germans cleared from ST. ETIENNE to hill N.E. Indirect M.G. fire on Main road to ST. ETIENNE, by O.P. Red Cross 1½ kil. sS. of ST. ETIENNE heavily shelled by planes at noon. Several waves of Boche attacking ST. ETIENNE woods at N.E. broken by artillery fire at noon."

Lee, or someone at his headquarters, sent Lt. Col. Earl Ellis a memorandum at some time during this day to advise that his regiment was in bad shape, with approximately 250 men in each battalion and few officers, adding that it was about 1700 hours and telling of a German "tremendous barrage" against his men "which is undoubtedly the preliminary of a counter attack."

The 95th Co. submitted their casualty list and they had 4 officers and 92 men out of a possible total of 250. The first battalion estimated they had about 275 total out of more than 1,000. Two/Six had 303, and 3/6 had 283. Total regimental strength, 861 officers and men out of 3,000 plus.

Macon Overton sent Barker a message with no time mentioned: "76th Co. is connected on left with 62nd French Inf. and is on outskirts of ST. ETIENNE dug in. Machine guns covering ravine leading into town on East. No liaison on right as there is no established line. 3rd Batt. echelon to my right rear."

9 October: Lee sent Overton of the 76th a long and windy message through Barker at 0305, which stated in essence that Overton was to make a reconnaissance just in front of the French right, to determine whether the works were occupied by the enemy. He was not to engage the enemy. If Germans held the works, Division wanted to know immediately to put artillery concentration on it. Overton responded to Lee and Neville, no time indicated: "The woods located on line 285 between 264-265 is held by enemy. Have reconnaissanced [*sic*] and Major of 102 says same would appreciate a battery concentration on woods and whole right front as enemy is massed in large numbers."

First Lieutenant Henry E. Chandler of the 75th Co. was killed in leading a final attack on 9 October 1918. This was to be the 75th Company's day. For extraordinary heroism in action at St. Etienne, Private Dean F. Smiley, also of the 75th Company, was awarded a Distinguished Service Cross, and, a very unusual event for a private, he was also awarded a Navy Distinguished Service Medal plus a Silver Star and the top of the line Croix de Guerre with Palm. He rushed a hostile machine gun nest single handed, killing three of the crew and capturing the remainder. While taking his prisoners to the rear this gallant Marine was killed by enemy artillery fire.

Lee sent all three battalion commanders another message at 1305 mentioning that the regiment would be "relieved tonight." He also added at 1630 that "all Browning guns and equipment now in the possession of the men of your command will be turned in ... as the troops pass by on their way to the rear." What happened, of course, was that the Marines had talked the "doggies" of the 36th Division into trading their Browning automatic rifles for their "much better" Chauchats. But complaints from the leaders of the 36th forced the men to return those superior firearms for the atrocious Chauchats, which all Marines hated.

Meanwhile, the 76th Company, 1st Lt. Macon Overton, commanding officer, was released when the 3d Battalion, 142d Regiment, relieved them. Apparently his was the last Marine unit to be relieved.

Meuse-Argonne

The Second Division had a few days to recover and absorb replacements before they began their march toward the Meuse River for a new campaign. The American Army units that had been fighting in and about the Argonne Forest since the end of September had been badly handled by the well-trained Germans facing them for the past month. Pershing had cancelled most activity awaiting a few more divisions to begin anew on 1 November. The Second and 89th Divisions were assigned the farthest right flank of the AEF. The 95th Company was removed from 1/6 and added to Major George Stowell's newly created Liaison Battalion, which was to be liaison between the brand new 80th Infantry Division and the 2d Division during the advance toward the Meuse River.

1 November: One of the first heroes of the day was 2d Lt. Wilbur Summerlin, of the 74th Company. On 1 November he displayed extraordinary qualities of leadership in holding his platoon together against heavy machine gun and artillery fire. When the regimental flank was exposed he led his men to cover it, capturing 155 men, one officer and 17 machine guns. He voluntarily led a patrol into the town of St. Georges and was the first to enter the town. On the evening of November 10 he was conspicuous for his bravery in exposing himself to enemy fire in order that he might find protection for his men. Also, as a sergeant with the 95th Company, he was cited at Soissons.

Early in the morning, Captain Macon C. Overton of the 76th was awarded an Oak Leaf Cluster for a second Distinguished Service Cross and two Croix de Guerre, one with Palm and one Gilt, at the Meuse-Argonne, for extraordinary heroism in action near St. Georges on 1 November in forming his company under heavy artillery fire, advancing and wiping out 5 machine gun nests and crews. He then personally guided a tank in operations against machine gun nests. He was struck and mortally wounded while so engaged by a German antitank sniper. Overton had been awarded a DSC and later a Navy Cross for his heroics at Blanc Mont. Here was another superb fighting machine.

Site (Lee) sent a message to Neville at brigade, 0905: "Site–1 (1st Bn. Barker) reports at 9:00 a.m. that Site E-1 (3rd Bn. 6th Shuler) had leapfrogged him. Reports indicate that they are close up to barrage."

Barker notified Lee at 1010:

> Reached objective at 8:00 a.m. Position sketch attached. Had following casualties.
>
> | | | |
> |---|---|---|
> | 75th Company | 1 Officer wounded | 8 Enl. wounded. |
> | 74th Company | 1 Officer wounded | 45 Enl. wounded. |
> | 76th Company | 2 Officers wounded | 60 Enl. wounded. |
> | | 1 Officer killed (Captain Overton). | |
> | 73rd M.G. Co. | 1 Officer wounded | 30 Enl. wounded. |
> | Totals | 5 Officers wounded | 143 Enl. wounded. 1 Officer killed. |
>
> Captured 200 prisoners.

At 1910 Lt. Col. Holcomb sent Barker an order to "have your telephone crew run line to Shuler's P.C. in BAYONVILLE, etc."

For exceptionally meritorious and conspicuous service, Major Frederick A. Barker, commanding officer of the 1st Battalion, 6th, was later awarded a Navy Cross to join with the two Silver Stars and Croix de Guerre with Palm for distinguished and exceptional gallantry at Sommerance on 1 November 1918. He skillfully led his battalion, which was in a front line position, from the "jumping off" place to the first objective. He kept his men close to the barrage, all the way subjected to a heavy fire of high explosives and a machine gun barrage.

He reached his objective on time and secured a number of prisoners and considerable material. He had also earned two Silver Stars at St. Mihiel.

2 November: Col. Lee sent all three battalion commanders a message at 0645 that the 23d Infantry would relieve the 5th and 6th Marines that day, hour to be decided later. This was mainly of interest to 2/6 and Stowell's battalion.

At 0940 an officer named Brown sent the following message to Maj. Pere Wilmer, 6th Regiment adjutant: "Major F. A. Barker was evacuated to hospital sick this date. The reason our telephone has not been connected is because the telephone and signal men have not yet come up. I have sent out men to locate them." For a few days it appears that the officer commanding the 73d Machine Gun Company, Major Louis Fagan, assumed command of 3/6. There were three officers named Brown in 3/6 so I have no idea which this one was.

Most of the messages during this entire period were not from the battalion commanders but rather from Neville at 4th Brigade, or his adjutant, Earl Ellis, or Lee, and frequently to other than the battalions, but rather to the various support companies, supply, trains, etc.

At 1910 Lee advised the three battalion commanding officers that the 3d Brigade would advance at 2000 that night. At 2215 Ellis from brigade sent an order that the 2d Division "is to advance in column of brigades, 4th Brigade in support, at 6:00 a.m. 3rd November '18."

Sometime during that day, the strength of the regiment was reported. First/Six reported 15 officers and 371 men, which didn't include the strength of the 95th Company.

4 November: It appears that Maj. Fagan supplied Lee with a map sketch of the position of 1/6 at 0900 "about 500 meters north of Bellevue Farm. Contact with 2nd Btn ahead."

That morning Lee sent a message to all three battalion commanding officers notifying them that "in case of advance of 5th in the morning, 5 Nov. 18, you will follow in support at distance of approximately one kilometer from rear of 5th to head of 5th, and same distance between Bns. of this regiment." However, he didn't tell them which position each would have.

5 November: Captain Maurice S. Berry assumed command of 1/6 and sent Lee a message at 0800 this date: "Our patrols have connected with the first and second Battalions of the 5th Reg. A patrol from the 2nd Bat. 5 Reg. was fired on from the left flank while trying to get in contact with the 9th Inf. We are also in liaison with Williams [2/6] and Shuler [3/6]." Major George Stowell sent Lee a message at 1115 via Lieut. Groat (? no record of): "Have joined the 1st Bn. with the 95th Co. and have assumed command of the Bn."

Lee advised the three commanders that the brigade was expected to cross the Meuse and "in this event the 5th Marines will move forward, effect a guarded crossing of the MEUSE at POUILLY and seize the heights to the northeast of POUILLY, heights west of AUTREVILLE and heights Bois d' Alma Gisors, pushing forward strong patrols and keep in contact with the enemy.... Be ready to move on short notice.... Keep liaison with 5th Regiment ahead, etc."

6 November: At 1815 Lee advised the three battalion commanders that they would probably not move until morning, and by a different route.

At no time indicated, Lieutenant Preston A. McLendon, assistant surgeon, USN, sent a message to the commanding officer of 1/6: "The physical condition of this battalion becomes increasingly worse. Diarrhoea, exhaustion and influenza are rampant, numerous cases of running a subnormal temperature, showing an exhaustive condition of the men. It has been found absolutely necessary to evacuate 26 men this date with above complaints."

7 November: Fagan, still in command of 1/6, sent a detailed message about the 73d Machine Gun Company to Lee in the afternoon at 1230:

> Total strength of the 73d Mach. Gun Co., with 1st Btn. exclusive of train and galley—1 Major—1 1st Lieut.—5 Sgts.—6 Cpls.—56 pvts—5 stretcher bearers—2 hosp. apprentices—11 a.m. car. from 1st Btn.—Total 2 officers—74 men and 11 a.m. carriers.
> Lt. Duncan reported in from school 5 Nov and assigned as train officer.
> Lt. Jackson evacuated sick 3 Nov
> Lt. Lee slightly wounded 1 Nov and evacuated—3 guns blown up in 3d platoon on 1 Nov and their crews killed or wounded—accurate report impracticable at present.
> Men suffering from diarrhoea, but are holding on—2 hot meals daily—well dug in and camouflaged—5 gun carts have been brought up for future movements of our 9 remaining guns and 40 extra blankets for men, issued out to them.
> We have 5 guns on our *left* at cross roads set up and loaded to enfilade all approaches on roads and to flank our front. 4 guns on *right* to flank and also to enfilade the road to our front. On rear is sketch of positions. Very quiet here, except that last night the Boche shelled our left at crossroads, without casualties.

8 November: Lee sent a message to the three battalion commanders, no time indicated: "The crossing is postponed and will not take place tonight."

9 November: Lee sent the three commanders a message at 1130: "Put your Bns. in march as soon as they have had hot meal for the Bivouac in the Bois du Fond de Limon. Upon arrival there make effort through small patrols to the eastward to locate Major Williams, Stowell, and Shuler, who are in that vicinity on reconnaissance and show them this order and they will proceed north in the vicinity of MOUZON and make reconnaissance of the river in that vicinity, as it is now intimated that our operations may occur in that vicinity."

10 November: Lee sent a message to all three at 2340 and to Larsen of 3/5: "After you have attained your objectives your northern limit will be the line MOUZON (inclusive) CARIGNAN (inclusive). Southern limit Hill 341 (inclusive) SAILLY (exclusive). You will send out to the front strong patrols within that sector as exploitation. Send frequent reports."

Shuler led the regiment plus 3/5 to the north and attempted to cross the river, but the German artillery continued to blast each bridge the 2d Engineers managed to erect. Shuler decided that it was impossible to cross the river and retreated south, saving his command. The next morning at 1100 the war was over.

For the following few days, most of the activity was in getting food to the remnants of both regiments. On the 12th Lee notified Major Louis E. Fagan, Jr. (1/6), Williams and Shuler that "it is contemplated that battalions will move to BEAUMONT this date, if billets can be obtained. Send Sergeant Murphy with car to these headquarters this morning." There were too many Sgt. Murphys in the 6th to identify this one.

On the 14th Maj. Pere Wilmer, 6th adjutant, sent message at 1030 to all stating that various ranks were to be assigned to various schools. At 1345 that message was revoked.

1 December: This date began a series of directions on how to behave, where to go, and when: "Thoroughly police ground you occupy for dinner.... March at attention for first ten minutes of each hour," etc.

On this date Major Franklin B. Garrett was now commanding 1/6, and his messages began going to Lee and others, frequently, and mostly telling where each company would be billeted as they stopped each day. The last of record follows.

13 December: Garrett to Lee at 1700: "Arrived at 10:30 a.m. The battalion is billeted as follows: 73rd M.G. Co. and 75th Co. in LEUTESDORF. 74th Co. in Obr. HAMMERSTEIN. 76th Co.—95th Co.—Bn. Hdq. and train are billeted here. Have interviewed Burgomaster and complied with orders regarding arms, etc. Interior guards, alarm posts and patrols have been established."

Occupation of Germany

According to the semi-official history of the 6th Regiment, as of 16 December, the companies were allocated as follows. Battalion Headquarters, 73d Machine Gun Company, 75th Company, and three platoons of the 74th Company were stationed in Honningen. The 95th Company was at Honborn Farm; 2 platoons of the 76th Company were at Ariendorf; one platoon of the 74th was in liaison with the 5th Regiment at Bremscheid; and two platoons of the 76th Company were at outposts Nos. 1, 2 and 3, on the outpost line.

From this date until mid–June the regiment, brigade, and division were all more or less living comfortably in various sections of western Germany. After the Germans signed the Allied proposed peace treaty, on 19 July 1919 the regiment left their quarters and the members of the 2d Division began their trip back to the United States, arriving on 8 August 1919. Then came the various parades and inspections before ending up at Quantico, where the term of war men were discharged on 13 August 1919.

6

Second Battalion, Sixth Marines, 1917–1919

Battalion Headquarters
78th [E] Company
79th [F] Company
80th [G] Company
96th [H] Company

Commanding Officers

From	To	
14 August 1917	9 August 1918	Major Thomas Holcomb
10 August 1918	December 1918	Major Ernest C. Williams
December 1918	unknown	Major Franklin B. Garrett

In August 1917 the Marines were collecting together a second regiment of infantry to send to France. This would be the 6th Regiment of Marines and would include three regular battalions plus assorted service units. Toward the latter part of August 1917 when the three newly organized companies—95th, 96th, and 97th, composed mainly of recruits from Parris Island—arrived at Quantico, Colonel Albertus Catlin could finalize his regiment. Meanwhile, the newly appointed officers, many old time noncommissioned officers among them, were assigned to their newly formed companies.

The first unit to leave for France was 1/6, in September 1917. Following was the Third Battalion, which shipped out in the latter part of October. For various reasons, 2/6 was the last battalion of the regiment to ship out and it wasn't until late January that it left the United States, arriving in France on 5 February 1918.

Verdun

Along with their earlier arrived comrades of the regiment, 2/6 began training under French soldiers until mid–March 1918 when the 4th Brigade was transferred to the near quiet Toulon sector near Verdun. The Second Battalion began the move on 17 March by train, detrained at Lommes on the 18th and marched 18 kilometers to Sommedieue, where it was stationed in reserve behind a part of the French 10th Army Corps. There the battalion

Corporal Noyes V. Moore, commanding officer (center), and his machine gun squad, 96th Company, 2d Battalion, 6th Regiment, pictured at Quantico in 1917.

remained until the night of 28 March when they relieved 3/6 at the battered towns of Mensil, Bonzee, and Mont-sous-les-Cotes. While in this area the main activity was the nightly patrols.

During the entire period the battalion and regiment was located at Verdun, nearly every message of record stated exactly the same entry: "Nothing of importance to report."

On the night of 10 May, 2/6 began its move to the west along with the balance of the regiment. The entire regiment was together once again at Serans where from 21 to 31 May it remained. Meanwhile, the Germans had broken through French lines and were rapidly reaching the Marne Valley threatening Paris.

The commanding general of the French Armies, General Petain, requested the assistance of the American Expeditionary Forces and General John J. Pershing responded by ordering the 2d Division (Regular) to report to the French command. The French ordered the division toward Chateau-Thierry and there they headed beginning late on 31 May. The defensive position selected for the 2d Division was at the apex of the German advance between Soissons and Rheims, launched by the enemy on 27 May 1918.

Belleau Wood

1 June 1918: Maj. Thomas "Tommy" Holcomb and 2/6 had reached Montreuil at 0400 after a day and a night in camions. Like everyone else in the division, they were exhausted, but at 1430 were moving again. After the trucks of the 2d Supply trains had dumped field rations and ammunition on the roadside, Harbord commandeered them. With a number of vehicles in tow he rode back to where Holcomb and his rearmost battalion of the 6th Marines was marching toward the front. After loading the troops, Harbord then returned to where

Surviving officers of the 6th Regiment following action at Belleau Wood.

the action was developing at Le Thiolet. Two/Six was the first Marine unit to arrive at the scene.

They jumped out of their trucks and soon were headed northward across the road from where the 9th had begun to dig in. The division line was thus extended along the eastern face of Bois Clérembauts, through Triangle Farm, and then to the west end of the Bois de Triangle, and finally to Lucy-le-Bocage. It was a thin line, but at 1705 Holcomb could report being in place. The battalion had three companies in line and one in reserve, according to the regimental unit history. The company that connected with the 9th Infantry, the 96th Company, Capt. Donald F. Duncan commanding, had its right on the Paris-Metz Road at Le Thiolet. To their immediate left was the 79th Company, Capt. Randolph T. Zane, occupying Triangle Farm. Captain Robert E. Messersmith with the 78th Company was next to the left, from the gully just northwest of the farm, to Lucy on their far left. Battalion headquarters was established at La Cense Farm; Capt. Bailey M. Coffenberg and his 80th Company were held there in reserve within a small wooded area just behind the 96th.

At 1705 Harbord notified Bundy, commanding general, 2d Division: "Second Bn 6th Marines in line from Le Thiolet through Clerembauts Woods and Triangle to Lucy. Instructed to hold this line." He also described positions for the other two battalions. French infantry was in front of the battalion on the night of 1-2 June, which passed quietly for the battalion. The enemy did not have his artillery up at this time because of the rapidity of his advance.

The advances of the Germans continued but seemed without their usual spirit or aggressiveness. They were, after all, becoming quite tired after advancing for the previous five days, and short of both food and water. The Germans were not supermen, later claims to the contrary not withstanding. They became even more cautious when they encountered heavy rifle and machine-gun fire, from the American lines. Some French artillery was in action but they were, unfortunately, more effective with short rounds into the 79th Company's position at Triangle Farm than against the Germans. Shortly after his arrival, Captain Zane had to report "five casualties from short rounds falling into this area."

As the division was settling in, the enemy began probing along the lines, and unknowingly came into contact with the recently arrived Americans. German troops could be clearly seen moving into the woods northwest of the Bouresches-Vaux line, opposite the 6th Marines. The Germans were aware that new, fresh troops were now occupying a line opposite them, but apparently did not realize they were not French.

2 June: Holcomb sent out a panic message to Catlin that the "enemy attacking along our whole front at 8:30 a.m. They were about twelve hundred yards from our position." The operations journal for the 2d Division reports for that day: "The 6th Marines had several casualties among the officers and men—wounded only. The 6th Machine Gun Battalion stopped the German advance several times." Obviously, the attack wasn't quite as serious as it seemed to Holcomb. There were very few panic attacks like that. Perhaps being a new father had caused some of the overreaction.

But based upon erroneous reports, Harbord concluded that Holcomb's 2/6 was falling back at Triangle Farm. Harbord sent Catlin an order at 1440 to "stiffen your lines."

Maj. Frank E. Evans, adjutant, 6th Marines, received from Holcomb at 1445: "In liaison with 5th Bn. 356th Regt. (French) on our left. Will send further information about French troops later. One killed and two wounded by our [French] Artillery firing into TRIANGLE FARM. Just rec'd 50,000 Chauchat. I brought up this morning 40,000. Now on easy street. Send in 30,000 Cal 30 at first opportunity." He meant rounds, obviously. At 1450 Harbord wrote to Holcomb: "Reported that your are giving way at TRIANGLE. Your are supposed to hold your line there at all cost. Keep Colonel Catlin informed of conditions, and [Major Edward B.] Cole [6th Machine Gun Battalion, Commanding Officer], and send me report now."

Holcomb, with a direct phone connection to Harbord, angrily replied to the admonition, "When this outfit runs it will be in the other direction. Nothing doing in the fall-back business." Later, upon learning the truth, Harbord apologized to Holcomb. Meanwhile, Harbord directed Sibley to provide "a fresh company" to Holcomb at La Cense Farm as a reserve because a German division was expected to attack the American right. Holcomb wrote Harbord at 1513: "Will you send some anti-toxin tetanus, also three Very pistol star shells."

The French fell back on and through U.S. Marine and Infantry lines. Enemy could be seen filtering into the woods northwest of the Bouresches-Vaux railroad line. They seemed to sense that formidable troops were opposite them, for enemy attempts to advance were not spirited. The Germans were stopped with machine gun and rifle fire, and artillery, which did very effective work. Several rounds, however, fell short into the 79th Company's position, causing five casualties. As ordered, Maj. Berton Sibley, commanding officer, 3/6, duly sent Capt. Robert W. Voeth and his 97th Company to strengthen the junction between the 6th and 9th Regiments.

3 June: Harbord sent Holcomb an original message at 1100 which must have been for Catlin:

> It appears that the French Bn. immediately in front of Holcomb's right does not belong to the division under which we have been serving and it has to be relieved tonight and the line which it holds, which is slightly in advance of that held by Holcomb, is to be taken over by enough men from Holcomb's Bn to hold it. On right that French Bn are some French units extending further to the right in front of the 9th Infantry who are not to be relieved and whose flank would be exposed unless Holcomb advances his line to join up with them. Please give Holcomb the necessary instructions to advance enough men to hold that line and inform him that guides for each platoon will report to him at his PC at midnight to conduct the men to the places.
>
> The CG 2nd Div [Omar Bundy] states that while our line now occupied is the one which we will hold he desires that any strongpoints in the French line in front of ours be occupied by detachments when the French are relieved at four o'clock in the morning. Such points to be occupied should be strongpoints capable of defense, such as farms, cuts, stone walls etc. This applies to the entire front of your regiment.

The enemy brought up more artillery and registered on the 2d Division positions and near the 2/6 Post of Command. Those Marines were by this time fairly well entrenched.

4 June: On the afternoon of this day the enemy shelled Battalion Headquarters and the reserve company, in La Cense Farm, with 150s. Captain Thomas S. Whiting and several men of the 80th Company were wounded. In evacuating the farm seven men were killed and about a dozen wounded. Battalion Headquarters and the 80th Company were located in the Bois de Clerembauts about two hundred yards to the rear of La Cense Farm where there was little shelling and no more casualties. The casualties in line, up to this time, were light. Lieutenant H. Leslie Eddy, U.S. Army Volunteers, attached to the 78th Company, was killed by shrapnel. Several men were wounded.

5 June: The day passed quietly with battalion and company locations the same. The enemy had apparently given up the idea of continuing his advance. Franco-American artillery was still very active and did excellent work. Orders from Harbord, no time indicated: "1. As soon as practicable after dark tonight, the following changes will be made: (c) The 2nd Bn. 6th Marines to be relieved by the 23rd Infantry of that portion of its present sector from the PARIS-METZ Road to TRIANGLE Farm inclusive."

6 June: The battalion was relieved by a battalion of the 23rd Infantry at about 0300, and proceeded to woods near Regimental Headquarters at Maison Blanc and south of Lucy-le- Bocage. Enemy artillery was very active against Lucy. Catlin sent to Harbord at 1505: "Maj. Holcomb requests that his runners now at Brig. Hdqrs. be sent to Plan and that they be instructed there by the runners for Plan N as to their itinerary. Runners were kept at FORM because it was closer. Decided best when F called up the night Major Holcomb went to Brigade Reserve." This was part of the record but with no further details.

At 1730 the battalion advanced, one company, the 96th, in line, and the other companies supporting the 3rd Battalion in its attack on the Bois de Belleau and Bouresches. The attack was made across 600 yards of open ground under intense artillery and machine gun fire, and the conduct of officers and men was excellent. Captain Donald F. Duncan of the 96th Company was killed by a shell just as his company started forward. First Lieutenant James F. Robertson assumed command and his conduct was very commendable, as was that of 2d Lt. Clifton B. Cates. These, with 24 men, the remainder of one platoon of the 96th Company, after a hard struggle took the town of Bouresches. Casualties were heavy. The spirit of the men, including those wounded, was deserving of special mention. Battalion Headquarters was established in a ravine about 800 yards to the southwest of Bouresches. Reinforcements from the 79th Company were sent into Bouresches and consolidation began.

Holcomb sent Catlin the following message at 2127, not aware that Catlin was wounded and out of action: "[1st Lt. James F.] Robertson says he holds BOURESCHES and woods to the right with most of company. Needs reinforcements. [Capt. Randolph T.] Zane [79th] has only one effective platoon left and cannot advance. Will ask 23rd Infantry to hold [Capt. Robert E.] Messersmith's [78th] line and if they will do so, will send him into town. Our line of resistance from LUCY to Messersmith should be reinforced at once."

Another message to Catlin at (estimated) 2200: "Am sending in German prisoner, who says his forces have withdrawn from town and is entrenching along railway. Am sending Zane's one remaining platoon into town to reinforce Robertson." In fact it was Cates holding the town, Robertson having left to seek reinforcements.

From Messersmith to Holcomb, who couldn't be located, and directed to Evans, then to Harbord at 2210: "[1st Lt. James McB.] Sellers has been wounded in groin. Most of his platoon is gassed pretty badly. Relief of platoon is necessary. [1st Lt. James P.] Adams platoon also has a good deal of gas. Let me know what can be done."

From Evans to Harbord at 2250: "Am sending in German prisoner who says his forces have withdrawn from the town of BOURESCHES and are entrenching along the railway.

Am sending Zane and one remaining platoon into town to reinforce Robinson [sic] 261.4-175.2. Puts him on a straight line between LUCY and 169, two thirds of the way out."

From Lt. Col. Harry Lee, commanding officer, 6th Marines, to Harbord at 2335: "Report by runner Holcomb to [Major Berton W.] Sibley [commanding officer, 3/6] says one of Holcomb's companies is in BOURESCHES and he wants reinforcements. Authorized Sibley use reorganized 82nd and 83rd Companies for this…. Need grenades and 37 m/m guns."

From Holcomb to "Reg. Comdr or Brigade Commander" at 2328, received at 0130 on 7 June:

Lieut. Robertson with part of 96th Co. holds E. edge of BOURESCHES. Enemy holds station and railway. I have sent in one platoon as reinforcements. Robertson says Bois de Belleau is held by the enemy. Unless Sibley can do something in the way of taking left part of objective, we are in a hole. We also need reinforcements to hold our line of resistance. Send me some word."

7 June: There was much reporting from Holcomb to brigade all day. At 0200 he reported to Harbord: "Am holding BOURESCHES with 2 1/2 platoons 96 Co. and 1 platoon 79th. They are connected up with Messersmith on the right who now holds the line running due south from BOURESCHES to TRIANGLE FARM. He is digging in and BOURESCHES is digging in. Have just sent out order to 80th Co. (Coffenberg) to go into BOURESCHES and connect up with Sibley on the left. 23rd Infantry asked me to advance line to BOURESCHES-VAUX road which I declined to do, as it meant moving 78th Co. forward and giving up their strong line. My P. C. 263.3-176.5."

At 0440 someone named Ballard, no unit mentioned, reported to someone: "Major Holcomb reports telephone communication to his P. C. re-established. Also reports things are going very nicely here. Have Major Evans call him when he gets up." Then another message to someone at 0600: "Connected up with Inf. on right. Germans hold R. R. Sta. at BOURESCHES. Germans entrenching behind R. R. Track. Ration and Amm. received last night by Holcomb. Said machine gun fire caused most of their casualties yesterday. 79th Co. loss very heavy & 96th Co. loss very heavy. In one platoon of 79th it was reported that there was only one man left."

Lee advised Harbord at 0650 that "Holcomb was in touch with Sibley of his left and 23rd Infantry on his right. The 96th Co. took Bouresches alone after a splendid fight with heavy losses. The 79th Co. has about one effective platoon left. The 78th Co. about eight casualties. The 80th Co. have few if any. Holcomb reports that he has plenty of ammunition but needs rations and requests they be sent to Bouresches by truck."

There were several messages reflecting the status of 2/6, none of which said anything different than what has already been stated above. Although Holcomb did advise someone at 1213: "Order of companies right to left 78th, 84th, 97th, 79th, mixed up with 78th on right nd 84th and 79th."

Holcomb sent "F-7" a request at 1555: "79th Co. reports parties of enemy advancing towards ravine which runs E N E left of our advance. Require 3 and 6 star rockets—2 stokes mortars—2 37 m/m guns—15,000 Springfield—Clips for Chauchat gun." He sent the same message to the ordnance officer.

That day the 6th Regiment sent in a casualty report: "78th Co.—1; 79th Co.—23; 80th Co.—2; 96th Co.—23."

8 June: Another quiet day, with some sniping and artillery activity. Enemy shelled the rear areas. The defense of Bouresches was well organized and enough troops were concentrated there to hold against strong odds. Lt. Col. Lee sent to Harbord at 1234. "An attack on Holcomb at 12:20."

Liaison officer, 6th Regiment, to Harbord, at 0200. "There was a predetermined fire attack on the town and machine guns arrived just before it started. Not as many as supposed to be. Line held beautifully. No German advance. Captain Zane and Robertson everything well organized." According to 2d Lt. Clifton B. Cates, Robertson never returned to Bouresches.

From Harbord to Holcomb at 2115: "Much to my regret I am unable to relieve your battalion in its turn from its present place [Bouresches]. The holding of that town is too important for me to risk a change at this time. It will be done just as soon as conditions permit. You and your battalion have done fine work and it is much appreciated by the Division Commander and myself. I want to advise you that I have taken out the Sibley battalion tonight and am not replacing it. About fifty batteries will play on the wood tomorrow and we will probably occupy the far edge in the afternoon."

9 June: The enemy attacked Bouresches at about midnight, but was beaten off by intense rifle and machine gun fire after about an hour of hard fighting. The badly battered 96th and 79th Companies were still the only Marines in that town. Later reports indicated that about 100 officers and men of the 96th and 90 officers and men from the 79th Company, plus 175 from the 2d Engineers, were the totals. Additionally, there were 44 men from the 73d Machine Gun Company and a detachment from the 6th Machine Gun Battalion as well. There was plenty of ammunition and water plus a hot meal on the night of the 8th.

10 June: The battalion was relieved by the 1st Battalion of the 6th Marines, Major Maurice E. Shearer commanding.[1] The companies went to the woods from which the attack had been launched, near Maison Blanc. Battalion Headquarters was established in Montgivrault Petit Farm where Major Franklin B. Garrett had been in command of the rear echelon.[2] The Second Battalion was sent back to the La Sablonniere woods, located about two kilometers from Montreuil, as corps reserve. Here the men received good, hot food, and, according to the records, plenty of it.

For the following few days their time was spent quietly, the troops resting in the woods after 11 days of hard and exhausting work. On the 13th at 1215 Holcomb and 2/6 were ordered to woods northwest of Lucy-le-Bocage by Brigade Commander Harbord. A statement of a dying German officer was to the effect that the enemy had brought up a fresh division and intended to attack at dawn. The battalion reached its new position just after dawn. The move was made through harassing artillery fire and 2/6 suffered two casualties. They had just settled under cover of the woods when a message was received from the brigade commander that the enemy had retaken Bouresches. Two companies from 2/6 were ordered to the woods southwest of Lucy-le-Bocage with a view to counterattack. The 78th and 96th Companies were sent on this mission and covered the dangerous two kilometers of open ground to the new position in open formation and without interference by the enemy's guns. The destination was reached about 0800, when the companies dug in. Battalion Headquarters was established at rear echelon of Montgivrault Petit Farm. Later developments proved that report was false and Bouresches remained in Allied hands. The 78th and 96th Companies spent the day under cover of the woods, subjected to intermittent fire from the enemy's artillery. A few casualties were sustained.

14 June: At 1230 the enemy shelled the woods southeast of Lucy-le-Bocage heavily with gas, high explosives and shrapnel. The battalion was ordered into the Bois de Belleau to relieve the 2d Battalion of the 5th Regiment at 0200.[3] The 78th and 96th Companies moved from the woods southeast of Lucy-le-Bocage at that hour. The losses from gas and shell fire were severe.

Wise sent Neville and Habord a message at 0605 concerning the condition of 2/6: "Holcomb arrived with 1¾ companies at 3 a.m. and other two companies badly broken up, from shells and gas. About 150 of these have showed up. My men physically unable to make another attack. Have just made another reconnaissance of the line and consider my present line unsafe unless whole woods are in our possession and not enough troops on hand."

The relief was accomplished but, by mid-afternoon, practically all of the 78th and 96th Companies had been evacuated as gas casualties. There were 157 enlisted men from the 78th Company evacuated. Captain Robert E. Messersmith and Lieutenants Cecil B. Raleigh, Ben L. Taylor and James P. Adams of the 78th, and Lieutenants James Robertson and George B. Lockhart of the 96th Companies were evacuated.[4] The position in the Bois de Belleau, of which the enemy still held a part, was most difficult, the line consisting almost entirely of dangerous salients. Two/Six suffered a few casualties from enemy field artillery and one-pounders. Battalion Headquarters was at the rear of the Bois de Belleau. At 1410 Harbord sent Holcomb a message apologizing for "putting 2/6 in again with so little rest."

The 15th passed with no infantry developments on either side. The enemy continued his harassing artillery fire. Lieutenant James S. Timothy, Infantry, U.S. Army Volunteers, was killed.[5] Casualties, as a whole, were slight, but the men were tired out. The following day was without incident. Two/Six was relieved at night by a battalion of the 7th Infantry which was coming in to take the place of the 4th Brigade. Before the relief was made two enemy attacks were repulsed on their positions in which the enemy sustained severe losses. Upon "relief complete" the battalion proceeded to Gros Jean woods, about 1.6 kilometers east-northeast of Montreuil, for a much needed rest.

From the 17 June until the 23d, the battalion rested and reorganized in the Gros Jean woods. Up to that date the casualties in the battalion were about 70 percent. Here the ranks were partially filled with replacements. Captains Egbert T. Lloyd and Wethered Woodworth and Second Lieutenants John W. Overton and Robert L. Duane reported for duty.[6] Each morning was devoted to gas, Chauchat, bayonet and machine gun instruction, the afternoons to recreation and rest. A swim in the Marne was enjoyed by the battalion. Mail was received. The food was good and abundant. According to the records, the Red Cross and Y.M.C.A. performed excellent services for the men.[7] The evening of June 23 found the battalion again on the march with its destination the woods northwest of Lucy-le-Bocage, where they relieved the 2d Battalion of the 5th Regiment, which, in turn, went in line to the left of Bois de Belleau.

On the 22d, the Battalion was not much troubled by the enemy's guns and their quartermaster continued to function in a very satisfactory manner. Hot food was brought up in marmites at night and an issue of American canned beef was very welcome after subsisting so long on "monkey meat," as the men jocularly termed the French canned meat ration. Through the 25th the days passed quietly enough. The Y.M.C.A. again did good work and presented the men with an excellent ration. Artillery put down a splendid artillery preparation on that portion of the Bois de Belleau still held by the enemy. The 3d Battalion of the 5th Marines, which Major Shearer commanded, attacked at 1700 and was completely successful, clearing the woods of the enemy and taking approximately 500 prisoners, 25 machine guns, some mortars and a quantity of material.

The following day, 26 June, 2/6 relieved 1/5 in the Bois de Belleau.[8] Just as they left the woods northwest of Lucy-le-Bocage, about dusk, the enemy shelled it with mustard gas but 2/6 sustained no casualties. Battalion Headquarters was located in a ravine in Bois de Belleau, about 1350 meters (bearing 12 degrees east of north) from Lucy, where was also the 78th Company in reserve, commanded by 1st Lieutenant Amos R. Shinkle.[9] During the relief they were subjected to intermittent shelling by the enemy. Their casualties numbered 17. Captain Randolph T. Zane and First Sergeant Simon D. Barber of the 79th Company were among those wounded, the latter seriously.[10] The companies in line were the 79th, 1st Lieutenant Graves B. Erskine commanding—right; 80th, Captain Egbert T. Lloyd commanding—center; and the 96th, Captain Wethered Woodworth commanding—left. The enemy lines were about 600 meters distant, following the general line Torcy-Belleau-Bouresches railway station.

26 June: From Harbord to every unit in 4th Brigade, sent at 0815, "1. The Second Battalion, Sixth Regiment, Marines, as soon as possible, tonight, June 26-27, will relieve the 3d Battalion, 5th Regiment, Marines in the North end of the Bois de Belleau. Battalion and Company Commanders will make reconnaissance today. The Third Battalion, Fifth Marines, when relieved will take station in the Bois Gros Jean. Command Passes when relief is completed."

From 27 to 30 June there were no infantry developments of importance on either side. Two/Six sent out several patrols which did good work. The enemy was quiet during the days, but shelled the battalion at frequent intervals during the night. Casualties, however, were negligible, perhaps 10 all told. Food came in satisfactorily, being brought up hot, each night, in light trucks, which, returning, were loaded with salvage. The enemy did not place a shell on the ration distribution point, which was rare good fortune, since he shelled all around it. On the night of 30 June, the reserve company, the 78th, undertook the work of wiring the battalion's entire front and made fair progress.[11] The enemy was quiet all along the front and engaged only in the usual shelling of back areas.

28 June: Maj. Holcomb sent to Neville at 1420, "It is my intention to advance to the foot of the hill, the position of my left company (96th) and to connect up with Cooper's [?] right. The new Trench should be properly sited and taped out by an engineer, Have taken matter up with Capt. Palmtag, 2nd Eng, and he suggests you ask division for an officer. He should bring in his tape, and do the work to-night. Difficulty with Maj. Sibley about rations last night prevented my" (message incomplete).

30 June: From Harbord to Neville, Lee, Waller (6th Machine Gun Battalion), Hughes, and Holcomb, sent at 1640:

When the 2d Bn. 6th Marines is withdrawn from the Bois de Belleau it will not be replaced. The 1st Bn. 6th Marines will hold the Bois alone. The wiring must be completed without delay. Positions selected as strong points should have the rifle pits connected for occupation by squads or platoons according to their location, field of fire, etc. The C.O. 1st Bn, 6th Marines will consult with the C.O. 5th Marines and the C.O., 6th Machine Gun Bn. in making the plans for taking over the defense of the entire Bois. The present intention is to relieve the 2d Bn. on the night of the 2d-3d. of July.

1 July: The day was quiet, and, at night, the 78th Company resumed wiring. The work, under favorable conditions, progressed so rapidly that by 2:00 a.m. on the following morning, the entire front of 1500 meters was completely wired.

2 July: Two/Six was relieved at night by the 1st Battalion of the 6th Regiment, which extended its left so as to take in that portion of the line formerly held by 2/6. This move was made possible by the complete wiring of the front. When the relief was completed, just at dawn, the battalion moved back to the woods northwest of Lucy-le-Bocage. During the following several days, until 5 July, the battalion rested quietly in the woods. Red Cross and Y.M.C.A. supplies were a source of much comfort to the men. Some mail also came in, the first in a long while.[12]

5 July: The battalion was relieved at dark by a battalion of the 103rd Infantry, 26th Division, and moved back, once more, to the Gros Jean woods. The following day was spent in rest.

From that day until the 16th of July, 2/6 took it easy east of the village of Bezu, chowing down, resting beside the Marne River and swimming in it to get themselves and worn out clothes clean. Late in the afternoon of July 13, the battalion moved to Nanteuil sur Marne, where, the same night, for the first time since May, the whole battalion slept under cover. The days here were spent in policing, rest and recreation. The Marne proved a great boon to the men. The battalion stood by on July 16 from 6:00 p.m. to board camions for an unknown destination, and finally entrained about midnight.

Soissons

Like all the battalions of the Second Division, 2/6 had a rough ride to their ultimate destination, just south of the ancient town of Soissons. Fortunately for the 6th Regiment, its men had a day's rest before they were called upon to waste themselves on the firmly entrenched German army waiting for them. Second Lt. Lucien Vandoren's unofficial history is summarized as follows. He was 2/6's adjutant.

17 July: Shortly after noon they detrained and rested in a nearby wood until about 1800, when they took to the road again. The battalion marched until deep in the Foret de Retz and halted for the night about 2230. Troops were concentrated in great numbers in the wood, and, from the incessant stream of traffic, it was obvious that an important development was imminent.

18 July: Early the next morning the battalion was on the march, and, before they had progressed very much farther into the great wood, the large number of prisoners headed to the rear attested the complete initial success of Marshal Foch's surprise thrust. The Fifth Regiment of Marines, along with both the 9th and 23d Infantry Regiments, had advanced on this morning and had driven deep into the German lines. Two/Six halted in the morning at Greenleaf Farm and remained there until later in the afternoon, when the battalion moved up and bivouacked for the night on the slope just east of Bon Repaire Farm where a captured enemy battery still remained in place, evidence of the successful Allied advance.

19 July: The next day, the 6th Regiment was to go it alone. Everything that could go wrong, did. Though not their fault, they were late getting to the starting line, the artillery preparation had preceded them, and the enemy were back in their holes just waiting for them.

One/Six was on the right and 2/6 was on the left with 3/6 in the support line. Hughes remained in command of 1/6; Thomas Holcomb had resumed command of 2/6 from Maj. Robert L. Denig, and Berton Sibley still commanded 3/6. All of the officers were capable but could do nothing to prevent what was about to happen that day.

At 0730 the regiment moved forward from their place of repose. Two battalions went into their first line at Vierzy. Hughes' battalion, 1/6, moved to the right flank and Holcomb's 2/6 the left flank. Sibley's 3/6 would support the first line. Hughes had gone forward and settled his men in an open wheat field, somewhat exposed to artillery and Maxims. Most of Holcomb's men were inside a walled cemetery that initially provided some protection. Several hours before the 6th Marines were to jump off, the artillery had already fired their rolling barrage. Hence, when the 6th took off from their positions at 0830 in and about Vierzy, there was no rolling barrage for them. Worse, the Germans were ready for them. The only artillery fire the 6th Marines witnessed was incoming and dropping on them. The regiment had to cross over two miles to their target. Most wouldn't make it.

The battalion was assembled as soon as possible after orders to attack had been given at 0500, and the march to the "jumping off place," a kilometer and a half east of Vierzy, was begun. Two/Six were on the left of the regiment in the attack, the 1st Battalion on the right and the Third in support. The zero hour was 0820, and they were supported by tanks. The advance to their own front lines, a kilometer distant, was across perfectly open wheat fields. Their pace, because of the necessity of following the tanks, was slow, and the advance over the entire distance was through a heavy barrage put down by the enemy. When they had passed the front lines the enemy's machine guns proved most troublesome. The battalion was halted after a gain of about one kilometer because they had nothing left with which to continue the attack.

Several times during the morning, the commanding officer of the 6th Marines, Col. Harry Lee, sent messages to Harbord telling him "attack moving nicely. Four casualties from shell and shrapnel." Capt. Woodworth, commanding officer, 96th Company, sent to Lee at 1000: "96th and 79 Cos. gained objective, but cannot hold for wounded are coming thick. I am hit. Lt. Robinson [Robertson] hurt badly. We must have reserves for we cannot hold."

Major Robert Denig, who went along as an observer, describes in a lengthy letter home what he saw in the first few minutes on that first day. He had been in the 5th Marines for a spell and many of the officers mentioned were friends of his, like Wass and Murray. Denig also described what his first day, 19 July, was like.

At 8.30 we jumped off with a line of tanks in the lead. For two "kilos" the four lines of Marines were straight as a die, and their advance over the open plain in the bright sunlight was a picture I shall never forget. The fire got hotter and hotter, men fell, bullets sung, shells whizzed-banged and the dust of battle got thick. Overton was hit by a big piece of shell and fell. Afterwards I heard he was hit in the heart, so his death was without pain. He was buried that night and the pin found.

A man near me was cut in two. Others when hit would stand, it seemed, an hour, then fall into a heap. I yelled to [Maj. Pere] Wilmer that each gun in the barrage worked from right to left ... looked for Hughes way over to the right: told Wilmer I had a hundred dollars and be sure to get it. You think of all kinds of things.[13]

At 1023 Holcomb, at road bed 178.4-286.4, sent Lee a message: "Woodworth wounded. Reports that one company is nearly all casualties. They have merged with the 79th Co.— left line company. He believes they reached Chateau-Thierry road and had to fall back. Have sent to all companies for reports. Will wait here."

At 1045, 2d Lt. Clifton Bledsoe Cates sent a message to Holcomb that stands the test of time. It clearly indicated that he was something else. "I am in an old abandoned French Trench bordering on road leading out from your P.C. and 350 yds. from an old mill. I have only two men out of my company & 20 out of some other company. We need support, but it is almost suicide to try and get it here as we are swept by machine gun fire and a constant barrage is on us. I have no one on my left and only a few on my right. *I will hold.*" What remained of the battalion took shelter in a line of semi-complete entrenchments constructed by the Germans, where, from 1030 until dark they were subjected to assault by the enemy's artillery, one-pounder and machine gun fire.

At 1545 Lee sent the following message to all three battalion commanders, "The Division Commander directs us to dig in and hold our present line at all costs. No further advance will be made, for the present. He congratulates the command on its gallant conduct in the face of severe casualties. Let me make a sketch of your position and disposition. Ammunition at crossroads 122 southeast of Vierzy."

They were relieved at midnight, by a battalion of Algerians, and marched out with fewer than 800 effectives, their losses in killed and wounded being about 70 percent for the day.[14] Only three company officers remained, Captain Lloyd, Lieutenant Shinkle and Lieutenant Cates. Lieutenants John W. Overton and Charles H. Roy were killed while advancing at the head of their platoons. Vandoren's account describes the next few days.

20 July: They marched back through Vierzy and reached Greenleaf Farm just after sun-up. The day was spent resting in the woods nearby. Overnight, the men found comfort in dugouts which, but a few hours before, had been occupied by the enemy. On the following day, in the early forenoon the battalion took the road an moved a few kilometres to an important cross-roads where the regiment was assembled. Here they rested for a few hours, and, later in the afternoon the regiment was off again. They bivouacked in the forest near a cross-roads about two kilometres from Taillefontaine, and for the next few days spent quietly resting in the woods.

24 July: They received orders to move and the battalion got under way at about 0730. The march was conducted until 1130 when the column halted in a wood near the roadside, for lunch. The march was resumed at 1300 and the column halted for the night at 1730. They then bivouacked in a wood. On the road the next day until they reached Nanteuil[15] in the middle of the morning. We went into billets. Spent next few days in Nanteuil. Close order drill, bayonet and Chauchat instruction for the companies in the mornings. The afternoons were devoted to rest and recreation.

On 30 July they entrained at night-fall and the train got under way the early morning. Entraining progressed smoothly and there was more room for the battalion than on former occasions. The next day the battalion detrained at Nancy. It then hiked nine kilometres to Chavigny, where we billeted for four days until 4 August. The Fifth Replacement Battalion joined us here, bringing the battalion back up to strength. Their next move was to Liverdun. On August 7 the battalion relieved the 347th French Regiment in the trenches at Pont-a-Moussan, a quiet sector, with the 1st and 3rd Battalions in reserve.

Marbache

On the night of August 8-9 the enemy put down a box-barrage to the right of the position held by the 2nd Battalion and everything pointed to a raid, but the enemy did not penetrate Allied lines. Only two men were slightly wounded. Effective work at reconnaissance was carried out and patrolling was successful. Apparently the enemy was content to rest within his own wire. There were no infantry developments, both artilleries were quiet, and each side was moderately active in the air.

9 August: Lt. Col. Thomas Holcomb sent Col. Lee a report with no time indicated: "1. At 4:00 a.m. Lieutenant [Walter] Powers, commanding the 79th Co., (front line), reported by phone that enemy artillery was firing on his front.—No barrage signal having been sent up, after consultation with Powers, I asked for artillery at 4:14 a.m. and requested 'Barrage # 10, Burgogne.'" From this point on, Holcomb described what he went through with different people on the phone trying to get the barrage going. "Our front line continued to send up barrage calls at five minute intervals, until 4:48 a.m. when our barrage started,—a period of 33 minutes from the time the first rocket was sent up." He asked for a continuance when the barrage shut down and it took another twenty minutes to get it going again. He was having difficulty with the 12th Field Artillery.

For the balance of the battalion's stay at this location, there seem not to be any further messages from or to 2/6. Holcomb was reassigned as second in command of the regiment and Major Ernest C. Williams replaced him in command of 2/6 on 16 August. On 22 August orders were given directing the various units of the 4th Brigade to begin marching toward their next destination—St. Mihiel. The entire division arrived at its site, Limey, on or about 11 September.

St. Mihiel

The best record for 2/6 at St. Mihiel is the report of operations covering the period from 12 September to 15 September 1918:

> At 4:45 a.m. September 12th, 1918, after a difficult night march from the BOIS DE LA RAPPE, this battalion was in position to the rear of LIMEY prepared to go forward, Artillery preparation had been in progress since 1:00 a.m. Promptly at 5:00 a.m. the first wave of attack left the parallel of departure followed at intervals of a few minutes by the succeeding waves.—We followed the

3rd. Battalion of the 6th Regiment at a distance of one thousand (1000) metres. The advance was steady and rapid with the enemy's artillery feeble. We passed through the BOIS D' EUVEZIN to the left of LOGE MANGIN where, because of the extent of the woods and thickness of the undergrowth, the maintenance of liaison was extremely difficult. Here for a time, we lost touch with the 78th, 79th and parts of the 96th and 80th Companies. On reaching the northern edge of the BOIS DU BEAU VALLON a halt was made for a few minutes and a wave of attack reorganized, consisting of Battalion Headquarters, and two platoons each of the 96th and 80th Companies. The advance was again resumed and we reached and passed through THIAUCOURT about 4:00 p.m. At this point the battalion was assembled and took up a position on the line of hills north of THIAUCOURT. Our casualties during the day were extremely light, numbering possibly ten (10) in all.—During the night we were subjected to light intermittent fire from the enemy's guns and sustained a few additional casuals.

We occupied this position until the afternoon of September 13th, 1918, when we were ordered to relieve, in place, a support battalion of the 23rd Infantry. This relief was effected by infiltration and we were in our new position by 6:00 p.m. In this position we were subjected to harassing fire by the enemy but our casualties amounted to practically nothing.

Here we remained until the afternoon of September 14th, 1918, when orders were received from Regimental Headquarters that the 3rd Battalion would take up a position to the right of XAMMES and that we would occupy the position vacated by the 3rd Battalion. A misunderstanding about certain company positions delayed this relief temporarilly [sic] but It wan finally effected about 9:00 p.m.

At 3:00 a.m. September 15th the following order was received from Regimental Headquarters,—"To—C.O. 2nd Bn., 6th: You will proceed immediately with your battalion and M.G. Co. north and occupy the line from XAMMES-CHAREY road, eastward across the southern edge of the woods lying between XAMMES and CHAREY along the unimproved road running east and west through the BOIS DE LA MONTAGNE and the X line 244.3 from Hill 331.5."—The Battalion was assembled at once and moved forward in accordance with the order above quoted. The head of the column reached the XAMMES-CHAREY road, at X line 244.3, at 5:00 a.m. The column was as follows:—Intelligence Section, Battalion Headquarters, 80th, 98th, 79th, 75th and 81st M.G. Companies. As we approached the crest of Hill 231.5, to turn off on unimproved road and take up our position a machine gun was heard firing from our right, but apparently not at us, for no losses were sustained. We turned off on unimproved road near crest of Hill 231.5 and encountered about forty (40) of the enemy withdrawing through the brush. They were commanded to halt and surrender by the Adjutant and Sgt. Major and we would have made them all captive had not someone fixed into them. They immediately took to their heels, with the Sgt. Major close behind them and he later succeeded in rounding them all up and bringing them in.—It was apparent that Hill 231.5 and the BOIS DE MONTAGNE were held by the enemy, and the companies were brought up and deployed as rapidly an possible. Because of machine guns fire from the left of the XAMMES-CHAREY road, it was necessary to protest this flank, to exceed our sector on the left. Lieutenant [James P.] Adams with two platoons of the 78th Company and 6 guns from the 81st M.G. Company, was sent over to handle the strip of woods to the left of the road. The battalion Commander gave the order to advance and clean the woods of the enemy which was accomplished in good time cleaned the woods without heavy losses, although the position was well organized and heavily defended with machine guns. We were not at first subjected to artillery fire because the enemy did not know the situation of his own troops. Owing to the confusion resulting from the initial surprise and from the difficulty of maintaining contact in the heavily wooded slopes, the units of the command became badly mixed, but the line was finally straightened out along the northern edge of the BOIS DE MONTAGNE and liaison established with the 5th Regiment on the right. Our left flank was in the air, the division to our left not having advanced. The 75th Company, 1st Battalion, and two platoons of the 83rd Company, 3rd Battalion, were sent up to reinforce our front at this point. When the enemy, through the withdrawal of his troops, ascertained that we held the BOIS DE MONTAGNE, we were subjected throughout the day to heavy artillery, mortar and machine gun fire. Battalion P.O. was located at 363.6-244.3 on the crest of Hill 231.5. By 2:00 p.m. in answer to a hurry call, the Regimental Munitions Officer had delivered to us 38,000 rounds of 30 calibre and 16,000 rounds of Hotchkiss ammunition. At 6:00 in the evening and again about dusk the enemy countered. Each time his attacks were proceeded by brief but violent artillery preparations. Each time he was repulsed by rifle and machine gun fire, with losses to himself. During the day the enemy had supremacy of the air. The night was quiet and we were relieved by a Battalion of the 310th Regiment, 78th Division. Of the officers, Lieutenants [Emmons J.] Stockwell [USA] and [Albert C.] Simonds were killed and Captains [John A.] Minnis, [Wethered] Woodworth and [Bailey M.] Coffenberg and Lieutenants [David R.] Kilduff, [Graves B.] Erskine and [Thomas H.] Wert were wounded.[16]

Reports of casualties and captured property are being submitted separately. The position captured was in the course of strong organization—we found spacious dugouts (concrete) reinforced with steel, a narrow gauge railway, some rolling stock, a cement mixer, large quantities of sand and gravel and big gun pits in the course of construction.

The next report is uncommon because a company commander sent his battalion commanding officer a descriptive report of his company's activities on one day.

22 September: First Lieutenant James P. Adams sent a report to the Battalion commanding officer, about the 78th Company's attack on the 15th:

1. This company left the crest of the hill in rear off Thiaucourt at about 3:30 a.m. in the formation column of tow's with three paces between men, and a twenty pace interval between files. We proceeded on to the valley, where the column was halted and enemy machine gun fire opened up on our column. The 78th Company was ordered by Captain Woodworth to move over to the left, in order to get protection from the harassing fire, and there we started digging in. A few minutes later the order was given "Over the Top." The 79th Company, being mixed with the 78th, started over at the same time. We proceeded from there down into the valley, destroying one machine gun nest under the cement bridge. Captain [George W.] Martin, Lieutenant [Archie W.] French and Second Lieutenant [William L.] Harding commanded the left flank. Lieutenant [James P.] Adams and Lieutenant [Gardiner] Hawkins commanded the left center. In this formation we proceeded up the side of the hill advancing to the crest of Hill 231. There I saw the left flank falling back, and proceeded over to the left flank, in order to hold our position. Upon my arrival the men were in disorder, as there were no officers to command them. I immediately formed a skirmish line across the left and sent a runner to Battalion Commander with a map showing our position. The extreme left we could not get liaison with. This was about 8:30 a.m. September 15th, 1918.

About 1:30 p.m. Lieutenant Harding reported to me with a detachment of men, which I immediately put in line with him, I found that extreme left flank under the command of Captain Martin had fallen back. A little later a platoon of the 83rd Company, and one platoon of the 82nd Company [both 3/6], reported to me, which I immediately placed in line with my men, and to the right of them, to fill up the gap on my right. One platoon of the 73rd Machine Gun Company reported to me, and I placed them in position, so that they would have enfilading fire on the enemy to our left and right flank. A half hour later, Captain Stowell reported with one company to help defend our position, and his company was put in line on the right of our position. The attack had quieted down, and we were straightening our position and digging in.

About 6:30 p.m. September 15th, 1918, the enemy started a counter attack on our right flank, and to our right. The left flank immediately opened fire on the enemy and helped drive them back.

At about 11:30 p.m. September 15th, 1918, I was relieved by one company of the 78th Division, and one machine gun platoon from the same division, and from there I proceeded back to the woods in which we were bivouaced for that night.

(signed) J. P. Adams, 2nd Lieut., U.S.M.C.

According to Adams' report, some of the officers were seriously lacking in skills, and perhaps courage. Adams, by the way, would soon be a first lieutenant.

Like the entire Second Division, 2/6 marched for many days until reaching their next area of combat. Like all the others, 2/6 arrived on 30 September. In a few days they would take over lines held by the French.

Blanc Mont

2 October: At 0920 Col. Lee sent a message to all three battalion commanders (see Chapter 5, Blanc Mont section). He gave instructions for unit placement and boundaries for regimental sectors.

3 October: In his message sent at 0350, Lee gave "H" hour for the attack at 5:50 a.m. on October 3, with further details for the plan of attack (see Chapter 5).

At 0500 Lee sent a message to the three battalion commanders describing their actions at 0550. The 6th Regiment would lead, followed by the 5th Regiment in a column of battalions, with a distance of 1,000 yards between them. After a 5 minute artillery preparation, at zero hour a rolling barrage would begin and precede the infantry by 100 yards. Twelve French tanks were assigned to the leading battalion, while the next battalion would have 12 tanks following them to repel any enemy counterattacks.

At 0800 Maj. Williams, 2/6, asked Barker if he was in contact with anyone on his right. Williams was evidently expecting a unit, perhaps from the 3d Brigade, to be in the Bois de Vipère. A few Germans left in those woods, but most had retreated up to the ridge under orders when the Second Division arrived.

Williams sent Lee a message at 0900: "Objective reached at 8:30 a.m. Position now being consolidated. From first information casualties appear to be light and the bag of prisoners good. Spirits of all very high. Barrage was beautiful." Then, at 1105 he requested support from Shuler on his left flank. "The French have not come up and our left is in the air. The enemy about 700 or 800 strong encircling movement."

Captain Walter Powers, at this time in command of the 80th Company, sent Williams the following message: "About 11:00 a.m. I was 150 yards in front of the line due north from your present P.C. and found 5 abandoned field pieces, 1 wounded German and many good dugouts in a pine woods cleared of underbrush. It might be well to put outposts there as there is good observation and good cover. Also guns might be remanned [*sic*] by the enemy."

A portrait of Private John Joseph Kelly, awarded a Medal of Honor for heroics on 3 October at Blanc Mont.

Williams sent Lee a message at 1350: "We

Top: **Survivors of the 96th Company, 2/6 Battalion, in Germany.** *Bottom:* **Survivors of the 79th Company, 2/6 Battalion, in Germany.**

Members of the 6th Regiment who were awarded Distinguished Service Crosses, in Lutesdorf, Germany.

are exposed to extremely punishing artillery and M.G. fire from both front and left flank. 12th Art. Liaison Officer has sent in our position to his Hqs. and it is requested that we be given counter battery work. Have suffered a number of casualties in this position, which is bad because enemy's fire enfilades our left flank, which we are obliged to hold. Position sketch herewith [None available]."

At 1530 Williams advised Lee: "Message received. No arrangements have been made for rations but of course we need them and would appreciate anything you can do toward getting them for us. Have established outposts and our position to the front is a commanding one for several kilometers. On the left, the 2nd Bn. of the 5th has moved in. The situation here is none to good, as we are constantly harassed by severe artillery, M.G. and minenwerfer fire. However if we can get effective cooperation from artillery, I believe we will be O.K. We connect with 3rd Brgd. on right."

Williams, expecting 2/5 to move forward that night leaving his left flank open, sent several message out concerning that, including one at 2230 to his company commanders. Of course, the 5th did not move that night. An interesting message from Corporal Frederick C. Ladd, 96th Company, no time indicated, told Williams, "Not yet reached destination (96th Co.) 96th Co. are at junction of front lines and Boy de Bromberg." He earned two Silver Star citations and a Croix de Guerre, Bronze, at Blanc Mont "for gallantry in action as a runner."

4 October: At 0830 Maj. Messersmith sent Williams a message: "20th Company held up by heavy fire on the left of sector along road. The company needs assistance and I have none to give. What can you do for us? About 265.4-281.5."

At 0910 Williams directed his company commanders to return all men from other companies to their own. He also asked for list of casualties and missing. Evidently, some of the men weren't keeping up with their companies. No wonder.

Lee sent a directive to Shuler at 3/6 to get in touch with Barker at 1/6 to "tell him to move forward to relieve the 5th of this fire, both on the left flank and from the right and left rear. Your Bn. and 2nd Bn. will stand fast, for the moment."

Williams notified Lee at 1355 that he was not in complete possession of Blanc Mont Massif. "The enemy holds a good portion of Blanc Mont and is about 150 yards distant from the line we hold along our eastern flank. From his position, which is as commanding ours, the enemy covers the low ground in front of us with his M.G. fire and advance, without heavy losses on this flank, is impossible without heavy artillery preparation on his positions on our left or until the French advance on the left and take this position. Our effectives are approximately as follows: 78th—95. 80th—60. 96th—65. 79th—85. Casualties in officers about 40 percent."

The Fifth Marines had been advancing and brutally hit by enemy artillery and machine gun fire. Consequently, the 6th Marines were ordered forward to save the 5th. Williams sent orders to the commanding officer of the 78th Company, Captain James McB. Sellers, "This Bn. will follow the 1st Bn. at 1000 meters. We will have 2 companies in front and 2 in local support, 2nd wave to follow first at 400 meters. The positions will be as follows: 78th—left front; 79th—right front; 96th—left rear; 80th—right rear. It is absolutely necessary to cover off entire sector assigned to us." He sent the same message to all four company commanders.

Powers at 80th sent Williams this message at 1910: "1. I am in my same position on edge of woods. 2. 96th Co. has fallen back a little distance. I think they should come up on line with me. 3. Drove back a little attack. 4. I Think it is all over."

Williams sent the commanding officer of the 96th Company, Lt. Cliff Cates, a message at 1945: "What position are you holding at present? I want you to hold the position which 96th occupied last night and today on line with the 80th unless you have good reasons for not doing so." Williams then asked Shuler for the positions of 3/6. He also sent a message to Lee at 1955, but not received until 2355, that his battalion needed water, badly.

At 2005 Powers of the 80th reported: "1. The 3rd Battalion fell back farther when they were shelled. I sent a runner out to find them and he judged they were 600 to 800 yds., behind my line. 2. The 96th Company has not come back and touched up with my left, so I am unprotected there."

Colonel Lee sent both Williams and Barker a message at 2100, "There will be no further advance tonight … take up positions in support of the 5th Regiment and dig in." At 2350 Williams notified Shuler at 3/6: "1st Bn. and our left flank company report being heavily shelled from right rear, seeming by our own artillery. Have fired rockets to lengthen range to no effect. Please relay this to Site [Lee], our phone connection broken."

5 October: Beginning at 1205 that morning Lee sent a series of orders that described what the artillery was going to do to the German machine guns in and on Blanc Mont from 0515 to 0615. Lee sent all three battalion commanders a message at 0815 saying they should be prepared to pass through the 5th Marines and continue when ordered. The formation, from head to rear, was Williams [2/6], Shuler [3/6] and Barker [1/6].

Williams sent his company commanders the following at 0830: "All men belonging to other companies will be sent to their proper units this morning. If impracticable to give list of casuals and missing by names. Companies will submit, at once, total effectives present, total number brought into action, and approximate number of killed, wounded and missing." At 1035 Williams sent Lee a record of his manpower:

Statement of effectives in 2nd Bn., this a.m.
78th Company   102 men including 3 officers
79th Company   82 men including 3 officers
96th Company   51 men including 3 officers
80th Company   55 men including 4 officers
Total in line   290 men including 13 officers
In addition Bn Hqrs 4 Off. present and 35 men.

Lee sent all three commanders a message at 1205 saying the French Division had advanced to the St. Pierre–St. Etienne road with little opposition. The regiment was to advance at once with the French Division on the left and the 3rd Brigade on the right. Twenty minutes later Lee sent a message to Shuler for Williams which stated that "the advance will not go beyond ST. ETIENNE without further orders." In fact, Lee sent two more messages saying the same thing.

Lee sent a message with directions to all three commanders at 1820 that 1/6 would relieve 3/6 in second line, 3/6 would then relieve 2/6 in the front line, and 2/6 would then become the third line.

Williams notified the commanding officer, 79th Company, at 1505: "When you connect up with the 23rd Infantry, who are somewhere to our right front notify me and we will halt and regulate our advance on them. Make every effort to get in touch with the leading elements of 23rd Infantry. Establish a line of skirmishers to your left flank with as large intervals as possible, in order to obtain contact with left company. I shall be in rear of center of Bn."

Williams to Lee at 1740: "Right held up by M.G. nests in woods at 266.65-282.73 to 266.8-282.8; 266.95-282.7 to 267.13-282.7 and extending to 267.13-282.83. Left reports trenches at center of coord. square 265, 266, 283.20 rapidly filling with enemy, who are coming in from rear brining M.G.'s with them. Heavy M.G. fire from both right and left. We have requested artillery fire on 3 nests on right; via artillery Liaison Officer. Request that artillery be put on trenches to left (coordinates above). Am holding in these positions."

Second Lieutenant Cates, commanding officer, 96th Company, sent Williams the following at 1750: "I now have 80 men from 79th Co. and 96th Co. combined. From my position it will be impossible to even flank them. The Major of the 23rd Inf. ordered us to halt here. There must be at least eight guns and a lot of wire in the woods. I am digging in here and consolidating. I have liaison with 23 Inf. on right. No liaison on left."

And at 1800 Cates sent the following message to Williams, "We have numerous wounded men in the woods where the nest is. A report is that Lt. [John A.] West is still alive but badly wounded and still in the woods. Should we shell the woods under those circumstances? It is impossible to get out the wounded. This same nest cut up the 23rd Inf. yesterday and the Major told us that we should not attack but we followed orders. We can hold here, but it will take an extra heavy barrage to get them out *and more men*."

Lee sent around the order, at 1820, for 1/6 to relieve 3/6. Three/Six would then proceed to relieve 2/6 now in the first line. Two/Six would retire to the third line. At 1950 he wanted to know how many "effectives have you got?" Williams replied that he had 13 officers and 240 men.

6 October: Lee advised all three Battalion commanders that they would provide his headquarters guides for the incoming 141st Regiment, 36th National Guard Division. He also sent an order that Williams would appoint a "board" to inventory guns, ammunition and other property captured by 2/6. Williams created a board consisting of 1st Lt. George Wale, Jr., 79th Company; 2d Lt. Jesse L. Crandall, 96th Company; 1st Lt. James P. Adams, 78th Company; and 1st Lt. Ross S. Wilson, 80th Company.

Captain Walter Powers, commanding officer, 80th Company, sent Williams the following message at 1115: "1. I need map of forward area, hand-grenades and a little chauchat ammunition. 2. The men have had only one meal a day for three days and have no reserve rations. They must have rations of some sort. 3. Should not the 80th and 96th Cos. come up on line with 78th and cover 3rd Batt?" In line 2, Powers, for once, was right on target. Not feeding the Marines, at least, was one terrible mishap during the entire war.

8 October: Lee directed Williams, at 1805: Sixty men of your battalion, equipped with rifle bayonet and gas mask, will report to these Hdq. immediately as a carrying party to take food to the 3rd Bn. They will be in charge of an officer from your Bn.

9 October: Lee sent each battalion the following message at 1630: "You will see that all Browning guns and Browning equipment in possession of your command are turned in to the Ordnance Officer of the 142nd Inf. who will be at 2nd Bn. P.C. at 5:30 p.m. to receive them." When the members of the 142d Infantry arrived, the Marines managed to talk them out of those fine, superior, brand new Browning Automatic Rifles in exchange for the lousy Chauchats the Marines were stuck with.

At 1935 Williams sent directions to all company commanders:

> The following will report to Lt. [Paul J.] Ogden at Bn. Hq. at once: Lt. [William L.] Harding, 78th, Lt. [Henley M.] Goode, 96th, Lt. [George Jr.] Ehrhart, 80th, Lt. [George] Wale, 79th, and *one* N.C.O. from each platoon of *each* company.
>
> The following will report to Capt. [Eugene F.C.] Collier at Bn. Hqs at once: Lt. [Jesse L.] Crandall, 96th, Lt. [George W.] Hopke, 80th, Lt. [Edward C.] Fowler, 78th, Lt. [Maurice E.] Barnett, 79th, and 1 N.C.O. from each platoon of each company.
>
> These details must be instructed as to the officers to whom they are to report and must be kept separate. Two Bns. of the relief will move into and occupy trenches now held by this Bn.
>
> The details made above are to act as guide for the 2 relieving Bns. and will remain behind 24 hours after relief is completed.

The relieving battalions were from the 36th Division.

17 October: Major Williams, commanding officer of 2/6, prepared the following lengthy report of operations which covers every aspect from 29 September through 10 October.

> At 5:30 p.m. on the afternoon of September 29, in accordance with orders received an hour earlier from Regimental Headquarters, the Second Battalion, 6th Marines, embussed at SARRY, where it had been billeted for several days, and started its journey to the front. At about 11:00 p.m. the troops left the camions one kilometre south of SUIPPE through which town the Battalion

marched, and bivouaced for the night in a trench, screened by a fringe of trees from hostile observation, about midway between SUIPPE and SOUAIN and to the left of the road. The night was chilly and wet, but the men were tired and slept soundly on the hard ground. At noon the following day hot rations were brought up and later in the day the kitchens arrived, restoring everyone's spirits. This position, one the French had constructed as a part of the reserve defenses, was occupied until late in the afternoon of October 1st when we were ordered forward to relieve the French in the front lines north of SOMME-PY. Before moving out the twenty percent of commissioned and enlisted strength were given orders to remain; one Officer, Lieutenant John D. Bowling, went in advance to reconnoiter the position we were to take over; ammunition and pyrotechnics were picked up on the way forward. At 8:30 p.m. the Battalion was off and made the march a good 12 kilometres, without a rest and over a road jammed with traffic of every description, nor did we lose a man. The position from which we relieved the French consisted of four lines of parallel trenches, of which we took over the first,—DE KREFELD. From right to left in trench DE KREFELD the companies were as follows: 79th, 80th and 78th,—"y" coordinates 7.75 and 68.4 marking limits. The 96th Company on the left, occupied the BOYOU DE BROMBERG to a point just south of trench DE L' ELBE, where it was blocked and beyond,—the Boches. Between the 96th and the 78th the enemy held the trench DE L' ELBE. More in advance, the enemy also held trench DU PACHE, trench DE ELBE and trench D' ESSEN and annoyed us, during the night, with his machine gun fire. Liaison was established on the left with the French, who were intermingled with the men of the 96th, and on the right with the 1st Battalion of the 5th Marines, Major George W. Hamilton commanding, located in the trench DES PRUSSIEN. Battalion P.O. was located at junction of GENZWEG and trench KREFELD. The relief was completed at 5:00 a.m. and report of dispositions made to Regimental Commander.

On the morning of October 2nd, orders were received from Regimental Headquarters to be prepared to attack at noon, but a later order informed us that the attack would be postponed for twenty four hours. During the afternoon the Stokes Mortar and one-pounder sections, which had dropped out of the column the night before, reported, and were sent over to [Lt. Clifton] Cates, on the left, to assist against the enemy's strong point at junction of BOY DES HOHENZOLLERN and principal parallels, from which his machine gun fire menaced our flank. Pursuant to orders received from the Regimental Commander, the following order was, in substance, sent to all, company commanders at 4:20 p.m. "At 6:30 p.m. you will occupy, by infiltration, the trenches DE PACHE, DE L' ELBE and D' ESSEN. Two platoons will be used. initially, followed by other two as successive trenches are reached. Consolidate and hold with two platoons in front trenches and two in rear." In addition, the limits of each company's occupancy were clearly defined. Everything went according to schedule. The following message, written at 8:00 p.m. by Lieutenant Cates, who had the difficult flank, was characteristic:—"Attack a success. Few Losses. Consolidated. Liaison with 78th on right and French on left. Everything in good shape."

Before midnight liaison officers from the 12th and 15th Artillery Regiments and thirty six pioneers, commanded by Lieutenant [William J.] Whaling, had reported to us. The pioneers were split up equally among the companies. From the artillery officers we learned that "H" hour was set for 5:50 on the morning of October 3rd. Everything pointed to an early morning attack, but no orders had been received. A telephonic communication with the Regimental Commander at about 3:30 a.m. disclosed the fact that orders would be sent us. At 4:30 a.m. no orders having been received, attack orders were, with the aid of a Field Message Book, poncho and flashlight, issued to Company Commanders. We had the "H" hour from the Artillery officers and the order which planned the attack for noon of the 2nd gave our sector limits. We attacked with all four companies in line, in four waves, each wave consisting of a platoon from each company. Promptly at 4:45 our artillery thundered away on its five minute preparation and promptly at 5:50 the Second Battalion went "over the top." Exactly at 5:40 a.m. a breathless runner from Regimental Headquarters delivered the orders for the attack. From the very first the progress was excellent. Machine gun fire from the left, as we cleared the parallel of departure, caused a few casualties in the ranks of the 96th and 76th Companies. For a short time the enemy put down a counter—

barrage but, before long, he was busily engaged in moving back his guns and his artillery opposition became more feeble. Our barrage was magnificent and our men kept right on the edge of it, even, at times, risking our own guns to dash ahead and silence a particularly troublesome Maxim. Numerous machine guns were encountered but these failed to hinder our advance and at 8:30 a.m. the following message was sent back:—"Objective reached at 8:30 a.m. position now being consolidated. From first information casualties appear to have been light and the bag of prisoners good. Spirits of all very high. Barrage was beautiful.—Williams."

The position consolidated was about seventy five yards in advance of the MEDEAH FME. road from 6.37 to 6.85. Battalion P.C. was located along the same road, at about 6.6. The enemy still held on our left, where no Allied advance had been made, and his machine guns, one-pounders and mortars proved particularly troublesome from this quarter. In addition, realizing that our advance was at an end, his artillery took position to our front and was very annoying, particularly his pieces of 88 calibre. In order to protect our left it was necessary to draw back the 96th Company and part of the 78th. Our stokes and One-pounders could not be located. A counter-attack from the left was impending, and both our front and flank were enfiladed by the enemy's fire. Four tanks, which had supported the attack, were conducted to position on the left and our machine gunners, as usual, proved equal to the occassion. When the counter-blow developed it was repulsed, after some hard fighting with severe losses to the enemy.

During the afternoon of the 3rd, our left was reinforced by a company and two platoons from the First Battalion, 6th Marines, and at 4:30 p.m. Major Messersmith, commanding the Second Battalion of the 5th Marines, reported that he had closed the gap on the left, between the 96th Company and the French, with his Battalion. This move relieved the troops of the First Battalion and they re-occupied their support position. At about 5:45 p.m. the following message was received from Regimental Headquarters. "Information has been received that the French division on our left has advanced. Our division will move forward at about 4:00 p.m. and occupy the ridge to the eastward and southeastward of ST. ETIENNE. The 5th Regiment will pass through the 6th Regiment in its present position and will advance to the new objective. When the 5th has passed through, the Battalions of this Regiment will immediately reform and be prepared to follow the 5th at a distance of about one kilometre should their advance make that necessary. This regiment will advance in column of Battalions in the order—Barker, Williams, Shuler, and will assure the protection of the left flank of the 5th Regiment. Should the rear Battalion of the 5th Regiment not advance more than one kilometre from the present position, this regiment will remain in place and assure the protection of the Left flank.—Lee."

The advance of the 5th, as described in the order just quoted did not take place until early on the morning of the 4th and was without artillery preparation. Heavy enemy artillery fire was encountered and after about two kilometre of progress, further advance was impossible because of heavy machine gun resistance. A message from Major Messersmith, written at 8:30 a.m. was as follows:—"20th Company [3/5] held up by heavy fire on left of sector along road. The Company needs assistance and I have none to send. What can you do for us? About 265.4-281.5." This was referred to the [1st] Battalion of the 5th which was third in the advance. At about 1:30 p.m., this message was received from Captain Shuler, commanding the Third Battalion:—"Colonel Lee directs that I transmit the following order to you. Barker is ordered forward immediately to cover left flank of 5th Regiment. Zero hour 2:30 p.m. You and I will remain in place until zero hour at which time we will advance."—This advance was not effected. The French division, which had advanced on our left, had skirted Blanc Mont to the westward, leaving a stronghold of considerable importance in the hands of the enemy, from which he continued to menace our left. At about 9:00 p.m. we received orders from Regimental to take up position in support of the 5th Regiment and dig in. This was done.

At about 5:00 o'clock on the morning of the 5th after an hour's artillery preparation, the Third Battalion attacked and took that part of Blanc Mont still held by the enemy without firing a shot and without the loss of a man. The prisoners numbered over two hundred and approximately seventy five machine guns were taken in the course of this operation. At 8:25 a.m. telephonic orders were received as quoted: "This regiment will at once be reorganized and be prepared to pass through the 5th Marines when ordered. Usual formation. Order of Battalions front to rear, Williams, Shuler, Barker." Companies were at once ordered to stand by, and, ammunition was drawn from dump near junction of SOMME-PY–MEDEAH FME. road. At 12:50 p.m. the following order was received over the wire: "The 6th Regiment advances at once. Advance to ST. ETIENNE, keeping in liaison with French on left and the Third Brigade on right. French have already advanced. Halt at St. Etienne and await orders, Lee." Before we moved forward, Lieutenant Colonel Holcomb arrived and ordered us to stop at ridge, south east of ST. ETIENNE. Regimental P.C. moved up to P.C. which we were vacating. At about 3:00 p.m. we went forward, the first wave, from left to right, consisting of the 76th and 79th Companies, and the second of the 80th and 96th Companies. Battalion Headquarters held the center of the Battalion sector in the advance, which was more than a kilometre and a half in width. At this time our effectives numbered a few more than three hundred. On the left we attained our objective. On the right a Battalion of the 23rd Infantry was found to be in our sector. Its commanding officer strongly advised Lieutenant [John A.] West, commanding the 79th Co., not to attempt a further advance because strong machine gun nests made progress without artillery preparation impossible. The preceding day his command had been badly cut up in attempting to take the position. Lieutenant West, however attacked with his company, and was carried from the field, severely wounded. Lieutenant Cates, 96th Company, took command on the right, and drew back to the line held by the Infantry. The situation was reported by him to the Battalion Commander, and, in turn, to the Regimental Commander. We were told to stand fast and not to attempt a further advance.

By dawn on the morning of the 6th we had been relieved by Shuler's Battalion, and, pursuant to orders, we moved back to the third line position along MEDEAH FME. road, on Blanc Mont, the companies occupying the same positions they held on the morning of the first advance. On the night of October 6th, one Battalion of the 141st Infantry came in and occupied, with us, our position. Later this Battalion, plus the other Battalions of the Infantry Regiment, moved up to the relief of the more advanced units of our Regiment. A Regimental memo of October 9th, written at 1:05 p.m. brought the good news that nightfall would see our relief. Two sets of guides and officers were furnished for the two Battalions of the 144th Infantry which were to relieve us. The relief was completed early on the morning of October 10th and the Battalion proceeded, by companies, to NAVARIN FME., where a good breakfast did much to put new life into a tired but confident Battalion. Later in the morning the Battalion moved back to Camp NAWTIVET, where the work of replacing, reorganizing and training was begun.

In summarizing the operation, much credit is due the initiative and dash of both officers and men. Many brilliant performances both individual and collective, marked the combat. The Battalion Medical Staff, in charge of Surgeon Robert Mueller, U.S.N., labored unceasingly and our evacuations were all that could have been desired, no patient remaining in an advanced dressing station for a longer period than thirty minutes. During the first three days, October 2nd to 4th inclusive, the problem of rationing was, because of heavy enemy fire on our positions, one of extreme difficulty. In this period but one meal a day was served the men. Thereafter the Battalion Quartermaster was able to function on a normal basis, and the question of food and water was handled in an entirely satisfactory manner. Enough Chauchat clips and musettee were salvaged from the French to supply our needs—as were hand grenades. Advanced dumps provided an abundance of small arms ammunition, but rifle grenades which time and again would have been of great value in the reduction of machine gun nests were not procurable. Our supply of pyrotechnics was not what it should have been. We went into the attack with only three Very pistols in the Battalion and but a very limited number of flares. In addition we were without signal panels, so that it was impossible to comply with the Division's plane's request to mark out our front lines. The tanks assigned to the Battalion did not come up in time to go over the top with us and the Stokes Mortar and one-pounder sections were never in line and did not, in any way, aid in the success of the operation. The 81st Machine Gun Company, which has always cooperated most efficiently with the 2nd Battalion again proved a splendid organization and in great measure the results obtained must be attributed to the zeal and untiring efforts of its officers and men.

(Sgd) Ernest C. Williams, Major, U.S.M.C., Comd' g. Battalion.

Meuse-Argonne

31 October: Major Williams sent Col. Lee the following message at 2356: "Companies located in ravine whose center point is 300.5-83.5 with "Y" coordinates 00 and 01 approximately marking limits of Bn. flanks. Bn. P.C. located at 300.5-83.5. We are ready to attack."

1 November: Williams sent to Lee at 0945: "We are on 1st objective which we reached at 9:05. Companies are in proper position. The 3rd Battalion is about 250 meters ahead of us and we are waiting for them to advance. Then at 1224 Williams notified Shuler at 3/6: "I am ready to pass through and continue but am held up by own artillery falling short. Please send this to Regimental P.C."

At 1250 Williams told Lee: "Left of the 3rd Bn. held up about 1 kilometer behind its objective by own artillery fire am now passing through their lines as they are now." Then at 1515 Williams told Lee: "We are on our objective. Front companies adjusting line and sending exploiting parties ahead. Have liaison with Major Stowell (1 company) on left with 5th Regt. on right. Some M.G. being encountered from that part of Bois de la Folie which we have not yet taken. Casualties among the men were not extremely heavy. Officers about 50 percent."

At 1800 Lt. Col. Thomas Holcomb advised Neville at 4th Brigade Headquarters that Williams was "on his objective. His front line Cos. are adjusting line and sending exploiting parties ahead." He added that "Williams telephone wire is in Bayonville and will soon be there." Holcomb followed that with a message to Williams, "It is vitally important that you should push exploitation to the northern, northeastern, and northwestern edges of BOIS DE LA FOLIE unless stopped by serious resistance, and prevent the enemy occupying this woods during the night."

First Lieutenant Gardiner Hawkins sent the 6th Regiment intelligence officer the following message at 1900: "80th Company just reports having pushed out and holding bulge in woods south of Fme-de-Mases bounded by 01.7-95. 01.6-95.5 and 02.0-95.7 Two platoons along edge of woods and two platoons southeast in support. 96th is slightly southwest of 80th." At 1920 Williams told Lee: "To hold edge of woods as required would cause us to hold a line 5 kilometers in length. We are now holding about 2 kilo's and have outposts and auto-rifle posts pushed to the front. Neither the 5th Regt., nor the 80th Division are up to our line."

This was followed by more instructions from Holcomb to Williams fifteen minutes later, telling him that patrolling to the northern and western limits of the Bois de la Folie was necessary and if it couldn't be done during the dark hours then it should be done in daylight.

2 November: Lee sent a common message to all battalion commanders at 0646 explaining that the 23d Infantry would relieve both Marine regiments "at an hour to be designated later." He added, "The leading Bn., 2nd Bn., (Williams) and the combat liaison force under major Stowell, after the passage of the 23rd Inf. will maintain their present positions in order to cover the ground to the west insofar as their present formation permits."

At 1600 Williams sent Lee the following: "The first Bn. 23rd Infantry, has conflicting orders with ours concerning relief and their advance. 2 of their companies are moving into line with us and 2 are remaining in rear. Can you advise me what action is contemplated." Apparently another message was sent from 4th Brigade to Lee at 1430 which he told Williams about at 1705. "[You] will withdraw to the rear about 500 meters, thereby leaving you in the woods."

Williams responded at 1820 with the following details: "4th Brigade memo referred to in your message calls for our withdrawal when leading elements of 3rd Brigade arrive to relieve our front elements. The 23rd has not relieved us. Our 96th, 'A' Co. (23) and 78th now form continuous line thru woods in that order from left to right. This line is same as 96th and 78th positions indicated to you by [2d Lt. Lloyd A.] Houchin today. Houchin 79th Co. is being withdrawn behind this line. Shall we pull back if other 3 companies of 23 do not arrive?"

3 November: Williams requested rations for his "entire Bn., on basis of strength," 16 officers and 603 men. At 1140 he notified Lee: "We are holding position on height slightly E. of N. along X line 99. (Cote Jeab). Bn. limits about 02–03. We are directly behind the 3rd Bn. of the 23rd Inf. No appreciable advance seems to have been made for over 2½ hours. Machine guns and heavy—light artillery fire is holding up the advance. Word just received that 23rd intends advancing 1000 meters and there dig in. We will conform to their movements."

Williams sent the 80th Company's commander orders at 1755: "Send 2 platoons from your company to take up positions on crest to your front which is marked by a row of tall pines. They will be established as outposts and will protect our left front and flank. One platoon machine guns is also being sent to this position. Shelters are already dug on this position." Powers had been relieved by Williams, and Capt. Kirt Green commanded the 80th until he was killed in action on 1 November. I don't know who replaced him in command.

4 November: Lee ordered Williams and 3/6 to take positions "on yesterdays objective and remain there until further orders."

5 November: From Williams to Lee at 0825: "We are in position as ordered in Field Order No. 28, Headquarters 6th, 1:30 p.m. 4 Nov. 18. Have located all Battalions of the 5th Regiment and 1st and 3rd Battalions of the 6th. We have liaison with a Regiment of the 89th Division on our right." At 1110 he replied to Major Larsen, commanding officer, 1/5, telling him that "we will continue to hold our present position unless you advance beyond the line you are about to take up."

Lee advised the three commanders that the brigade was expected to cross the Meuse and then the 5th Marines would cross the Meuse at Pouilly and seize the heights to the northeast of POUILLY, west of AUTREVILLE and the heights Bois d' Alma Gisors. Strong patrols were to push forward and keep in contact with the enemy.

6 November: Lee sent the three battalion commanders a message at 1815: "There will be no movement tonight. We will probably move early in the morning, but by a different route from that indicated. Further information will be furnished about this as soon as received." This had to do with the crossing of the Meuse River which would not take place until the night of 10 November, and then the 6th Marines would not cross as did 1/5 and 2/5.

8 November: Lee sent a message to the three battalion commanders, no time indicated, that the crossing was postponed would not take place this night.

9 November: Lee advised the three commanding officers to bivouac in the Bois du Fond de Limon. Then he told them to locate Williams and Shuler, who were "in that vicinity on reconnaissance."

11 November: Major Ernest Williams gave this operations report of the Meuse-Argonne campaign:

> At 11:58 p.m. on the night of October 31st, pursuant to Regimental Field Orders No. 23, the following field message was sent to Regimental Headquarters: Companies located in ravine whose center point is 300.5-83.5, with "Y" coordinates 00 and 01, approximately marking limits of Battalion flanks. Battalion P.C. located at 300.5-83.5. We are ready to attack.—Williams.
>
> Our batteries were fairly active throughout the night, but promptly at 3:30 a.m., the two hours preparation commenced. The enemy countered to an appreciable extent. At 5:30 a.m., the code word "Paris" was telephoned to Regimental Headquarters and the Second Battalion moved forward as reserve. Our formation, from left to right, was as follows: line—80th and 78th. Companies in two waves; local support 96th and 79th Companies, also in two waves.
>
> We moved forward in accordance with orders, following the 3rd Battalion at a distance of about 1,000 metres, and suffering but few casualties. At 9:45 a.m. we reported to the Regimental Commander that we had reached the first objective with companies in proper position were about 250 meters behind the 3rd Battalion, and were waiting for them to advance.
>
> About noon the right of the 3rd Battalion signalled that it had reached its objective. One gun from a battery of our heavies was firing short and causing some casualties in our ranks. At 2:50 p.m. this message was sent to the Regimental P.C.:—"Left of the 3rd Battalion held up about one kilometre behind its objective by our artillery fire. Am passing through their lines as they are now.—Williams."
>
> The passage of the lines was effected and we continued to our objective about three kilometres further. The enemy offered practically no resistance until we had reached our objective and pushed on in advance.
>
> At 3:15 p.m. we were able to send back message #3, as follows; "We are on our objective. Front companies are adjusting line and sending exploiting parties ahead. Have liaison with Major Stowell on left and have sent to 5th on right. Considerable machine gun fire being encountered from that part of the Bois de la Folie still held by the enemy. Casualties among the men not extremely heavy—Officers about fifty percent.—Williams."
>
> During the advance Captain Kirt Greene, 80th Company was killed.; Lieutenants [John G.] Schneider [Jr.], [George] Ehrhardt, [Arthur S.] King and [Maurice E.] Barnett [Jr.] and Captain [Eugene F.C.] Collier were wounded.
>
> In accordance with orders received the preceding night, the 79th company was pushed forward to the northern edge of the Bois de la Folie the morning of November 2nd,—on the left side of the Nouart road. No serious resistance was met with, but the 96th on the left was held by machine gun and one pounder fire from vicinity of Fme. Masmes.
>
> Early on the morning of November 3rd, in pursuance of orders issued on the evening of the 2nd a battalion of the 23rd Infantry passed through our lines and took up the advance. We followed in support, at a kilometre distance. At 11:45 a.m. this message was sent to the Regimental P.C. "We are holding position on heights slightly east of north from Fosse (Cote Jean) along "X"

line 99. Battalion limits about 02–03. We are directly behind the 3rd Battalion of the 23rd Infantry. No appreciable advance has been made for over three hours. Machine gun and heavy light artillery fire is holding up the advance. Word just received that the 23rd Infantry intends advancing 1,000 metres and digging in. We will conform to their movements. Williams."

At dusk the 23rd continued their advance, and we followed at the prescribed distance. Late that night, the advance having ceased we took up a position along the road from 03.25-00 to 03.75-00.58. Early the following morning, November 4, we were continuing ahead in support of the 23rd, which had resumed its advance, when orders were received from Regimental to take up a position on the line running from Vaux to Le Champy Bas and remain there until further orders. This was done.

Late in the afternoon of the same days pursuant to Regimental Field Orders #25, this Battalion moved to the Foret de Belval and took up a position along the ridge running from 7038 to 7830. Here we were in support of the 5th Regiment. On the morning of November 5th, we sent the following message to the Regimental Commander:—"We are in position as ordered. Have located all Battalions of 5th Regiment and 1st and 3rd Battalions of 6th. We have liaison with a Regiment of the 89th Division on our right.—Williams."

The Battalion remained in this position for two days, pending the reconnaissance of the river banks by the 5th Regiment, and the determination by it, of the possibilities of a crossing.

On November 7th, by Field Orders #27, we were ordered to the Bois de Yoncq but, by an operations memorandum of the same date, our destination was changed to a position in the western part of the Bois de Four, along the Beaumont-Sommesuthe road. At 2:15 p.m. this message was sent to the Regimental Commander:—"In accordance with Field Orders #27, 2nd Battalion is proceeding to new bivouac in Bois de Four—Williams."

Our destination was reached after dark and position taken up as ordered. Here we remained until the evening of November 8, when we moved to the woods about a kilometre Southwest of La Thibaudine Fme., where we bivouaced for the night. At 4:30 p.m. on the afternoon of November 9th, the Battalion resumed its march and went into bivouac along the southwestern edge of the Bois de Fond de Limon.

On the night of November 10th, the Battalion was ordered to cross the Meuse river north of Mouzon, in support of the 3rd Battalion, 6th Marines. "H" hour was 9:30 p.m. with two hours artillery preparation. At 10:15 were in position along the railroad tracks northwest of Mouzon. The enemy, by a direct hit, destroyed the footbridge upon which we were to effect a crossing. It could not be repaired and at 4:00 a.m. on the morning of November 11th, the Battalion marched back to its bivouac in the Bois de Fond de Limon. At 11:00 a.m. on the same day hostilities were suspended in pursuance of the terms of the armistice signed by the German representatives at 5:40.

Ernest C. Williams, Major, U.S.M.C. Comd'g. Battalion.

The war was over and in a few days the entire Second Division would take a long hike through Belgium and Luxemburg to the frontier with Germany, then cross the Rhine River into their individually assigned occupation points. The Second Battalion, 6th Regiment of Marines, occupied the village of Rheinbrol. Further duties would include guard posts, drill, marching, sports, attending schools, and some would float on the Rhine River aboard gunboats.

Finally, after the Germans signed a peace treaty, the entire 4th Brigade headed for France and in mid–July boarded ships for their trip back to the United States, beginning on 19 July and arriving in Hoboken, New Jersey, on 5 August 1919. After parades and a stop in Quantico, discharge for most of the officers and men was on 13 August 1919.

7

Third Battalion, Sixth Marines, 1917–1919

Battalion Headquarters
82d [I] Company
83d [K] Company
84th [L] Company
97th [M] Company

Commanding Officers

From	To	
1 August 1917	18 September 1918	Major Berton W. Sibley
18 September 1918	18 July 1919	Major George Shuler
19 July 1919	13 August 1919	Major George A. Stowell

The 3d Battalion, 6th Regiment of Marines, was organized at the Marine barracks, Quantico, Virginia, on 1 August 1917. The companies composing 3/6 were as follows: 82d with Capt. Dwight F. Smith in command; the 83d with Capt. Albert R. Sutherland; the 84th, Capt. Harry G. Bartlett, soon to be major; and the 97th, Capt. Robert W. Voeth as skipper.

After numerous enlisted men from Parris Island, South Carolina, and junior officers arrived, training for the trench warfare in France began. On 24 October 1917, 3/6 left Quantico in two trains, upon orders received the previous day, for 3/6 to entrain for League Island, outside Philadelphia. They arrived at 1800 and immediately boarded the USS *Von Steuben*, which was anchored in the Delaware River. Officers and men awoke the next morning as their ship was steaming down river. On the morning of the 26th the ship dropped anchor in New York Harbor, remaining there for five days. On the night of 31 October 1917 the ship began its voyage to France convoyed by the cruiser *North Carolina* plus several destroyers and other transports.

The night of 9 November, the *Von Steuben* and another transport, the *Agamemenon*, collided and a large hole was torn in the former. The convoy was disrupted but gathered back together the following day, with modest repairs to the *Von Steuben*. The journey through the submarine zone was completed without further incident and early on the morning of 12 November the shore of Brittany was sighted and the ship docked at Brest, France.

While awaiting debarkation orders and transportation to the final destination, the battalion commander ordered one company ashore each day for a practice march. On November

17 the 83d and 84th Companies with Battalion Headquarters paraded in Brest. Early Monday morning, November 19, the troops. disembarked and entrained in a French troop train which left at 1230 on the Chemin de Fer de L' Ouest Southward, arriving at Lormont, France, a suburb of Bordeaux, at midnight, 20 November 1917.

The battalion here rejoined the regimental headquarters 73d Machine Gun and Supply companies and was assigned to duty with the 18th Engineers building docks at Bassens. The following detachments were detailed for provost and engineer duty in the neighboring camps and towns: Captain Voeth, provost marshal at Tours, 27 November–21 January; First Platoon, 97th Company, provost duty, Tours, 27 November–21 January, 1st Lieutenant Albert G. Skelton in command; the 84th Company, provost and fatigue duty, La Corneau, 18 December–5 January, Major Harry G. Bartlett, commanding; First Lieutenant Ralph W. Marshall and twenty men from the 97th Company, La Cortine, 8 December to 5 January, fatigue and provost duty; First Lieutenant Louis F. Timmerman, Jr., and 30 men, 83d Company, at Marche Prime, 6 December to 4 January, fatigue duty; First Lieutenant Charles D. Roberts and 1st Platoon, 82d Company, Cenon, provost duty, 27 December to 6 January.

The regiment was relieved by the 162nd Regiment Infantry (Montana National Guard) on 8 January and entrained 9 January 1918 at Carbon Blanc for the Second Division training area. After a three day trip, officers in 3d class and troops in box cars, the regiment was detrained at Damblain, Haute-Marne, 12 January 1918 and marched to Chaumont-la-ville, a distance of five kilometers.

Here intensive training for trench and open warfare began at once. This training was very severe due both to strenuous schedule and the winter season which arrived in earnest about this time. However, grueling as it seemed then, it so hardened the men that they were able to bear up under the strain of continuous fighting which later became the lot of the Second Division. The schedule included hikes, close order drill, extended order, bayonet fighting, games, practice in both rifle and hand grenade throwing, rifle range practice, storming trench systems, taking strong points, defense against gas attacks and all modes of signaling then in use. Steel helmets were received shortly after arrival in this area and included in the uniform for drill in order to accustom the men to wearing them at all times when in the line. A great deal of gas drill was included in the schedule and men were required to shoot, march, throw grenades and perform every possible duty with the masks on.

In March, trench knives, extra clothing, etc., were received and issued; preparations were made for storing extra baggage, and men were allowed to keep only what clothing they could carry in their packs.

Orders were received that the Second Division was going in the line just south of Verdun for thirty days' training under fire, and on 14 March the battalion marched to Breuvannes and entrained for the front, moving at 2142 that night.

Verdun

Three/Six detrained at Dugny after arriving from Verdun at noon on 15 March. The unit was under orders to clear the loading platform within two hours to avoid shelling; the men moved out quickly by companies.

A walk of about 16 kilometers took them to the support position of the Toulon sector, where they were billeted in camps. Battalion Headquarters was established at Camp Ronde Fontaine. The 82d Company was assigned to Camp Richert and Camp Ronde Fontaine; the 83d Company to Camp Marquenterre; 84th Company to Camp Massa; and the 97th Company, Camp Fontaine St. Robert.

On March 18 in the evening, the battalion went into line in the Bonchamp sub-sector of Montsous-le-Cotes, the center of resistance. The 82d, 83d, and 84th Companies were in line; the 97th Company was in reserve at Camp Fontaine St. Robert.

The battalion was relieved March 28 by the 2d Battalion, 6th Marines, and marched overnight to Sommedieue for billet, arriving at daylight. At dark on March 31 the 82d and 84th Companies and Battalion Headquarters moved to Camp Douzains; the 83d Company went to Camp Sommedieue and 97th to Camp Eveche. They remained until April 7 working on defenses, digging trenches and building entanglements. That evening at dark they relieved 2/6 at Mont-sons-le-Cotes with three companies in line and one in reserve.

They were without incident until 0110 hours on 21 April, when the 84th Company of 3/6 repulsed a raid around the town of Villers by the "Hindenburg Circus," a group of *Sturmtruppen* that had been raising hell on the line. The Germans were equipped with flamethrowers, grenades, knives, and pistols, and assaulted just after a box barrage. From the report of the operations, the Germans used hand grenades exclusively, even after they occupied the same trench as the Marines. They also used flares to light up the night; one man in particular was seen firing flares continually from another trench.

When Marines tried firing their own flares, they failed six times. When they tried two three-star flares, they fared as poorly as before. "All lines of communication were cut ... someone found two more six-star flares and they fired." A barrage from friendly artillery immediately answered the call raised by the flares, but knowing it was to cease in ten minutes, two volunteers raced to the guns to request a continuance of the fire. Pvts. Earl H. Sleeth and Frank H. Hullinger ran through an intense bombardment on the road from Villers to Mont. Hullinger fell exhausted upon reaching Mont, but Sleeth made the run and returned from the artillery with new flares. Soon afterward the enemy ceased to trouble the 84th Company. The report stated that Cpl. Clarence H. Babb was wounded within thirty yards of his post as he was going on duty. He crawled to his post and was found lying there exhausted with 18 wounds. Second Lieutenant Allan C. Perkinson, Corporal Babb, Hullinger and Sleeth were all awarded the Croix de Guerre.

Three/Six was relieved the night of April 24 by the 3rd Battalion, 20th French, and marched into reserve at Camp Chiffoure.

One officer and two noncommissioned officers from each company were sent to 1st Corps Schools at Gondrecourt on 1 May. The following day, 3/6 relieved 1/6 in strong point Haudiomont. Two companies were in the line; one was in support and one in reserve at Camp Chiffoure. Battalion Headquarters and the 84th Company (in support) were at Post of Command Bordeaux. The next 10 days in this sub-sector were quiet.

Lieutenant Marshall and four noncommissioned officers left to secure billets in a new area on May 9. Then on 13 May, 3/6 was relieved by a battalion of the 174th French and marched to Haudainville, arriving at 0200. At 0100 on 14 May the battalion moved to Ancemont and entrained, departed at 1830, and arrived at Blesmes on the Marne at 0330 the next morning.

The battalion marched without breakfast to new training area. Battalion Headquarters and the 83d and 84th Companies were billeted at Vavray-le-Petit. The 97th Company was assigned with Regimental Headquarters at Doucey, and the 82d Company was billeted in Vavray-le-Grande. Training lasted until 19 May. At that time the 97th Company was assigned as a loading detail for the 2d Division and proceeded to Vitry-le-Francois.

On 19 May at 2100 the 82d, 83d, and 84th Companies and Battalion Headquarters marched 27 kilometers to Vitry-le-Francois, arriving at 0430. Breakfast was served a half hour later on the train loading platform, and then the entire battalion departed on the train at 0530.

At 1755 on 20 May, the battalion arrived at L'Isle-Adam, detrained, and marched to Nesle-le-Ville five kilometers away for billets. The next day at 0800 the battalion marched to the town of Marines, arriving at 1644 for the night's billet. On 22 May, 3/6 marched at 0600 to Montagny-en-Vexin, where they were billeted with 2/6 until 31 May. A training program included divisional terrain exercise; men were issued clothing and equipment, and the battalion was put in first class condition.

On 30 May 1918, Regimental Field Order No. 2 contemplated a march to a new area to begin at 1100 on the 31st. Then, at 1800 on the 30th, a memorandum arrived from Headquarters, Sixth Marine Regiment, which directed the regiment to move at 2200 by wagons to Serans. Then, at 2200, another memorandum arrived: "The 3d Battalion will take Camions at Serans at 4:45 a.m. tomorrow, 31 May, for 8 hour trip…. Destination Meaux."

Belleau Wood

1 June 1918: Colonel Albertus Catlin, commanding the 6th Marines, led Sibley's battalion off the highway at Paris Farm and placed it in reserve in the woods north of Voie du Châtel. He briefly took up residence there.

2 June: As ordered, Sibley duly sent Capt. Robert W. Voeth and his 97th Company to strengthen the junction between the 6th and 9th Regiments. Around noon, the 82d Company (Capt. Dwight Smith) of 3/6 was ordered to support 2/5. When they arrived, they moved to the right of Capt. Lloyd Williams (51st Company, 2/5) who was at the far right of 2/5's line.

Major Frederick Wise, commander of 2/5, had been positioned on the far left (west) of the division's line holding a large farm, Les Mares Ferme, and most of 3/6 had been placed to his right holding a large wooded area lying west of the village of Champillon.

3 June: At 2020 Capt. Dwight E. Smith, skipper of the 82d Company, notified Major Berton Sibley that he had not been attacked yet but "a French major on our right … expects attack tonight or early morning. Situation much better than I thought at first…. I have filled up entire gap of French troops that did withdraw…. Ammunition not yet received." Harbord told Catlin that he was "very glad [Smith] declined retire." He also made mention that "one of Wise's companies … also declined." That was Williams' 51st Company.

Shortly after its arrival the 82d was in trouble. Four men were killed and several others were wounded by artillery fire. Sometime afterward, Headquarters Company under 1st Lt. David Bellamy, the 83d Company commanded by 1st Lt. Alfred Noble, and one platoon from the regimental 73d Machine Gun Company led by Capt. Roy W. Swink were sent to bolster the 82d Company. Since most of his battalion was now located in line there, Maj. Berton W. Sibley of 3/6 assumed command of that portion of the line running from Hill 142 in an easterly direction for about a thousand yards. Most of the line was along the edge of Belleau Wood, and at some points the Germans were also in the woods, only fifty or so yards away. It was a difficult spot for both groups to be in.

4 June: Major Sibley had remained with his three detached companies in the area of Hill 142. When he reconnoitered his position he found that the French had withdrawn from Belleau Wood and Bouresches, leaving a large gap uncovered on the right, as well as the territory between him and 1/6.

5 June: At 2100, Frank Evans, adjutant of the 6th Marines, sent Sibley a message telling him that he and his two companies would be relieved by Turrill's 1/5 "sometime tonight," and that he should go to Ferme Blanche, on the Paris-Metz Highway, where he would find the balance of 3/6 and go into reserve.

6 June: This was the day of the three major efforts, by 1/5, 3/5, and 3/6, plus the push to Bouresches by elements of 2/6. All battalions would suffer heavy casualties, especially 3/5.

Three/Six went into the southern portion of Belleau Wood and were cut to pieces by the well-placed and entrenched German soldiers. Their Maxim machine guns were interlocked and located in such a way that the Marines of 3/6 were caught in continuous crossfire.

At 1905 Sibley sent message to the commanding officer, 6th Regiment. With Catlin wounded and out, this was now Lee: "Reported that front line of 82 Co. has reached far edge of woods. They have apparently passed around the M. G. stronghold, am having it investigated."

At 1921 First Lieutenant William B. Moore, intelligence officer of the 6th Regiment, sent a message to Harbord: "83rd Co. hold railroad station at BOURESCHES. 97th was held up slightly by M.G. on right. No further news. 19 prisoners on the way." I don't believe either company was in the town but just in Belleau Wood opposite it.

Frank Evans, 6th adjutant, sent message to Harbord at 2015: "Machine gun emplacement on the rock plateau on the left of the LUCY-BOURESCHES road. Sibley's (3d Bn. 6th) has it surrounded but has not reduced it. He has asked for Stokes Mortar and I have sent to the rear to rush it up. He also reports right half up, not advanced as far as the left. The 97th Co. has asked for reinforcements.

Then Sibley sent this message to Lee at 2024: "In absence of further instructions we are advancing to point designated as objective in beginning of battle." At 2045 Sibley sent Lee another message: "Unable to advance infantry further because of strong machine gun positions and artillery fire. Have given orders to hold present positions at far edge of woods. Losses already heavy. Await instructions."

The above information was sent by Lee to Harbord at 2115. He added: "83rd Co. also reorganizing at this point. Seems impossible to take hostile M.G. position, without artillery. Request instructions." Lee advised Harbord at 2335: "Holcomb to Sibley says one of Holcomb's companies is in BOURESCHES and he wants reinforcements. Authorized Sibley use reorganized 82nd and 83rd Companies for this." Obviously, Lee had no idea how badly off Sibley's companies were.

Holcomb sent a message to Lee and Harbord at 2328, a portion of which stated: "Unless Sibley can do something in a way of taking left part of objective, we are in a hole. We also need reinforcements to hold our line of resistance. Send me some word."

7 June: This message was from Maj. Berton W. Sibley, commanding officer, 3/6, to Lt. Col. Frank E. Evans, regiment adjutant, 6th Marines, at 1220: "Copy of your message to Col. Lee push attack by way of Hill 135 and take BOURESCHES just received. Am sending 84th Co., to take and occupy town. It is rumored that three platoons of 95th Co., are already there. Am trying to verify this by patrol. 97th Co., moving forward to Hill 138. 82nd Co., and 83rd Co., remain in position in woods. Still unable to get in touch with Berry's Battalion on left. Major Dwight Smith advised Evans of most recent orders for line, to dig in and hold. Also told him that BOURESCHES is in our possession." Most probably Maj. Holland McT. Smith, then with 4th Brigade Headquarters as liaison officer with Second Division.

A casualty report was given on this date: "83rd Co.—8 killed, 54 wounded or missing; 84th Co.—29; 82nd Co.—9 killed, 25 wounded; 97th Co.—27."

From 1st Lt. David I. Garrett, to Evans, 6th Regiment adjutant, at 1255: "I called Sibley and he informs me he sent one company in at 11:50 p.m. That his troops are still advancing but final objective not yet reached. I have notified Holcomb by runner." My records indicate that Garrett was a member of the 83d Company.

The next verbal message was received at 6th Regiment Headquarters by "W.H.S.," probably Capt. Walter H. Sitz. "Three (3) platoons 96th Company, all 97th and 79th [2/6] hold BOURESCHES. 84th Company on right flank. 78th Company [2/6] on right of 84th. 82nd Company on left flank. 83rd Company on left of 82nd. No communication with 3rd Bn. of 5th Regiment."

Messages indicate that at 0650 Holcomb was in close contact with Sibley on his left flank. Later, at 0720, further information stated that F.M. Wise, 2/5, was in close contact with Sibley's left flank. But that was refuted twenty minutes later.

8 June: Adjutant Frank Evans sent a report to the commanding officer, 23d Infantry, at 0505 about Bouresches: "Attack made on BOURESCHES and its immediate right 12:25 a.m. Heavy M.G. firing at 1:00 a.m. reported quiet. We had withdrawn 84th and 97th Cos from town into support positions S of our P.C. of the 2d Bn. Received later word 20 casualties. Action ended 1:20 a.m. Our 3rd Bn now engaged destroying M.G. positions in B. de Belleau. No reports as to progress received. Will keep you advised."

Evans sent to Harbord at 0545: "Message from C.O. 3d Bn. 6th: Some machine guns out of action. Mowing our men down pretty fast. 83rd Co. reports many machine guns delaying advance. Good progress in some points. This information from wounded." At about the same time Evans reported that Holcomb was supporting Sibley's right by fire.

Sibley told Harbord at 0555: "82nd Co. reports advance with slight M.G. fire in front. Have taken two. One platoon 80th Co. [2/6] to support of 82nd. Take Lieutenant Roberts place who is wounded. Asking for some barrage. Laying out four wires to your P.C. At present not connected." First Lt. Charles D. Roberts was commanding officer, 1st Platoon, 82d Company.

At 0640 Lt. Col. Lee sent Harbord a message: "At 5:30 Captain Smith reported wounded. Nest of machine guns on his left. Captured two and are going on. At 5:50 83rd Co. reports two captured and surrounding the others. At 6 o'clock the advance held up. 84th and 83rd mixed together finding new emplacements everywhere. 82nd asking for reinforcements, 2 platoons. Engineers standing by awaiting orders from C.O. 3rd Bn. Runners sent out to advise him of situation. Are holding where held up and will advance when situation permits. One Lieutenant of 80th Company wounded."

From Evans to Harbord at 0658: "Captain Zane [79th Company, 2/6] at Bouresches says that a wounded man from 82d Co. in town and said Major Sibley had all but one machine gun and thinks he has that one now. Could hear him crying from woods: "Get that S. of a B." has no liaison but thinks it ok." The man said "Get that son of a bitch."

At 1027 Sibley finally admitted to Evans:

> They are too strong for us. Soon as we take one M.G. the losses are so heavy that I am reforming on the ground held by the 82nd Co last night.
> All of the officers of the 82nd Co are wounded or missing and it is necessary to reform before we can advance. Unable to do much with trench mortars because of being in the woods. These M. Guns are too strong for our infantry. We can attack again if it is desired. The 97th Co of platoon and the one pounders for point of advance. 61.5-76.0 now reforming 61.2-76.3. Can place Barrage 61.5-76.0 I can withdraw to the south edge of the woods and with artillery liaison to adjust the fire back a barrage from the first hill north. We did not take the hill but did take some of the guns on it. There are three hills they went up and surrounded the one hill and we went up and have taken some of the guns on the second.

Sibley and 3/6 were obviously finished.

A couple of minutes after noon, an engineering lieutenant sent Sibley a message stating that they "have taken three guns." He mentioned his heavy casualties but would "post 10 engineers there. Have posted 20 engineers at point midway between Bouresches and Messersmith's right." The latter was commanding officer of the 78th Company. Harbord sent Sibley a message at 1230: "Get cover for your men in the ravine (gully) at south edge of woods. Let your men rest. I will have artillery play of the wood. Any further orders will be given you later for other movement by you. Send reply by the runner who brings this as to the hour at which you will be in your gully." Even Harbord was finally getting the word.

Evans reported to Harry Lay, brigade adjutant, at 1255 that he was having difficulties getting food and water to Sibley's men and "I am sick thinking about it." At 1355 Sibley reported to Harbord that his men were "too exhausted for further attack on strong resistance until after several hours rest." For the following several hours he was asking for food for 3/6 and the attached 80th Company.

Later that evening plans were being developed to relieve 3/6 with Major John Hughes' 1/6 battalion, but that was changed. "Major Sibley is to be withdrawn tonight after dark with any engineers that may be with him." No one was to take their place.

9 June: First Lieutenant Allan Perkinson, commanding officer, 3d Platoon, 84th Company, with twenty men was holding the right flank outside Bouresches.

12 June: From Evans, adjutant, 6th Regiment, to Sibley: "Will work in replacements according to plans you give Sgt. Maj. Quick. Will have them go in with extra bandoleers, reserve rations & with any pyros that are available. Lt. Jackson will take up ammunition with you. Have two (2) Captains but they are green & don't think you want them. Will do all I can to see you get what you need. Expect to be over there this afternoon. Hughes getting along well & quiet out there. Colonel Lee now located here." I have no idea who each of those 2 captains were; Jackson was probably 2d Lt. George R. Jackson of the Supply and later 73d Machine Gun Company. On the 13th he was adjutant, Third Battalion Hughes of course was Maj. John Hughes, commanding officer, 1/6.

From Harbord to Neville, probably earlier evening:

> At dark tonight the 3d Bn., 6th Marines now in Brigade Reserve in woods northwest of Lucy will pass under your command to relieve the 1st Bn., 5th Marines [Turrill], which when relieved will take station at Brigade Reserve in same woods now occupied by 3d Bn., 6th Marines. Have the relief accomplished as early as possible after dark. Give Major Sibley explicit instructions as to reconnaissance by small patrols.
>
> In the open country between the Y line 174 and the Lucy-Torcy Road. It is important that the enemy not "dig in" along the ravine which runs north of west from the cross-roads a kilometer south of Torcy. With control of that ravine Major Sibley can probably establish a strong point held by a company near the cross roads mentioned, and with the machine guns as they now are around the salient half a kilometer south of there, can economize in men so that you can withdraw the company of the 3rd Bn. 5th Marines now there. Sibley's line would then hold from the Champillon brook at 176.6-263.6 to approximately 174.4-263.4; with an interval to a strong point approximately N. W.–S. E. near X 262.6. Talk this over with Major Sibley today.

13 June: From Maj. Sibley, commanding officer of 3/6, to Col. Neville, sent at 1200:

> Referring to Brigade Commanders Memo. June 12 relative to the ravine north of west of the X-roads. 1 kilometer south of TORCY, it is found that this ravine is already "dug in," or contains trenches of a sort. To what extent we have been unable to learn or to ascertain how strongly enemy is holding the ravine. Patrols were sent out last night as soon as this battalion arrived in this C.R., but were soon drawn in upon instructions from Regimental Commander relative to artillery fire. The heavy shelling by both our own and enemy batteries continued until after daylight, so we were unable to again send out patrols last night. The ravine has, however been left under careful observation today.
>
> 2. It is desired to send out patrols tonight between 9 p.m. and 3 a.m. for the purpose of ascertaining just what is in that ravine, and to locate a position for a strong point in the vicinity of 171.5-263.0.
>
> 3. It is requested that the artillery be advised of the presence in the ravine between the hours above mentioned, of our patrols so they will not be fired upon by our own artillery. Coordinates of ravine expected to be patrolled are 174.0-263.4 and 173.8-263.1.

From Capt. Alfred H. Noble, commanding officer, 83d Company, to Sibley, at 1200 M.(midnight?):

> Patrol returned and reported a number of the enemy were heard in the right end of the ravine. Could hear them talking. My patrol was not discovered by the enemy. We now have listening posts out front but cannot occupy the ravine as intended. Believe the artillery should be notified to be prepared to drop barrage in ravine when called for. Am notifying 84th Co and M.G's that our patrols are in. Dare not to attempt to occupy ravine tonight as they seem to be there in some force. Could not get an exact estimate of their strength. We are ready to stand to at any time and will hold this position till further notice.

From Capt. Charles Gill (?), intelligence officer, 5th Marines, to Neville, by phone at 0400, "Shelling continuous, Much H. E. and gas. Some shrapnel, Casualties unknown. No rifle fire. Replacements joining company now." From Lee to Sibley at 0530: "Brig. directs do not attack. Hold your line, take measures for security sending small patrols to keep informed of positions and movements of enemy. Report any movement or concentrations. Make frequent reports. Arrangements for artillery have been made."

14 June: Col. Lee, commanding officer, 6th Marines, sent word to the commanding officers of 3/6 and 2/5 at 1925 that the enemy was moving by foot and auto toward Bois de Belleau.

Sibley sent Lee notice that he had sent the commanding officer, 1st Battalion, 174th French Infantry, the following message: "Orders have been sent to our companies that in case of enemy attack we will hold our positions to the last man, Sibley, Major Commanding." Lee sent Sibley a message, no time indicated: "Upon being relieved by the 167th French Div., you will take a station in the woods about 170.0-259.5 as [2d] Div. Reserve."

On the 15th at 0255 Sibley kept Lee up to date by informing him that his telephone was out of order and his battalion was taking incoming plus some sniping. Later that morning at 0755 he added another message to the effect that a French officer had notified him that 3/6 would be relieved "tonight." He also suggested that some of his men who had been runners be sent back to him. He said the men were tired and movement slow, so notify him early of any new position to take.

Lee sent Holcomb and Sibley a message at 1045: "Notify this office of number of replacements required—place and time of rations needed and any other things need for health and comfort of your command—every effort will be made to supply you during your reorganization."

Three/Six was relieved by the 167th French Division and sent south to recover a bit with plenty of good food, new clothes, and plenty of sleep. But they like the rest of the brigade, they were back on the line a week later.

22 June: From Harbord to Sibley thru Neville, no time indicated:

1. As soon at you are established in the BOIS DE BELLEAU hurry the completion of the wiring on the east side.
2. Start detail to cutting some paths from east to west through the BOIS so your supports can get through to your front line.
3. Establish communication with the 23rd Infantry in BOURESCHES.
4. Push patrols out from several places in your line to locate the enemy. If possible get in some live or dead Germans for identifications. The location of the enemy is most important for you, and the identifications are necessary. The space between you and the Germans belongs to us. Take possession with night patrols.

25 June: From Harbord to Sibley, through Neville, no time indicated: "I have asked the artillery to not put any shells tonight east of BOIS DE BELLEAU, south of X line 262 west of the railroad unless you request it. This is to give you an opportunity to send patrols out in this region and secure Prisoners. Please caution patrols that rank, regimental insignia and papers must be brought in from bodies of any dead German encountered."

26 June: From Major Charles B. Elliott, commanding officer, 3d Battalion, 23d Infantry, to Sibley at 1430: "This Bn is to be relieved to-night. Request that my runners be sent here so as to arrive by 11:00 p.m. I will have C.O. Bn which relieves me send runners as soon as he arrives."

27 June: From Sibley to Neville, sent at 2200:

> There is neither artillery liaison officer nor noncommissioned officer attached to this battalion for liaison with artillery. The P.C. of the battalion on our left has moved some distance away and we no longer have the benefit of that art. Liaison officer being near by. It is requested therefore that an artillery liaison officer or NCO be detailed to this P.C.
> Arrangements have been made for patrols and wiring tonight.
> Enemy has been shelling-vicinity of this P.C. intermittently to day and some section of the C.R. has been under artillery fire most all day, which situation is normal.

28 June: From Harbord to Neville, Turrill, Lee, Hughes, and Sibley, at 2200: "The 1st Bn. 6th Marines will relieve the 3d Bn, 6th Marines in the BOIS DE BELLEAU as soon as practicable after dark, night of June 29-30. Reconnaissance by Battalion and Company Commanders during the day June 29th. 3d Bn. 6th Marines to BOIS GROS JEAN south of PARIS-METZ Road as Division Reserve. 1st Bn. 5th Marines to woods N.W. of LUCY night of June 29-30 as Brigade Reserve."

30 June: From Harbord to Shearer and Sibley, sent at 1200: "In accordance with Field Orders No. 9, Headquarters 2d Division, 30 June 1918 (Note: this order has to do with a contemplated attack by the 3d Brigade) the 3d Battalion 5th Marines and 3d Battalion 6th Marines, are placed at the disposal of the Division Commander. These Battalions will remain in the Bois Gros Jean until further orders and maintain a liaison officer at Division Headquarters from and after the receipt of this order."

On 2 July Sibley notified the commanding general, 2nd Division, that he had sent "80 men and 4 officers to PARIS to take part in parade." And on 3 July Lee notified Sibley that the following officers were being "assigned to your Bn. for instruction … Capt. Woodend L. Co., Lt. Frazier I Co., Lt. Garrison K Co., and Barron M Co., 110th Infantry. Lt. J.J. Pirtle I Co., Lt. Rhem K Co., Lt. Conover L Co., Lt. Crance M Co., 59th Infantry. Please assign them accordingly." The 110th Infantry was in the 28th National Guard Division; 59th Infantry was in the 30th National Guard Division.

When the 2d Division was truly relieved by the 26th National Guard Division, they went south to various villages and towns for rest and relaxation. Three/Six withdrew to Nanteuil and spent a few free days until called upon, once again, to enter the arena.

Soissons

19 July 1918: The attack lineup placed 1/6 with Hughes in command on the right; 2/6 was on the left with 3/6 in the support line. Thomas Holcomb, now a lieutenant colonel and assistant to Lee, had resumed command of 2/6. Maj. Berton Sibley still had 3/6.

The operations report from the *History of Third Battalion, Sixth Regiment* for 16–25 July 1918 covers their agony better than any other source that I could find.

> At 2300 entrained in camions and rode all night and until noon July 17th when Battalion was put down from camions by order of the French officers in charge at the crossroads at point 135,

one kilometer southwest of BRASSOIR (Soissons Map). The Battalion rested in the field while its commander rode ahead in an effort to secure orders and gain information about the situation. Not finding other headquarters he was able from Corps Headquarters to get orders to bring the Battalion into the Foret-de-Retz from the west via the BRASSOIR railway station. The march was begun at 3:00 p.m. At 4:00 p.m. as the Battalion was about to enter the forest, Lt. Marshall, Battalion Scout Officer joined it, having gone ahead for information and succeeded in location Division Headquarters. He reported that regiment was to participate in an attack the following morning.

The march was continued into the forest and at about 6:00 p.m. temporary Regimental Headquarters were located and passed. Orders were received then from the Regimental Commander to push on to the vicinity of Cross Christine (Point 168,2-268.3 Villers-Cotterets map) and bivouacked there. This position was reached in a violent thunderstorm at 11:20 p.m. The march has been rendered difficult by the extremely congested condition of the roads owing to the forward movement of all manner of military transportation. The Regiment was then in Divisional reserve for the general allied attack which was to begin the next morning at daylight. The battalion bivouacked at that point and took what rest it could until violent allied artillery action at daybreak in surrounding forests gave notice that the attack had begun. Orders were received at 9:15 a.m. from Regimental Headquarters to be on the alert and be prepared to move forward. The order came at 11:45 a.m., to move to VERTE FEUILLE FERME 3.9 kilometers northeastwards on the edge of the forest. There the Bn. rested until orders were received about 6:00 p.m. to move to the vicinity of the BEAUREPAIRE FERME about 3 kilometers to the southeast. This battalion bivouacked for the night of July 18 & 19 in the woods near the point 129, one kilometer south of BEAUREPAIRE FERME. Up to this time Battalion had been subjected to little hostile fire and there had been no losses. During the day advance had been made four kilometers over what had been previously occupied by the Germans and this was still two kilometers behind the now battle line. Many hundreds of prisoners had been seen passing to the rear and the tremendous amount of traffic on the roads of all description indicated the large support that might be expected in our attack. Officers and men were in high spirits and eager to take their part in the work of the advance.

Major Sibley was called to Regimental Headquarters in the field south of BEAUREPAIRE FERME about 4:25 a.m. the next morning July 19. There it was explained to him that this Regiment would attack the German line east of VIERZY that morning. Ha was given a map and ordered to report with the Battalion to the Regimental Commander at VIERZY. The 1st Bn. was to attack on the right of the Regimental sector, the 2nd Bn., on the left with the 3rd Bn., in reserve. It was understood that the hour set for the attack was 8:00 a.m. with previous artillery preparation. Battalion was put on the march as soon as possible, congested roads and the fact that it had to halt to permit the two Battalions going into the front line to pass, prevented its arrival in the town of VIERZY until about 8:15 a.m. The 1st and 2nd Bns. were at that time forming for the attack. Verbal instructions were received from Regimental Commander at his Headquarters, which were then established under a cliff in the southeastern edge of the town of VIERZY, that this Battalion should follow the advance of the other two Battalions at a distance of about one thousand yards and to be in a position to support the other battalions. Company Commanders were called together, the situation explained and the objective of the Regiment pointed out to them on the one available map. They were also informed that the Battalion P.C. would advance to the eastward along a designated trail.

5. There being no cover available, the companies immediately began taking their positions in the open wheatfield under aerial observation and subjected to shell fire. Each company was in four lines (lines of combat groups), the 97th Company on the right, the 84th right center, the 83rd left center and the 82nd on the left.

6. The P.C. of the Battalion was established, at about 9:00 a.m., in the eastern end of the ravine half a kilometer due east of point 112 and all companies notified of this. At that time and place the following organizations reported to Major Sibley for duty and support. One platoon

each from the 73rd and 81st machine gun companies and also the 15th and 77th machine gun companies complete. The Regimental Headquarters Company reported, less certain signal groups and other details. The Stokes mortar and one pounder platoons were without their Stokes mortars and 37 mm. guns as these had been left with the Regimental train which had not arrived from NANTEUIL. The detachments from the 73rd, 81st and Headquarters companies were placed in the ravine in rear of the Battalion P.C. Machine gun companies were directed to take cover in VIERZY and hold themselves in readiness.

By 9:15 a.m., all companies of the Third Battalion had reported in position.

At about 9:45 a.m., the following message was received:
From: C.O. 6th Regt.
At: P.C.
19 July 1918—8:55 a.m., No. 5 By runner.
To C.O., 3rd Bn.

Upon arrival of the attack on the line now held by our troops about one and one half (1-½) kilometers east of VIERZY, you will be succeeded by the 1st Bn. 2nd Engrs. as reserve. You will then reinforce the line in the center between the 1st and 2nd Bns, two Cos. in the line in waves and two in local, support. (signed) Lee.

Upon receipt of this message the 84th Company was sent to reinforce the left of the First Battalion and the 83rd Company to reinforce the right of the Second Battalion, it being understood that there was an uncovered gap between the two battalions. The 97th and 82nd companies remained in support. The following message was then sent to Colonel Lee:
From: Hdq., 3rd Bn. 6th.
At: P.C.
19 July 1918—9:50 a.m.
To: C.O. 6th.

Attacking line is moving forward. No details received. Have sent 84th company to reinforce left of First Battalion and 83rd company to reinforce right of 2nd Bn., 97th is in position on right of 84th with orders to hold that position as support. 82nd Company is in a position on left of 83rd company with orders to hold that position as a support. My P.C. is now at the east end of ravine just east of cemetery. Expect to advance along road to the eastward. Headquarters company and two M.G. platoons are in same ravine with me. 15th and 77th M.G. companies are in vicinity of cemetery. (Signed) Sibley.

At 10:10 a.m., these messages were sent.
From: Hq. 3rd Bn.
At: P.C.
19 July 1918—10:10 a.m.
To Noble (83rd Co.)

Keep In touch with Karstaedt on your right so as to fill any gap between the 1st and 2nd Btns. Move up into line with these Btns. at once. (signed) Sibley.

7. Necessary movement of runners and scouts in the vicinity of P.C. and observation from low flying enemy planes soon brought down a very heavy fire from the enemy artillery upon the ravine in which P.O. was located. Several of these high explosive shells landed directly in the ravine and caused rather heavy casualties among the Battalion Scouts, Headquarters Company and some of the machine gun units. Some machine guns were put out of commission.

8. By 10:30 a.m., the 84th and 83rd sent forward to reinforce the first and 2nd Battalions, had joined the first line and were participating in the attack. Reports from the Scout Officer who had been sent forward about 9:10 a.m., and had established an observation post at the point where the Battalion P.C. was later established indicated that the advanced line was at that time (10:30 a.m.) two kilometers east of VIERZY. The Scout Officer's report also stated that the troops were being subjected to very heavy direct enemy artillery fire and to the cross-fire from numerous German machine guns advantageously placed in the woods to the front and flanks. During this time nothing was heard from our own artillery.

9. At about 10:40 a.m. reports came from both the 84 and the 83rd companies that they had suffered very heavy casualties, at that time estimated to be over sixty percent, and that further advance was almost impossible without reinforcements. Liaison between adjoining companies was maintained but was rendered extremely difficult because of the open country and the activity of snipers, machine guns and direct artillery fire. At about 10:45 a.m., the Battalion P.C. began moving to cross-roads about 200 yards south of the point 8160 at 10:55 a.m., the following message was sent:

From: Hq. 3rd Btn.
At: P.C.
19 July 1918—10:55 a.m., By runner.
To: C.O. 6th.

Your message saying your P.C. moving just received. My P.C. at that point at present. Am looking for another one. Shelling in this vicinity now. (Signed) Sibley.

10. Shortly after 11:00 a.m., a runner from the 83rd Company Commander reported that the 83rd Company was held up by machine gun fire on the left. The general situation on that flank appeared to be serious and the 82nd Company, held in support was ordered to reinforce the front line advancing eastward along the line taken by the 83rd company, (Left center), and to connect up the line between that company and the 2nd Battalion.

11. On the right the 84th Company, after suffering heavy casualties, dashed across the remaining open space and occupied a strong point in the woods half a kilometer north of TIGNY. The company commander having been evacuated, what was left of the company was now led by Lt. [Horatio P.] Mason, 26 men, including 1 officer, 4 machine guns, 1 trench mortar, and a projector were captured. The position taken was an unusually strong one and as shown by information subsequently received was considered by the enemy an important strong point. Just prior to this the reports received from the 84th company and from the first battalion indicating heavy casualties, caused Major Sibley to order the 97th company from a support position into the line with orders to reinforce the left of the first battalion and connect up with the 84th company.

12. At that time the town of TIGNY was still held by the Germans and, according to report received from Major Hughes of the first battalion, nothing less than a regiment would be able to drive them out. The following message was sent to Col. Lee, the Regimental Commander:

From: Hq. 3rd. Btn. 6th. At: P.C.
19 July 1918 By runner. To: C.O. 6th.

Scout officer has just returned from Major Hughes. Says that Hughes is in a cut in road whose coordinates are 285-178.90 and that he has but about 100 men left. 97th as well as 84th have reinforced him and they are nearly all casualties. Germans still hold TIGNY, Major Hughes stated needed reinforcements badly, nothing less than a regiment sufficient (Signed) Sibley.

13. During the progress of the fight the platoon of the 81st company and the 77th machine gun company had been detached from this command by Regimental orders and assigned to duty elsewhere. The separate platoon from the 73rd company and the 15th machine gun company and also the headquarters company, however, still remained as reserve for this battalion. Shortly before mid-day an urgent request was received to reinforce Lt. Mason in the strong point held by him and the remaining officers and men of the 84th company. The following message was then sent to Regimental Commander:

From: Hq. Third Btn. 6th. At: P.C.
19 July 1918—12:05 p.m. By runner. To: C.O. 6th.

In reply to your verbal message, 97th company is now with Major Hughes, approximately 179–285, has about 50 men left. 84th company is between 97th and 83rd. Has about 40 men. 83rd company is about 179–288 estimated about 50 percent casualties. 82nd Co. has been sent to reinforce 83rd Co. on its left; casualties unknown said to be heavy. Headquarters Co. is now advancing to support 84th Co. on its right. Their casualties unknown. Vicinity of this P.C. now being shelled. (Signed) Sibley.

(Note): Information had not reached the Battalion Commander at this time that the 77th

Company and the platoon of the 81st Co. had been disposed of by the Regimental Commander.

The 15th Machine Gun Company was ordered to reinforce the reserve line occupied by the 2nd Engineers.

At about 12:40 p.m. the following message was received from the Regimental Commander:
From: C.O. 6th. At: P.C.
19th July 1918—12:15 p.m. No. 9 By runner. To: C.O. 3rd Btn.

Has the town of TIGNY been taken by our troops? If you don't know find out. If you are stopped dig in. There are French troops on our right. Ammunition for M.O. and Chauchat has been asked for.

(Signed) Lee.

At 12:45 p.m. the following message sent to all companies:
From: Hq. 3rd Btn. 6th.
A: P.C.
19 July 1918—12:45 p.m.
To: All companies.

Hold the line you now have—dig in—get in touch with Cos. on your right and left. Reinforcements coming. (Signed) Sibley.

At 13:50 p.m. the following message was sent to Regimental Commander:
From: C.O. 3rd Btn. 6th.
At: P.C.
19 July 1918—12:50 p.m. By runner.
To: C.O. 6th.

TIGNY had not been taken by our troops at 12:00 noon. Believe it has not been taken since. Am sending to verify this. Have just received information that enemy is massing troops to front and left of our 84th Company. Have no further troops to send to their assistance or to stop enemy counter attack. Reported ammunition getting short. Can some be sent from rear. I have no troops to send back for ammunition. Have ordered companies to dig in.

(signed) Sibley.

At 1:20 p.m. the following was sent to Regimental Commander:
From Hq. 3rd Btn. 6th.
At: P.C.
19 July 1918—1:20 p.m. By runner.
To: C.O. 6th.

1:15 p.m. Scout has just returned and says that TIGNY has not been taken. Major Hughes sent word that he was trying to hold what he now has and that he was expecting reinforcements from this Battalion. I have no more troops to send him. (Signed) Sibley.

14. At about 2:30 p.m. it became necessary to have the exact location of the companies and Lieutenant Marshall, the scout officer was sent to get this information.

15. At about 4:00 p.m. the Battalion P.C. was moved about 200 yards to the southward and located in a cut in the road to give a little better cover.

16. At about 4:30 p.m. the following message was received:
From: C.O. 6th Regt.
At: P.C.
19 July 1918—3:45 p.m. No. 10 BY runner.

To C.O. 1st, 2d, 3d, Hqrs. Co., 1st Bn. 2nd Engrs. The Division Commander directs us to dig in and hold our present line at all costs. No further advance will be made for the present. He congratulates the command on its gallant conduct in the face of severe casualties.

Let me have a sketch of your position and dispositions. Ammunition at cross-roads 112 southeast of Vierzy. (Signed) Lee.

This message was sent in reply:
From: Hq. 3rd Btn. 6th Marines.
At: P.O.

10 [19] July 1918—5:00 p.m. No. 6 By runner.
To: C. O. 6th Regt.

Your No. 10 Just received—trying to consolidate positions and get companies into some kind of a line where they can dig in and hold. Accompanying sketch shows best information we have regarding disposition. Believe positions of companies somewhat inaccurate. Am checking this up and will forward another sketch later. (signed) Sibley, per Bellamy.

17. After Lieutenant Marshall's return from the front lines with definite information as to the positions of the companies, the following report was sent to the Regimental Commander:
From: C.O. 3rd Btn.
At P.C.
19 July 1918—8:05 p.m. No.? By runner.
To: C.O. 6th Regt.

Lieut. Marshall has just returned from most perilous trip which he voluntarily made to our entire front line. Am enclosing sketch of positions held at present. Situation worse than I had wished to believe. According to best information received present strength is as follows;

97th Co.	4 Officers	50 Men
84th	3	50
83rd	4	100
82nd.	4	140
Hdqs	(?) 1	45
Total	16	385

Also Battalion Hqrs. 4 officers 30 men, Strength of Bn. (estimated) this morning was 36 officers, 850 men. So far as known these unaccounted for are casualties. Quite likely some can be located later. It is reported that the fields between our P.C. and the front contain many killed and wounded. No facilities here for sending out wounded unable to walk.

Under present conditions it will be very difficult to reorganize companies even under cover of darkness. Will continue holding line until we can be reinforced or relieved. Companies have done all digging possible under circumstances. Will continue to dig all that conditions permit.

On account of greatly weakened fighting force impracticable to send out carrying parties to bring enough necessary water and rations. In front line canteens are practically all empty and very few remaining rations. Can water and rations be sent to us or a relief sent. We have no flares—pyrotechnics or flare pistols. Have no hand grenades. Considerable amount of rifle ammunition remaining. Also some Chauchat. Many of their Chauchats out of action because of loss of men. (Signed) Sibley.

18. During these operations and during the entire day communications were accomplished with extreme difficulty. The Battalion P.C. was under continuous hostile artillery fire, also aeroplane observation and occasional fire from their machine guns. There was great need for water all along the line and wounded were sent to the rear only with great difficulty. Because of the lack of stretchers only walking cases could be moved. It had not been possible to serve a meal before the march was begun that morning and a small amount of reserve rations were all that the men had to eat.

Notwithstanding the greatly reduced fighting strength of the companies and the exhaustion of the men and their lack of food and water for eighteen hours, preparations were made for the consolidation of the positions gained during the battle. Plans were made with the assistance and cooperation of the first Battalion, and Engineers under Major Fox, to dig trenches and put up wire. As soon as dusk obscured enemy observation it was possible to move the wounded from the front line to the rear. Motor trucks from the supply train assisted in this work.

19. At 8:30 p.m. the following message was received:
From: C.O. 6th Regt.
At: P.C.
19 July 1918—7:30 p.m. By runner.
To: C.O. 3rd Bn. 1st Bn. 2nd Bn.

You will have guides for three companies of your battalion at the cross-roads southwest of VIERZY about south of letter R in VIERZY, coordinate 176.2-285.7 at nine thirty (9:30) p.m. tonight. Your entire Battalion will be relieved and also Hdqs. Co., but guides for but three companies are required as a French battalion only consists of three (3) companies. Bring in all wounded when relieved. By direction (Signed) W. H. Sitz, Capt. U.S.M.C.

In accordance with the above order guides from this battalion arrived at the designated rendezvous at the hour specified and at midnight were in turn, met by the first Battalion of the 11th Tirrailleurs (French). Relief by this Battalion began about 1:00 a.m., and was completed at 4:30 a.m.

20. The companies when relieved rendezvoused in the woods south of BEAUREPAIRE farm where rations had been provided by the Battalion quartermaster and they were given breakfast. In accordance with orders received from the Regimental Commander the Battalion was marched at 8:15 a.m., to the edge of the FORET DE RETZ near TRANSLON FARM and bivouacked there with the rest of the Regiment. At this time a check was made and losses during the previous day's fighting were estimated as follows:

July 18	Company Strength		Killed		Wounded		Missing		Total Casualties		Present Strength	
	O.	M.	O.	M.	O.	M.	O.	M.	O.	M.	O.	M.
Btn. Hdqrs.	5	6									5	6
82d Co.	6	217	0	4	1	55	0	10	1	69	5	148
83d Co.	6	212	0	5	3	51	0	2	3	58	3	154
84th Co.	7	201	0	6	4	72	0	23	4	101	3	100
97th Co.	7	213	0	12	4	105	0	15	4	132	3	81
Total	31	849	0	27	12	283	0	50	12	360	19	489

The casualties amount to 39 percent of the officers and 42 percent of the men present with the Battalion on the morning of July 19th.

The advance which this Battalion made in the battle was over an open stretch of two and one half or three kilometers. Half of this distance, however, was behind the lines already occupied by our troops, but nevertheless exposed to continuous enemy artillery fire. The advance of the companies was in all cases cool and fearless in the face of tremendous hostile fire. They were stopped only when loss of numbers made further advance impossible.

While in bivouac near Translon Farm, July 20th, the Battalion suffered three casualties from falling tree trunks and during the night of July 20-21 was subjected to intermittent long range shelling from Austrian 130s. Seventeen casualties, including one death, resulted from this.

At noon July 21 Battalion moved about three kilometers westward to a point near St. Christine where a halt was made until 7:25 p.m. when, in accordance with orders from Regimental Headquarters, the Battalion moved about ten kilometers due west to a point near TAILLEFONTAINE. On July 23 some clothes were issued.

This battalion joined Regimental column at 8:00 a.m. 24 July. Regiment marched westward approximately fifteen kilometers and bivouacked for night in woods one kilometer southwest of town of LEVIGNEN. At 6:00 a.m. next day Regiment marched to the town of NANTEUIL-LE-HAUDOUIN and Battalion was billeted there.

By order of Lt. Col. Sibley,
(Signed) David Bellamy
1st Lt. U.S.M.C.,
Adjutant.

The entire Second Division acquitted itself extremely well, however, because the Germans were better prepared on that second day than they had been the first day, and had to face but one regiment, not three; the 6th Regiment was literally cut in half. Fortunately for the Second Division they were allowed more than a month to recuperate.

Marbache

The 6th Regiment detrained at Nancy on 1 August and by 7 August headquarters was established at Liverdun. Three/Six and 1/6 went into reserve positions behind 2/6 in the trenches at Pont-a-Moussan. This was a normally a quiet location but on the night of 8-9 August the Germans laid down a heavy box barrage on the right of 2/6's position. Patrols went out but there was little enemy activity. Three/Six located in the town of Sexey-le-Bois along with the French 145th Territorial Infantry and remained there until 14 August. Other units located there were 2/23, 15th Machine Gun Company, assigned to 3/6, and numerous French units.

On 8 August, Major Sibley was notified that he had been promoted to lieutenant colonel, and the following day leave for seven days was awarded to 5 percent of the officers and men. The men were not actually granted leave until 25 August.

The battalion moved to Autreville on 15 August and remained there until 21 August when they moved to Camp Bois-de-l'Eveque. On the 19th the regiment absorb badly needed replacements, officers and men who were trained in maneuver and firing. Three/Six made another move on 25 August arriving at Harmonville at 0200 the following day.

On 2 September the battalion received orders to march, which they began at 2100 that evening. This was the beginning of the march to the St. Mihiel salient which terminated on 11 September. After the usual set-aside, 20 percent of officers and men, the battalion had 21 officers and 918 men plus one officer and 30 men in the 3 gun Stokes mortar platoon, one officer and 14 men in the one-pounder section with one gun, 40 pioneers for wire cutting, and one officer and seven engineers for cooperation with tanks.

On 6 September, Captain Louis M. Bourne, Jr., arrived with 2d Lt. Neil F. Dougherty with 93 replacements and casuals. Bourne was assigned to command the 84th Company, Dougherty as a platoon leader with the 83d. Two days later, Capt. James H. Johnston arrived and assumed command of the 82d Company. The battalion continued its march toward the St. Mihiel salient.

St. Mihiel

In the evening of 11 September, 3/6 received orders to arrive at the starting point by 0200 on 12 September. At 0108 Lt. Col. Sibley announced that 3/6 was there but missing the Stokes mortar and one-pounder platoons, though the 15th Machine Gun Company was there.

At 0500, 12 September, the 23d Infantry jumped off, followed by 3/6 at 1,000 yards. The conditions were not pleasant. Heavy rains plus a huge amount of traffic on muddy roads made travel difficult.

12 September: From Sibley to Col. Lee at 0830: "Entering Bois Haie l'Eveque and sill progressing." Two hours later 3/6 had passed through those woods and reorganized for further advance. Two companies, 82d and 97th, had, in going through the woods, moved to the left of the sector. That was soon straightened out. Sibley sent another message to Lee via 2/6 at 1300: "Advancing on THIAUCOURT and about 1½ K. from it. Casualties light."

By 1400 3/6 was beyond the town but they were still having problems with the 82d and 97th Companies lagging behind. Two hours later he sent another message. Sibley to Lee, at 1600:

> About an hour or two or more ago we passed to the north of THIAUCOURT and took up position about 1,000 yards behind the 23rd Infantry with the two companies that remain with us. Enemy shelling our lines, and Infantry fell behind us. Now we are in position again.
>
> Our two remaining companies have just reported in, and are being placed. However, all units are badly disorganized and out of position.
>
> We need rations if possible, some ambulances for a few wounded, and counter work. Artillery has been silent for several hours.

It is unclear from that message which companies he was writing about. What was clear was that the 23d Infantry was in trouble. German guns were firing directly into them and they were beginning to fall back. Then the 82d and 97th Companies arrived and were assigned to support the 23d's right flank, where they remained that night.

13 September: From Sibley to commanding officers of all companies, at 1800:

> In accordance with Regimental orders the companies of this battalion will take over positions as reconnoitered this p.m. 82nd Co. right front line, 83rd Co. left front line, 84th Co., left support, 97th Co., right support. This will be accomplished at dusk and completed at dark. Report to these headquarters as soon as relief is completed. One platoon of 15th M. G. Co. will support right front company another will support left front Co. and another will be in reserve; Stokes Mortars and one-pounder detachment will remain in reserve and will occupy position now held for present.

Relief was completed at midnight and soon patrols were sent out to establish enemy positions.

14 September: Lee sent Sibley the following order at 1740: "In compliance with verbal instructions from the Brig. Comdr. you will advance your line to the army line this evening as soon as light conditions are favorable. By this is meant the high in your front extending from a point northeast of JAULNY to the north of Xammes. Arrange the disposition of your local support to suit the terrain and your own judgement."

Sibley sent the following to Lee at 2340:

> Have just returned from reconnoitering the "army line" and established a P. C. in the southeastern edge of woods (Pill Box) co-ordinates 363.5-242.3.
>
> Company commanders were taken out to center of this line and shown the positions which their companies are to occupy. Companies are now getting into position as best they can in darkness. 97th Co. will be on right front and 84th Co. on left front, 82nd and 83rd Cos. have been ordered to hold in present positions until they can be more advantageously located. This cannot be done in darkness. Will send further report when front line has been established. Two platoons of 15th m. g. Co. have been ordered to support new front line. They are also getting into position. Stokes Mortars and One-Pounders are left in reserve for present.
>
> Major Barker [1/6] and his companies passed on their way north about 9:00 p.m. Both new and old front line positions are being heavily shelled. At about 11:00 p.m. aeroplanes dropped bombs in vicinity of cross roads 363.3-242.7, near our old front lines, where battalion P. C. was then located.

Report of casualties not received, not believed to be heavy.
(Signed) Sibley, D. B.

The night of the 14th-15th was marked by heavy shelling throughout the entire sector. At daylight on the morning of the 15th, 2/6 under Major Ernest Williams passed through the 3/6 lines to occupy the Bois de la Montagny. Their advance drew heavy shell fire. There was some uncertainty as to the location of the 1st and 2nd Battalions, and the following message was sent to all companies at 0930 a.m. on the 15th.

15 September: From Sibley to commanding officers, 97th and 84th Companies:

Following message just received from regimental: 8:10 a.m. Stay in place on army line till further orders, 2nd Battalion is separated into two bodies, one under Williams and one under [Capt. George W.] Martin. 1st Btn. is in front in Bois de Montagny don't know where. Send patrols to front to locate them and have him (Major Barker) report over phone up at front. Phone in on line with Williams, follow wire up. "Lee" 84th and 97th Cos. will each send a patrol immediately to comply with this order. Runners bearing this message may be able to give information relating to location of phone wire running to front. You will also make an effort to get in touch with both detachments of our 2nd Battalion.

Please send us all information you have relative to conditions and keep us informed.

At 10:30 a.m. a verbal message was received from Lieutenant Colonel Holcomb to send two platoons to support the front line on left in Bois de la Montagny (Hill 231.5) where it was reported that the Germans were counterattacking. Two platoons of the 83rd Company were dispatched at once and took up positions with the left of 2/6, remaining there until 1800 when they were recalled by regimental order.

Word was received that the 6th Marines would be relieved at dark. They were replaced by the 310th Infantry of the 78th Division by 0345 on the 16 of September. The total casualties for 3/6 during this period were seven men killed and forty-three wounded plus one officer wounded, and fifteen men missing.

On 18 September, Lt. Col. Berton Sibley was evacuated to a hospital with a severe eye infection. The battalion's successes could rightfully bear his signature and the members of 3/6 were very fortunate in the man that replaced him—Captain George K. Shuler, soon to be major.

The battalion would soon be moving in the direction of its next campaign: Blanc Mont Massif, just to the west of the Argonne Forest. The 6th Regiment left on 27 September and arrived on the 19th. The following day, 30 September, they would be at that area of Somme-Py-Suippe. For the next few days various plans were made to attack the enemy on Blanc Mont; however, it was delayed and the Marines moved above taking positions before the massif.

Blanc Mont

2 October: At 0920 Col. Lee sent a message to all three battalion commanders concerning "D" day and "H" hour (see Chapter 5 for full text). The regiment was to advance in three echelons to enemy positions in trenches Pacha and d'Essen, and northwest to Blanc Mont. Troops were to prepare to move by noon.

3 October: At 0350 Lee informed all three battalion commanders that "H" hour was at 5:50 a.m. this date. The 17th Company of 1/5 took the Essen Hook in the action that followed. The 17th turned it over to a French army unit, which lost it to the Germans that afternoon.

At 0500 Lee sent details of the "H" hour action to the battalion commanders. The 6th Regiment was to lead, with the 5th Regiment next. At zero hour a rolling barrage would precede the infantry by 100 yards. French tanks were assigned to repel possible enemy counterattacks. All troops would be in position at 0345. Shuler and 3/6 would be in a support position with 1/6 in second place following the lead of Williams' 2/6. Shuler would send many messages to Lee during this day and those following. I have included only those that are very important.

At 0615 Shuler wrote to Lee: "Went over at 5:50 a.m. : First Line: 83 Co. on right, 97 on left. Second Line: 82 Co. on right, 84 on left. I am advancing along Boyau Landshut. Will use this boyau as line of my own advance and as line of communication. One Co. of 3rd Bn. of 5 Reg. has occupied my old trench." At 0712 he reported to Lee: "Am now at trench D' Essen at junction of trench d' Augsbourg. All going well." At 0740 he wrote that "97th Co. now going forward." Lee responded at 0807: "Fine, keep it up. Look out for left flank."

Captain Hugh McFarland, commanding the 97th Company, sent the following message to an unknown person, perhaps to Shuler, received at 0810: "There are three (3) tanks working on our left, now. The French are still on our left. Our casualties are two killed and a few wounded." Five minutes later Shuler sent a message to Lee: "My scout officer [1st Lt. Ralph Marshall] reports that my scouts are on the heels of the 1st Btn which is in the woods. McFarland, commanding the 97th Co. reports three tanks working on our left. 97th Cos. casualties—2 killed—3 wounded."

Shuler sent a highly detailed description of his battalion layout to Lee at 1010:

> I understand 1st Btn. has passed through 2nd Btn. and holds objective. I am now ordering my 83rd Co. which at present extends from road west to Boyau d' Augsbourg at 267.3 and 280.2 to line 267.0. My 97th Co., which has reported in touch with 83rd I will move to the west so as to occupy with that company 1/3 of the line. My 84th Co., will be placed on the left of the 97th. I have no report from 84th Co., but know that it has advanced in rear of 97th. My 82nd Co., is now in rear of 83rd. I will move it to a position in rear of center. My P.C. is at present 267.3-279.4 in the trench d' Augsbourg. I intend to move along trench running to the left. 2nd Btn. 5th Regt. Btn. Commander [Capt. Charley Dunbeck] is about 200 yds. to my rear. I have sent word to him to watch the left. No further report of casualties received.

Barker of 1/6 notified Shuler where he was located at 1130 with 2/6 on his left and 23d Infantry on his right. "Left flank exposed. Expect counter attack. Have you seen 5th Marines."

At 1143 Shuler notified Williams, 2/6: "I have ordered my 84th Co. to take up position extending from our left line north-east to 266.5-280. My line extends from there to 267.6-280.3. I can help you support the left. Advise me what position would be best. Will you inform this runner of the location of Barker's P.C. and disposition of his Co's, if possible." Seven minutes later Shuler again to Williams: "Officer from 2nd Bn 5th Regt. just came here and showed me orders from [Capt. Robert] Messersmith to fill in gap between 6th Marines on left and the French. He is proceeding to do so."

Shuler sent the following message from Williams to Lee at 1155: "The following message just received from Major Williams. 'We need support on our left flank. The French have not come up and our left is in the air. The enemy about 700 or 800 strong, are going around our left and are threatening and encircling movement. Can you give us any help.'" At 1210 Shuler advised Barker of Williams' desperate message and Messersmith's request. Then at 1240 Barker was asking Shuler for help. Shuler replied at 1331 with a sketch showing his dispositions and asked where Barker needed his support.

Lee sent a message to both commanding officers of 1/6 and 3/6 at 1445 telling them that the French division to his left had advanced. His division would move forward at 4:00 p.m. and occupy the ridge to the east and southeast of St. Etienne. The 5th Marines would pass through the 6th and the new objective. Then the reorganized 6th would follow the 5th.

At 1500 Lee requested that Shuler do the following: "Please reconnoiter Bois-de-Somme-Py with a view to placing kitchens and carts there tonight. Let us have your recommendations as quick as possible."

First Lieutenant Kortwright Church of the 84th Co. sent following to Lee at 1500: "74 and 43rd Companies ahead, North-westerly direction enemy machine guns ahead of them. 55th Co. South Rec. 3:40." Church had been shell-shocked and relieved at Soissons; he would suffer the same fate on 4 October and Captain Charles D. Roberts would replace him.

Lee sent an informative message to all three battalion commanders at 1650 telling them where a small arms dump was located, and "am arranging to send your kitchens somewhere in the BOIS DE SOMME-PY and will probably do so tonight."

Shuler to Lee at 1700: "Machine gun firing (enemy) still continues in rear of us on our left. Understand than 9 French battalions have gone in on our left flank but the woods there are apparently not clear of the enemy. Shelling of vicinity of our P.C. continues."

Barker sent Shuler a message at 1915: "As far as I know we will remain here tonight. Have just received a message from Regt. Commander that kitchens, water carts etc. will be up tonight. You will send a continuous patrol all night on your left flank and front. I will send out a patrol to our rear and left to connect with yours at the edge of the woods."

4 October: Barker was still in trouble and sent Shuler this message at 0220: "Information that Boche will attack on our left about 4:00 a.m. Our left flank is still exposed. Can you move your battalion so that two companies join our left flank and face west. At least two companies are necessary. Whole battalion if possible. Fresh Division facing us."

At 0750 Lee notified Barker, Williams and Shuler that "the French 22nd Division attacks on our left … will jump off from a position abreast of the Shuler Bn. at 9:50 a.m." Then Lee notified Shuler that 5th Regiment was "subjected to heavy M.G. fire from left flank." He was to notify Barker to "move forward to relieve 5th of this fire.... Your Bn. and the 2nd Bn. will stand fast." At 1500 Lee ordered Shuler to "send back to your rear a small patrol to get in touch with the French 17th Inf, in your rear." Then he ordered Shuler to "hold up advance until 3:55 and let us have report. Have you got in liaison with 17th in rear."

At 1530 the following message from Capt. McFarland, commanding officer, 97th Company, was received by someone: "The Second Battalion has not advanced. We are up with them now. I am trying to find the 2nd Battalion Hdq."

Twenty minutes later Barker sent Shuler a desperate query: "Are you in liaison with the French division on our left, if so please give us their extreme north and eastern limits, as they have not arrived at our lines yet, and we are receiving severe machine gun fire from our left rear. Answer at once."

At 1600 Shuler by phone requested "artillery fire on woods be put on again. The enemy is laying down a heavy M.G. fire. Make our fire as heavy as you can. Between 280 and 281. Artillery notified at 4:05 by Liaison Officer. Expect to have three additional batteries this time."

At 1635 Shuler notified Lee how bad the situation at, around, and in Blanc Mont was, saying, "It is impossible to clean out Blanc Mont without adequate artillery preparation.... It is strongly held." Soon afterward Lee asked Shuler to pass on any messages received from the other two battalion commanders. He could read them and "if you think they are safe you may phone them in."

At 1715 Shuler conversed with Holcomb by phone:

Shuler—I am unable to take the woods. The artillery fire does not seem to have reduced the machine guns. Let me have a concentration of heavies on this point from six to six-thirty.
   Col. Holcomb—is the 17th French Inf. near you? Are they doing anything?
   Shuler—They are behind us.
   Holcomb—Call on them for assistance if needed. We will give you the heavy stuff from 6 to 6:30 around the words "Blanc Mont" on 1/20,000 map (over)
   Coordinates:
   265.7-280.3 to
   266.2-280.6
   155a & 75s
   from 6 to 6:30 p.m.

Shuler called Lee at 1742 and said: "Do not fire on woods unless I call for fire. Artillery notified at 5:45 p.m." Then Shuler notified Holcomb by phone at 1835, "Have taken seven prisoners. They say there are three German Bns. and 12 guns to a bn. in the woods. Holcomb—you had better call on the French to cooperate with you. We will give you two bns. of 155's and 1 Bn. of 75's on the woods."

Then Lee sent Shuler a lengthy message which boiled down to "be careful and on the alert of information from prisoners. Most of them lie like hell to worry you ... French troops on left and front ... sit tight and luck be yours." Shuler's final message this date went out at 2235, to Lee: "My Battalion in same position as this morning. This Battalion will attack Mont Blanc [sic] tomorrow morning after Artillery preparation."

5 October: At 0610 the commander of the 82d Company, Captain James H. Johnston, sent Shuler the following message: "Am at rest in Position marked, have had so many conflicting orders that I do not know what to do. The Art. is not shelling the woods to our front. The 80 Co. of 2nd Batt. 6th Regt. is in our front. Advise." At 0645 Johnston sent the following to Shuler: "Have reached our objective and digging in just rear of R.R. track have taken about 75 prisoners and have sent them to the rear. Am in touch with 97th on right. French on left." Shuler notified Lee at 0745 by phone: "84th Co. support has reached its objective and is digging in. I think it must have gone up on a line with the left of the 82nd Co. Have four officers and three more Pvts."

At 0800 Johnston sent Shuler a message giving his position and saying his unit had captured 200 Germans. "Turned them over to 80th Co. Almost 60 machine guns. 80th Co. salvaged most of them. We followed barrage so close the enemy did not get out of ___ until we were on them." At 0805 Shuler let Lee know that "the 97th Co. gained their objective and connected with 82 Co. on the left and 2nd Bn. on the right."

Lee sent all three battalion commanders the following message at 0815: "This regiment will at once be organized and be prepared to pass through the 5th Marines and continue the advance when ordered. Usual formation—order of battalions, head to rear, Williams [2/6], Shuler [3/6] and Barker [1/6]." At 0930 McFarland sent the following, probably to Shuler, "We have sent patrols well to the front from 600 to 1000 meters and have found no one."

At 1115 First Lieutenant Alfred H. Noble, commanding officer, 83d Company, sent Shuler a message:

> Have located 2nd Btn. of this Regt. It is as indicated on Maps.
> They do not know where 5th Regt. is.
> Our front line companies report not one in their front.
> French have advanced to point indicated on map (approximately) [Not included].
> There is in my opinion no better place forward for this company than its present position as we are now within 5 min. walk to our front line and the trenches between us are filled with 96 Co. men.
> In view of our shifting behind the 2nd Btn. to go forward soon I will not move from my present position without further orders from you.
> P.S. Is there anymore definite news as to positions of other units or when we advance etc.

At 1200 1st Lt. Ralph Marshall, the battalion scouting officer, sent Lee a message:

> Just returned with 2 scouts from patrol to ST. ETIENNE. Proceeded from Parc du Genie at crossroads on BLANC MONT to within 500 yds of the town as shown on sketch. Started across open towards Germans' trenches when one of the 2 men with me was hit by sniper possible French from neighborhood of town. Patrol brought the casualty in. French are west of road as far as town. Germans are in trenches as indicate. 3rd Batln of 5th Marines is digging in as indicated. Big tractor truck in good condition on road as shown [no sketch].

Lee informed all three commanders at 1205 that the French Division on the left has advanced to the St. Pierre—St. Etienne road with little opposition. This regiment would advance at once, with the French Division on our left and the 3rd Brigade on the right.

At 1215 Shuler sent Williams a message from Lee:

> The French had advanced on our left thru ST. ETIENNE. This Regt. will advance immediately in the following order. Williams-Shuler-Barker passing thru the 5th Regt. on our front. Objective is beyond a line connecting CAUROY and MACHAULT. The liaison will be kept up with the French on our left and the 3rd Brig on our right. Should the 3rd Brig. be held up so that by our advancing liaison with them will be broken this Regt. will halt. The movement will conform to the movement of the French on our left. The advance is along the lines laid out for the attack of yesterday. The Regt'l P.C. will move to Major Williams' present P.C.

Then a few minutes later Shuler told them that Lee did not want them to go beyond St. Etienne and "this order supersedes other messages."

At 1800 Barker asked Shuler to send him a guide from each company to guide to Shuler's positions. Lee sent a message to all three commanders at 1820 that 1/6 would relieve 3/6 in the second line; 3/6 would then relieve 2/6 in the front line and 2/6 would become the third line.

Shuler wrote to Lee at 1845: "If this Btn. is to resume the attack tomorrow I believe it would be much better if this Btn. passed thru Williams Btn. in the morning than to attempt a relief in the dark tonight. Our companies are well in hand and in good position to take up the advance. A scout was at ST. ETIENNE and found Germans there. Regarding Williams position, we know it approximately but it would be a hard job relieving him tonight." Lee agreed and sent a change of orders for the relief to take place "just before daylight in the morning."

6 October: At 0715 Shuler called Lee and told him: "My men have crossed the first line of trenches and are held up by M.G. fire between first and second line. Two Co. Comdrs. Hurt—Johnston and Roberts." And Lee replied: "We will arrange data for fire on 2nd Trenches but will not fire until we hear from you." Shuler continued sending phone messages. At 0724, "97th Co. being held up by our own fire. They are dropping short." At 0735, "Last report is they have crossed through and got the 2nd line, but there is a hell of a nest in the woods." Shuler continued in contact all morning until 0929 when he advised, "We have attained our objective ... we are in perfect liaison with the 23rd Inf. on our right who have also attained their objective ... 30 percent casualties." At 1030 he reported on the phone that three Frenchmen from the 62nd Regiment were at his post of command and told Shuler that the Germans weren't in St. Etienne.

At 1410 Shuler reported to Lee: effectives—15 officers, 290 men. Lee instructed all three battalion commanders at 1840 to provide his headquarters with guides for the incoming 141st Regiment, 36th National Guard Division.

Lee ordered Shuler at 2120 as follows: "If you have not certain liaison with the troops on your left and there is any considerable space try to get in touch and establish with him in the interval between you and he, strong combat liaison. Let me know by return runner what action you will take and if successful call me on the 'phone and speak the single word 'Appomattox.'" I have no idea what troops were on Shuler's left except possibly Frenchmen.

7 October: Shuler sent a message to Lee at 1230 that morning: "After many difficulties have gotten in touch with French on left. They counter attacked about 1800 [6 October] and drove enemy from ST. ETIENNE and now hold the place. Their line extends from ST. ETIENNE (inclusive) westward and connects with other French on their left. They are not coming east of ST. ETIENNE so the line between that place and my 82nd is open. I have ordered a strong patrol from 83rd to cover ground."

And forty-five minutes later, Lee to Shuler: "The 142nd Inf. will relieve this regiment. The 2nd Bn. will occupy the position with your Bn. The troops are expected momentarily. Please see that your officers assist the corresponding officers of the 142nd in making the necessary reconnaissance in view of the fact that they will probably attack."

At 0947 Shuler wrote Lee with the information that 2/142 was with 3/6 and the various companies were as follows: 142d E Company on right with 97th Company; Company G in center with 82nd Company; Company H on left with 84th Company; and Company F in support with the 83rd Company.

Shuler continued sending messages all day. A French captain notified Barker, who then notified Shuler that the French held St. Etienne, then didn't, then did, but the Germans "are still in the edge of the trench 100 meters to the south of the outskirts on the east of the village." Early afternoon, at 1335, Shuler told Lee all of the activity of the Germans that he could see. Then he mentioned, "I have hard luck about officers." Then told him that the commanders of the 82d, 84th, and 97th Companies had all been wounded, as had his scout and gas officers: "82 has 1 officer, 84 has 2, 97th 3, and 83 has 6."

Regardless of what the French said, the Germans were still in and about St. Etienne all that day and the men of the 6th were still very busy even though they had been "relieved" by the 142nd Infantry. One of the stalwart company commanders, 1st Lt. Alfred H. Noble, sent the following message to Shuler, who immediately forwarded it on to Lee at regiment at 1440.

> It is estimated that at least 200 of the enemy are in the town and more are seen filtering from over the hill into the town. It is believed that they are trying filter into the N.E. end of the town and drive the remaining French out. Their barrage did not play on part of town to the N.E. of the church.
>
> They occupy a trench near the town. They are probably trying to strike the French right flank and, later our left flank. It is believed necessary for the Americans to advance some troops (probably a Bn) to occupy trench between us and the town as soon as possible, or else advance here soon.
> A. H. Noble
> When are the infantry with us going to advance?
> (2) Shuler agrees with this. I have asked him about best way to accomplish this.
> T.H. [Lt. Col. Thomas Holcomb]

Shuler wrote to Lee at 1500 telling him that he was going to reconnoiter a stream lying before St. Etienne that night. Holcomb responded that Lee was away and he couldn't make decision as to occupation of trenches lying before 3/6, and asked a multitude of questions as to how Shuler attempted to accomplish it. Then at 1750 Lee responded that the occupation would be by "the Barker Bn, during the course of the evening." Later, at 1845, Shuler reported to Lee that two scouts did not reach stream north of St. Etienne "as enemy are between French and stream." Then he added, "The French are in the west end of town *only*. They are not in the east nor north part." Later but no time indicated, Major General Lejeune, commanding officer, 2d Division, requested information as to "whether the enemy have or have not withdrawn from the front."

8 October: Shuler wrote Lee at 1325: "The men of this battalion are getting in very bad shape physically. Their spirit is good and I haven't heard a complaint, but the fact remains that they have been through hell and are under constant shell fire now and no let up. I believe the machine gun nests that have worried our lines so much are now wiped out. I am getting in liaison with whatever units are on my right and left."

Lieutenant Colonel Earl H. Ellis, brigade adjutant, replied to Lee at 1535, agreeing with what Shuler wrote and asking about where the 141st Infantry was located, the strength of the effectives, and more information about what was occurring in the east sub-sector.

Second Lieutenant Earl F. Lucas, now the commander of the 82d Company, wrote to Shuler, no time indicated: "142nd Reg. retreated to our position. Reorganized men and established new position on edge of woods to left front. Two of our platoons in front line.

Captain and three Lieutenants present from 142 Reg. Very good position and our two platoons used as nucleus for position. Patrols out to find stragglers thought to be in front."

9 October: The next message from Lee ordered the men to turn in all Browning guns and equipment. The Marines had conned the infantrymen out of their great new weapons for their cheesy Chauchats. Now they had to give them up. However, some Marines managed to retain their ill-gotten goods through the last campaign.

The next message described what shape 3/6 was in as they were being relieved.

Approximate strength of companies.

82	1 officer	69 men
97	3 officers	63 men
83	6 officers	90 men
84	2 officers	66 men
Total	12 officers	288 men

Each company normally had 250 officers and men each or a total of at least 1,000 in each battalion. And, they were all in that same bad shape.

The 6th Regiment of Marines was finally relieved from its terrors at Blanc Mont, marching out of the line at midnight. When they arrived at Suippe the following morning at 0800 they received a fine hot breakfast and afterward were allowed to take showers and get deloused. On the 11th, Captain Arnold W. Jacobsen arrived and was given the command of the 84th Company. On the 14th the battalion marched to the town of Vadenay and billeted.

13 October: Shuler completed and submitted the most complete report of operations:

From 1st to 6th October, 1918, operating near St. Etienne on the Champagne Front.

1. In accordance with Regimental instructions the following report of operations of this battalion during the period 1–10 October 1916, is herewith submitted.

2. Preceding the operation of Oct. 2–9, 1918, the Third Battalion, Sixth Marines was billeted in the Division area south of Chalons, this battalion occupying the town of MONCETZ. The battalion embussed from this town at 6:00 p.m. 29 September 1918, and proceeded northward through Chalons to Suippe where the Battalion disembarked at 10 p.m. and marched two and one half kilometers northward on the SUIPPE-SOUAIN road. The night of 29-30 Oct. passed in the trenches at that point together with other battalions of this regiment.

The following day, Oct. 30, this battalion moved to more comfortable quarters in a nearby French camp, where the kitchens were brought up. At 4 p.m. on the 1st of October, verbal instructions were received by the Battalion Commander that the battalion would move forward at dusk through SOUAIN to the trenches south of SOMME-PY. At 8:00 p.m. the Regimental Commander called the Battalion Commander, Scout Officer and one officer from each company to his P.C. for a conference and a brief explanation of the procedure to the above mentioned trenches. The Scout Officer and one Officer from each company were sent forward to reconnoiter, it being then thought that this battalion would occupy trenches immediately to the south of the railroad. running west from SOMME-PY.

The 20 percent reserve as designated was left behind and the march of this battalion was begun at 8 p.m. following the First Battalion. Attached to this battalion were the 15th Machine Gun Company, Captain [Matthew H.] Kingman, two Stokes Mortars and one One Pounder section. The road was heavily blocked with traffic and progress was slow. Pyrotechnics, hand grenades and engineering tools, but no V.B. grenades, were picked up enroute. The following message was received enroute:

"From; Hq. 6th Regt. 1 Oct. 1918—9:35. p.m. To: C.O. 3rd Btn.

"Your position in trenches DUSSELDORF and GOTTINGUE. Our regimental P.C. at 7863. Guides will meet you a little south of place we told you to go. Explain to them that you are third line battalion. By order of Col. Lee (Signed) Holcomb."

At 4:30 a.m. this battalion took position in the trenches DUSSELDORF and GOTTINGUE southwest of SOMME-PY where the following order was received at 9:25 a.m. October 2nd.

[Col. Lee in this message informed the three commanders that the regiment would advance toward enemy positions on "D" day and "H" hour. His instructions were to prepare for flank protection and combat liaison (see Chapter 5). The operations report continued:

At 10:50 a.m. an order from Regimental Commander was received postponing the attack for 24 hours.

The following morning 3 Oct at 5:10 a.m. the following order was received:

"From: C.O. 6th Marines. At P.C.

"3 Oct 18 a.m. BY runner.

"To: C.O. 1st, 2nd. and 3rd Bns 6tn. Marines.

"This division attacks this morning at 5:50 a.m. 3rd Brigade on right, 4th Brigade on the left. Direction of attacks and objectives as shown on attached sketch. This Brigade will attack in column of regiments: the 6th Regiment in the first line and the 5th forming the 2nd line or support. This regiment will take the usual form of attack, column of battalions; one battalion first line, one battalion in the second and one in the third. Distance between battalions about 1000 yards.

"2. There will be five minutes' artillery preparation before the infantry attack at zero hour a rolling barrage will begin and will precede the infantry advance at the rate of 100 metres in four minutes to the objective there a standing barrage will be put on 300 metres beyond the objective for 30 minutes where the rolling barrage will continue for 1400 metres further for the support of patrols and establishment of out post lines.

"3. Tanks will be assigned as follows:

"One company (12 tanks) to the leading battalion of this regiment in the usual front line attack formation.

"One company (12 tanks) to the battalion of the second line this regiment taking position in rear of right and left flank to repel attacks and counter-attacks.

"These tanks will be under the command of the battalion commanders to which assigned. Each battalion will provide suitable flank protection for his own organization. The Commanding Officer of the 5th regiment will detail his rear battalion to watch the hook from the trenches on our left flank. If it is not necessary to attack the hook this battalion will advance as left flank guard.

"4. All troops will be in position at "H" minus two hours.

"5. Attached is copy of division order just received 4:45 a.m.

"6. P.C. of this regiment will remain in present position until the first objective is reached when it will be moved to a point 680.5-5-768.0 (Signed) Lee."

According to above instructions this battalion advanced at 5:50 a.m. at 1000 yards in rear of 1st Battalion. The companies were placed as follows: 83rd on right, supported by 82nd; 97th on left supported by 84th. Our P.O. advanced along the BOYAU LANDSHUT.

The battalion advanced steadily until about 7 o'clock, when the 97th Company reported that it was held up by enemy machine gun fire from the left, which caused a few casualties. At 7:30 four tanks were seen advancing upon these machine gun nests. Forty minutes later the 97th reported that machine guns were silenced and that they were advancing.

We advanced without further trouble and with few casualties until about 9:40 a.m., when Lieutenant Noble, 83rd. Co. reported that the 1st Battalion had passed through the 2nd Battalion and had reached objective on the BLANC MONT ridge. This battalion halted in reserve position 800 yards in rear of 2nd battalion where it dug in.

The following messages were sent as indicated and explain the situation at the end of the first phase of the attack:

"From: 3rd Bn 6th Regiment
"3 Oct 10:10 a.m. No. 3 By runner
"To: C.O. 6th Regiment.

"I understand 1st Bn has passed thru 2nd Bn and holds objective. I am now ordering my 83rd Co. which at present extends from road west to BOYAU D'AUSBORG at 267.3 and 280.2 to line 267.0. My 97th Co. which has reported in touch with 83rd. I will move to the west so as to occupy with that company one third of the line. My 84th Co. will be placed on the left of 97th. I have no report from 84th Co. but know that it has advanced in rear of 97th. My 82nd is now in rear of 83rd. I will move to a position in rear of center. My P.O. is at present at 267.3-279.4 in the trench D'AUSBORG. I intend to move along trench running to the left. 2nd Battalion 5th Regiment Commander is about 200 yards to my rear. I have sent word to him to watch the left. No further report of casualties received.

"Signed Shuler."
"From: C.O. 3rd Bn
"3 Oct. 18 11:43 a.m. No. 7 By runner
"To: C.O. 2nd Bn. 6th Marines.

"I have ordered my 84th Co. to take up position extending from our left line northeast to 266.5-260.0. My line extends from there to 287.6-880.3. I can help you support the left. Advise me what position would be best. Will you inform this runner of the location of Barker's P.C. and disposition of his companies if possible. (signed) Shuler."

"From C.O. 3rd Bn.
"3 Oct. 11:50 a.m. No. 9 By runner.
"To C.O, 2nd Bn. 6th Marines,

"Officer from 2nd Battalion 5th Regiment just came here and showed me orders Messershmidt [Messersmith] to fill in gap between 6th Marines on left and the French. He is proceeding to do so. (signed) Shuler."

"From: C.O. 3rd Bn.
"3 Oct. 12:10 p.m. No. 10 By runner
"To: C.O., 1st Bn. 6th Regiment.

"My P.C. 267.2-279.6 in trench. I am now getting my line established from 267.3 to 280.6 to 266.1 to 279.7. Just received message from Williams stating enemy was circling left and asking for help. At same time this message was received Messerschmidt commanding second battalion 5th Marines showed me his orders 'to immediately fill up any gap between 6th Marines and French on our left." (Signed) Shuler."

The line of this battalion as ordered in the above messages was exactly taken up.

The following messages further explain the situation which developed on left and the action taken:

"From: C.O. 1st Bn. at P.C.
"3 Oct 18 11:30 a.m. No. 11 By runner
"To: C.O. 3rd. Bn. 6th Marines.

"Have reached our objective and consolidating line. 2nd battalion on our left 23rd infantry on right. Left flank exposed. Expect counter-attack. Have you seen 5th Marines. Let us know your exact location of P.C. and your coordinates. (signed) Barker."

"From: C.O. 3rd Bn.
"3 Oct. 11:55 a.m. No. 6 By runner
"To: C.O. 6th Regiment.

"The following message just received from Major Williams 'We need support on our left flank. The Trench have not come up and our left is in the air. The enemy about 700 or 800 strong are going around our left and threaten an encircling movement. Can you give us any help.' I sent message to Williams that I would give him support and asked his advice as to location for same. Between sending that message and writing this one Messerschmidt commanding 2nd Bn. 5th Regiment showed me his orders from Commanding Officer 5th Regiment 'To immediately fill in any gap between 6th Regt. and the French on our left.' His order was to do so without further orders. I have sent Major Williams runner to Messerschmidt to take back any message and have sent message to Major Williams informing him of Messerschmidt's orders. (Signed) Shuler."

"From: C.O. 3rd Bn.

"3 Oct 1:30 p.m. No. 11 By runner

"To C.O. 1st Btn.

"My Co's disposed as sketch shows. According to your coordinates fartherest point on my line is about 800 metres in your rear with good communication through trench D'AUSBOURG. However if you want line closer can move it forward. Give me an idea of where you would like my line to better support you. (signed) Shuler."

"From: C.O. 1st Btn. at P.O.

"3 Oct. 18 12:40 No. 13 By Runner

"To: C.O. 3rd Btn.

"1st and 2nd Batt. on front line with no support. In need of a support line. Can you help us out. (signed.) Barker."

When the line of this battalion was established in support of the 1st and 2nd Battalions the following situation became evident. The advance of our regiment had been unimpeded to the objective on the BLANC MONT ridge. But the French on our left had not advanced and in fact there was an exposed flank to the left of two or three kilometres. Our leading battalions in order to keep in touch with our brigade on the right had veered slightly to the right and the dense woods on and approaching BLANC MONT had not been cleared of enemy machine guns. It was to protect this flank that the line of the battalion was swung in a partial semi-circle as support to the left as indicated in the above messages.

During the afternoon the 22nd Division, French crossed our rear from the right and began cleaning up the woods on our left flank, from which a great deal of machine gun fire had been enfilading our positions. Elements of the 170th Division, French also came up in support of us.

Elements of the Fifth Regiment, which during the afternoon and early evening had been supporting our left and center moved forward ahead of the line of this regiment (ridge road) during the evening and took up positions somewhat in advance. Our left flank was protected during the night of 3-4 October by liaison patrols which connected up with the French.

Water carts and ration carts with hot food were brought up in the evening. Thereafter each night hot food was brought up to the men in the trenches by Battalion Quartermaster Lieut. [Bert O.] Herreid from the rolling kitchens which were placed in the BOIS DE SOMME-PY.

At 6:35 a.m. October 4 a message was received from c.o. 6th stating that measures had been taken to strengthen our flank by the addition of chasseurs on our left and of other French troops on their front to our left. A lateral artillery barrage of heavy calibre was arranged for on the neutral ground on our left according to report. Combat liaison was established on left with 3rd Battalion, 67th Regiment, 22nd French Division at 9:30 a.m. This French Division attacked on our left at 9:50 a.m. and advanced to the east. This advance however did not drive the enemy from their strong positions on BLANC MONT on our left flank. This was because the French turned to the left of BLANC MONT which point had been erroneously reported as taken.

During the early morning and most of the day our positions were heavily shelled causing a number of casualties. At 11:05 a.m. Lieut. Church commanding 84th Company send word that he was shell shocked and could not retain command of company. Lieut. [George R.] Rowan was sent to take command of company. At 2:20 p.m. verbal message from 84th company that all but two officers were casualties was received. Lieut. [Charles D.] Roberts of 82nd Co. was ordered to take command of the 84th.

Phone message was received at 12:50 p.m. from Col. Lee stating that the 5th Regiment would attack at 2:30 p.m. in accordance with Division Field Order No. 37. The 6th Regiment would move off at same time, as support in following order: Second Battalion, Third Battalion and First Battalion. First Battalion was ordered to move out immediately to cover the left flank of the 5th Regiment on our front.

Although the attack was to begin at 2:30 p.m. the following message was received from the C.O. 2nd Battalion at 2:20 p.m. and sent in immediately to C.O. 6th.
"From C.O. 2nd Bn. at P.C.
"4 Oct 18—1:55 p.m. No. 1 By runner
"To: C.O. 6th Marines.
"The limits now actually held by this Bn. are eastern, 266.9-281.2 western, 266.2-280.7 instead of as previously reported. Location of barracks and roads on our left flank (present) confused us with what should actually have been our left flank, about 450 metres more to the left. The enemy consequently holds a good portion of BLANC MONT and is about 150 yards distant from the lines we hold along our eastern flank. Their position here heavily held with machine guns and exposure at this point in daylight hours subjects the men to heavy sniping from his position, which is as commanding as our own, the enemy covers the low ground in front of us with his machine gun fire and advance without heavy losses on this flank is impossible without heavy artillery preparation on his position on our left or until the French advance on our left and take this position. Our effectives are approximately as follows:
78th Co.—95 80th Co.—60 96th—65 79th—85
"Casualties in officers about 40 percent. (Signed) Williams."

This meant that the BLANC MONT stronghold had not been reduced and was still a menace on our left. At the "H" hour, 2:30 this battalion advanced but the P.C. remained in same place. The companies advanced until they approached on first battalion, which was still in the vicinity of the Ridge road and then halted. At 2:40 phone message from C.O. 2nd Battalion, stating that he was not going to advance because of machine gun fire of enemy on left.

Verbal orders (phone) were received from Col. Lee at 3:05 p.m. to halt all companies and to clean out the machine gun nests on our left. Artillery fire was to be concentrated on nests until 3:35 p.m. The battalion commander sent instructions to 97th and 82nd Companies to halt until 3:35 and then advance on machine gun nests and reduce them. The 83d and 84th Companies were ordered to "Stand By" to support 97th and 82nd in this attack.

These orders for attack were delayed, however, and because also of insufficient artillery preparation this attack on the machine gun nests, was postponed until 4:45 p.m. at which time artillery was to lift its fire from the BLANC MONT area. Instructions were sent to companies that the attack would begin at 4:45 p.m.

After reports by the Adjutant and Scout Officer on enemy positions and the ineffectiveness of artillery fire the Battalion Commander sent the following message to C.O. 6th Regiment at 4:35 p.m.
"From: 3rd. Bn. C.O.
"4 Oct 18—4:35 p.m. No. 3 By runner
"To C.O. 6th Regiment.
"It is impossible to clean out BLANC MONT without adequate artillery preparation. There has been no real heavy artillery fire put in the woods up to the present time. They are now firing an occasional seventy-five, which is not effective. Machine guns are firing from there all the time. It is strongly held. I have ordered C.O. 97th Co. to use his judgement about taking machine gun nests. It will require a heavy concentration to properly prepare for an attack. A concentration of one half kilometre around the words "BLANC MONT" (TAHURE map 1/20,000) would be right. Will call you up as soon as phone is working. (Signed) Shuler."

At 5:12 the Commanding Officer 6th Regiment was requested to concentrate heavy artillery fire on one half kilometre square around words "BLANC MONT" from 6 to 6:30.

At 5:15 Lieutenant Marshall carried the following verbal order to companies, "Fall back to road; attack if possible at 6:30." And at 5:40 the following message phoned to Commanding Officer 6th Regiment, "Don't start barrage unless I call for it. I want to be sure companies are clear of woods."

Meanwhile the 97th and 82nd Companies at 4:45 p.m. had advanced upon the machine gun nests. The 97th Co. encountered two machine gun nests with crews which they captured. These two companies were still advancing when orders reached them to fall back.

Thirteen prisoners were taken by the 97th Co.

Word was received at 6:10 p.m. that the 97th, 82nd, and 84th Companies had withdrawn from BLANC MONT. Inasmuch as it was decided to postpone the attack until morning the four companies were then ordered to retire to the positions they had at 2:30 p.m. before they advanced.

Heavy shelling of our positions continued all afternoon resulting in a number of casualties. Intermittent shelling of positions continued throughout the night of October 4-5. Our own artillery had been feeble in its preparation for the attack on BLANC MONT. Enemy fire on our positions had been much heavier than our own "destructive" fire had been in the area which was to be reduced. In the attack of the following morning the artillery preparation was heavier but by no means destructive.

At 11:00 p.m. the following order was received:

"Headquarters 6th Regiment,

"Marine Corps, A.E.F.

"France 4 Oct. 18.

"Hour 9:27 P/M.

"*FIELD ORDERS*

"1. The enemy have established a machine gun nest on BLANC MONT.

"2. The 3rd Battalion, 6th Marines, will attack and drive the enemy from this position.

"3. (a) Artillery preparation with 155s and 75s will be given between 5:15 a.m. and 6:15 a.m., 5 Oct., firing on the area included between the points 265.79-281.0; 266.04-281.12; 265.9-280.3; 266.2-280.4; and after 8:15 a.m. artillery will rake woods to the north of this area.

(b) The 3rd Battalion will be in position to attack at 6:15 a.m. and will attack as soon as the artillery fire shifts to the north of the occupied area.

"4. Messages to present P.C. of 3rd Battalion and thence by telephone to Regimental P.C. (signed) Lee.

"Copies to C.O. 1st Bn 6th Marines; C.O. 2nd Bn 6th Marines; CO. 3rd Bn. 6th Marines; C.G. 4th Brigade; C.O. 5th Marines; C.G. 22nd Div. (French); 170th Inf. (French)."

In accordance with this order this battalion attacked at 6:15 a.m. advancing on left flank from the east; 97th Co., 82nd, and 83rd. on line and 84th in support. At 7:35 a.m. word was received from 82nd, 83d and 97th Companies that their objectives (BLANC MONT) was reached, and that they were digging in. During this short engagement they captured 4 officers, 269 prisoners, 80 machine guns, a number of trench-mortars and other materiel. No casualty was sustained.

At 8:45 a.m. the following message was sent to the companies of this battalion:

"From: C.O. 3rd Bn. at P.C.

"5 Oct. 18—8:45 a.m. No. 1 By runner

"To: C.O. 82, 83, 84 and 97th Companies.

"The following just received from Regimental Headquarters, From site. Time 8:15. This regiment will at once be organized and be prepared to pass through the 5th Marines when ordered. Usual formation. Order of Battalions, front to rear, Williams, Shuler, Barker—Lee.' This battalion will follow the 2nd Battalion in this order: front line, 82nd Co., left, 97th Co., right, 2nd Line, 84th Co. left 83d Co. right. The 97th Co. will keep in touch with battalion headquarters, 2nd Battalion, and inform the 82nd, 83d, and 84th Companies of any orders received. This battalion will follow 2nd Bn at usual distance of 1000 metres. The regimental C. O. congratulates us on this morning's work. (signed) Shuler."

The following was received by phone from C.O. 6th at 12:15 p.m. and copies sent to 2nd and 1st bns.: "The French have advanced on our left through ST. ETIENNE. This regiment will advance immediately in the following order, Williams, Shuler, and Barker passing through the 5th Regt. on our front. Objective is beyond a line connecting CAUROY and MACHAULT. The liaison will be kept up with the French on our left and the 3rd Brig. on our right. Should the 3rd Brig. be held up so that by our advancing liaison will be broken, this regiment will halt. The movement will conform to the movement of the French on our left. The advance is along the lines laid out as for tile attack of yesterday. The regimental P.C. will move to Major Williams present P.C."

The following order was received at 12:20 p.m. from the C.O. 6th Reg. by phone and copies sent to 1st and 2nd Battalions: "Regt'l Commander directs that the advance will not go beyond ST. ETIENNE without further orders. This is the latest order and supersedes other message."

At 1:00 p.m. this P.C. advanced to BLANC MONT. At 4:30 this battalion advanced in support of the second battalion 1000 yards to the rear; 82nd Co. left front supported by 84th. 97th. right front supported by 83rd. The battalion advanced as directed through light enemy artillery barrage until 5:10 p.m. when it was forced to halt and dig in, as the second battalion was held up by enemy machine gun fire from their right front. Information was sent to the C.O. 6th regiment. Our P.C. was established in cable man-hole 265.6-282.1. At 6:45 the following order was received from the Commanding Officer 6th.

"From C.O.   6th at P.C.
"5 Oct 18. 6:20 p.m. By runner.
"To: C.O. 1st, 2nd, and 3rd Bns.

"As soon as light conditions will permit the first Bn. now in third line will proceed to relieve the 3rd Bn. now in their front in 2nd line. As soon as relieved by the 1st Bn. the 3rd Bn. will proceed from the 2nd Line and relieve the 2nd Bn. now in the 1st line. The 2nd Bn. as soon as relieved by the 3rd Bn. now in the 1st line will retire to the third line, position just south of the road. Water carts, rolling kitchens etc. will be up shortly and when they arrive meals will be cooked and battalion commanders notified.

(Signed) Lee."

A message was immediately sent to the commander of the 6th suggesting that if this battalion was to attack the next morning it would be better if this battalion passed through the 2nd battalion in the morning than to attempt a relief in the dark that night. Later in the evening an order was received for the relief to be held in abeyance until just before daylight the following morning. The night passed quietly. At 1:00 a.m. Oct. 6th time was moved back one hour.

On the 17th Captain Pink H. Stone arrived and he was handed the command of the 82d Company. The 6th took up marching once again on 21 October, as the 2d Division had been ordered to relieve a French division, but that command was rescinded on 22 October and they marched to Leffincourt instead.

Back to the towns of Somme-Suippes on the 23d, at 0845 the battalion boarded camions to be taken to Les Islettes where they disembarked at 1300 and marched to Camp Lochere in the Argonne Forest. They were on their way by the 27th to relieve the U.S. 42d Division, which they did on the 30 of October. Then Field Order No. 24 was received ordering the regiment to prepare to attack the enemy the following morning, 1 November.

Meuse-Argonne

1 November: Shuler complained to someone at 0720 that information "was extremely hard to get." His battalion was ahead of him, he had no reports from any of his companies, and all were advancing slowly. At 0814 he sent Lee a message: "My two leading companies are on first objective, following companies on ridge in position to advance at proper time. Few casualties. Barker is near me. Have met two companies of Williams back of S. Georges. Made good time since last message." Then, at 1100 he notified Lee: "We are in Chennery and

Bayonville and pressing up to 2nd objective. Took about 100 prisoners here by using tanks assisted by riflemen. About 100 enemy retreated from their guns southeast of SIVRY. That woods north of the 2nd objective should be well shelled. Have taken 6 88's. Scouts just reported we hold Chennery and Bayonville. Enemy are shelling from woods north of Bayonville."

First Lt. Alfred H. Noble, still commanding the 83d Company, sent Shuler the following at 1105: "I am North of Bayonville. My first line is at marked on the other side. The enemy is at Do not know. They are still retreating. Remarks: If they could follow up now the enemy could be kept on the run. We captured about 15 officers and men that I know of. The 97th Co. will meet no resistance if it advances to its position *now* for we ran at least 200 clear over the hill."

At 1245, Shuler in a report to probably Lee. "97th Co. is on left of 83rd. The 82nd is in rear of 97th and the 84th is in BAYONVILLE. The 97th Co. was compelled to drop back about 300 M to avoid our own barrage. As soon as barrage lifted they took up position on objective." The next message from Shuler to Lee was at 1720: "Our liaison platoon has returned reporting 5th and 6th connected. Regt. I.O. has position of companies plotted on his map."

2 November: Colonel Lee sent a message to all 3 battalion commanders at 0645 telling them they were going to be relieved by the 23d Infantry but he wasn't sure at what hour. At some time on this date the 6th Regiment reported its manpower and 3/6 had 22 officers and 648 men. Also in that report was the position of 3/6, and it was in reserve.

3 November: At 1100 from his post of command 800 meters south of Fosse, Shuler sent a message to Lee: "Position sketch submitted. 1st Batn 6th Regt. 1 KM north of my front. Fosse is being shelled. Wounded from 23rd say they are several Kms north of Fosse. No casualties in my Batn." At 1400 Shuler advised Lee that his post of command was located "in town 100 yds east of Reg'l P.C."

4 November: Lee sent another message to his three commanders at 1130 that morning: It explained that on the 5th the 5th Marines were going to lead and the 6th would follow "approximately one kilometer from rear of the 5th to head of 5th, and same distance between Bns. of this regiment." There was no mention of which position each would be in. At 1950 Shuler sent a sketch of his positions to Lee.

At no time indicated, Colonel Allen, the commanding officer of the 356th Infantry Regiment, 89th Division, sent Shuler a lengthy message describing his difficulties and asking him to notify "your assaulting Bn. Very desirable that he clear south edge of Foret de Jaulnay of machine guns before our front line advances to river."

5 November: Lee advised the three commanders that the brigade was expected to cross the Meuse. The 5th Marines would move forward, cross the Meuse at Pouilly and seize the heights to the northeast of Pouilly, west of Autreville and Bois d' Alma Gisors.

6 November: Lee to all three commanders at 1815 that the next move would be early in the morning, and by a different route than that previously indicated. "Further information will be furnished about this as soon as received."

In a report to the 4th Brigade, the 3d Battalion reported a complement of 23 officers and 541 men.

8 November: Lee sent a message to the three battalion commanders, time not specified, that the crossing would not take place that night.

9 November: Lee instructed the three commanding officers to bivouac in the Bois du Fond de Limon. Then told them to locate Williams and Shuler, who were on reconnaissance in that area. The 3d Battalion would occupy the last position.

10 November: At 2340 Lee notified all three, Barker, Williams, and Shuler, "after you have objectives ... you will send out strong patrols ... as exploitation." I find no record of how and why it happened, but for some reason Lee, nominal commander of the 6th Regiment since 6 June 1918, disappeared and instead, Major George K. Shuler was his replacement, at least for the next day or so. This was the time when the 5th Marines would send two battalions, 1/5 and 2/5, across the Meuse River at 10 to 11 at night to gain ground on the eastern side of the river. The 6th Regiment, plus 3/5, was to march north to the town of Mouzon and there cross over the river on bridges the 2d Engineers would construct.

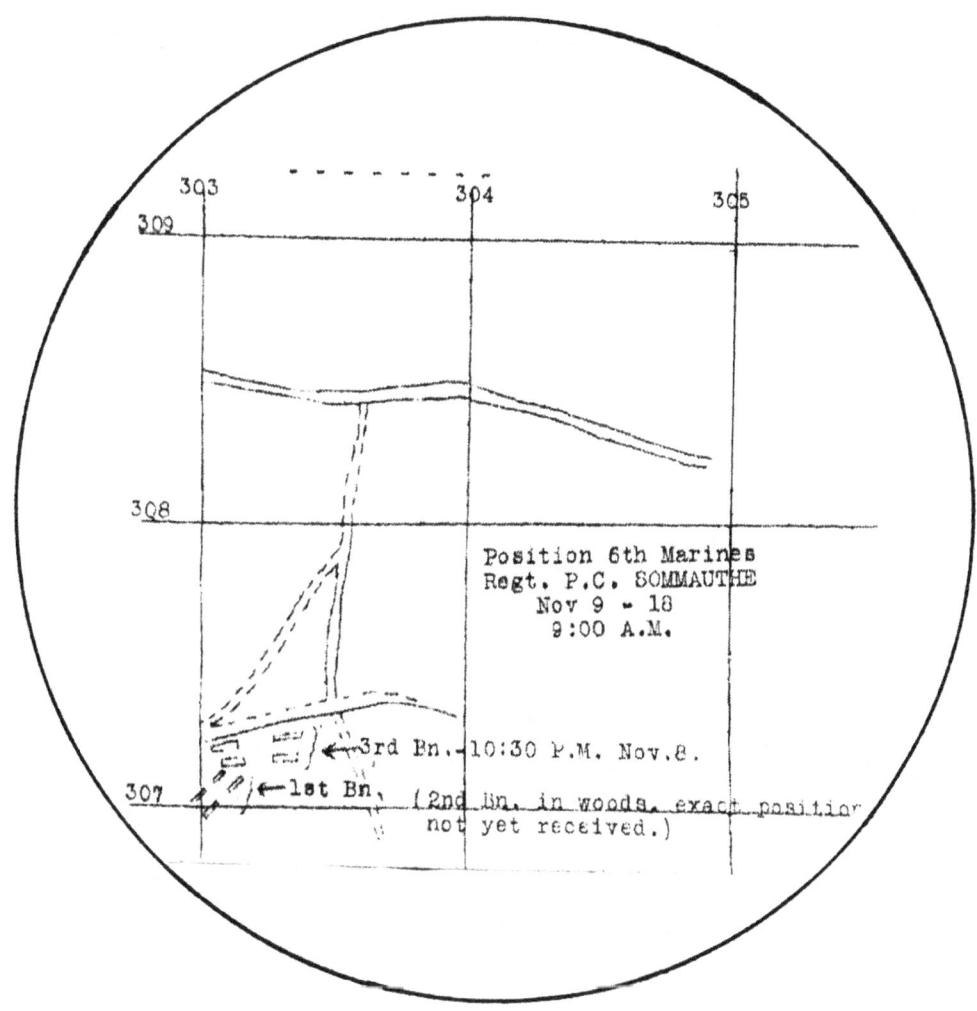

Location of 6th Marines.

Top: Survivors of the 84th Company, 3/6 Battalion, in Germany. *Bottom:* Battered buildings at Mouzon on the Meuse River.

Captain David Bellamy, adjutant of 3/6 Battalion, in Germany.

The effort went to naught because every bridge the engineers put across the German artillery would smash. At 0400 the morning of the 11th, Shuler decided not to try and cross in daylight hours, thereby saving most of his command. They marched back south to the Bois du Fond de Limon.

Occupation of Germany

On 13 November 3/6 relieved the 23d Infantry at Villemontry and on the 17th the 2d Division units, including 3/6, began their long march to Germany. On 13 December the 6th Marines crossed the Rhine River and on the 16th the 6th took over the left half of the

4th Brigade sub-sector and 3/6, as regimental reserve, was stationed at the village of Leutesdorf.

Like all members of the occupying force, the 6th Regiment began duties more pleasant than any they had been engaged in for the previous twelve or so months. After nearly eight months, the German government officials signed the unequal treaty and the 2d Division began its movement toward the United States, arriving on 5 August 1919 at Hoboken, New Jersey. After a few parades, the remnants of the 4th Brigade arrived at Quantico and the war-time men were discharged on 13 August 1919 and went home.

8

Sixth Machine Gun Battalion

Battalion Headquarters
15th [A] Company
23d [B] Company
77th [C] Company
81st [D] Company

Commanding Officers

From:	To:	
17 August 1917	10 June 1918	Major Edward B. Cole
10 June 1918	11 June 1918	Capt. Harlan E. Major
12 June 1918	19 June 1918	Capt. George H. Osterhout, Jr.
20 June 1918	13 August 1919	Major Littleton W. T. Waller, Jr.

The Sixth Machine Gun Battalion was organized 17 August 1917 at Quantico, Virginia, by order of the major general commandant, United States Marine Corps. It was designated the First Machine Gun Battalion, comprising a headquarters detachment and the 77th and 81st Companies, with two companies to be added later. It was renamed the 6th Machine Gun Battalion, and the 15th and 23d companies joined while the battalion was in France in early 1918. Captain Edward B. Cole had as assistants in the headquarters detachment Second Lieutenant Thomas J. Curtis, adjutant, and Second Lieutenant John P. Harvis, quartermaster. The first two companies had the following as officers.

77th Company
First Lieutenant Louis R. de Roode, Commanding
Second Lieutenant Clifford O. Henry, Company Officer
Second Lieutenant William B. Croka, Company Officer
Second Lieutenant Lothar R. Long, Company Officer
Second Lieutenant Robert M. Montague, Company Officer

81st Company
Captain L.W.T. Waller, Jr., Commanding
Second Lieutenant Jack S. Hart, Company Officer
Second Lieutenant Edmund P. Norwood, Company Officer
Second Lieutenant Shaler Ladd, Company Officer
Second Lieutenant William J. J. Elger, Company Officer

The companies were each equipped with 16 Lewis machine guns and 33 machine gun carts. These light carts had two wheels and were drawn by hand. According to the Table of Organization of that time, there were two of these carts to every gun. One carried the gun and five boxes of ammunition (1410 rounds) and was designated the gun cart. The other, known as the ammunition cart, carried six boxes of ammunition (1692 rounds).

The battalion remained in Quantico from 27 August to 7 December and went through a course of intensive training. Instruction included the nomenclature of the Lewis machine gun, machine gun drill in close and extended order, the tactical use of machine guns, and terrain exercises. They also learned to dig machine gun emplacements in conjunction with infantry, build concrete pillboxes, and skills for organization and direction of fire. Target practice included signals, flags, flash and sound; other training was in transmission of orders and messages by telephone and in reconnaissance reports and sketches.

While at Quantico, the following named officers were commissioned in the next, higher, grades:

Captain Edward B. Cole, to be Temporary Major.
Captain L.W.T. Waller, Jr., to be Temporary Major.
First Lieutenant Louis R. de Roode, to be Captain.
Second Lieutenant Thomas J. Curtis, to be Temporary First Lieut.
First Lieutenant Thomas J. Curtis, to be Temporary Captain.
Second Lieutenant John P. Harvis, to be Temporary First Lieut.
Second Lieutenant Clifford O. Henry, to be Temporary First Lieut.
Second Lieutenant Jack S. Hart, to be Temporary First Lieut.
Second Lieutenant Edmund P. Norwood, to he Temporary First Lieut.
Second Lieutenant William B. Croka to be Temporary First Lieut.
Second Lieutenant Lothar H. Long, to be Temporary First Lieut.
Second Lieutenant Shaler Ladd, to be Temporary First Lieut.
Second Lieutenant Robert M. Montague, to be Temporary First Lieut.

The following named officers joined the battalion at Quantico and were assigned as follows:

Asst. Surgeon Ogden D. King, U.S.N., to Headquarters Detachment.
Asst. Surgeon William H. Whitmore, U.S.N., to Headquarters Detachment.
Second Lieutenant Lucius L. Moore, to 77th Company.
Second Lieutenant Phil. G. Stiles, to 81st Company.

On 7 October, First Lieutenant John P. Harvis, Battalion Quartermaster, was detached temporarily and accompanied the 1st Battalion, 6th Marines, to France.

On 6 December 1917 orders were received that the battalion would hold itself in readiness to leave on 8 December 1917 for overseas expeditionary duty. Preparation started immediately for departure.

At 6:00 a.m. on 8 December 1917, the battalion with Headquarters, 77th and 81st Companies, entrained and left Quantico, Virginia, for Newport News, Virginia, arriving at 3:00 p.m. the same day, and embarked on board the USS *DeKalb* for overseas expeditionary duty. The 12th and 20th Companies and aviation detachment embarked on board the USS *DeKalb* and joined the battalion, which became a provisional battalion. The ship left on 11 December and arrived off France on 28 December 1918.

On 31 December all troops disembarked and climb aboard a train leaving at 1800 to proceed to their training area. At 0600 on 3 January the battalion arrived at Damblain and detrained. It was at this time that all the battalion's Lewis guns, gun carts, and tripods were turned in. At the same time the 12th and 20th Companies were detached and transferred to the 5th Marines. On 12 January the 2 company battalions were issued their 24 Hotchkiss machine guns and ammunition carts. On the 14th, Capt. John P. Harvis rejoined the battalion. The following day, General Order No. 4, from Headquarters, Second Division, was received which changed the designation of the 1st Machine Gun Battalion to the Sixth Machine Gun Battalion.

The following joined the 15th Company: Captain Matthew H. Kingman, commanding; Captain Harlan E. Major, second in command; Captain Augustus B. Hale, train officer; and First Lieutenant James F. Moriarty, company officer.

These officers joined the 23d Company: Captain John P. McCann, commanding; First Lieutenant Ralph L. Schiesswohl, company officer; and First Lieutenant Harold D. Campbell, company officer.

Verdun

On 14 March orders were received that the Second Division would begin to move to a new area and on 16 March the units marched to a railroad station at Breauvannes and began loading. They soon after arrived at Lemmes in the Verdun Sector and unloaded.

On the 17th each company was assigned to a unit to support: 15th Company with the 3d Battalion, Sixth Marines; 23d Company with the 2d Battalion, Fifth Marines; 77th Company with the 3d Battalion, Fifth Marines; and 81st Company with the 2d Battalion, Sixth Marines.

On the night of 28-29 March the 81st Machine Gun Company relieved the 73d Machine Gun Company in the front-line trenches at Mont-sur-la-Cote in support of 2/6. At 0400 the following morning the 23d Machine Gun Company relieved the French in the front-line trenches, supporting 2/5 in the Chatillon-Bourbaki Sector. The next night, 30-31 March, the 15th Machine Gun Company relieved the French supporting 2/6 in the Cote des Hures Sector. At 0500 the 77th Machine Gun Company, supporting the French, relieved 3/5 in the Moulainville Sector.

During the period the battalion was in the front-line trenches the various companies participated in repelling raids, patrolling No-Man's Land, repairing barb-wire and constructing trenches plus machine gun emplacements.

Various changes in personnel took place during this period. Major Waller in the 81st Company was transferred to command the 8th Machine Gun Battalion of the 3d Division on 29 August. Captain Allen M. Sumner replaced Waller in command of the 81st. On 11 May, 1st Lt. Clifford O. Henry was detached from the battalion and sent to the U.S. as an instructor in machine gun usage.

Otherwise, like the rest of the Second Division, the 6th Machine Gun Battalion was reduced to boring service in trenches until relieved in the middle of May and sent to an area called Montjavoult where they trained, trained, trained, and participated in maneuvers. They received orders to prepare for a movement north to relieve the tired First Division; however, as we know, that changed and instead, the Second Division headed eastward to stop a major German drive toward Paris.

Belleau Wood

June 1: Battalion assembled at 4:30 a.m. at junction of Beaugrenier and Dieppe-Paris roads, embarked in camions, carrying guns and ammunition by hand, and proceeded to Mayen-Multien; the supply train followed by marching. The battalion proceeded at 4:30 a.m. by camion to Montreuil-aux-Lions, halted until 4:00 p.m. and then continued on to Ferme Paris. From this crossroads the 15th and 23d went north through la Voie du Chatel to Champillon, disembarked there and took up position in line, from Hill 142 to Lucy-le-Bocage, forming the left group of the battalion line (Captain Kingman, group commander). In the right group the infantry line was composed of the 2d Battalion, 23rd Infantry (right), and the 2d Battalion, 6th Regiment (left). The infantry battalions on the left group front were in reserve, the French holding the first line in this half of the brigade sector until the next day. Two guns from the 81st Company were placed on the Paris-Metz road between Lucy crossroads and Bois de Clerembauts, flanking the right wing of the brigade front.

While 2/6 was deploying, Maj. Edward B. Cole and the 6th Machine Gun Battalion arrived in camions and debused near Hill 201. The men dismounted from their "prisons" with genuine enthusiasm. One young Marine asked, as he and his buddies dismounted and went across the fields from the highway, "Which way is this here line?" A sergeant responded, "Line, hell! We're going to make one." Turning north on the Lucy road Cole established headquarters at Montgivrault-le-Grande, then sent guns forward to support the line established by 2/6. These were men and guns from the 77th and 81st Companies. The entire group was commanded by Capt. Louis R. de Roode of the 77th Company with Captain Augustus B. Hale of the 81st Company as his second.

June 2: The 15th and 23d companies of the 6th Machine Gun Battalion were assigned to provide cover for the 5th Marines on the division's northern flank. The 81st and 77th, north to south, remained in their locations just behind 2/6 and 3/6. These guns kept the "wolf from the door" during the first few days of the Aisne Defense. The .03 in the hands of trained marksmen also helped a great deal. The story has been told, many times, of the surprise inflicted upon the German attackers at finding their comrades falling in the wheat and not hearing sounds of any enemy fire, the distance being that great. So was the accuracy.

The usual American method of supplying machine-gun support to the various units was to assign a machine-gun company to each battalion. The regimental machine-gun companies, the 8th in the 5th Marines and the 73d in the 6th, were usually each assigned to the first battalions of their respective regiments. Each company received a platoon of guns. Consequently, the commanding officer of the 6th Machine Gun Battalion, Major Cole, and his successors, had little direct control over the entire unit while they were engaged in combat. Fortunately the leadership down to platoons was more than satisfactory in most cases, and consequently the battalion always functioned at the top of their form.[1]

Enemy attacked along the brigade front at 8:30 a.m. Right group guns were in action. Pursuant to orders received from the brigade commander, six guns from 81st Co. were withdrawn about noon from back of Bouresches and the crews proceeded by way of Voie du Chatel north to section of front line between Hill 142 and Bois du Veuilly (Col. Wise's battalion held this part of line). Before 81st Company guns arrived, the infantry battalion here was protected as it deployed by guns of 15th Company echeloned in depth. To fill the gap left by withdrawal of 81st Company guns from right group, the 77th Company positions were extended to left.

June 3: The 8th Machine Gun Company made a rapid recovery from their long walk. Not many hours after arrival they had supplied twelve guns to support 2/5's left. The 81st Company supplied four more for the right flank and the 15th Company provided another four.[2]

The counter attack of the French troops on left was not participated in by U.S. infantry. The 23d Company guns moved forward 500 meters to a new line. The 77th and 81st Companies guns were in position in the repulse of attack on the right group front. Right group ration and ammunition dump was established on Lucy road near Montgivrault le Grand, and the left group dump was in the woods on the road between la Voie du Chatel and Champillon. These were designated as #1 and #2 respectively.

June 4: No material change.

June 5: No change.

June 6: The 1st Battalion, 5th Regiment, attacked from Hill 142 northward to Lucy-Torcy road at 3:45 a.m. assisted by ten guns of the 15th Company. Excellent direct overhead fire by these guns hit enemy reserves and assembly points. New gun positions to conform to line were established. At 5:00 p.m. Bouresches and the western edge of the Bois de Belleau were attacked by the 3d Battalion, 5th Regiment, and the 3d Battalion, 6th Regiment, respectively. With the former, guns of the right group cooperated, and with the latter, 23d Company guns cooperated, in the second instance laying down two barrages—one a covering barrage over U.S. troops before zero hour, and the other on the enemy lines during the attack. Guns of this company went forward for consolidation.

June 7: 23d Company guns laid a barrage on road west from Torcy at 3:30 a.m. 77th Company guns participated in the repelling of an attack against right group front. Four guns of the 15th Company moved forward for better consolidation of the line of the 1st Battalion, 5th Regiment. The 77th Company's guns assisted in repelling an enemy counter attack during night.

June 8: No material change.

June 9: 23d Company guns were withdrawn west of Lucy-Torcy road at 12:10 a.m. to allow artillery to shell Bois de Belleau.

June 10: Six guns of the 23d Company went forward with the 1st Battalion, 6th Regiment, in the attack on Bois de Belleau.

June 11: 2d Battalion, 5th Regiment, attacked Bois de Belleau at 4:30 a.m. Four guns of the 23d Company went forward with infantry; 77th Company guns were also used in consolidation. Received 43 rounds.

June 12: No material change.

June 13: 2d Battalion, 5th Regiment, attacked Bois de Belleau at 4:00 p.m. The 23d Company's guns went forward with infantry and consolidated a new line.

June 14: 23d Company guns laid down a heavy barrage in anticipation of enemy attack, which failed to materialize.

June 15 to June 19: No material change.

June 20: The 23d Company was relieved by Company "A," 4th Machine Gun Battalion, at 4:30 a.m. This company went into rest in the woods on south side of Paris-Metz road one kilometer east of Montreuil-aux-Lions.

June 21: No change.

June 22: No change. Received 63 rounds.

June 23: 77th Company relieved by "B" Company, 4th Machine Gun Battalion, and went into rest adjacent to camp of the 23d Company near Montreuil.

June 24 to June 27: No material change. The two companies of the 4th Machine Gun Battalion in the line operated under orders of battalion commander 6th M.G.B.

June 28: 15th Company was relieved by the 8th Company, 5th Regiment, and proceeded to camp east of Montreuil.

June 29: 81st Company was relieved by the 73rd Company, 6th Regiment, at 1:00 a.m. and proceeded to camp east of Montreuil.

June 30: All companies at rest. Battalion supply train was at St. Aulde. The four companies which relieved the 6th Machine Gun Battalion in the line operated under the orders of the battalion commander, 6th Machine Gun Battalion, located at post of command Waller, in the ravine running through the Champillon woods northwest of Lucy-le-Bocage.

Soissons

The next campaign the Fourth Marine Brigade participated in was near the ancient city of Soissons, about 50 miles north of Chateau Thierry. The Second Division was rushed northward beginning in mid–July. The first day the 5th Marines and their cohorts of the Third Brigade, the 9th and 23d Infantry Regiments, advanced against the German lines making several kilometers' advance. On the following day, 19 July, the 6th Marines advanced alone and were met by a ferocious artillery and machine gun fire that cut the regiment in half. Records for the 6th Machine Gun Battalion for this campaign are scarce. The information on this battle is from Thomas Curtis's *History of the Sixth Machine Gun Battalion*.

On 18 July the battalion arrived in an exhausted condition at the north end of the Bois de la Retz, where, because of the physical condition of the officers and men, the battalion rested. Battalion Headquarters post of command was established at the Beaurepaire Farm as was the 15th Company, in reserve. At 1800 the 15th was ordered to support the 9th Infantry in its attack upon on the enemy north of the town of Vierzy. Upon the success of the 9th, the 15th was then ordered to take up a reserve position about 200 yards northwest of that town.

At noon the 23d Company was ordered to support 2/5. At 2100 their new orders were to take up with the 23d Infantry. The 77th Company received orders to support the 9th Infantry when it went over the top at 1800. The 81st Company received orders at 1700 to go to the Beaurepaire Farm and take up reserve positions. The infantry they were supporting moved forward at an incredible speed and the machine gun companies had a difficult time carrying their heavy French guns and maintaining their support.

The following day, 19 July, it was the 6th Marines' job to advance and the various machine gun companies were spread about. The 15th joined 3/6, which was in reserve south of Vierzy. But at 1600 they received orders to support the 2d Engineers about a kilometer east of that town. The 23d Company replaced the 15th in their old positions. The 77th Company was ordered to move at 1630 into Vierzy as support for the 6th Marines. At 0800 two platoons were sent to support 1/6 near Tigny.

More splitting up: The 81st Company moved at 0500 to Vierzy, where its 1st Platoon joined 1/6 and the 3d Platoon joined 3/6 as support for that battalion as it moved forward.

On 20 July at 0100 French troops relieved the entire battalion located in or near the Bois de la Retz. The following day all units of the 6th Machine Gun Battalion marched to the woods at Carrefour de la Croix and bivouacked.

According to the unit history, the accurate and heavy shell fire on 19 July did not allow the gunners any chance to establish a line of, and rate of, effective fire. Their losses in killed included six from the 81st Company, including Capt. Allen M. Sumner plus five more that died of their wounds, four officers and men from the 23d, and 2 men from the 15th, plus many wounded. This was the end of the Battle of Soissons. From here the entire Second Division was moved to the quiet sector of Marbache.

Marbache

During this period of relative quiet, the 6th Machine Gun Battalion absorbed 171 replacements on 3 August. During this sojourn I could find just one report, and this one from junior officers in the 81st Company.

12 August: From Second Lieutenant George Bower of the 81st Company to First Lieutenant Jack S. Hart, commanding officer of the 81st: "Working with Burdette [2d Lt. Vernon B. Bourdette]. Only two guns in position due to shortage of ammunition and men. Six men fell out on the way up—Pvts. [Carl C.] Colby, [Earl J. Vrendenburg] Viendenburg, [Paul C.] Pearce, [Edward C.] Bass, [Byron R. Tennant] Tinnant, [Marion E.] England. Have on hand twenty-four (24) boxes of amm. but cannot carry more without more men."

St. Mihiel

The 6th Machine Gun Battalion along with the rest of the 4th Brigade and the entire Second Division, moved next to their forthcoming engagement at the St. Mihiel Salient. They arrived on 11 September and the battle began the following morning.

The first official report we have is that of the 15th Company. It shows as Company "A" because it seems that this battalion utilized company letters unlike the rest of the Marines. But we will stick with numeric assignments, as all other reports have.

Company "A" (15th Company)
Sixth Machine Gun Battalion
September 22, 1918.

A memorandum for the battalion commander stated: "The report of operations submitted herewith is complete, covering fully the operations of Company 'A.' (Sgd) Matthew H. Kingman, Captain, U.S. Marine Corps, Commanding Company 'A.'"

Report of Operations of Co. "A" 6th M.G. Bn. from Sept. 12th–15th. Incl.

Sept. 12, 1918

At 12:45 a.m. this was in position north of Limey grouped into 3 batteries, of 4 guns each, the batteries positions as shown by the following map coordinates;—

Rt. Battery	365.37-233.97
	365.44-233.98
Center Battery	365.28-233.98
	365.34-233.99
Left Battery	365.22-233.94
	365.27-233.97

At 5:00 a.m. zero hour we laid a barrage on the enemy, important trenches and strong pts. by firing indirectly over the heads of the 3d Brigade which advanced at zero hour.

At 5:48 a.m. we ceased fire, as our friendly troops reached the dangerous zone, having fired about 15000 rds.

At about 6:00 a.m. we joined the 3d Bn 6th Reg. Marines which were passing thru our gun positions and took up the advance with them. Their formation was two companies in advance and two companies in local support. Two of the M.G. platoons were attached to the support companies and 3d platoon followed in rear center. Infantry rate of advance was about 25 yds per minute and the M.G. gun company had no difficulty in keeping up.

Arrived Thiaucourt about 2:00 p.m. and went into support position about 1 kilometer north of town using the same formation as in the advance, the two leading platoons having positions on high ground for direct overhead fire in case of attack, and the rear platoon being placed in position, for indirect fire or anti-avion work. The night was spent in this position.

Sept. 13

At 11:00 a.m. received message from Major Waller that 4th Brigade would relieve 3rd Brigade tonight and to reconnoiter positions for M. Guns.

In company with my platoon leaders and Lt. Col. Sibley 3rd Bn. 6th Marines, we selected positions and moved into place about 10:00 p.m. The 3d. Bn had 2 cos. in the front line (82 Co. rt. and 83d Co. left) with 97th and 84th supporting them respectively. Our 2nd platoon was with the 82d Co and 3d Platoon with 83d Co. 400 yds south of a line running between Xammes and Jaulny. These platoons covered the front with a belt of fire. The first platoon was rear center about 400 yds. Remained in this position until next day.

Sept. 14

At 8:30 a.m. received following message from Maj. Waller: "Your rations are at the ammunition dump. Kitchens have not yet arrived. Let me know what you want done with them. I have no idea where you are—where your guns are, let me know right away." Waller.

At 8:40 a.m. sent following message to Major Waller "Will send detail for rations. We did not get into position until late last night. Will send sketch as soon as I can get completely over the line which is difficult on account of shelling" Kingman.

About 11:45 a.m. sent Maj. Waller sketch of our positions.

At 7:10 p.m. sent following message to Maj. Waller:

"The 3d. Bn. takes over the Army line between Jaulny and Xammes tonight. Am moving two platoons for their support. Will send sketch of new positions as soon as guns are definitely located." Kingman.

About dark the 3d Bn moved their line forward to the Army line by passing the 97th and 84th Cos. thru the 82d. and 83d Cos. who remained in place. Our 2nd platoon moved with the 97th (rt) and 1st platoon joined the 84th on the left. The 3d platoon remained in place.

Sept. 15

About 11:00 a.m. received message from Maj. Waller that 78th Div. would relieve the 2nd. Div. tonight and that details of the relief would be sent out later.

At noon the 2nd platoon fired about 300 rds at a German plane flying low over our positions. The tracer bullets were seen to pass thru the wings of the machine and close to the body but he was not brought down.

At 5:00 p.m. received message from Major Waller that relief of machine guns would not take place till following evening.

Remained in this position till the relief Sept. 16. During the day and evening it was fairly quiet with occasional shelling with H.E.

REMARKS

It is recommended that the men be furnished shelter halves and that they carry a roll over the shoulder of a blanket and shelter halve.

We experienced [sic] in getting hot meals. I believe the train officers can handle the kitchens better by working directly with the companies than thru the orders of the Q.M.

The bottoms of the strip containers are not substantial enough for a long advance where they receive rough handling by tired men.

We carried 2500 rds ammunition per gun. This would not have been possible had we not an excess of about 25 men over our authorized complement [possibly prepared by 1st Lt. Edmund P. Norwood, who took the place of commanding officer 1st Lt. Jack Hart after he was wounded on 14 September].

Headquarters Sixth Machine Gun Battalion,
Marine Corps, Am. E. F., France Sept. 22, 1918.

MEMORANDUM: For Company Commanders.

1. There is returned herewith report of operations recently submitted by you, and you are directed to submit a supplementary report if the original does not cover fully all the operations of the company under your command. If the original report is complete so state.

2. This supplementary report must be submitted to this office by 3:00 p.m. this date as a report from this office to Division is required to be at Division by Noon.

Copy to A Co.   By Order of Major Waller:
    B Co.   J.[ames] P. Schwerin,
    D Co.   2nd Lieut. M.C.R. C Co.

Memo for Battalion Commander:
There is nothing further to add to this report.
(Sgd) J.[ohn] P. McCann
Capt. M.C.

23 Co. 6 M.G. Battalion, U.S. Marines.
France Sept. 17, 1918.

From: C.O. Company "B" [23d Machine Gun Company]
To: Battalion Commander
Subject: Operations report. Sept. 12 to Sept. 15, 1918 inclusive.

1. The following is a report of operations of Company "B" from September 12, 1918 to September 15, 1918.

2. At 8:45 p.m. September 11, 1918 moved out of Bois des Hayes, took up Barrage position 500 yards N. E. of Limey (366.1-234.1 map Thiaucourt 1/10,000) at 5:00 a.m. September 12,

1918 put down a machine gun Barrage, indirect overhead, lasting 50 minutes, expending 20,000 rounds of ammunition, upon the completion of Barrage men were ordered into trenches and dugouts in the vicinity of the gun positions, there awaiting the arrival of the 2nd Battalion, 5th Regiment, Marines.

At 8:15 a.m. I reported to the Battalion Commander, of the 2nd Battalion, and received orders for the company to join his battalion, forming in the rear. Advanced with the 2nd Battalion in squad column formation, by hand, each gun crew having 9 boxes of strip ammunition. I took my post with the Battalion Commander, 2nd Battalion, and advanced during the day through Remenauville, Bois du Four and Bois d'Heiche, nothing out of the ordinary happened during the advance. Arrived at Hill #282.1, at about 7:00 p.m. the Battalion formed here, 365.5-240.9, in support of 3rd Battalion 5th Regiment. Machine guns taking up position on both flanks and in rear of battalion. Remained in this formation until about 9:30 p.m. when I received instructions to have the men bivouac for the night at 365.4-240.5. There were no rations so the men were allowed to eat part of reserve rations. Nothing happened during the night. Remained at this point until 5:00 p.m. Sept. 13 1918, when by order of the Battalion Commander the Company moved forward in rear of the 2nd Battalion where a position was taken on ridge north of road leading to Thiaucourt. One platoon was put in position on right of line, to protect right flank, One platoon on left to protect left flank; and one platoon in rear to fire overhead to the front. 1st platoon on right 365.8-241.4, 2nd platoon 364.8-241.3, 3rd platoon rear 365.3-241.35, no rations received, men ate their reserve rations, each man dug in and dug emplacements for guns. I did not relieve any machine gun organization here, when the 2nd Battalion took over, there was a little desultory shelling during the night, one private being wounded slightly.

At about 9:00 a.m. Sept. 14, this position was shelled by the enemy at intervals for about 30 minutes, this Harassing fire was kept up by the enemy during the day, one private being wounded slightly. At about 3 p.m. received first cooked rations from Company. At about 5:15 p.m. a German plane was brought down, presumably by machine gun fire from this Company, fell about 50 yards in rear of the 1st platoon, the aviator was badly wounded and was taken prisoner by the infantry and evacuated. At about 10:55 p.m. received word from Battalion Commander, 2nd Battalion, that there was a Counter attack expected at 1:00 a.m. All guns were notified and kept on the alert. Word was received at 2:00 a.m. that the counter attack did not materialize. Shelling by the enemy was continued at intervals during day & night. At 6:15 a.m. Sept. 15 Private Porter E.[rnest] W. was killed by fragment from aerial bomb, which also wounded Corporal [Fred H.] Underwood slightly. Pvt. Porter was buried near where he was killed, 364.80-241.31. 8:10 a.m. P.O. heavily shelled by enemy. 11:00 a.m. P.O. was moved to the ravine in rear of ridge 364.5-241.3. At 3:30 p.m. received word that the Company would be relieved night of 15-16, reconnoitered the position with the Machine Gun Captain, from the 78th Division, At about 8:00 p.m. was informed that company would not be relieved until nights of 16–17 Sept. 4:00 a.m. Sept. 16 the 2nd Battalion moved out of this position relieved. At daybreak by authority of Battalion Commander, M.G. Battalion withdrew guns from hill, and placed them on the reverse slope, two men from each platoon being kept on watch as observers. Nothing occurred during the day. At 8:00 p.m. by order of Battalion Commander evacuated this position, and proceeded to Bois d'Heiche where we bivouaced. for the night.

REMARKS

After the 14th of September, hot meals were received regularly from Company kitchen twice a day, meals were not allowed to be brought up during daylight, as they were under observation of enemy observation balloons.

The most important fault noticed was the failure of all men of all organizations, to keep under cover.

(Sgd) John P. McCann.

Night of Sept. 11th-12th enroute to barrage positions on right flank of 2nd Division line of advance base gun right gun 366.53-234.46 (maps used Thiaucourt 1/10,000 & Hayeville 1/10,000) went in battery "grid north" guns echeloned by platoons to left rear at 4:00 a.m. Sept.

12th, 1918. 5:00 a.m. the 12th opened fire at zero hour with all guns on enemy's targets previously designated by Battalion commander maintained fire on barrage schedule for twenty-eight (28) minutes. Shifted fire of guns firing on nearest targets to those farthest away as our infantry advanced. All guns eventually concentrated on most distant target, all guns functioned fine, expended 30,000 rounds of ammunition, changed barrels and cleaned guns upon completion of firing, remained in position till 8:30 a.m. the 12th. Joined 3rd Battalion 5th Marines as they passed through in support of the 9th Infantry, assigned 1st platoon under command of 2nd Lt. Galtowski[3] to operate with 16th Company 5th Marines, the 3rd Platoon under command of 2nd Lt. [Fitzhugh Lee] Buchanan to the 20th Co. 5th Marines, and the 2nd Platoon under command of 1st Lt. [John O.] Hyatt held in reserve, halted north side of Harricot hill 9 a.m. During advance 2nd Lt. [Herbert G. Joerger] Joeryer and six enlisted men wounded by grenade mine in wire entanglements and one gun so damaged that it was put out of action, resumed advance at 9:10 a.m. to point 364.50-241.30. Took up reserve position at 18:00 hours north side of ravine, nothing of importance occurred during advance to this point. Encountered very little enemy's fire during advance, at 20th hour upon request of Commanding Officer 9th Infantry, who feared for his front line, Major Shearer comdg 3d Battalion 5th Marines sent two Co's to assist in holding front line. All machine guns accompanied 16th and 20th Co's 5 Marines and took up position on hill from cross roads 261.10 to and including woods 277.70 continued in this position until 4:30 hours when relieved by 23rd Infantry and their machine gun unit withdrew to position on crest of hill on northside of ravine 364.50-241.30 continued in these positions with the following exception until 23d hour Sept 14th at 18:30 hour the 45th Co 5th Marines and two machine guns left with orders to patrol to the north edge of Bois de Hailbat the 47th CO 5th Marines and two machine guns left with orders to patrol to the northern edge of Bois de la Montagne to establish lines at these points—at the 23rd hour Sept 14th the two remaining Co's (16th and 20th) and balance of machine gun company consisting of seven guns broke camp to go into position to support 1st Battalion 5th Marines who held front line, against threatened counter-attack, followed ravine to western edge of Bois du Fey, thence followed edge of wood and river road to Jaulny and took up position about on hill 400 yds southeast of Jaulny at 1:00 o'clock.

Sept. 15th at 3:30 enemy put over an intense artillery barrage our front lines and position occupied by us which lasted for one hour and a half no attack followed. At 5330 in compliance with orders regimental Commander 5th Marines 16th and 20th Co's 5th Marines and Machine Guns moved forward to consolidate front lines northern edge Bois de Montague and Bois de Hailbat, the 2nd Platoon Machine Guns accompanied the 20th Company to Bois de Montague and the 1st Platoon, the 16th Co. to the Bois de Hailbat, established my P.C. at 3rd. Bn. Hdqs 5th Marines point 365.60-243.40. During this advance 2nd Lt. Buchanan (who started out in command of these guns) 1 corporal and two privates were wounded by shell fire and evacuated. The 47th Co. stopped in the North west side of the Bois de la Montague the line being held by the 95th & 78 Companies attached to 47th Co. Sgt. Long in command of the two MG. took up position to assist Co. D 6th MG. B. 363.40-245.50. The 20th Company took up support position in south and Bois du Rupt. Machine Guns remained with company and took up positions 364.45-243.4.

The 16th Co. and M.G.s joined the 45th Co. about 8:30 the 15th established along Northern edge Bois de Hailbat 365.0 to 368.30—Machine Guns were placed at 365.20-243.60, 365.40-243.40, 385.70-243.80, 365.80-243.95, 365, 85-243.60 and 366.10-243.70. Relieved from line the evening the 16th by the Regt. M.G. Co. 309th Infantry.

A.[ugustus] B. Hale
Capt. USMC
Commanding Co. C, 6th M.G.B.

Report of Operations
Co. C 6th M.G.B. [77th]
Sept. 12th to 15th 1918
Supplementary.

Sept 14th at 5:15 #12 gun in charge of Pvt. [Edward J.] Hamp fired on and brought down German airplane—The pilot badly wounded in the legs by machine gun bullets was made prisoner. Lieut. [John O.] Hyatt was evacuated to Hospital, sick.

A. B. Hale,
Capt. M.C.

Headquarters Sixth Machine Gun Battalion,
Marine Corps, Am. E.F., France, Sept. 22, 1918.

MEMORANDUM: For Company Commanders.

1. There is returned herewith report of operations recently submitted by you, and you are directed to submit a supplementary report if the original does not cover fully all the operations of the company under your command. If the original report is complete, so state.

2. This supplementary report must be submitted to this office by 3:00 p.m. this date, as a report from this office to Division is required to be at Division by Noon.

Copy to	By order of Major Waller:
A Co	
B Co	J. P. Schwerin,
D Co	2nd Lieut. M.C.R.
C Co	Acting Adjutant

At 8:30 p.m. Sept. 11, we broke camp and moved into positions on the right Limey (366.15-233.695—reference Thiaucourt map 1/10,000).

At 5:00 a.m. Sept. 12 began 40 mm. barrage (62 rounds per gun per min) Targets: 1st Platoon, Communicating trench

(366.05-235.80 to 365.85-236.35)

2nd Platoon, Communicating trench

(365.86-235.74 to 365.62-236.42)

3rd Platoon Barracks

(365.70-236.75 and 365.85-236.85)

At 5:40 moved forward in support of 2nd Bn 6th Reg. Reached main objective (Thiaucourt) at 6:30 p.m. Dug in in the northern outskirts of Thiaucourt where we staid until 4 a.m. Sept 15.

At 4 a.m. we moved forward to take up position in support of 3rd Bn 6th Reg. At about 5 a.m. the 3rd. Bn. not being in position it was thought to be in, we were fired on by enemy machine guns, we were at 364.2-243.2. An enemy artillery barrage was put down behind us and we were ordered by Bn. Com. to attack. The 1st Platoon, under Lt. [Robert L.] Young, was sent to the right flank, the 3rd Platoon under Lt. [George] Bower was sent to the left flank. The 2nd Platoon was held in reserve. The right flank advanced until it was held up by machine guns stationed around Mon Plaisir farm. Positions were then taken up in the trenches about 600 yds southwest of M. Plaisir Farm. The left flank advanced to about 800 yds south of Charey. The guns were in position along the unimproved between Charey and Bois de Montagne. The enemy counter attacked and the infantry was driven back to the edge of the woods. 2 guns were blown up & one had to be abandoned when the infantry was ordered to fall back. Lt. Bower was wounded and Sgt. [Marmaduke] Sharp, the senior N.C.O. took the 3rd platoon and three guns back to Thiaucourt. At about 5 p.m. after a heavy barrage of about 10 min, the enemy counterattacked our Center, but was driven off with heavy losses. Two of the reserve guns under Lt. [Vernon] Bourdette were put in position at 364.3-245 (Chamblay 5–6 map) and got enfilading fire. (Heavy G[erman] casualties).

At about 11 p.m. the infantry was relieved by 2nd Bn of 310th Inf and their machine guns were put in position. At about 11:30 P. L Sgt. Sharp returned from Thiaucourt and his platoon was held in reserve behind the left flank.

Relieved at 9:30 p.m. Sept. 16—relieved by Rgt Co. of 310th who were in for 24 hours prior. (Thought 3rd Bn was ahead—told so by Williams.)

When the infantry began falling back 2 guns from the reserve platoon were sent to the left flank.

10:10 a.m.

8. Sixth Machine Gun Battalion

Headquarters, Sixth Machine Gun Battalion
Marine Corps, Am. E. F., France, Sept. 22, 1918

From: Commanding Officer, Sixth Machine Gun Battalion.
To: Commanding General, Second Division.
Subject: Operations Report September 12 to 15, 1918.
Reference: (a) Memo. Hq. 2nd Div. Sept. 20, 1918.

1. The Operations Report submitted by the undersigned on the 17th instant is complete and there is no additional data to be added thereto.

(Sgd) L.W.T. WALLER, Jr.

Headquarters Sixth Machine Gun Battalion,
Marine Corps, Am. E. F., France, Sept. 17, 1918.

From: Commanding Officer, Sixth Machine Gun Battalion.
To: Commanding General, Second Division.
Subject: Operation Report from Sept. 12 to Sept. 15, 1918.
a) MEMO. 74 HQ 2nd Div. dated 9-16-18.
Enclosures: 3

1. List of casualties sustained, approximate list of captured property brought out by battalion and complete inventory of the personnel are attached.

2. In submitting operation report for the Sixth Machine Gun Battalion each company has submitted separately as they were attached to different battalions and assigned different parts of the line.

3. Prior to September 12th this battalion moved to the vicinity of the line, where it prepared machine gun barrage positions, carried forward and established ammunition dumps, and prepared everything for laying down a barrage.

Company "A" [15th]

September 12: At 12:45 a.m. this company was in position North of LIMEY, grouped into three batteries of four (4) guns each:

The Right Battery   365.37-233.97, 365.44-233.98
The Centre Battery   365.28-233.98, 365.34-233.97
The Left Battery   365.22-233.94, 365.27-233.97

At 5:00 a.m. a barrage was laid down covering important trenches, strong points, P.C.s, etc., of the enemy, using indirect overhead fire over the 3rd Brigade.

At 5:48 a.m. the barrage ceased, having fired about 15,000 rounds.

At 6:00 a.m. Company "A" joined the 3rd Battalion of the 6th Marines, to which it was assigned and which passed through gun positions at about that time, and took up the advance with them. One platoon was on line with the supporting companies on the right flank, one on the left flank, and one in rear of the centre. Platoons leap-frogged forward during the advance, rate of advance 100 meters in 4 minutes. The machine guns had no difficulty in keeping up.

About 2:00 p.m. arrived at THIAUCOURT and went into support position about one (1) kilometer North of town. Formation same in during advance.

September 13: The guns of "A" Company were changed a little in order to belt-fire the position, and remained in that position all day.

September 14: About dark the 3rd Battalion, 6th Regiment, moved forward to the Army Line with the 97th and 84th Companies. The Second Platoon moved up with the 97th Company, the First Platoon joined the 84th Company on the left, and the Third Platoon remained in place.

September 15: Infantry Battalion was relieved, machine guns remaining in position until the night of September 16th, when they were relieved by the 78th Division.

Company "B" [23d]

September 12: Barrage positions of B Company were about 500 yards Northeast of LIMEY—366.1-234.1. Barrage lasted 50 minutes. Upon completion of barrage B Company remained in place awaiting arrival of the 2nd Battalion, 5th Regiment, Marines. At 8:15 a.m. joined 2nd Battalion advancing in squad column formation with the support line of the Battalion.

The Battalion reached hill 282.1, Southeast of THIAUCOURT at about 7:00 p.m. and formed in support of the 3rd Battalion, 5th Regiment, the guns taking up positions on both flanks and in rear of the centre of the Battalion.

September 13th:—At about 5:00 p.m. moved forward with the 2nd Battalion and took position on ridge north of road leading to THIAUCOURT (385.8-241.4). Dug gun emplacements for guns.

September 14: At 5:15 p.m. a German plane was brought down by machine gun fire of B and C companies, falling near their positions. The aviator was captured.

September 15: Remained in place.

September 16: The 2nd Battalion, 6th Regiment, was relieved, machine guns remaining in position. At 8:00 p.m. this Company withdrew, there being no company from the 78th Division that could relieve it.

Company "C" [77th]

September 12: Company C's barrage position (366.53-234.46) Upon completion of barrage fire C Company remained in place until about 8:30 a.m., when they joined the 3rd Battalion, 5th Marines, as they passed through the barrage position. During the advance one (1) officer and six (6) men were wounded, and one gun destroyed by a grenade mine in enemy's barb wire entanglements. At about 6:00 p.m. took up position on North side of ravine to the East of THIAUCOURT. About 8:00 p.m. C Company accompanied the 16th and 20th Companies, 5th Marines, which went forward to support the 9th Infantry who feared a counterattack. Remained in position 261.10 until about 4:30 p.m. September 13th, when relieved by the 23rd Infantry. Guns withdrawn to crest of hill 364.50-241.30.

September 14: At 6:30 p.m. two machine guns were sent to accompany the 45th Company, 5th Marines, on patrol to the North edge of BOIS DE HAILBAT, and two guns to the 47th Company, 5th Marines, which was to patrol the Northern edge of BOIS DE LA MONTAGNE.

At 11:00 p.m. remainder of the company went forward with balance of the Battalion to support the 1st Battalion, 5th Marines, and took up position 400 yards Southeast of JAULNEY.

September 15: At 5:30 a.m. moved forward to consolidate the Northern edge of BOIS DE LA MONTAGNE and BOIS DE HAILBAT, machine guns being placed on that line on both sides of the road, where they remained until the evening of September 16th when they were relieved by the Regimental Machine Gun Company of the 309th Infantry.

D Company [81st]

September 12: Barrage positions of Company D (366.15-233.69). Barrage lasted 36 minutes. At 5:40 a.m. moved forward in support of 2nd Battalion, 6th Regiment. Reached Thiaucourt at about 6:30 p.m. Dug in on Northern outskirts of town where they remained until about 4:00 a.m. September 15th.

September 15: At 4:00 a.m. moved forward to take up position in support of 3rd Battalion, 6th Regiment, as it was thought. At about 5:00 a.m. at 384.2-243.2 fired on by enemy machine guns, and an artillery barrage was put down behind the companies. Attacked on orders of Battalion Commander, the 1st Platoon supporting right flank, the 3rd Platoon the left flank, and the 2nd Platoon held in reserve.

Right flank platoon advanced with the infantry until the line was held up by enemy machine gun fire from MONPLAISIR FARM, and positions were taken up in drill trenches about 500 yards Southeast of the farm.

The left flank platoon advanced to about 800 yards South of CHAIREY, and the guns took position along the unimproved road between CHAIREY and BOIS DE LA MONTAGNE.

The enemy counter-attacked and the infantry fell back to the edge of the woods. Two (2) reserve guns were sent to the left flank, making a total of six (6) guns on that flank. Two (2) of these guns were blown out with artillery fire and one (1) had to be abandoned. Owing to the speed with which the infantry fell back it was impossible to keep up, the machine guns at one time on that flank being surrounded on three sides by the enemy.

The left platoon was badly scattered and fell back to THIAUCOURT where it was reformed. At about 5:00 p.m. accompanied by a heavy barrage, the enemy counter-attacked the right flank but was repulsed with heavy losses. In retreating the enemy's advance wave presented itself to infilade fire from one section of two (2) guns and was entirely wiped out, position of guns 364.3-245.

September 16: At about 1:00 p.m. the infantry was relieved by the 2nd Battalion of the 310th, their machine guns accompanying the relief.

Company D remained in position until 9:30 p.m. when it was relieved.

4. During the time this Battalion was in support with the 4th Brigade very few casualties were sustained and nothing of note happened.

5. In the positions around THIAUCOURT the machine guns were at all times subjected to artillery fire, and in some instances under very heavy fire.

6. Companies C and D were practically the only companies who had much fighting to do, and this occurred in extending of the line of observation beyond the Army Line.

7. It is to be noted that D Company as well as the 2nd Battalion, 6th Regiment, in their advance beyond the Army Objective, did not know that they were in the front line and thought until they were attacked that they were acting in support of our own troops; consequently the formations were those of a support and not of a combat line. The left platoon of D Company was held well in place until Lieutenant [George] Bower, platoon commander, was wounded. And the retreat from that flank took place when they were caught in a depression of the ground and subjected to intense machine gun and artillery fire. The platoon was scattered and retreated to THIAUCOURT, where it reformed and returned to the Company.

(Sgd) L.W.T. Waller, Jr.
Headquarters Sixth Machine Gun Battalion,
Marine Corps, Am. E. F., France, Sept. 17, 1918.

CAPTURED PROPERTY
4 Horses
6 Wagons
8 Light Machine Guns, Maxim
4 Heavy Machine Guns, Maxim
10000 Rounds Maxim Ammunition.
(Sgd) L. W. T. Waller, Jr.
Major, U.S.M.C.
Commanding 6th M. G. B.

This was the end of the St. Mihiel campaign by the 4th Brigade. General John Pershing, commanding the American Expeditionary Forces, had already committed the Second Division to the French Army in order to break a strong German position on the Blanc Mont Heights, just west of the Argonne forest. The Germans had held this position, overlooking the great city of Rheims, since the war had begun.

It was a threat to that city and the French line for years, and the French had suffered huge losses trying to retake it. Now it was the "opportunity" of the Second Division to drive the Germans, who had many strong positions, towards the north and the Aisne River.

October 1–10, 1918
"B" Company 6th Machine Gun Battalion, U.S. Marine Corps
France, October 13, 1918.

The following report of events covers October 1 to October 10, 1918, Map Tahure 1/20,000.

October 1, 1918.
Joined the 2nd Battalion, 5th Regiment at 5:45 p.m. on Ano ne Chaussee Romaine route in Bois de la Cote 170 at 267-270. 1-4. Weather fair and cold.

Marched from Bois de la Cote 170 at 7:15 p.m. along Ano ne Chaussee Romaine route in an easterly direction to national route #77 Nevers Sedan, where we turned toward the north on the latter, traveling almost due north through Souain to Somme-Py.

Machine guns were carried by hand from point 268-274-10-7. Each crew carrying 9 containers of ammunition. All the remaining ammunition was dumped here by order Company Commander no guard being left on the same. One runner being detailed to remember the location of said dump. No information given the platoon commanders regarding dump locations. Result: 36 belt containers and 128 Strip containers were salvaged by some one. The same consisting of kitchen, water cart, and ration cart received orders to follow the company. Roads were bad and blocked by traffic. Lieut. [Axel] Enholm in charge of the train had no orders as to where he would take the train in case he lost the company, which he did near Navarin Farm. He on the morning of the 2nd of October joined the supply train of the 2nd Battalion, 5th Regiment, off road near Navarin Farm we were shelled lightly near the Farm, but suffered no casualties.

October 2, 1918.

Company arrived at Somme-Py at or about 2:00 a.m., where we relieved the French in the support positions along the railway running through the southern edge of the town.

Our left being the Railway station and our right being along railway embankment at 269-277-2-2 Company P.C., being at 268-276-7-9. Relief was made without being shelled but under a harassing machine gun fire by enemy. No casualties. During day October 2nd enemy shelled. Suffered one casualty. At 8:00 p.m. all platoon commanders reported to Company Commander's P.C., and, were notified of the planned attack at 6:00 a.m. October 3rd, and of the infantry formation and our own in said attack.

October 3, 1918.

At 6:00 a.m. the 2nd Battalion, 5th Regiment, moved to left of Somme-Py along railway, with the right at point 7666 the Battalion formed two companies in first line and two in second line. Companies being formed in combat groups. Machine gun company followed second line in line of squad or gun columns. We moved forward in rear of the 3rd Battalion, 5th Regiment, followed by the 1st Battalion, 5th Regiment at about 7:45 a.m. The Sixth Regiment being the attacking Regiment.

October 3, 1918.

As we advanced we were subjected to a heavy shell fire and machine gun fire from our left flank, we suffered few casualties in this advance as everyone took advantage of all available cover. The Sixth Regiment having gained their objective, the 2nd Battalion 5th Regiment took up front line on left of Sixth Regiment, along old improved road from point 266-280-4-5 in trench de Etienne south to point 286-260-4-0. In taking up this position we were subject to heavy shell and machine gun fire. Two platoons of Machine Guns were put in line and one platoon held in support near Company Commander's P.C., in trench near cross roads at 267-279-9-8.

At 10:00 p.m. received orders to draw back to point 267-280-7-0. Remained here until 6:00 a.m. October 4th.

October 4, 1918.

5th Regiment formed for attack on road side. Right flank at point 266-260-7-10, left flank at 266-260-4-7. Formed in this order head to rear. 3rd, Battalion, 2nd Battalion, 1st Battalion, were subject to violent shell fire and some gas while forming.

Two machine guns crews were knocked out here. Two platoons of machine guns were supporting and one platoon in reserve slightly to rear. Distance between Battalions 400 meters. Direction of attack toward St. Etienne and parallel to St. Etienne–Somme-Py road. Met no resistance, but under shell fire from an arc.

Enemy machine gun fire came from both flanks, right and front. Reached point 285-283-3-2 at about 12:00 a.m. The Infantry withdrew at once to point 265-282-5-9, where the line was established. Two platoons remained at farthest point of advance for three hours until the line had been formed then come back on line with the Infantry, which had its right in the woods on right of St. Etienne–Somme-Py road at 268-282-1-5.

Line extended along same road to 285-282-5-9, then west to point 265-282-8-4. Had liaison with 5th Machine Gun Battalion, Company on right no one on left. In afternoon company commander and second in command were casualties. Train under Lieut. Enholm moved up to Somme-Py from where we received two hot meals per day and established an ammunition dump at 267-7-279-9.

October 5, 1918.
Held same position.

October 6, 1918.
Held same position.

October 7, 1918.
At or about 10:00 p.m. 2nd Battalion, 5th Regiment and [8th] Machine
Gun Co. withdrew and took up reserve positions along trench de St. Etienne from 266-8-281-2 to 267-5-281-1.

October 8, 1918.
Held reserve positions.

October 9, 1918.
Received orders to effect that the company was relieved and started at 3:00 a.m. October 10, 1918.

October 10, 1918.
Marched through Somme-Py picked up train there, then along national highway #77 Nevers Sedan road through Souain back by way of Battalion train located in Bois de la Cusines Boches, where company had breakfast, picked up packs left there and marched through Suippes to Camp Marchand, arriving there at about 4:00 p.m.

W.[illiam] B. Croka
Captain, USMC
Commanding.

October 1–10, 1918
(Brigade) Report of Operations
SIXTH MACHINE GUN BATTALION
October 1 to October 10, 1918. inclusive.

Map: Tahure 1/20,000.

October 1, 1918:
Received orders for an advance toward Somme-Py; advance to position to be made largely at night, and as the roads were not well defined and liable to become conjested, the Companies of this battalion were ordered to join the Infantry Battalions with which they usually worked. No orders had been received as to the disposition of machine guns, but it was thought that they would be assigned to the infantry. Companies were assigned as follows:

    A Company   3rd Battalion, 6th Marines.
    B   "   2nd   "   5th   "
    C   "   3rd   "   5th   "
    D   "   2nd   "   6th   "

A COMPANY established liaison with the 3rd Battalion, 6th Marines, about 3:00 p.m. At 6:00 p.m. it broke camp and marched along the Souain–Somme Suippe Road, where it joined the 3rd Battalion. At a point about 2 kilometers south of Somme-Py, position was taken in the trench de Gottinque about 4:00 a.m., Oct. 2nd.

B COMPANY joined the 2nd Battalion, 5th Marines at 5:45 p.m. at 267-270 and marched with them at 7:15 p.m. via the route National to Somme-Py, arriving there at about 2:00 a.m., October 2nd and relieved the French in the support positions along the railway running through the southern edge of town: Left of Company at railway station, and the right along embankment at 269.-277.

C COMPANY joined the 3rd Battalion, 5th Marines on the Chaussere–Romaine, and marched with it. Relieved the French units in reserve line trench de Gottinque at 275.6-288.5,—two platoons relieving the French in Gottinque and one platoon relieving the French in trench Stuttgart 275.9-268.7. Relief completed at 3:30 a.m., October 2nd.

D COMPANY joined the 2nd Battalion, 6th Marines, and relieved the French units west of Somme-Py, in vicinity of 288-277.4. Relief completed at about 4:00 a.m., October 2nd. French were confused and uncertain about their own positions and those of enemy

Roads badly congested.

October 2, 1918:

A COMPANY remained in place all day. Attack scheduled for 11:00 a.m. postponed for 24 hours.

B COMPANY remained in place. Subjected to harassing fire from machine guns all day.

C COMPANY remained in place. Guns set up for and fired at enemy avions. Shelled intermittently by enemy artillery.

D COMPANY remained in place. Established two new gun positions 266.8-277.6.

October 3, 1918:

A COMPANY attacked at 5:00 a.m.; 1st Platoon with 82nd Company on right flank, 2nd Platoon supporting rear center of battalion, and 3rd Platoon supporting left flank. Company Commander, Captain Kingman, was with Battalion Commander. Reached objective without incident, taking up line 279.8-266.8-280.3-267.6. Remained in this position until October 4th.

B COMPANY formed for attack with 2nd Battalion, 5th Marines, along railway embankment west of Somme-Py. Machine guns followed in 2nd wave in squad columns. Advance begun at 745 a.m.

Company was subjected to heavy artillery and machine gun fire from left flank. The 6th Marines was the assault regiment, and on gaining its objective, the 2nd Battalion, 5th Marines, took up position on left of 6th Marines along old improved road from point 266-280 in trench de Etienne, toward the south, two platoons of machine guns in line and one platoon held in support. At 10:00 p.m. drew back, acting on orders, to point 267-280. Remained here until 5:00 a.m. October 4th.

C COMPANY took up positions in trench Dusseldorf 275.7-267.8, at 5:00 a.m.; 1st platoon with 3rd Battalion Headquarters as reserve, 2nd platoon with 18th Company, and 3rd platoon with 45th Company. Attacked in general direction of 343 degrees compass bearing, battalion in support of 5th Regiment. Attack started at 5:50 a.m. Advance made to Bois de Somme-Py, arriving there at 2:00 p.m. Remained in this position until 6:30 p.m. then moved forward to road 281-266.7; right flank at crossroads 281.07-267.2, left flank about 900 metres west of crossroads. Gas and shell fire on crossroads at night. Remained in this position until 6:00 a.m. October 4th.

D COMPANY received orders to advance at 5:50 a.m.—orders received at 5:40 a.m.; 1st platoon advanced with right support Company, third platoon with left support Company, and 2nd platoon held at Battalion Headquarters as a reserve. All platoons slow in moving out due to lateness of receipt of orders. Objective gained at 8:30 am., and consolidated; 4 guns on right flank, one gun with each center Company, and 3 guns on left flank. One gun with 5th Regiment, having become lost from the Company it joined the 5th Marines on its advance.

October 4, 1918:

A COMPANY, at 5:00 p.m. 1st and 3rd platoons supported 82nd and 84th Companies in advance on machine gun nests on Blanc Mont. At 6:00 p.m. withdrew and remained in place until next day.

B COMPANY attacked with 5th Regiment, acting with support battalion. Two crews knocked out while forming for attack. Much gas and shell fire. Two platoons supporting and one in reserve.

Direction of attack toward St. Etienne and parallel to St. Etienne–Somme-Py road. Were shelled from arc of 300 degrees but met with no resistance. Reached point 265-283 about noon. Infantry fell back to point 265-282 and consolidated, two platoons remaining in advanced positions 3 hours to cover consolidation. Right of line in woods on right of St. Etienne–Somme-Py Road at 266-282.

Line extended along the road a short way and then toward the west. Company Commander and 2nd in Command were casualties.

C COMPANY at 8:00 a.m. leap-frogged the 6th Marines and advanced in general direction

343 degrees compass bearing. Advance made without artillery preparation, and met with considerable artillery and machine gun fire. Platoons assigned as follows 1st with 20th Company as left flank protection, 2nd with 16th Company, left flank of leading wave; and 3rd with 45th Company, right flank of leading wave. Advance was made to point about 3 kilometers north of crossroads. Encountered much opposition on right of line. On left, units met heavy machine and one pounder fire from front end left flank, and suffered heavy casualties. The 47th and 45th Companies advanced through woods toward St. Etienne, 3rd platoon using direct overhead fire to assist the advance. The infantry and machine guns were suddenly subjected to heavy machine gun fire from the front and flanks, apparently the woods had not been cleared out during the advance.

The infantry retired harassed by machine gun fire, and the advance was stopped due to heavy casualties and lack of support on flanks, notably the left flank. All guns were organized on line 265.5-282.4, 266.3-282.3. Company now had only 9 guns; others destroyed by shell fire or crews casualties in the advance.

About 7:00 a.m., the 2nd platoon with the 16th Company encountered the enemy at close quarters, who attacked with hand grenades and tried to put the gun crews out of action before guns could be set up. The attack was held up by pistol fire until the guns could be put in action.

D COMPANY remained in place.

October 5, 1918:
A COMPANY moved into support position behind 2nd Battalion, 6th Regiment, and held front line for remainder of day. This line was from 284.2-265.4 to 284.2-268.1. The objective was 287.1-283.0 to 287.6-266.0, but was not reached.

B COMPANY remained in place

C COMPANY remained in place.

D COMPANY remained in place.

October 6, 1918:
A COMPANY at daylight moved forward to attack enemy positions on the ridge due east of St. Etienne, passing through 1st Battalion. Artillery preparation from 5:30 a.m. to 6:30 a.m. Attack succeeded. Formation of guns the same as for previous attacks. All platoons on the line for consolidation.

B COMPANY remained in place.

C COMPANY at about 7:30 p.m. drooped back to trench de St. Etienne on the slope of Blanc Mont.

D COMPANY remained in place, becoming reserve on advance of 5th Regiment. At 4:30 p.m. moved forward, taking up positions along the ridge south of St. Etienne.

October 7, 1918:
A COMPANY remained in place. During the night the 142nd Infantry arrived and occupied same positions.

B COMPANY, at about 10:00 p.m. withdrew, and took up reserve positions along trench de St. Etienne, from 266.8-281.2 to 287.5-281.1.

C COMPANY remained in place.

D COMPANY withdrew and took up reserve positions on Blanc Mont ridge.

October 8, 1918:
A COMPANY remained in place. 141st Infantry advanced at 5:20 a.m.

B COMPANY remained in place.

C COMPANY remained in place.

D COMPANY remained in place.

October 9, 1918:
A COMPANY remained in place. 3rd Battalion, 6th Marines, relieved.

B COMPANY remained in place during day. Started relief at 3:00 a.m. October 10th. Marched back along route National, arriving at Camp Marchand 4:00 p.m. October 10th.

C COMPANY remained in place during the day. Relieved at 2:30 a.m. October 10th. Marched to Camp Marchand, arriving at 3:00 p.m. October 10th.

D COMPANY remained in place during day. Relieved at night by machine guns from the 36th Division, relief completed at 1:30 a.m. Marched to Camp Marchand, arriving during afternoon of October 10th.

October 10, 1918:
A COMPANY relieved about dark. Marched to Camp Marchand, arriving about 4:00 a.m., October 11, 1918.

On the relief by the 36th Division, one officer per Company and one non-commissioned officer per platoon were left for 24 hours. All maps and data were turned over to the relieving units.

Relief was made in some instances and in others Companies were withdrawn on the passage of lines of the 36th Division. This relief was badly bungled, the relieving division having no orders, instructions or idea of what they were to do. The relief started on October 8th and was completed on October 10, 1918.

The Battalion Commander of the machine gun battalion relieving this battalion was never seen, nor could he be located.

(Sgd) L. W. T. Waller, Jr.
Major, U.S.M.C.
Commanding.

Meuse-Argonne

That was the end for the Blanc Mont campaign. The Second Division and all its units moved farther east to help Pershing's army to break the massive German positions and slash through to the Meuse River. By 1 November they were at the starting gate.

"B" Company, 6th Machine Gun Battalion, U.S. Marine Corps,
Luxemburg, November 26, 1918.

From: Company Commander.
To: Battalion Commander, Sixth Machine Gun Battalion.
Subject: Report of operations October 31, 1918 to November 11, 1918

1. For the operations covered by the above dates under Field Order #49, two Platoons of Company "B," Sixth Machine Gun Battalion were assigned to the 2nd Battalion, 5th Regiment Marines, joining that unit at 'H' Hour November 1, 1918 after laying down harassing fire from prepared positions for two hours before 'H' hour. The third Platoon was assigned to duty with the liaison company which connected on the right with the 89th Division. Detailed report of operations is as follows:

2. October 31st, 8:00 p.m. commenced construction of machine gun emplacements for eight guns on ridge one and one half kilometers north east of Sommerance completing same at midnight.

November 1st. At 3:30 a.m. commenced firing harassing fire with two platoons (eight guns), continuing until 'H' hour or 5:30 a.m. Rate of fire 25 per minute. This fire was concentrated on designated areas in the vicinity of Landres St. Georges at ranges from 1700 to 2000 meters each section (two guns) covering one area. As the 2nd Battalion, 5th Regiment, which was formed in rear of our position, passed us on 'H' hour these two platoons joined the support company of the battalion, one platoon on either flank, this battalion being the support battalion in the attack until the first objective. The platoon with the liaison company advanced in their rear.

In this formation we reached the first objectives when the 2nd Battalion went through the attacking unit and continued the advance to the second objectives which was reached at 12:20 p.m. without serious resistance and no opportunity on target appearing for the use of machine guns.

Upon attaining the second objective the 3rd (?) Battalion, 5th Marines, passed through our lines and took up the advance, the 2nd Battalion following as support 1000 meters in rear, with the guns in the same formation. The attacking battalion attained the days objective at 3:20 p.m. and the support entrenched for the night, our guns being placed to cover front and flanks.

November 2nd. Remained in place in support of front line without advancing.

November 3rd. The 3rd Brigade having passed our front line during the night the 2nd Battalion, 5th Marines with the Machine Gun Company followed as the leading element of the 5th Marines in support, the advance continued until 3:00 p.m. when we entrenched in a support position on line from le Champy Haut (east limit) to les Fontenelles Farm (west limit).

November 4th. The 3rd Brigade advanced during the night to a position two kilometers south of Beaumont the 2nd Battalion and machine gun company marched to the Bois du Port Gerache taking up a support position in northern edge of woods directly south of Beaumont at 9:45 a.m. Held this position during which time covering concentrated fire on our lines; twenty percent casualties in this machine gun company at 7:00 p.m. battalion marched to Belle Tour Farm and established, without opposition, a line at that place, connection on the left with the 3rd Brigade. Strength of company seven guns.

November 5th. Remained in place.

November 6th. 7:00 a.m. Battalion moved to position in support of 2nd Battalion, 5th Marines in woods at 308.1-304.4 remaining there during that day and night.

November 7th. Orders being received to shift to left of 3rd Brigade. Battalion moved at 11:00 a.m. and bivouaced at 6:00 p.m. in the Bois de Sommauthe for the night.

November 8th. Remained in place.

November 9th. After making reconnaissance of Meuse River in vicinity of Bois de Hospice with a view to effecting a crossing the battalion marched to the Bois du Fond de Limon and bivouaced there at 8:00 p.m. for the night. Evacuated two gun crews on march for sickness. Strength 5 guns.

November 10th. Remained in place during day and at dusk advanced to Meuse River for crossing. One gun was sent forward to cross with 1st platoon of infantry going over to concentrate a bridge guard. The balance of the company (four guns) held with reserve company of battalion on account of delay in crossing due to destruction of one of the bridges the battalion was subjected to a heavy concentration of enemy artillery fire and because of casualties the four guns with the reserve were abandoned, being salvaged by the company on the following day. The one gun which had crossed the river with the bridge guard remained in place until the armistice became effective at 11:00 a.m. November 11, 1918, when all operations ceased.

3. During the period of operations the company was rationed from the kitchen after the third day and the ammunition supply in the carts was always available after that time. Due to traffic congestion the company supply train was not able to connect with the advance until November 3rd but after that time we experienced no difficulty in that way.

4. Very little opposition was met with the advance until the crossing of the Meuse and casualties were principally due to enemy shell fire which in support positions. No opportunity on targets offered for machine guns. And in a rapid advance such as the first four days with the enemy in retreat it taxed the men to keep up with the Infantry with their loads.

J.[ames] P. Schwerin.
"D" Company
6th Machine Gun Battalion,
Marine Corps, A. E. F., France.
November 27th, 1918.

Report of operations in the Argonne Sector from November 1, 1918 to November 11, 1918.
From: Company Commander.
To: Battalion Commander.

1. This company took up a position, about a half a kilometer north of Sommerance, at 8:30 p.m. October 31st, 1918. From 3:30 a.m., until 5:30 a.m., November 1st, an indirect-barrage was

fired. At 5:40 a.m. one gun was hit and put out of action. At 5:50 a.m. the company moved forward about three kilometers to take up position to fire another indirect-barrage, but upon arrival at that point, it was found to be impracticable, as this was the point at which the company was to join the 2nd Battalion, 6th Regiment, and the first waves of that battalion were already moving forward, upon our arrival.

2. This company joined the 2nd Battalion, 6th Regiment, Major [Ernest] Williams, U.S.M.C. Commanding, at about 9:00 a.m. One platoon was ordered to the support company, right flank, one platoon to the support company, left flank, and one platoon held in reserve. The objective was reached at about 3:30 p.m. and a line was established about one half a kilometer from the northern edge of the Bois de Folie. Captain William H. Taylor Jr., was evacuated, wounded during the day. The Company was then commanded by Lieutenant [Cornelius H.] Reece.

3. November 2nd, we remained in the same positions, this time serving as support to the 9th Infantry, which moved forward at about 8:00 p.m.

4. From November 3, 1918, to November 10, we remained in support, moving forward.

5. At about 7:00 p.m. November 10, 1918, the 1st, 2nd and 3rd Battalions, 6th Regiment, moved forward to effect a crossing of the river Meuse about four kilometers north of Mouzon. Owing to the wrecking of the pontoon bridge, this crossing could not be made. The 2nd Battalion returned to its former position about eight kilometers south of Mouzon, at about 6:00 a.m., November 11.

6. Orders were received at about 9:30 a.m. November 11th 1918, that the enemy had signed an armistice, and that hostilities would cease at 11 a.m. that date.

Jack S. Hart,
Captain, U.S.M.C.

SUMMARY OF OPERATIONS BY THE 77th COMPANY
OCTOBER 25, 1918 to NOVEMBER 13, 1916.

October 26, 1918.

While in bivouac at Camp Cabaud, situated in the Foret d'Argonne, about 3 kilometers north of Les Islettes, orders were received from the Commanding Officer, 6th Machine Gun Battalion, to join and operate with the 3rd battalion, 5th Regiment, U.S. Marines, in connection with operations of the First Army, American E. F.

At 2:00 p.m. the Company marched independently of the battalion generally north and about 1:00 a.m. October 26th bivouaced in the wood, 79.7-02.4 Buzancy Special, 1½ kilometers S. E. of Exermont.

October 27, 1918.

The Company moved at daybreak to a more favourable position on higher ground in the same wood. A reconnaissance of the front lines was made by the Commanding Officer. During the night there was intermittent shelling of artillery positions near us and a gas alarm was given, but nothing of importance occurred.

October 28, 1918.

Front line positions were reconnoitered by the Company Commander. The Company remained in position. The intermittent shelling of the previous night was again experienced.

October 29, 1918.

During the afternoon the Company moved to the wood, 79-01.8 Buzancy Special, and joined the 3rd Battalion, 5th Regiment Marines. A further reconnaissance of front line positions was made by the Company Commander.

October 30, 1918.

Orders were received to proceed to support positions on a line extending generally east and west and about one kilometer north of the road from Sommerance to the Bois de Romagne near Hill 263. The march was started at 5:30 p.m. but enroute the orders were cancelled and the Company stopped with the battalion in the woods 91.9-04.3 Buzancy Special.

October 31, 1918.

A reconnaissance of the front lines was made by all company officers. While in bivouac in the wood 91.9-04.3 Buzancy Special. The Company Commander was ordered about 3:30 p.m. to reconnoiter positions for firing a barrage. Further orders received about 6:30 p.m. named D-day the following morning and H-hour 5:30 a.m. The Company proceeded independently of the battalion and arrived about 1:30 a.m. and established positions near the road running easterly from Sommerance to the Bois de Romagne between two small woods 84.9-01.3 Remonville.

November 1, 1918.

Positions were taken up near the road running easterly from Sommerance to the Bois de Romagne between two small woods, 84.9-01.3 Remonville. At 3:30 a.m. in conjunction with the artillery a barrage was fired for two hours objective the southern entrance of Landres et St. Georges. About 30,000 rounds of ammunition was used during the barrage. Firing ceased at 5:30 a.m. and the platoons joined their infantry organizations, the second platoon with the 20th Company, the third platoon with the 47th Company and the first was held in reserve. The jump-off occurred at 5:30 a.m. from east and west positions about 1½ kilometers south of Landres et St. Georges 86.4-030 to 86.5-03.6 Remonville. The 4th Brigade attacked accompanied by a rolling barrage, the 3rd Brigade supporting, and the 5th Regiment objectives were in the right half of the division sector 1st battalion attacking, 2nd battalion in support and the 3rd battalion in reserve. The line of the first objective extended from 89.5-300 to 89.5-03 Remonville. At this point the barrage became standing for 30 minutes while the 2nd and 3rd battalions passed through in the order named, and the 1st became the reserve. In Landreville some machine gun opposition was met. The advance continued successfully to the second objective, a line extending from 93.2-01 to 92.3-04.4 Remonville. On the slopes southeast of Bayonville et Chennery machine guns were set up and overhead fire was directed into the woods on the right of the sector. At this point also some trouble was experienced by the short fire of our artillery.

The 3rd and 1st battalions moved up in the order named and the 2nd became reserve. After a half hour's standing barrage the advance was continued to the third and Corps objective, a line extending from 94.7-01.2 to 95.2-03 to 94.7-04.9 Remonville. This line was reached at 2:10 p.m. and was established after clearing out many machine gun nests in the woods. At this point over 100 prisoners and a large quantity of artillery, machine guns and other material were taken.

November 2, 1918.

The positions reached the afternoon before were further strengthened and consolidated. There was considerable artillery and machine gun firing on both sides. Aerial observation by the enemy was active.

November 3, 1918.

Before daybreak the 3rd Brigade moved through our lines the 9th Infantry on the right and the 23rd Infantry on the left. The 4th Brigade moved in support, the battalions of the 5th Regiment arranged 1, 2 and 3 from front to rear. Around Magenta Farm and on the slopes to the northeast there was considerable shrapnel fire. The advance extended several kilometers beyond the exploitation line, where the 3rd battalion dug in, about ½ kilometer northwest of Nouart, in the wood 97.8-04.75 Remonville.

November 4, 1918.

At daybreak we continued forward to a point ½ kilometer northeast of La Fontaine au Cronq Farm and dug in on the southern slope in a position 99.5-05.5 Remonville. A burst of shells from our right flank caused a number casualties. There was considerable aerial activity.

About 4:30 p.m. we were relieved by units of the 26th Division and proceeded east and northeast over bad roads via Le Champy Haut and Le Champy Bas to a point in the Bois de Belval, 303.3-307 Stenay. A line was established and strong patrols sent forward.

November 5, 1918.

At 9:00 a.m. the battalion proceeded through the Bois de Belval and the Foret de Dieulet, crossed the main road from Beaumont to Stenay and entered the Foret de Jaulnay establishing a line facing Pouilly. Positions were reconnoitered and patrols sent forward. Our position was approximately 10.5-05.5 Buzancy Special.

November 6, 1918.

The battalion was relieved at dusk by units of the 89th Division and proceeded to bivouac in the northern part of the Foret de Dieulet near the Wamme River and the Farm de Belle Tour, 06.6-04.5 Buzancy Special.

November 7, 1918.
Proceeded at 11:00 a.m. to reserve positions in the Bois de Sommauthe 02.5-05 Buzancy Special, arriving about 4:30 p.m.

November 8, 1918.
The battalion remained in place during the day and night.

November 9, 1918.
At 4:30 p.m. march was made to a bivouac in the Bois du Grand Dieulet about 2 kilometers southwest of Thibaudine Farm, 301.3-307 Vendreese (prelim edition).

November 10, 1918.
Proceeded at 4:30 p.m. to the Bois du Fond de Limon 305.5-311 Mouzon (prelim edition) and joined the 2nd battalion, of the 6th Regiment. The two battalions acted together. Orders were received to proceed at once via Mouzon to the bank of the Meuse River where a crossing was to be effected on pontoon bridges. H-hour was 9:30 p.m. A standing barrage was fired by our artillery, followed by a rolling barrage. Although the river was not reached until about 1:00 a.m. the bridges were not in place. On account of the heavy shell and machine gun fire, the Engineers had been unable to push the bridges across. At 4 a.m. it was still unaccomplished, and in view of the approach of daylight and the fact that the nearest cover was four miles distant, a return was made. The 3rd Battalion of the 5th Regiment reached a position in the Bois du Fond de Limon (304.5-312) Mouzon (prelim edition) about 8:00 a.m.

November 11, 1918.
Orders announcing the signing of the armistice with the enemy effective at 11:00 a.m. this date were received. Support positions along the road and in the Bois des Flaviers on the east bank of the Meuse, near Villemontry 308.2-322 Mouzon (prelim. edition) were reconnoitered. The battalion moved to these positions and relieved the 1st battalion of the 9th infantry at 10 p.m.

November 12, 1918.
The battalion remained in place during the day and night.

November 13, 1918.
The battalion moved at 3. p.m. to the town Letanne.

November 1–11, 1918
Headquarters, Sixth Machine Gun Battalion,
Marine Corps, Am. E. F.
November 28, 1918.
REPORT OF OPERATIONS

1. The following is a report of the operations of this battalion covering the period November 1 to November 11, 1918, both dates inclusive, in the Argonne Sector:

The four companies of this battalion during these operations were attached to infantry battalions as follows:

15th Company to	3rd Battalion,		6th Marines
23rd "	2nd "		5th Marines
77th "	3rd "		5th Marines
81st "	2nd "		6th Marines

This assignment was the same as those in the Soissons and Champagne operations.

November 1, 1918

In accordance with orders contained in Field-Order No. 34 the Fourth Brigade passed through the 42nd Division, holding the line St. George–Landres St. George, and attacked at 5:30 a.m., with the 5th Marines on the right and the 6th Marines on the left. Previous to zero hour all four companies laid down a barrage on enemy front line, and joined their battalions as the latter followed the 1st Battalion of the 5th Marines and the 1st Battalion of the 6th Marines. The 15th Company, closely following its battalion, advanced to Barronville and established P.C. in rear of the church. The 1st and 3rd Platoons ware in town with the 84th and 82nd Companies, and the 2nd Platoon was divided between the 83rd and 97th Companies. The 23rd Company accompanied its battalion to the first objective where it passed through the attacking units and continued the advance to the second objective. The 77th Company, attached to the reserve battalion, followed to first objective line, where the 2nd and 3rd Battalion passed through the first. Machine Gun opposition was met in Landreville. Machine guns were set up southeast of Bayonville, and overhead fire was directed into the woods on the right of the sector. Trouble here was experienced by the short fire of our artillery. The advance was continued to the Corps objective (Fosse-Nouart), which was reached at 2:10 p.m. At this point over 100 prisoners and a large quantity of artillery, machine guns, and other material was taken. The 81st Company less one (1) gun put out of action during barrage firing, advanced with its battalion about 3 kilometers to the point where the indirect barrage for the purpose of facilitating the passing through of the support battalion was to be laid, but upon arrival at that point barrage was found to be impracticable, as the attacking battalion had already advanced too far. For the advance of this battalion one Platoon of machine guns was attached to the support company, right flank; one platoon to the support company, left flank and one Platoon held in reserve. The first halt was made about one-half kilometer from the Northern edge of the Bois de Folie.

November 2, 1918

15th Company, 1st Platoon in Bayonville, 2nd Platoon with the 83rd and 97th Companies, 3rd Platoon 2 guns in battery North of town and 2 in reserve. 23rd Company remained in place in support of our front line without advancing. The 77th Company remained in place on the line reached the afternoon before, strengthening and consolidating their positions. There was considerable enemy artillery and machine gun fire and an aerial reconnaissance. 81st Company remained in position, and became the support of 9th Infantry units when the latter passed through at about 8:00 p.m.

November 3, 1918

15th Company moved up and first Platoon took position 300 metres east of Fosse, second Platoon at Company P.C. (01.95-97.95 Remanoville 1/20), the third Platoon close by. Company P.O. moved into Fosse at 230 p.m. 23rd Company with its battalion followed the leading elements of the 5th Marines in support of the 3rd Brigade, the advance continuing until 3:00 p.m. and dug in in a support position on line from le Champy Haute to les Fontenelle Farm. 77th Company moved up with its battalion, experiencing considerable shrapnel fire near Magenta Farm and on the slopes to the Northeast. The advance extended several kilometers beyond the exploitation line, where the company with its battalion dug in, in the woods 500 metres North of Nouart. 81st Company, remaining in support, moved up behind the 5th Marines line.

November 4, 1918

15th Company moved as follows (Reference Stenay Map 1/20): P.O. to 306.35-301.4, 1st Platoon to 306.40-301.7, 3rd Platoon to 306.5-301.5, and 2nd Platoon to 306.85-301.15, protecting flank and in battery to Northeast front.

23rd Company advanced to the Bois du Pont Gerache, taking up a support position in northern end of woods directly south of Beaumont at 9:45 a.m. Delivered frontal fire from this position, and in the evening experienced some losses from enemy shelling. At 7:00 p.m. advanced to Belle Tour Farm and established without opposition a line running Northwest and Southeast through that place. Strength of Company, 7 guns.

77th Company at daybreak advanced to point 500 metres Northeast of La Fontaine Farm and dug in. Some casualties from shell fire. At 4:30 p.m. moved forward via road through le Champy Haute and le Champy Bas to the Bois de Belval, where line was established and Infantry Patrols sent out. 81st Company remained in support.

November 5, 1918

No change of positions or distribution of guns in 15th Company. 23rd Company remained in place with battalion. 77th Company moved forward at 9:00 a.m. through the Bois de Belval and the Foret de Dieulet, crossing the main road from Beaumont to Stenay, and entered the Foret de Jaulnay, establishing line facing Pouilly. The 81st Company with its battalion remained in place.

November 6, 1918

The 23rd Company moved at 7:00 a.m. to position in support of 5th Marines in woods at 308.1-304.4 (Stenay) and remained there during the day and night. The 77th Company with its Infantry Battalion was relieved at dusk by units of the 89th Division, and proceeded to bivouac in the northern part of the Foret de Dieulet, near the Wamme River and Belle Tour Farm. The 81st Company remained in support.

November 7, 1918

The 15th Company at 12:45 p.m. moved to Bois du Four, arriving there at 6:00 p.m. and bivouaced at 302.0-304.4 (Raucourt 1/20)

The 23rd Company with its battalion, receiving orders to shift to left of 3rd Brigade, moved at 11:00 a.m. to the Bois de Semmauthe, bivouacing there at 6:00 p.m. The 77th Company moved to same locality at Noon. The 81st Company remained in place.

November 8, 1918

15th Company moved at 6:30 p.m. to 303.6-306.6 (Stenay) and bivouaced. Fire eschelon reduced to 63 men and 6 guns.

November 9, 1918

The 15th Company moved at 9:30 p.m. to Bois du Fond de Limon on road from Beaumont to Mouzon. 23rd Company moved to same locality. 77th Company at 4:30 p.m. moved to and bivouaced in the Bois du grand Dieulet, about 2 kilometers SW of Thibaudine Farm.

November 10, 1918

23rd Company at dusk advanced with its Infantry Battalion to the point South of Villemontry selected for the crossing of the Meuse River. One gun was sent forward to cross with the first Platoon of Infantry going over to concentrate a bridge guard. The Balance of the Company (4 guns) was held with the reserve company of infantry on account of the delay resulting from destruction of one of the bridges by shell fire. This one gun and crew which had crossed the river with the bridge guard remained in place until the armistice became effective at 11:00 November 11, 1918. The crews of the 4 guns left on west side of river experienced such losses that all 4 guns had to be salvaged.

77th Company proceeded at 4:30 p.m. to the Bois du Fond du Limon, 305.5-311.0 (Mouzon), and joined the 2nd Battalion of the 6th Marines. In accordance with the orders concerning the crossing of the river by the 2nd [6th Marines] and 3rd Battalions of the 5th Marines the Company proceeded to the river at a point 2 kilometers north of Mouzon, where a crossing was to be effected by pontoon bridges. The bridges were not in place upon the arrival of the attacking units at 1:00 a.m., nor was this task completed that night. The two Battalions withdrew to cover, the 77th Company proceeding with its battalion to the Bois de Fond du Limon.

The 81st Company with its infantry battalion proceeded at 7:00 p.m. to the point North of Mouzon designated for the river crossing, and upon the change of orders moved to and bivouaced in the Bois de Fond du Limon.

November 11, 1918

Armistice took effect at 11:00 a.m. All units remained in place.

Liaison with Companies.

Company P.C.'s at all times were with Infantry Battalion P.C.s. On account of the frequent changes of P.C. and the consequent failure to notify Battalion P.C. beforehand of movements, there were times when location of Companies was not known. Communication was on the whole, however, good and no great difficulty in transmitting orders and so on was experienced.

Ammunition and Supplies.

The supply of machine gun ammunition was at all times unfailing. During the whole of the operations the roads were in very bad condition and this coupled with the enormous traffic (artillery and supplies) made the bringing up of rations difficult. Rolling kitchens followed up their Companies as closely as possible.

Tactical use of Machine Guns.

The areas indicated in the attached sketch [not available] were thoroughly covered by the 4 Companies and machine gun units of the 42nd Division preparatory to the jump-off on November 1st. This fire was delivered from prepared emplacements at ranges from 1700 to 2000 metres, separate areas being allotted to Companies and Sections. The barrage lasted 2 hours, and in comparative intensity corresponding to the artillery barrage. The machine gun Companies joined their Battalion when they passed through after 5:30 a.m.

Battalion P.Cs.

During the night of October 31st-November 1st, the Sixth Machine Gun Battalion P.C. was at point in woods 1½ kilometers NE of Sommerance. It moved to St. George the night of November 1st, and to Bayonville the night of November 2nd, to Fosse the night of November 3rd. P.C. established in Belval November 4th and moved to Beaumont November 8, 1916. The P.C. was at all times in close proximity to 4th Brigade P.C. No telephone communication necessary.

Casualties, Evacuations, Etc.

The casualties sustained by the 23rd Company near Belle Tour Farm and during the crossing of the Meuse on the Night of November 10th were heavy, but with this exception evacuations resulting from wounds were light. All companies, however, suffered heavy losses by evacuation on account of sickness. All sick men were evacuated through 5th and 6th Marines.

Administrative Work.

Owing to the fact that the advance was rapid and the rear eschelon was left so far behind administrative work was maintained under the greatest difficulties.

(Sgd) Matthew H. Kingman
Major, U.S.M.C.
Commanding.

Occupation

Like the rest of the Second Division, the 6th Machine Gun Battalion entered Germany, crossed the Rhine and were assigned to the following towns by 16 December:

Headquarters and Train:	Melsbach
15th Company	Melsbach
23d Company	Bremscheid
77th Company	Hausen
81st Company	Rheinbrohl

On 23 December the 23d Company changed location to Waldbreitbach. The entire battalion remained in the locations assigned and until leaving Europe continued to train.

The battalion reported a total of 606 casualties during the war, of which seven officers and 117 enlisted men were killed. The following is a chart showing each company's combined casualties.

	Killed	Missing	*Severely Wounded*	*Slightly Wounded*	Gassed	*Totals*
Headquarters	3		1	9	1	14
15th Co.	30		22	52	15	119
23d Co.	44	2	45	113	18	222
77th Co.	19	2	21	86		128
81st Co.	28	5	64	54	7	158
	124	9	153	314	41	641

As with the balance of the 4th Brigade, the 6th Machine Battalion left Europe aboard the *Santa Paula* and arrived in the United States on 5 August 1919, the last of the 4th Brigade. On the 8th a parade was held in New York City, and then in Washington, D.C., until finally all Marine units assembled at Quantico and by the 13 of August, all Marines, save those intending to continue their service, were discharged.

Portrait of an unidentified World War I Marine.

Chapter Notes

Chapter 3

1. Elliott Cooke, *We Can Take It and We Attack* (Pike, NH: Brass Hat reprint, 1979), 4.
2. Craig Hamilton and Louise Corbin, eds., *Echoes from Over There* (New York: Soldier's, 1919), 69–70.
3. Tharau was killed later in the usually "quiet" Marbache sector but not before he had been decorated at Soissons.
4. See George B. Clark, *Hiram Iddings Bearss, U.S. Marine Corps: Biography of a World War I Hero* (Jefferson, NC: McFarland, 2005).
5. Lieutenant Colonel Frederic M. Wise, formally the battalion commander, was now variously sick or in training at the army school at Langres and wouldn't return until after the battle terminated.
6. There are many stories of what happened on 18 July. Some are quite unusual, and many unbelievable.
7. Corbin, a former Marine gunner, was rather lackadaisical, and didn't push very hard. He sort of disappears from the records after Soissons.
8. Roberts paid for his courage with his life on the night of 10-11 November while crossing the Meuse River.
9. The 9th Infantry must also have been catching hell for a captain to be leading a battalion.
10. Lack of maps, poor directions, and lack of cohesion were all major problems at Soissons, which Maj. Gen. Harbord later admitted in his memoir.
11. Cooke, op. cit., 27. Really spelled "Crabbe."
12. Cooke was the only U.S. Army officer who commanded a Marine company for an extended period, even though he was but a first lieutenant and there were many USMC captains available. He was extremely well-liked.
13. There was a large gap, about a half mile, on its left rear. Upton's later report indicated that he had no idea where 2/5 was located.
14. Barczykowski received an Oak Leaf Cluster in place of a second Distinguished Service Cross, awarded for his actions at Belleau Wood on 11 June 1918. Later he would also receive a Navy Cross for 18 July.

Chapter 4

1. Major General Harbord ordered one company, the 47th (Case), to provide a provost guard of 2 officers and thirty men at Cré-de-Montgobert. The balance of the company was used to escort prisoners to the rear and to bring ammunition forward.

Chapter 5

1. Martin Gus Gulberg, *A War Diary* (Pike, NH: Brass Hat, 1993), 22.
2. Gulberg, *A War Diary*, 26.

Chapter 6

1. Shearer would also receive a Navy Cross and Distinguished Service Cross, two Silver Star citations, a Croix de Guerre and the Legion of Honor for clearing the Bois de Belleau of all Germans on 25 June 1918. Shearer had recently relieved Major Benjamin S. Berry, in command of the 3d Battalion, who had been badly wounded on 6 June in the assault upon the Bois de Belleau, losing his hand and much of his arm in the process. Consequently the notation that it was the 1st Battalion, 5th Regiment, was incorrect. Even though the term "Marines" to denote a Marine regiment did not become officially used until the early 1930s, that designation was consistently used during the war, by nearly everyone.
2. Garrett was later to command the 1st Battalion, 6th Regiment, before being assigned to Di-

vision Headquarters as provost marshal. Prior to that he had commanded the 80th Company. He was awarded a Silver Star citation for his actions at St. Mihiel.

3. The Second Battalion commanded by Lt. Col. Frederic M. Wise, often called "Fritz" and sometimes "Dopey."

4. Messersmith was later commanding officer of the 2d Battalion, 5th Regiment. Taylor was awarded a Silver Star and Croix de Guerre for his actions at Belleau Wood. He was again wounded at Soissons. He was commissioned from the ranks during June 1918. Adams earned a Distinguished Service Cross, Navy Cross, 3 Silver Star citations and a Croix de Guerre at Blanc Mont. Lockhart had been wounded on 6 June. Later that day a total of 378 officers and men were evacuated from those two companies.

5. Timothy, another fine Army officer, was a platoon leader in the 80th Company. He earned a Distinguished Service Cross that day.

6. Egbert T. Lloyd assumed command of the 80th Company from Coffenberg. Woodworth became skipper of the 96th, after Robertson, and was wounded at Soissons and St. Mihiel. Overton earned the Distinguished Service Cross and Navy Cross at Soissons on 19 July 1918 the hard way. Duane was with the 96th Company until he was wounded at Soissons.

7. As is well known now, that statement would usually be held in contempt insofar as the enlisted members of the A.E.F. were concerned. The exception would be to the Salvation Army and to a lesser extent the Knights of Columbus.

8. The 2d Battalion actually took over Hill 142, which had been the scene of ferocious fighting on 6 June when the 1st Battalion, 5th Regiment, launched the first assault made by the 4th Brigade during the war.

9. The roster of the semi-official history of the 78th Company and a listing for him in the Navy Register for 1920, as a retired captain in 1919. He is mentioned prominently in Sellers' memoirs.

10. Barber died of his wounds, having received a Silver Star citation.

11. There is an excellent description of the problems entailed in this wiring exercise in the semi-official history of the Seventy-eighth Company, pages 3–4.

12. A company composed of the older men in the battalion was sent to Paris to participate in the parade to celebrate that holiday. Presumably each Marine battalion followed this same procedure.

13. Cowing and Cooper, op. cit., 253. The pin mentioned was one that John Overton asked his friends to send to his mother, Mrs. John M. Overton in Nashville, TN, if he didn't make it. He was awarded a Distinguished Service Cross and later a Navy Cross.

14. The regiment had nearly 2,800 officers and men all told, of which 350 were set aside as reserves to help rebuild the battalion. The actual number engaged was 2,450, of which 1,300 were killed or wounded. Therefore this was the worst day of the war for the 6th Regiment of Marines. Not even Belleau Wood or Blanc Mont was as bad for the regiment.

15. Located some thirty miles south on the then main road and about halfway between Soissons and Paris.

16. Stockwell was a U.S. Army officer, and must have been one of the last still serving with the Marines. Minnis had recently arrived to serve with the 4th Brigade, having served with the 38th Infantry, 3d Division, at Mezy on 15 July, where he was awarded a Distinguished Service Cross and later a Navy Cross.

Chapter 8

1. Because the machine gunners were interspersed throughout the various front-line units, they will not receive the attention they deserve, but, like the engineers, corpsmen, doctors and other service people, they were there when they were needed.

2. *Records of the Second Division*, Vol. 5.

3. This must mean 2d Lt. William Zoltowski, who would be killed in action at Blanc Mont on 6 October. Cannot locate anyone named "Galtowski" in any unit.

Bibliography

Primary Source

Records of the Second Division. No place, No date. 10 volumes.

U.S. Government

American Battle Monuments Commission. *American Armies and Battlefields in Europe.* Washington, DC: U.S. Government Printing Office, 1938.

American Battle Monuments Commission. *2d Division Summary of Operations in the World War.* Washington, DC: U.S. Government Printing Office, 1944.

Annual Report of the Secretary of War, 1919. Washington, DC: U.S. Government Printing Office, 1919.

Annual Reports of the Navy Department for the Fiscal Year 1920. Washington, DC: U.S. Government Printing Office, 1921.

Blanc Mont (Meuse-Argonne-Champagne). Monograph No. 9. Reprint, Pike, NH: Brass Hat, 1994.

The Genesis of the American First Army. Washington, DC: Historical Section, 1938.

The Medical Department of the United States Navy with the Army and Marine Corps in France in World War I. Washington, DC: U.S. Navy, 1947.

Navy Yearbook 1920 and 1921. Washington, DC: U.S. Government Printing Office, 1922.

The Navy Book of Distinguished Service. Washington, DC: 1921.

Order of Battle of the United States Land Forces in the World War. Reprint, vols. 1 and 2 of 5 vols. Washington, DC: U.S. Government Printing Office, 1988.

Pershing, John J. *Final Report of Gen. John J. Pershing.* Washington, DC: U.S. Government Printing Office, 1920.

Report of the First Army, American Expeditionary Force, Organization and Operations. Fort Leavenworth, KS: 1923.

Smith, Gibson B. *Thomas Holcomb, 1879–1965, Register of his Personal Papers.* Washington, DC: History and Museums Division, Headquarters, U.S. Marine Corps, 1988.

U.S. Army, *Records of the Second Division (Regular),* 9 volumes. Washington, DC: Army War College, 1927.

U.S. Navy, *Annual Report of the Secretary of the Navy for the Fiscal Year 1918.* Washington, DC: 1918. [Corrected to 18 October 1919.]

United States Army in the World War 1917–1919. vols. 1, 3, 4 and various other volumes. Washington, DC: Historical Division, 1948.

Wood, Charles A. *Clifton Bledsoe Cates, 1893–1970, A Register of His Personal Papers.* Washington, DC: History and Museums Division, Headquarters, U.S. Marine Corps, 1985.

Personal Papers and Unpublished Memoirs

Barnett, George. "Soldier and Sailor Too." No place, no date [1923?].

Campbell, Albert J. "A Man's Journey into Hell." Np, nd, complied by his son, A.J. Campbell, Jr.

Cordes, Onnie J. "The Immortal Division." Np, nd, by a veteran of the 17th Company, 1st Battalion, 5th Marines.

Gorin, Joe. "Letters from the Front." Np, nd, by a grandson about 1st Lt. Neil Dougherty, 83d Company, Third Battalion, Sixth Marines.

Moore, William E. Personal letters to his mother, 15 February–31 March 1919, np, nd.

Paris, Gus. "Hold Every Inch of Ground." Unpublished biography of Logan Feland. Owensboro, KY: nd.

Richmond, Clarence L. "Recollections of a Buck Private." Somewhere in France, 43d Company, 2d Battalion, 5th Marines, nd.

Scoarse, Denzil I. "Diary of Pvt. Denzil I. Scorase,

April 1918–April 1919." Provided by S. Vic Glogovic, M.D.

Thomas, Eugene R. Letters, untitled, np, nd, sent to me by his daughter.

Thompson, Edward C. Memoirs. Np, nd, 45th Company, 3d Battalion, 5th Marines. Prepared by grandson.

Zischke, Peter H. "Recollections of My Father, Herman A. Zischke." Np, nd, 18th Company, 2d Battalion, 5th Marines. Provided by his son.

Official and Semi-Official Unit Histories

Akers, Herbert H. *History of the Third Battalion, Sixth Regiment, U.S. Marines*. Hillsdale, MI: Akers, MacRitchie and Hurlburt, 1919.

Burton, Allan. *A History of the Second Regiment of Engineers, United States Army from Its Organization in Mexico, 1916, to Its Watch on the Rhine, 1919*. Engers on the Rhine: 1919.

Clark, George B., editor. *A Brief History of the Sixth Regiment U.S. Marine Corps, July 1917–December 1918*. Reprint, Pike, NH: Brass Hat, 1992.

_____. *History of the Fifth Regiment Marines (May 1917–December 31, 1918)* Reprint, Pike, NH: Brass Hat, 1995.

_____. *The History of the Third Battalion 5th Marines 1917–1918*. Pike, NH: Brass Hat, 1995.

_____. *The Marine Brigade at Blanc Mont*. Pike, NH: Brass Hat, 1994.

_____. *The Second Infantry Division in World War I*. Jefferson, NC: McFarland, 2007.

_____. *Their Time in Hell: The 4th Marine Brigade at Belleau Wood*. Pike, NH: Brass Hat, 1996.

Curtis, Thomas J., and Lothar R. Long. *History of the Sixth Machine Gun Battalion*. Reprint, Pike, NH: Brass Hat, 1992.

Donaldson, G. H., and W. Jenkins, *Seventy-eighth Company, Sixth Marines, Second Division Army of Occupation*. Reprint, Pike, NH: Brass Hat, 1994.

Field, Harry B., and Henry G. James. *Over the Top with the 18th Company, 5th Regiment, U.S. Marines: A History*. Rodenbach, Germany [1919?].

Jones, William K. *A Brief History of the 6th Marines*. Washington, DC: Headquarters, U.S.M.C., 1987.

Macgillivray, George C., and George B. Clark, eds. *A History of the 80th Company, Sixth Marines*. Reprint, Pike, NH: Brass Hat, 1991.

Mitchell, William A. *The Official History of the Second Engineers in the World War, 1916–1919*. Regimental Headquarters, San Antonio, 1920.

Money, Willard I. *History of the 96th Company, 2d Battalion, Sixth Regiment, United States Marine Corps*. Washington, DC: Headquarters, U.S. Marine Corps, 1967.

The Ninth U.S. Infantry in the World War. Np, nd [Germany] [1919?].

Owen, Peter F. *To the Limit of Endurance: A Battalion of Marines (2/6) in the Great War*. College Station: Texas A&M University Press, 2007.

Second Division Association. *Commendations of Second Division, American Expeditionary Forces, 1917–1919*. Cologne, Germany, 1919.

Second Division Memorial Day, June 2nd, 1919, 75th Company, 6th Regiment U.S. Marines. Reprint, Pike, NH: Brass Hat, 1995.

74th Company, 6th Regiment, Second Division, A.E.F. Reprint, Pike, NH: Brass Hat, 1994.

Spaulding, Oliver L., and John W. Wright. *The Second Division, American Expeditionary Force in France 1917–1919*. New York: Hillman, 1937.

Strott, George G. *History of Medical Personnel of the United States Navy, Sixth Regiment Marine Corps, American Expeditionary Forces in World War, 1917–1918*. Reprint, Pike, NH: Brass Hat, 1995.

Thomason, John W., Jr., edited by George B. Clark. *The United States Army Second Division Northwest of Chateau Thierry in World War I*. Jefferson, NC: McFarland, 2006.

U.S. Army. *The 3rd Battalion 17th FA in 1918*. Coblenz, Germany, nd.

_____. *Twenty-third Machine Gun, Twenty-third Infantry, Second Division, Army of Occupation 1917–1919*. Np [1919?]

U.S. Marine Corps. *History of the First Battalion, 5th Regiment, U.S. Marines. 1919*. Reprint, Foster, RI: Brass Hat, 1980.

_____. *History of the Second Battalion, Fifth Marines*. Quantico, VA: Marine Barracks, 1938.

_____. *History of the Second Battalion, 5th Regiment, U.S. Marines*. Reprint, Foster, RI: Brass Hat, 1980.

_____. *History of the Sixth Regiment, U.S. Marines*. Tientsin, China, 1928.

_____. *History Third Battalion, Sixth Marines*. Np, nd.

Vandoren, Lucien H. *A Brief History of the Second Battalion, Sixth Regiment, U.S. Marine Corps, During the Period June 1st to August 10th, 1918*. Reprint, Pike, NH: Brass Hat, 1995.

Waller, Littleton W.T., Jr. *Final Report of the 6th Machine Gun Battalion*. Along with *Demobilization of the Marine Brigades, 1919* by Frank Evans. Pike, NH: Brass Hat, 2004.

Selected

Alvarez, Eugene. *Where It All Begins: A History of the United States Marine Corps Recruit Depot*

Parris Island, South Carolina. Blountstown, FL: Gayle, 1984.
Americans Defending Democracy: Our Soldiers' Own Stories. New York: World's War Stories, 1919.
Andriot, Captain R. *Belleau Wood and the American Army*. Trans. by W. B. Fitts. Washington, DC: Belleau Wood Memorial Association, nd.
Asprey, Robert B. *At Belleau Wood*. New York: G. P. Putnam's Sons, 1965.
Bellamy, David. *Dave Bellamy's War, from His Diary*. Pike, NH: Brass Hat, 2008.
Boyd, Thomas. *Points of Honor*. New York: Scribner's, 1925. Short stories by a Marine participant.
_____. *Through the Wheat*. New York: Scribner's, 1923. Fiction by a Marine participant.
Brannen, Carl A. *Over There: A Marine in the Great War*. College Station: Texas A&M University Press, 1996. Edited by Col. Rolfe Hillman II and Lt. Col. Peter Owen.
Carter, William A. *The Tale of a Devil Dog*. Washington, DC: Canteen, 1920.
Catlin, Albertus W. *With the Help of God and a Few Marines*. New York: Doubleday, 1919.
Clark, George B. *Decorated Marines of the Fourth Brigade in World War I*. Jefferson, NC: McFarland, 2007.
_____. *Devil Dogs: Fighting Marines of World War One*. Novato, CA: Presidio, 1999.
_____. *Hiram Iddings Bearss, U.S. Marine Corps: Biography of a World War I Hero*. Jefferson, NC: McFarland, 2005.
_____. *Legendary Marines of the Old Corps*. Pike, NH: Brass Hat, 2002.
_____. *A List of Officers of the 4th Marine Brigade*. Pike, NH: Brass Hat, 1993.
_____. *Major Awards to U.S. Marines in World War One*. Reprint, Pike, NH: Brass Hat, 1992.
_____. *Retreat Hell! We Just Got Here*. Pike, NH: Brass Hat, 1992.
Collins, Harry. *The War Diary of Corporal Harry Collins*. Pike, NH: Brass Hat, 1996.
Cooke, Elliott. *We Can Take It and We Attack*. Pike, NH: Brass Hat, 1995.
Cowing, Kemper F. *Dear Folks at Home*. Boston: Houghton Mifflin, 1919.
Daniels, Josephus. *The Cabinet Diaries of Josephus Daniels, 1913–1921*. Lincoln: University of Nebraska Press, 1963.
De Chambrun, Jacques Aldebert de Pinton, Comte de, and Captain De Marenches. *The American Army in the European Conflict*. New York: Macmillan, 1919.
DeMario, Joseph. *Fifty Years to Erase*. New York: Carleton, 1971.
Derby, Richard. *Wade in, Sanitary! The Story of a Division Surgeon in France*. New York: G.P. Putnam's Sons, 1919.

Gibbons, Floyd. *And They Thought We Wouldn't Fight*. New York: George H. Doran, 1918.
Gordon, George V. *Leathernecks and Doughboys*. Pike, NH: Brass Hat, 1997.
Gulberg, Martin Gus. *A War Diary*. Pike, NH: Brass Hat, 1993.
Hallas, James. *Doughboy War*. Boulder, CO: Lynne Rienner, 2000.
Hamilton, Craig. *Echoes from Over There*. New York: Soldier's Publishing, 1919.
Harbord, James G. *The American Army in France 1917–1918*. Boston: Little, Brown, 1936.
_____. *Leaves from a War Diary*. New York: Dodd, Mead, 1925.
Hemrick, Levi E. *Once a Marine*. New York: Hearthstone, 1968.
Hewitt, Linda L. *Women Marines in World War I*. Washington, DC: Headquarters, U.S. Marine Corps, 1974.
Kean, Robert W. *Dear Marraine, 1917–1919*. Np, private printing, 1976.
Kennedy, David M. *Over Here: The First World War and American Society*. New York: Oxford University Press, 1980.
Krulewitch, Melvin L. *Now That You Mention It*. New York: Quadrangle, 1973.
Leatherneck. Numerous articles.
Lejeune, John A. *Reminiscences of a Marine*. Philadelphia: Dorrance, 1930.
Leonard, John W., and Fred E. Chitty. *The Story of the United States Marines, 1740–1919*. Np [1919?].
Liggett, Hunter. *AEF Ten Years Ago in France*. New York: Dodd, Mead, 1928.
Ludendorff, Erich von. *Ludendorff's Own Story*, Vol. 2. New York: Harper Bros., 1919.
Mackin, Elton E., and George B. Clark. *Suddenly We Didn't Want to Die*. Novato, CA: Presidio, 1993.
March, William [pseud.]. *Company K*. New York: Harrison Smith and Robert Haas, 1933. High level of accuracy in fiction by a former Marine participant.
Marine Corps Gazette. Numerous articles.
McClellan, Edwin N. *The United States Marine Corps in the World War*. Washington, DC: U.S. Government Printing Office, 1920.
McEntee, Girard L. *Military History of the World War*. New York: Scribner's, 1937.
Michelin. *The Americans in the Great War: Illustrated Guides to the Battlefields*, 3 volumes. France, 1920.
Morgan, Daniel E. *When the World Went Mad*. Boston: Christopher, 1931.
New York Life Insurance. *War Stories: Being a Brief Record of Service in the Great War of Soldiers-Sailors-Marines*. New York, 1920.
Otto, Ernst. *The Battle at Blanc Mont*. Annapolis, MD: U.S. Naval Institute Press, 1930.

Pattullo, George. *Hellwood*. Philadelphia: Curtis, 1918. About Belleau Wood.

———. *Horrors of Moonlight*. New York: private printing, 1939. About Belleau Wood.

Pershing, John J. *My Experiences in the World War*, 2 vols. New York: E. A. Stokes, 1931.

Rendinell, Joseph E., and George Patullo. *One Man's War: Diary of a Leatherneck*. New York: J. H. Sears, 1928.

Russell, James C., and William E. Moore. *The United States Navy in the World War*. Washington, DC: Pictorial Bureau, 1921.

Sellers, James McB. *World War Memoirs of Lieutenant Colonel James McBrayer Sellers, USMC*. Pike, NH: Brass Hat, 1997.

Scanlon, William T. *God Have Mercy on Us*. Boston: Houghton Mifflin, 1929.

Smythe, Donald. *Pershing: General of the Armies*. Bloomington: Indiana University Press, 1986.

Stallings, Laurence. *The Doughboys*. New York: Harper, 1963. Marine participant.

Strickler, J. Harold. *My Diary*. Pike, NH: Brass Hat, 2002.

Stringer, Harry R., ed. *Heroes All!* Washington, DC: Fassett, 1919.

Thomason, John W., Jr. *Fix Bayonets*. New York: Scribner's, 1926.

Tucker, Spencer C. *The European Powers in the First World War: An Encyclopedia*. New York: Garland, 1996.

U.S. Army. *Army of Occupation in Germany*. Pike, NH: Brass Hat, 1998.

Vandiver, Frank E. *Blackjack: The Life and Times of John J. Pershing*, Vol. 2. College Station: Texas A&M University Press, 1977.

Venzon, Anne Cipriano, ed. *The United States in the First World War, An Encyclopedia*. New York: Garland, 1995.

Westover, Wendell. *Suicide Battalions*. New York: G. P. Putnam's Sons, 1929.

Where the Marines Fought in France. Chicago: Park and Antrim, nd. [1919?].

Wise, Frederick May. *A Marine Tells It to You*. New York: J. H. Sears, 1929.

Index

Adams, 1st Lt. James P. 190, 193, 199, 200, 201, 206, 280
Adams, Maj. Robert E. 119, 149–151
Ashley, 2d Lt. Thomas W. 39
Ashwood, 2d Lt. Forrest J. 173

Babcock, 2d Lt. Robert C. 140, 142
Barker, Capt. Frederick 3
Barnett, MG George 5, 6, 66, 106, 281
Barnett, 2d Lt. Maurice 206, 212
Bartlett, Capt. Harry G. 5, 214, 215
Baston, Capt. Albert P. 36
Bearss, Lt. Col. Hiram I. 18, 43, 89, 107, 164, 166, 279, 283
Beauchamp, Capt. Felix 56–58
Becker, 2d Lt. Fred H., USA 69–71, 96
Bellamy, Capt. David 218, 228, 229, 249, 283
Belleau Wood battles: (1/5) 30–42; (2/5) 69–91; (3/5) 110–124; (1/6) 152–166; (2/6) 187–195; (3/6) 217–223; (6th MG) 254–256
Belmont, 2d Lt. George 173
Bennett, 2d Lt. Floyd W. 145
Bernier, 2d Lt. Oliver D. 146
Berry, Maj. Benjamin S. 12, 15, 16, 38, 39, 77, 106, 108, 109, 111–115, 158, 219, 279
Berry, Capt. Maurice S. 182
Blake, 1st Lt. Robert 36, 40, 41, 64
Blanc Mont battles: (1/5) 49–60; (2/5) 100–102; (3/5) 129–140; (1/6) 173–180; (2/6) 201–210; (3/6) 233–245; (6th MG) 266–270
Blanchfield, Capt. John 72–74
Bourdette, 2d Lt. Vernon B. 257, 262
Bourne, Capt. Louis M., Jr. 230
Bower, 2d Lt. George 257, 262, 265
Brennan, 2d Lt. James J. 128, 129, 153
Broderick, 2d Lt. Joseph D. 177, 179
Buchanan, 1st Lt. Fitzhugh L. 261

Burnes, Capt. James F. 162, 163
Burr, 1st Lt. Carelton 151, 170
Busby, 2d Lt. William H. 173
Butler, Col. Smedley D. 150

Campbell, 1st Lt. Harold D. 253
Carhart, 2d Lt. Joseph B. 97
Case, Capt. Philip T. 112, 121, 122, 125, 279
Cates, 2d Lt. Clifton B. 170, 190, 192, 197, 204, 205, 207, 209, 281
Catlin, Col. Albertus W. 15, 72, 76, 111, 113, 150, 152–156, 185, 188–190, 217, 218, 283
Cauldwell, Capt. Oscar 153, 154
Chandler, 1st Lt. Henry E. 164, 178, 180
Church, 1st Lt. Kortwright 234, 242
Churchman, 1st Lt. Charles J. 87
Cochran, Capt. Harry K. 57, 59, 60
Coffenberg, Capt. Bailey M. 188, 191, 200, 280
Cole, Maj. Edward B. 5, 12, 133, 158, 159, 189, 251, 252, 254
Collier, Capt. Eugene F.C. 206, 212
Conachy, Capt. Peter 39, 111–115, 117, 121
Conner, 2d Lt. Robert E. 51
Conroy, 2d Lt. Edward E. 108
Conroy, 2d Lt. John I. 162, 164
Cooke, 1st Lt. Elliot, USA 70, 74, 84, 86, 92–95, 125, 151, 161, 279, 283
Corbett, 2d Lt. Murl 40, 45, 56
Corbin, Capt. William O. 85, 92–96, 279
Cornell, Capt. Percy 55
Crabbe, Capt. William L. 44, 93, 95
Crandall, 2d Lt. Jesse L. 206
Croka, 1st Lt. William B. 251, 252, 261
Crowther, 1st Lt. Orlando C. 33, 35, 39
Cukela, 2d Lt. Louis 29, 46
Culnan, 2d Lt. John H. 34
Cushwood, 2d Lt. Forrest J. 156, 173

Dalton, 2d Lt. Charles F. 178
Davenport, 2d Lt. Edwin J. 177
Davies, 1st Lt. Thurston 134, 139, 140
De Carre, Capt. Alphonse 131, 133, 135, 137, 140, 141, 143–145
Denig, Maj. Robert L. 5, 167, 196
Dennis, 2d Lt. Clarence 159
de Roode, Capt. Louis R. 109, 140, 251, 252, 254
Dirksen, Capt. Raymond F. 26, 47, 58
Dougherty, 2d Lt. Neil F. 230, 281
Doyen, BG Charles A. 3, 5, 6, 7, 9, 89, 107, 150
Duane, 2d Lt. Robert L. 193, 280
Duckham, 1st Lt. William A. 116, 146
Dunbeck, Capt. Charley 60, 62, 63, 67, 70, 75, 76, 78–80, 99, 101–103, 105, 233
Duncan, 1st Lt. David 153, 183
Duncan, Capt. Donald E. 155, 188, 190

Eddy, 2d Lt. H. Leslie, USA 190
Eddy, 2d Lt. William A. 12, 165
Ehrhart, 2d Lt. George, Jr. 206
Eickelberg, 2d Lt. Wilbur 173
Elliott, 2d Lt. Steven 173
Ely, BG Hanson, USA 46, 47
Enholm, 2d Lt. Axel 266, 267
Erskine, 1st Lt. Graves B. 194, 200
Etheridge, 1st Lt. Charles A. 162
Evans, Maj. Frank E. 77, 87, 88, 123, 153, 161–165, 188, 190, 191, 218–221, 282

Fagan, Maj. Louis 182, 183
Farwell, LTCMD Wrey G., USN 165
Fay, Capt. John H. 107, 130, 141
Feland, Lt. Col. Logan 22, 26, 28, 31, 37, 45, 47–52, 55, 57–61, 63, 72, 76, 77, 82, 92, 93, 97–100, 102, 103, 113, 114, 116, 126–137, 140–146, 153, 154, 176
Ferch, 1st Lt. Aaron 39, 60
Fifth Regiment: 8th MG Company

285

32, 35, 36, 39, 41, 44, 48, 50, 58, 63, 72–75, 108, 124, 130, 141, 254–256, 267; First Battalion (aka 1/5) 2, 11, 12, 15, 20, 23, 24, 26–66, 70, 75–77, 85, 90, 92–94, 101, 102, 108, 109, 111, 112, 117, 125, 129, 132, 133, 141, 144, 146, 147, 150, 166, 174, 176, 177, 182, 194, 211, 212, 218, 233, 247; (17th Company [A]) 20, 26, 28, 31–33, 36, 38–45, 48, 50, 51, 54, 55, 58, 60–63, 65, 67, 75, 94, 115, 129, 144, 174, 233; (49th Company [B]) 26, 29, 31, 32–41, 44–50, 54–56, 58, 60, 62, 63, 65, 112, 128, 129; (66th Company [C]) 26, 29, 30, 32, 33, 35–39, 41, 44–46, 48, 50, 51, 54–58, 60, 63–65, 75, 92, 93, 95, 112; (67th Company [D]) 26, 28, 30, 32–39, 42–46, 48, 50, 51, 54, 56, 58, 60, 63, 65, 112, 129, 132, 144, 150; Second Battalion (aka 2/5) 15, 16, 21, 24, 32, 33, 37, 40, 41, 43, 47, 49, 51, 52, 62, 67–105, 111, 116, 118, 122, 124, 125, 130, 132, 153, 154, 158, 161, 166, 212, 217, 219, 222, 247, 253, 255, 257, 279; (18th Company [E]) 67–70, 72, 75, 77–81, 84, 88, 92–102, 108, 136, 142–144, 148, 185, 268; (43rd Company [F]) 36, 67, 70–72, 75, 77–81, 90, 92–95, 98–100, 140, 146, 176; (51st Company [G]) 11, 12, 16, 37, 40, 52, 67, 68, 70–74, 76–80, 85, 87–90, 92–97, 99, 100, 132, 154, 161–164, 217; (55th Company [H]) 52, 67, 70, 72, 73, 79–81, 84, 86, 92–95, 97–100, 125, 132, 135, 136, 161, 234; Third Battalion (aka 3/5) 12, 15, 16, 21, 24, 29, 38, 39, 48, 50–52, 61, 63, 76–78, 85, 86, 92, 101, 102, 106–148, 155, 156, 158, 166, 171, 183, 208, 218, 247, 253; (16th Company [I]) 44, 47, 50, 86, 87, 106–109, 112–117, 121–125, 127, 128, 131–133, 135, 137–142, 144, 146, 147, 261, 264, 269; (20th Company [K]) 44, 47, 106–108, 112–116, 120, 121, 123–125, 127, 128, 131–133, 135, 138, 139, 141, 142, 144, 147, 203, 208, 252, 253, 261, 264, 269, 273; (45th Company [L]) 39, 47, 48, 58, 106–109, 111–116, 121, 122, 124–128, 131–134, 136, 139, 141, 142, 144, 147, 172, 261, 264, 268, 269; (47th Company [M]) 47, 48, 77, 106–108, 112–116, 121–128, 131, 133, 138, 141–147, 171, 172, 261, 264, 269, 273
Foster, 2d Lt. James E. 57, 146
Foster, Capt. John R. 7, 102, 136, 143, 144, 146, 148
Fowler, 2d Lt. Edward C. 206
Fraser, 2d Lt. Chester H., USA 70–71

Frazier, 2d Lt. Walter D. 34, 39, 223
French, 1st Lt. Archie W. 200
Fuller, Capt. Edward C. 118, 158, 159, 163

Galliford, 1st Lt. Walter T.H. 33, 115
Gargin, 1st Lt. Joseph F. 157
Garrett, 1st Lt. David I. 219, 279
Garrett, Maj. Franklin B. 155, 156, 165, 166, 184, 185, 192, 279
Garvin, 2d Lt. Earl W. 36
Geer, 2d Lt. Prentice S. 35
Gilfillan, 2d Lt. Max 29, 35, 37
Gill, Capt. Charles C. 114, 115, 222
Gissell, 2d Lt. Bernhardt, USA 36
Glendinning, 2d Lt. Henry P. 102
Goode, 1st Lt. Henley M. 206
Goodman, 1st Lt. Benjamin F. 7
Green, Capt. Kirt 212
Greene, Maj. Edward A. 26, 28, 29

Hale, Capt. Augustus B. 253, 254, 256, 261, 262
Hamilton, Maj. George W. 21, 26, 28, 31, 33–35, 37–40, 44, 45, 47, 49–53, 55, 58–65, 101, 102, 112, 132–136, 141, 142, 207
Harbord, BG James G., USA 6, 7, 11–13, 15–16, 31–32, 42, 46, 70, 76–82, 84–89, 94, 96, 111, 112, 114, 115, 117–120, 122–124, 152, 153, 155, 156, 158–167, 187–194, 196, 217–223, 279, 283
Hardin, 2d Lt. John R. 173
Harding, 1st Lt. William L. 200, 206
Hart, Capt. Jack S. 251, 252, 257, 259, 272
Harvis, Capt. John P. 251–253
Hawkins, 1st Lt. Gardiner 200, 210
Hawkins, 2d Lt. Lloyd A. 211
Heckman, 1st Lt. Jacob H. 122
Henry, 1st Lt. Clifford O. 251, 253, 262
Hermle, 1st Lt. Leo D. 135, 176
Holcomb, Maj. Thomas 11, 81, 82, 88, 114, 117, 153, 156, 164 167, 170, 181, 185, 187–198, 209, 210, 219, 222, 223, 232, 235, 238, 240, 281
Hope, 2d Lt. Edward B. 39, 108, 109, 112
Hopke, 2d Lt. George H. 206
Houchin, 2d Lt. Lloyd H. 211
Hughes, Lt. Col. John A. 77, 81, 118, 149, 150, 152, 155, 156, 158–167, 169, 170, 194, 196, 197, 220, 221, 223, 226, 227
Hulbert, MG Henry L. 37, 55
Hunt, Capt. LeRoy 20, 26, 44, 45, 50–52, 54, 58, 60, 62, 64, 65, 94, 141
Hyatt, 1st Lt. John O. 261, 262

Israel, 2d Lt. Frederick 134

Jackson, Capt. David 118, 139
Jackson, 1st Lt. George R. 183, 221

Jackson, Capt. Gilder D. 80, 118, 123
Jacobson, Capt. Arnold W. 239
Joerger, 2d Lt. Herbert G. 261
Johnson, 1st Lt. Gillis A. 50, 54
Johnston, Capt. James H. 230, 235, 237
Johnston, 2d Lt. Scott 170

Karstaedt, Capt. Frederick 225
Kearns, Capt. John 170
Kelly, 1st Lt. Francis J. 53, 55, 56, 58
Keyser, Maj. Ralph S. 43, 67, 84–90, 92–97, 118, 121–124
Kieren, Capt. Francis 39, 49, 58
Kilduff, Capt. David R. 200
King, 2d Lt. Arthur S. 212
King, AS Ogden D., USN 252
Kingman, Capt. Matthew H. 239, 253, 254, 258, 259, 268, 277
Kirkbridge, 2d Lt. Roger B. 173
Knapp, Capt. Raymond E. 112, 125, 146

Ladd, 1st Lt. Shaler 251, 252
Larsen, Maj. (later CO of 3/5) Harry L. 21, 52, 58, 60, 61, 101, 102, 106, 112, 114–117, 129–137, 139–148, 155, 183, 211
Lawler, Lt. Cmdr. Robert J., USN 141
Lay, Maj. Harry 7, 47, 165, 220
Lee, 2d Lt. Charleton P. 183
Lee, Lt. Col. Harry 42, 43, 82, 84, 96, 117–120, 123, 124, 156, 158, 159, 161–167, 169–171, 173–184, 191, 192, 194, 196–198, 201, 203–206, 208–212, 218–223, 225, 227, 230–240, 242–247
Legendre, 2d Lt. James H. 92
Lejeune, MG John A. 19, 24, 47, 49, 50, 58, 66, 98, 127, 132, 134–137, 238, 283
Lienhard, 2d Lt. Jacob 50, 54
Lindgren, 2d Lt. Edward E. 50, 54
Lloyd, Capt. Egbert T. 193, 194, 197, 280
Lockhart, 1st Lt. George B. 193, 280
Locy, Lt Francis E., USN 165
Long, 1st Lt. Lothar R. 251, 252, 282
Loughberry, 2d Lt. R.H., USA 163, 169
Lyle, D.S. Alexander G., USN 109

Maack, 1st Lt. Fred W. 178, 179
Major, Capt. Harlan E. 251, 253
Marshall, 1st Lt. Robert W. 215, 216, 224, 227, 228, 233, 236, 243
Martin, Capt. George W. 200, 232
Martineau, 2d Lt. Earl T. 139
Matteson, 1st Lt. Clyde 165
Matthews, 1st Lt. William R. 77
McCann, Capt. Joseph P. 253, 259, 260
McClain, 2d Lt. Dave W. 51
McFarland, Capt. Hugh 233, 234, 236

Index

McLendon, ASurg. Preston A., USN 182
Messersmith, Maj. Robert E. 21, 49, 51, 52, 58, 59, 67, 99–101, 130–136, 175, 188, 190–193, 203, 208, 220, 233, 234, 241
Meuse-Argonne battles: (1/5) 60–65; (2/5) 102–105; (3/5) 141–148; (1/6) 180–183; (2/6) 201–210; (3/6) 233–245; (6th MG) 270–277
Mills, 2d Lt. Morgan R. 153, 163
Milner, 2d Lt. Drinkard B. 80, 81
Minnis, Capt. John A. 200, 280
Montague, 1st Lt. Robert M. 251, 252
Moore, 2d Lt. Lucius L. 252
Moore, 1st Lt. William B. 158, 218, 281
Morgan, 2d Lt. Peter 153–154
Moriarty, 1st Lt. James F. 253
Moseley, Capt. Gaines 122, 126, 127, 133
Mosher, 2d Lt. William J. 177
Mueller, Surgeon Robert, USN 209
Murphy, 2d Lt. Lewis J. 173
Murphy, 2d Lt. Raymond F. 173
Murray, 2d Lt. Henry C. 51
Murray, Capt. Joseph D. 72, 75, 81, 83, 86, 88, 92–94, 196

Neville, Col. (later CO 4th Brigade) Wendell C. 6, 15, 22, 29–32, 36, 38, 39, 42, 47, 48, 61, 62, 66, 68, 70, 72, 73, 75–78, 80–82, 86, 89, 94, 109, 111–116, 118–120, 123, 126–128, 142, 154, 162–167, 178, 180–182, 193, 194, 210, 121–123
Nice, Marine Gunner William E. 61
Noble, Capt. Alfred H. 176, 218, 221, 225, 236, 238, 240, 246
Norstrand, 1st Lt. Carl J. 35, 36, 50, 58, 64
Norwood, 1st Lt. Edmund P. 251, 262, 259

Ogden, 2d Lt. Paul J. 206
O'Leary, Lt. Col. Arthur J. 26, 47, 49
Osterhout, Capt. George H., Jr. 251
Overton, 2d Lt. John W. 193, 197, 280
Overton, 1st Lt. Macon 78, 160, 161, 179–181, 197, 280

Parsons, Maj. Harold L. 98, 99
Parsons, 2d Lt. Miller V. 50
Peck, Capt. DeWitt 52, 99
Perkinson, 1st Lt. Allan 216, 220
Peterson, 2d Lt. William C., USA 37, 39
Plambeck, 1st Lt. George A. 130
Platt, 1st Lt. Jonas H. 34, 39
Platt, Capt. Richard N. 44, 47, 112, 120, 121, 125, 127
Poe, 1st Lt. Edfar Francis, Jr. 118, 162

Popham, 1st Lt. John N., Jr. 173
Powers, Capt. Walter 198, 201, 204, 206, 271
Puryear, Jr. Maj. Bennet 7

Quigley, Capt. Thomas 41, 42

Raleigh, Capt. Cecil B. 193
Rea, 2d Lt. Leonard E. 48, 56, 64, 146
Reamey, 2d Lt. Brewster 156
Redford, 1st Lt. David A. 170
Reece, 1st Lt. Cornelius H. 272
Roberts, Capt. Charles D. 215, 219, 220, 234, 237, 242, 279
Robertson, Capt. James F. 117, 156, 190, 191–193, 196, 280
Robinson, Capt. Fielding S. 7
Rockey, Capt. Keller E. 36, 38, 77, 117
Rowan, 1st Lt. George R. 242
Roy, 2d Lt. Charles H. 197

St. Mihiel battles: (1/5) 48–49; (2/5) 99–100; (3/5) 126–128; (1/6) 171–172; (2/6) 198–200; (3/6) 230–232; (6th MG) 258–265
Scheld, 2d Lt Frederick, Jr., USA 165
Schiesswohl, 1st Lt. 253
Schneider, 1st Lt. John G., Jr. 212
Schwerin, 2d Lt. James P. 259, 262, 271
Sellers, Capt. James McB., USA 190, 204, 280, 284
Shannon, Capt. Harold D. 155
Shea, Lt Richard O'B., USN 37
Shearer, Maj. Maurice E. 7, 16, 48, 71, 72, 75, 85–87, 106, 116–120, 122–129, 149, 151–155, 161, 192, 194, 223, 261, 279
Shelton, 1st Lt. Albert G. 215
Shepherd, 1st Lt. Lemuel 72–74, 76
Shinkle, 1st Lt. Amos R. 194, 197
Shuler, Capt. George K. 19, 63, 79, 109, 117, 118, 120, 122, 123, 136, 171, 172, 175–179, 181–183, 201, 204, 205, 208–210, 212, 214, 232–239, 241–247, 249
Sibley, Maj. Berton W. 72, 82, 86, 114, 123, 124, 154, 158, 165–167, 189, 191, 192, 194, 196, 214, 219–232, 258
Silverthorn, 1st Lt. Merwin 109
Simmonds, 1st Lt. Albert C. 200
Sitz, Capt. Walter H. 170, 219, 229
Sixth Machine Gun Battalion 1, 29, 68, 73, 109, 127, 139, 152, 158, 159, 166, 174, 188, 189, 192, 194, 195, 251–277; (15th [A]) 26, 28, 72, 74, 175, 225–227, 230, 231, 239, 251, 253–258, 261, 263, 274–277; (23d [B]) 23, 49, 67, 68, 100, 251, 253–257, 259, 263, 274–277; (77th [C]) 29, 109, 129, 139, 140, 225, 226, 251–257, 261, 264, 272, 274–277; (81st [D]) 72–74, 174,

199, 209, 225–227, 251–257, 264, 274–277
Sixth Regiment: 73d Machine Gun Company 171–173, 175, 181–184, 192, 200, 215, 218, 221, 225, 226, 253, 256; First Battalion (aka 1/6) 8, 15, 16, 42, 58, 71, 72, 77–79, 81, 116, 118, 135, 149–185, 196, 204–206, 216, 218, 220, 221, 223, 230, 231, 233, 234, 236, 257; (74th [A]) 8, 118, 135, 149–151, 155, 156, 158–160, 162, 163, 169–173, 176–178, 181, 184, 216, 222; (75th [B]) 118, 149, 150, 152, 153, 155, 156, 158, 159, 162–164, 170–173, 177–181, 184, 199, (76th [C]) 72, 78, 149, 150, 153, 154, 156, 160, 161, 163, 169–173, 175, 177–181, 184, 207, 209; (95th [D]) 75, 149–151, 153–156, 163, 169–173, 175, 177, 180–182, 184, 185, 219, 261; Second Battalion (aka 2/6) 15, 19, 24, 48, 58, 82, 88, 114, 117, 132, 133, 150, 156, 166, 167, 170, 172–178, 182, 185–213, 216–220, 223, 230, 233, 236, 237, 253, 254, 282; (78th [E]) 172, 175, 185, 188, 190–195, 199, 200, 204–208, 211, 212, 219, 220, 232, 243, 280; (79th [F]) 156, 185, 188–192, 194, 197–200, 202, 204–207, 209, 211, 212, 219, 220, 243; (80th [G]) 156, 158, 159, 185, 188, 189, 191, 192, 194, 199, 201, 204–207, 209–212, 219, 220, 236, 243, 280; (96th [H]) 15, 117, 149, 156, 170, 185, 186, 188, 190–194, 196, 199, 202–212, 219, 243, 280; Third Battalion (aka 3/6) 15, 16, 19, 24, 29, 71, 72, 82, 86, 109, 113–116, 123, 136, 158, 166, 167, 170, 175–178, 180, 182, 185, 186, 189, 191, 196, 200, 204–206, 208, 210, 211, 214–250, 254, 257; (82d [I]) 71, 72, 154, 165, 191, 200, 214–220, 224–226, 228–231, 233, 235, 237, 238, 240–246, 258, 259, 268, 275; (83d [K]) 121, 122, 176, 191, 199, 200, 214–221, 224–226, 233, 236, 237, 240, 241, 243–246, 258, 259, 275; (84th [L]) 109, 191, 214–217, 219–221, 224–235, 237–248, 258, 259, 263, 268, 275; (97th [M]) 149, 185, 189, 191, 214–220, 224–226, 228–238, 240, 241, 243–246, 258, 259, 263, 275
Smith, 2d Lt. Clarence W. 153, 155
Smith, Maj. Dwight F. 71, 72, 152, 214, 217, 220
Smith, Maj. Holland McT. 6, 7, 9, 12, 106, 107, 219
Soissons battles: (1/5) 43–47; (2/5) 92–97; (3/5) 124–125; (1/6) 167–170; (2/6) 195–197; (3/6) 223–229; (6th MG) 256–257
Somers, 2d Lt. Vernon L. 29, 35, 39

Index

Stallings, Capt. Laurence, Jr. 122, 284
Stiles, 2d Lt. Philip G. 252
Stockwell, 2d Lt. Emmons, Jr., USA 200, 280
Stone, Capt. Pink H. 245
Stowell, Maj. George A. 72, 102, 149, 153, 154, 156, 171, 172, 179, 181–183, 200, 210–212, 214
Sturdevant, Maj. (also CO 84th Co.; later CO USA 30th Regt.) Edward W. 5, 106, 108
Summer, Capt. Allen M. 73, 253, 257
Summerlin, 2d Lt. Wilbur 173, 181
Sundvall, 2d Lt. August L., USA 68, 69
Sutherland, Capt. Albert C. 121, 214
Swink, Capt. Roy W. 218

Taylor, 2d Lt. Ben H. 193, 280
Taylor, Capt. William H., Jr. 272
Thatcher, [?] Herbert H., USN 146
Thomas, 1st Lt. Fred 131
Thomason, Capt. John W. 24, 39, 46, 101, 282, 284
Tillman, 1st Lt., USA 72
Timmerman, 1st Lt. Louis F., Jr. 215
Timothy, 2d Lt. James S., USA 193, 280
Torkelson, 2d Lt. Timon J. 130, 131, 133, 135, 137, 140, 141, 143–145

Turner, Capt. Arthur H. 151, 163, 170
Turrill, Maj. Julius S. 11, 26, 29–33, 35, 37, 38–43, 45–48, 60, 61, 70, 76, 90, 92, 93, 111–113, 115–117, 125, 127, 144, 166, 218, 221, 223

Voeth, Capt. Robert W. 189, 214, 215, 217

Wagoner, 1st Lt. Frederick W., USA 179
Wale, 1st Lt. George, Jr. 206
Waller, Lt. Col. Littleton W.T., Jr. 5, 127, 166, 194, 251–253, 256, 258, 259, 262, 263, 265, 270, 282
Wass, Capt. Lester S. 70, 71, 75, 77, 78, 80, 81, 84, 88, 89, 92, 94, 96, 196
Waterhouse, 2d Lt. Hascall F. 72
Wert, 1st Lt. Thomas H. 200
West, 2d Lt. Eugene 54
West, 1st Lt. John A. 205, 209
Westcott, Maj. Charles T. 106, 107
Whaling, 2d Lt. William J. 207
Wheeler, 1st Lt. Frederick C. 151, 155
White, Dr.[?], USN 165
Whitehead, Capt. Frank 44, 45, 56, 57, 129, 132
Whiting, Capt. Thomas S. 189
Whitmore, AS William H., USN 252

Wicks, 2d Lt. Tom E. 173
Wilcox, 1st Lt. Ralph M. 62
Wilkinson, 2d Lt. Alfred 50
Williams, Maj. Ernest C. 19, 100, 133, 172, 173, 175–178, 182, 183, 185, 198, 201, 203–206, 208–213, 232–234, 236, 237, 241–245, 247, 262, 272
Williams, Capt. Lloyd W. 11, 12, 37, 40, 70–72, 74, 76, 78, 79, 154, 162, 217
Wilmer, Maj. Pere 182, 183, 197
Wilson, 1st Lt. Ross S. 206
Winans, Capt. Roswell C. 33, 35, 36, 38–42, 60
Wise, Lt. Col. Frederick M. 9, 12, 16, 32, 33, 40, 41, 67, 68, 70, 72–84, 90, 91, 98, 111, 116, 117, 153, 154, 160–164, 193, 217, 219, 255, 279, 280, 284
Withington, 2d Lt. James 145
Woodworth, Capt. Wethered 193, 194, 196, 197, 200, 280

Young, 1st Lt. Robert L. 262
Yowell, Capt. Robert 44, 47, 86, 114–116, 121, 122, 125, 127, 133, 140

Zane, Capt. Randolph T. 188, 190–192, 194, 220
Zinner, 2d Lt. Fred J. 55
Zoltowski, 2d Lt. William 280

www.ingramcontent.com/pod-product-compliance
Lightning Source LLC
Chambersburg PA
CBHW081543300426
44116CB00015B/2731